A COMPANION GUIDE TO SENTENCING

PART TWO : GENERAL ISSUES AND PROVISIONS

NIGEL STONE

Shaw & Sons

A Companion Guide to
Sentencing: Part Two

Published by
Shaw & Sons Limited
Shaway House
21 Bourne Park
Bourne Road
Crayford
Kent DA1 4BZ

www.shaws.co.uk

© Shaw & Sons Limited 2001

Published November 2001

ISBN 0 7219 1620 1

A CIP catalogue record for this book is
available from the British Library

Printed in Great Britain by
Bell & Bain Limited, Glasgow

CONTENTS

FOREWORD

Part Two of this *Companion Guide*, trailed well over a year ago in Part One on Specific Offences, has been rather longer in completion than anticipated. The text has had to be substantially revised to take account of important sentencing legislation reaching the statute book in the past few months. In a welcome move to bring together most of the provisions pertaining to sentencing, the Powers of Criminal Courts (Sentencing) Act 2000 has consolidated the 1973 and 1991 Acts, as amended, thus requiring practitioners to learn the new location and citation of familiar sections and schedules. But even before the Act received Royal Assent it was being amended by the Criminal Justice and Court Services Act 2000 so that the ideal of a one-stop shop for all the relevant statutory law has not enjoyed even a brief period of life. Quite apart from introducing the national probation directorate, the latter measure has expanded the community sentencing stable, abolished the sentence of YOI detention and, most prominently, renamed probation, community service and combination orders. At time of writing, this rebranding has not yet been implemented and the old terminology will doubtless live on in common parlance. The text here has sought to adapt to the new language of 'punishment and rehabilitation' but, for convenience sake, frequently continues to use the old terms on the assumption that this will remain more recognisable for a while at least.

As ever in preparing these Guides, the difficulty is in knowing when to stop, given the pace of change in criminal justice. While we still await the conclusions of the review of the criminal courts being conducted by Lord Justice Auld, the *Review of the Sentencing Framework*, announced last year, has been published while the book has been in production. In justifying this Review, the Home Secretary (Home Office, 2000) identified that public confidence in our system of justice is too low because sentencing:

'pays insufficient weight to the needs of victims. Too many offenders are returning to court on too regular a basis. There is insufficient consistency or progression in sentencing practice and sentencers receive insufficient information about whether their sentencing decisions have worked. The sentencing decision itself focuses too much on the offence and not sufficiently on offenders and their future behaviour.'

We have thus been promised 'more flexible frameworks for sentence decision-making and sentence management, which will join up custodial and community penalties, ... protect the public and take full account of the interests of victims', and place greater emphasis on offenders' 'lifestyles'. More recently, the Secretary of State has indicated (*Guardian*, 1 February 2001) that he wishes to target the country's '100,000 most persistent offenders' (a half of whom are under 21) who should, he argues, receive significantly longer sentences on re-conviction than is the case under the 'just deserts' framework of CJA 1991. Meantime, the new Lord Chief Justice (Woolf, 2001), while in support of new sentencing options that emulate the 'seamless' approach of the detention and training order served partly in custody and partly in the community and of keeping the judiciary better informed of the progress made by offenders on both custodial and community sentences, has urged:

'The judiciary must play their part in reducing the use of custody to what is the acceptable and appropriate minimum. In particular, when a custodial sentence is necessary, the shortest sentence which is appropriate within the relevant sentencing bracket, should be imposed. Frequently, one month will achieve everything that can be achieved by three months, and three months will achieve everything that can by six months and so on.'

This authoritative call for parsimony in sentencing, aimed to avoid or reduce the problem of chronic overcrowding in the prison system, what Lord Woolf calls the 'AIDS virus of the Prison Service', appears in remarkable contrast to the Home Secretary's wish to set aside the vision of the 1991 Act after a decade of consolidation. To aid readers to anticipate the likely changes, a summary of the Halliday Report is included as Appendix 2. In the meantime, it is hoped that the following text provides a succinct, accurate yet comprehensive friend to practitioners, particularly those with probation and youth offending responsibilities, who work at the interface of sentencers and offenders, interpreting the one to the other. The manuscript was delivered to the publisher at the end of May 2001 and updated in late August. Every effort has been made to state the law as it stood at that time.

Nigel Stone

REFERENCES

Ashworth A. (1993) – 'Victim Impact Statements and Sentencing', *Criminal Law Review*, 498-509.

Ashworth A. (1995) – *Sentencing and Criminal Justice* (2nd edition), Butterworths.

Ashworth A. *et al.* (1995) – 'Bespoke Tailoring Won't Suit Community Sentences', *New Law Journal* 145, 970-72.

Ashworth A. and von Hirsch A. (1997) – 'Recognising Elephant Traps: The Problem of the Custody Threshold', *Criminal Law Review*, 187-200.

Ball C. *et al.* (2001) – *Young Offenders: Law, Policy and Practice* (2nd edition), Sweet & Maxwell.

Bingham Lord (1997) – 'The Sentence of the Court', *Justice of the Peace* 161, 700-03.

Bottoms A. (1989) – 'The Concept of Intermediate Sanctions and its Relevance for the Probation Service', in Shaw R. and Haines K. *The Criminal Justice System: A Central Role for the Probation Service*, University of Cambridge.

Carlisle Lord (Chair) (1988) – *The Parole System in England and Wales*, HMSO.

Charles N., Whittaker C. and Ball C. (1997) – 'Sentencing without a Pre-Sentence Report', *Research Findings No. 47*, Home Office.

Clarkson C. (1997) – 'Beyond Just Desserts: Sentencing Violent and Sexual Offenders', *Howard Journal* 36(3), 284-92.

Darbyshire P. (2000) – 'The Mischief of Plea Bargaining and Sentencing Rewards', *Criminal Law Review*, 895-910.

Elliott R. and Airs J. (2000) – *New Measures for Fine Defaulters, Persistent Petty Offenders and Others: the report of the Crime (Sentences) Act 1997 Pilots*, Occasional Paper, Home Office.

Fenwick H. (1997) – 'Procedural Rights of Victims of Crime: Public or Private Ordering of the Criminal Justice Process?', *Modern Law Review* 60(3), 317-33.

Flood-Page C. and Mackie A. (1998) – *Sentencing Practice: an examination of decisions in magistrates' courts and the Crown Court in the mid-1990s*, Research Study 180, Home Office.

Harris M. (2000) – *Risk Assessments in Pre-Sentence Reports: their impact on the sentencing process*, Inner London Probation Service.

Hedderman C. *et al.* (1999) – *Increasing Confidence in Community Sentences: The Results of Two Demonstration Projects*, Research Study 194, Home Office.

Henham R. (1994) – 'Attorney-General's References and Sentencing Policy', *Criminal Law Review*, 499-512.

Herling D. and Dear I. (2000) – 'Bail from the Magistrates pending Appeal against Sentence: A Flawed Jurisdiction', *Criminal Law Review*, 987-90.

HM Inspectorate of Probation (1997) – *Tackling Drugs Together: Report of a Thematic Inspection on the Work of the Probation Service with Drug Misusers*, Home Office.

Home Office (2000) – *A Review of the Sentencing Framework*, Home Office.

Hoyle C. (1998) – *Evaluation of the 'One Stop Shop' and Victim Statement Pilot Projects*, Report to Home Office.

Lovegrove A. (2001) – 'Sanctions and Severity: To the Demise of von Hirsch and Wasik's Sanction Hierarchy', *Howard Journal* 40(2), 126-44.

Magistrates' Association (1995) – *Discretion to Dispense with a Pre-Sentence Report*, Magistrates' Association.

Mair G. and Mortimer E. (1996) – *Curfew Orders with Electronic Monitoring*, Research Study 163, Home Office.

Mattinson J. (1998) – 'Criminal Appeals England and Wales, 1995 and 1996', *Statistical Bulletin* 3/98, Home Office.

Morgan R. and Sanders A. (1999) – *The Uses of Victim Statements*, Occasional Paper, Home Office.

Mortimer E. and May C. (1997) – *Electronic Monitoring in Practice: The Second Year of the Trials of Curfew Orders*, Research Study 177, Home Office.

Moxon D. (1988) – *Sentencing Practice in the Crown Court*, Research Study 103, Home Office.

Raynor P. (1997) – 'Some Observations on Rehabilitation and Justice', *Howard Journal* 36(3), 248-62.

Rex S. (1998) – 'Applying Desert Principles to Community Sentences: Lessons from Two Criminal Justice Acts', *Criminal Law Review*, 381-91.

Sentencing Advisory Panel (2000) – *Racially Aggravated Offences: Advice to the Court of Appeal* (www.sentencing-advisory-panel.gov.uk/racadv.htm).

Stone N. (1994) – 'The Suspended Sentence since the Criminal Justice Act 1991', *Criminal Law Review*, 399-408.

Stone N. (1997) – *A Companion Guide to Life Sentences*, Owen Wells.

Stone N. (1999) – *A Companion Guide to Enforcement* (3rd edition), Owen Wells.

Stone N. (2000) – *A Companion Guide to Sentencing: Part One*, Owen Wells.

Stone N. (2002) – *A Companion Guide to Mentally Disordered Offenders* (2nd edition, forthcoming), Shaw & Sons.

Thomas D. (1979) – *Principles of Sentencing* (2nd edition), Heinemann.

Thomas D. (1997) – *The Times*, 11 March 1997.

Turnbull P. *et al.* (2000) – *Drug Treatment and Testing Orders: Final Evaluation Report*, Research Study 212, Home Office.

Victim Support (1994) – 'Victim Impact Statements', *Victim Support* 56, 7.

Vincenzi C. (1994) – 'Deportation in Disarray: The Case of EC Nationals', *Criminal Law Review*, 163-75.

von Hirsch A. and Ashworth A. (1996) – 'Protective Sentencing Under Section 2(2)(b): The Criteria for Dangerousness', *Criminal Law Review*, 175-83.

von Hirsch A. and Jareborg N. (1991) – 'Gauging Criminal Harm: A Living Standard Analysis', *Oxford Journal of Legal Studies*, 1-38.

von Hirsch A. and Wasik M. (2001) – 'Proportionate Sanctions and Sentence Substitutibility: A Reply to Austin Lovegrove', *Howard Journal* 40(2), 145-47.

Walker N. and Padfield N. (1996) – *Sentencing: Theory, Law and Practice* (2nd edition), Butterworths.

Wasik M. (1985) – 'The Grant of an Absolute Discharge', *Oxford Journal of Legal Studies*.

Wasik M. (1997) – 'Discharge Provisions and the Restricted Meaning of "Conviction"', *113 Law Quarterly Review*, 637-66.

Wasik M. (1998) – 'Youth Court: Maximum Custodial Sentences', *Justice of the Peace* 162, 1011-12.

Wasik M. (2001) – 'The Vital Importance of Certain Previous Convictions', *Criminal Law Review*, 363-73.

Wasik M. and von Hirsch A. (1988) – 'Non-Custodial Penalties and the Principles of Desert', *Criminal Law Review*, 555-71.

Wasik M. and von Hirsch A. (1994) – 'Section 29 Revisited: Previous Convictions in Sentencing', *Criminal Law Review*, 409-18.

Woolf Lord (2001) – *The Woolf Report: A Decade of Change?* (Address to Prison Reform Trust, January 2001).

GLOSSARY

ACO	attendance centre order
ACR	automatic conditional release
All ER	All England Reports
APO	action plan order
BA	Bail Act 1976
CAA	Criminal Appeal Act 1968
CCR	Crown Court Rules 1982
CDA	Crime and Disorder Act 1998
CJ	Lord Chief Justice
CJA	Criminal Justice Act
CJCSA	Criminal Justice and Court Services Act 2000
CJPOA	Criminal Justice and Public Order Act 1994
CMLR	Common Market Law Reports
CPIA	Criminal Procedure and Investigations Act 1996
CPO	community punishment order
CPRO	community punishment and rehabilitation order
CPS	Crown Prosecution Service
Cr App R	Criminal Appeal Reports
Cr App R(S)	Criminal Appeal Reports (Sentencing)
Crim LR	Criminal Law Review
C(S)A	Crime (Sentences) Act 1997
CSCOR	Community Service and Combination Order Rules 1992
CYPA	Children and Young Persons Act 1933 & 1969
DPP	Director of Public Prosecutions
DTA	Drug Trafficking Act 1994
DTO	detention and training order
DTTO	drug treatment and testing order
F(OD)A	Football (Disorder) Act 2000
FSA	Football Spectators Act 1989
HOC	Home Office Circular
HRA	Human Rights Act 1998
J	Judge of the High Court
JP	Justice of the Peace News
LCD	Lord Chancellor's Department

LJ	Lord Justice of Appeal
MCA	Magistrates' Courts Act 1980
MC(C&YP)R	Magistrates' Courts (Children and Young Persons) Rules 1992
MCR	Magistrates' Courts Rules 1981
MHA	Mental Health Act 1983
PCCA	Powers of Criminal Courts Act 1973
PCC(S)A	Powers of Criminal Courts (Sentencing) Act 2000
PSA	petty sessions area
PSR	pre-sentence report
QB/KB	Queen's/King's Bench Reports
RIC	remand in custody
RTA	Road Traffic Act 1988 and 1991
RT(ND)A	Road Traffic (New Drivers) Act 1995
RTOA	Road Traffic Offenders Act 1988
RTR	Road Traffic Reports
SCA	Supreme Court Act 1981
SED	sentence expiry date
SOA	Sex Offender Act 1997
SSR	specific sentence report
STP	short term prisoner
TA	Theft Act 1968
TIC	offence taken into consideration
WLR	Weekly Law Reports
YOI	young offender institution
YOT	youth offending team

1
OFFENCE-SERIOUSNESS: GENERIC ISSUES

The concept of commensurability or proportionality has been central to the framework of sentencing, particularly since the Criminal Justice Act 1991. This foundation chapter thus seeks to explore how the seriousness of an offence is gauged and expressed in principle, statute and practice, in the light of record, plea, totality of sentence, victim views and the importance of parity between co-offenders. This exploration begins on a somewhat theoretical note which may feel rather heavy going and may thus be of more interest to students. However, it is hoped that this provides some brief reflection of the deeper conceptual under-pinnings on which practical sentencing is based and the dilemmas that are faced. The text soon rejoins the main legal track of statute and case law.

Weighing Seriousness

Following Ashworth (1995), it is now common parlance in sentencing theory to identify the two main elements of offence-seriousness as *harm* and *culpability*.

Harm

Proportionality as a key concept in the evaluation of offence-seriousness has two distinct dimensions, sometimes referred to as *ordinal* and *cardinal*. Ordinal proportionality captures the seriousness or harmfulness of an offence relative to other offences, while cardinal proportionality refers to the challenge of translating that weight of seriousness or gravity into some proportionate point on the scale of available punishments. In making comparative judgements regarding ordinal proportionality, what parameters can be called upon to provide a degree of objectivity and consistency so that we are not at the mercy of somewhat vacuous notions based on the judgement of a 'right-thinking person' (see page 70)? One elementary starting point would be to adopt the criterion suggested by the Court of Appeal in *R v Stewart* (1987) 9 Cr App R(S) 135, namely to ask whether the offence is 'non-violent, non-sexual and non-frightening'.

The quest for a more sophisticated but suitably generic tool has proved very difficult but the most prominent attempt, albeit confined to cases involving individual victims, is the 'living standard' analysis developed by von Hirsch and Jareborg (1991). They propose that harmfulness can be best assessed by trying to gauge the effect of a typical instance of a particular crime upon the living standard, economic and non-economic, material and non-material, of the victim. By 'living standard' they mean 'not so much the victim's actual life quality but the means or capabilities for achieving a certain quality of life' (Ashworth and von Hirsch, 1997).

Interests Violated or Threatened Their starting point is to identify the interests of the victim violated or threatened by the offence. They suggest four tiers of 'interests' at stake or potentially undermined by crime:

    (a)   physical integrity: health, safety, avoidance of physical pain;

1

(b)   material support and amenity: including nutrition, shelter and other basics;

(c)   freedom from humiliation or degrading treatment;

(d)   privacy and autonomy.

(In so far as this seeks to suggest a descending order of significance, it may be argued that some aspects of (c) arguably rank above (b) or even (a), though serious instances of criminal behaviour violating interest (c) will almost inevitably violate interest (a) too.) Arguing for this tool of analysis in adopting a more principled approach to determining seriousness, Ashworth and von Hirsch observe:

'Why should the intentional causing of GBH generally be regarded as worse than burglary? It is because the overall quality of a typical victim's life has been so much more affected. The living-standard notion also permits drawing from a richer array of experience, including that outside the criminal law; in considering the degree of harmfulness of an arson, we can ask how it compares with an accidental fire.'

Impact of Violation Having decided the nature of the interest violated, von Hirsch and Jareborg's second step is to assess the effect of the violation upon the living standards of the typical victim, effects being banded into four descending levels of seriousness, according to the degree by which the crime undermines the victim's quality of life:

(a)   Subsistence: survival with maintenance of elementary human functions;

(b)   Minimal well-being: maintenance of a minimal level of comfort and dignity;

(c)   Adequate well-being: maintenance of an 'adequate' level of comfort and dignity;

(d)   Significantly enhanced well-being: above the merely adequate level.

To illustrate the application of the tools, it may be helpful to cite one or two of the authors' examples:

(i) *Assault*: A beats B up causing substantial bruising and some lacerations but not enough to require hospitalisation and with no lasting physical consequences. In terms of physical integrity, the impact is no worse than the harm caused by a relatively less serious accident. The offence does not undermine the victim's basic survival ('subsistence') or their minimal or adequate well-being but it impacts temporarily upon enhanced well-being. From the viewpoint of freedom from humiliation, the intrusion can be viewed as more serious, because being beaten up is demeaning, and so the assault can be seen to intrude at the level of adequate well-being.

(ii) *Domestic Burglary* involving removal of common items of property and without ransacking. In material amenity terms, the intrusion on material comfort is low but in regard to autonomy and privacy, the intrusion is more significant, affecting the enhanced well-being of the occupant. (The authors debate the issue of 'psychological harm', mentioning that a burglary may cause great fear of future attack, but they suggest that this is likely to be without regard to the actual risks and opt to disregard such responses in their analysis.)

(iii) *Armed Robbery* in which A robs B at gunpoint, taking his wallet and a small amount of cash. The property loss is quite minor, having only marginal impact on living standard but the threatened bodily intrusion is high, an immediate threat to kill that intrudes at the level of basic subsistence, albeit that this needs to be discounted to some extent to take account of the fact that it did not materialise.

(iv) *Forcible Rape* in which A rapes B at knifepoint. The threat to survival or subsistence is at the same level as the armed robbery but supplemented by a high level of intrusion into privacy and freedom from humiliation, undermining the victim's maintenance of a minimal level of dignity and comfort.

The authors then seek to devise a harm scale and offer a simple 5-point scale, from (i) 'grave' (intrusion at subsistence level) to (v) 'lesser' harm (only marginal intrusion), via (ii) 'serious' (intrusion upon minimal well-being), (iii) 'upper-intermediate' (intrusion upon adequate well-being) and (iv) 'lower-intermediate' (intrusion upon enhanced well-being). This mapping achieved, Ashworth (1995) suggests that the appraisal of seriousness should be tuned and modified to take account of factors pertinent to the individual case, particularly culpability:

Culpability

Adjust the level of seriousness to reflect whether the offence was planned, 'impulsive' or spontaneous, knowing, reckless, negligent etc.

Remoteness This concept embraces various considerations such as the degree of proximity between the offender's actions and the resulting harm (as in the offence of affray, or theft from a public telephone that happens to have the serious consequence of preventing an urgent call to the emergency services unrelated to the offence), or the extent to which the offender's intention was actualised in reality, matters that may indicate a need for adjustment to the weighing of seriousness.

Aggravation and Mitigation This requires consideration of features of the offence that are established in sentencing practice as factors that increase or reduce seriousness (addressed in respect of particular kinds of offence, in Part One of this Guide (Stone, 2000)).

Supporters of the living standard approach acknowledge that the tools offered are not precise and capable of fully consistent application but nevertheless suggest that this approach has integrity and can serve to avoid the kind of sentencing that leads to imprisonment for theft value £35 or a probation order for shop theft value £3.50, as detailed elsewhere in this Guide.

Particular Aspects of Offence Seriousness

At this point it may be worth noting three aspects of a generic nature relating to offence seriousness that may be encountered:

'Stale' Offence Apart from the provision of MCA 1980 s127 that an information alleging a summary offence should be laid within 6 months of commission, there is no provision preventing prosecution after a specified period of lapse of time. The question may thus arise whether the defendant should be afforded some mitigation of sentence in recognition of the so-called staleness of the offence if prosecution proceeds after a substantial lapse of time. The Court of Appeal in *R v Nicholson* (1992) 14 Cr App R(S)

3

311 indicated that 'the mere passage of time cannot attract a great deal of discount', in the context of a familiar scenario where a sexual offence is prosecuted only after the victim felt ready to report or disclose it.

A partial exception arises where the offender was a juvenile or adolescent at the time of his sexual offending against a younger relation, as in *R v Cuddington* (1995) 16 Cr App R(S) 246 where a partial reduction of custodial sentence was allowed. The Appeal Court indicated that the proper approach is to treat the sentence that would have been imposed if the matter had come to light at the time as a 'powerful factor' in passing sentence. Thus the offender's culpability should be assessed on the basis of his age at the time of commission. The sentencer may also have regard to sentencing practice at the point of offence when the kind of offending under consideration might have been different. *Cuddington* has recently been affirmed by the Appeal Court in *R v Bowers* [1999] Crim LR 234 where an offender aged 42 pleaded guilty to offences of buggery of boys aged 8 to 11, committed in the early 1970s when he was between 15 and 18 and had sexually abused younger members of a Lads Club. He had since married and had not re-offended. The Court reasoned that in the 1970s he would probably have been sentenced to Borstal and thus served around a year in custody. A term of $3^1/_2$ years was thus quashed in favour of a sentence of two years imprisonment (an order under CJA 1991 s44 was also set aside). In *R v Matthews* [1999] 1 Cr App R(S) 309 the offender aged 49 pleaded guilty to attempted rape and indecent assault committed when he was 18 against a girl then aged 10. She stated that she had been affected by this experience over many years. He was said to have been affected by learning difficulties and limited intellect at the time of his offending and he had been of exemplary character since his crimes. The Appeal Court upheld the correctness of a custodial sentence but, in view of the 'very exceptional delay' of some 30 years, reduced the term from 30 to 12 months.

The offender may be able to gain personal mitigation from their achievements since their offence showing their proven capacity to distance themselves from their offending past. In the case of paedophile behaviour, the court may not be easily persuaded of such distancing simply on the basis of the absence of any prosecution for crime of that nature in the interim. If the time delay before prosecution has been caused by the defendant's efforts to escape apprehension then clearly the 'staleness' argument lacks any weight. A guilty plea in instances of 'stale' offending may earn particular credit, given the difficulties that can arise in proving the allegation in contested cases several years on. In *Bowers* (above), however, the defendant was given a sentence equivalent to that which he would have received 25 years earlier, despite his guilty plea and the Court's acceptance that he had successfully established sexual relations with adult women and had no continuing sexual interest in children.

Offence Motivated by Addiction As the Court of Appeal made clear in *R v Lawrence* (1988) 10 Cr App R(S) 463:

> 'It is no mitigation that a crime was committed to feed an addiction, whether to drugs, drink, sex, fast cars or anything else.'

The appellant's appeal against three years for burglary committed to gain the funds to support a £90 a day heroin habit was dismissed.

Foreign Offender's Ignorance of the Law It may be argued that an offender new to this country should be entitled to some mitigation if they had a mistaken perception on the basis of their experience in their own jurisdiction that the conduct in question was not as serious as it is actually viewed in the United Kingdom. Thus in *R v Aidebayo* [1998] 1 Cr App R(S) 15 the offender, aged 36 with no previous convictions, who had come to the UK seeking political asylum had sought to acquire a driving licence for ID purposes by arranging for an impostor to take a driving test in his name. The PSR argued that he was 'in ignorance of the consequences and culture of this country' but sentence of 6 months' imprisonment for conspiracy to obtain by deception was upheld.

For the statutory requirements to regard an offence as aggravated because it was committed while on bail or more serious because it was racially aggravated, see page 79.

Sentencing Legislation

The Court of Appeal has often indicated that it is the responsibility of counsel at Crown Court to draw the judge's attention to the relevant statutory sentencing provisions if the judge is seeking to or has purported to pass a sentence that is unlawful or inapplicable or otherwise wrong, e.g. *R v Hartrey* [1993] Crim LR 230.

Weight of Court of Appeal Decisions

In the past the Appeal Court has indicated that sentencing is a matter for the discretion of the sentencing judge, that each case depends heavily on its own facts and that decisions of the Court of Appeal are more examples of approach rather than binding authority. However, the Court has more recently indicated that counsel for the prosecution at Crown Court should draw to the sentencer's attention relevant sentencing authority from decided cases, particularly where such authority goes contrary to the approach being suggested by the defence in mitigation: *R v Panayioutou* (1989)11 Cr App R(S) 535, where the Court stated that 'if this Court has laid down guidelines, ... judges are entitled to have those guideline cases drawn to their attention'. Further, in *R v Ozair Ahmed* (1994) 15 Cr App R(S) 286 the Court encouraged defence counsel to refer to relevant appellate decisions in mitigation. Contemporary sentencing practice certainly should prevent a judge from expressing disagreement with Court of Appeal guidelines and opting to ignore them. In *R v Johnson* (1994) 15 Cr App R(S) 827 the judge made the unwisely explicit point of stating that he did not agree with the principles drawn to his attention (in dealing with a robbery by mugging), believing that the Appeal Court had been wrongly reducing the length of custody in such cases, and stated that he would not act upon them. He imposed a total of 7 years' YOI detention. On appeal, the Court stated:

> 'A judge when sentencing must pay attention to the guidance issued by this Court and sentences should be broadly in line with guideline cases, unless there are factors applicable to the particular case which require or enable the judge to depart from the normal level of sentence. In such special cases the judge should indicate clearly the factor(s) which ... allow departure from the tariff set by this Court. What a judge must not do is to state that s/he is applying some personal tariff because s/he considers the accepted range of sentences to be too high or too low.'

Though the sentence passed was considered to be at the upper end of the appropriate sentencing bracket and would not ordinarily have been interfered with, the Court felt obliged to substitute a term of 5 years in the light of the judge's 'unfortunate remarks'.

Pre-Sentence Reports

PCC(S)A 2000 s162(1) defines a PSR to mean:

> 'a report in writing which "with a view to assisting the court in determining the most suitable method of dealing with an offender, is made or submitted by an appropriate officer."'

Where the offender is aged 18 or over, an appropriate officer means a probation officer or a social worker of a local authority social services department. In the case of a younger offender, a member of a YOT is also empowered to act in this capacity.

The statutory function and contribution of a pre-sentence report in sentencing is addressed at various parts of this text, particularly at pages 77 and 133 in the context of custodial and community sentences, and in Chapter 2 in respect of various procedural considerations associated with adjournment, establishing the factual basis of sentence, fairness to the defendant in respect of indications given by the court when a report is requested and disclosure to the prosecution. At this point it is worth noting that the content of PSRs is regulated by *National Standards* (for adult offenders, currently: Home Office, 2000; juveniles are subject to separate *Standards for Youth Justice*, Youth Justice Board, 2000), as follows:

Process Reports must (i) be based on at least one face-to-face interview with the offender, (ii) 'specify information available from the CPS, any hostel placement (undertaken on remand), or from any other relevant source', (iii) 'be prepared within, at most, 15 working days of request, or such shorter timescale as has been agreed in protocols with the court', (iv) 'be objective, impartial, free from discriminatory language and stereotype, balanced, verified and factually accurate' (para. B4). Additionally, reports will in future utilise 'the Offender Assessment System' (OASys, currently being piloted) 'to provide a systematic assessment of the nature and causes of defendants' offending behaviour, the risk the defendant poses to the public and the action which can be taken to reduce the likelihood of re-offending'.

Content Every report must contain:

(a)   a *frontsheet* giving basic factual details and identifying sources of information used to prepare the report;

(b)   *Offence Analysis* analysing the offence(s) and highlighting 'key features in respect of the nature and circumstances in which committed'; assessing the offender's culpability and level of premeditation; assessing the consequences of the offence (see page 29 in respect of victim impact); assessing the offender's attitude to the offence and awareness of its consequences; indicating whether or not any positive action has been taken by the offender to make reparation or address offending behaviour since the offence was committed;

(c)   *Offender Assessment* stating the offender's status as regards accommodation, employment and literacy; assessing the implications of any special personal circumstances directly relevant to the offending; giving details of any substance abuse and response to treatment, past or present; considering 'the impact of racism on the offender's behaviour where directly relevant to the offence'; addressing 'any relevant personal background which may have contributed to the offender's motive';

(d) *Assessment of Risk of Harm to the Public and Likelihood of Re-Offending* containing (i) 'an assessment of the offender's risk of causing serious harm to the public'; (ii) 'an assessment of the offender's likelihood of re-offending based on the current offence, attitude to it, and other relevant information'; (iii) identification of any risks of self-harm'.

(e) *Conclusion* evaluating the offender's motivation and ability to change, identifying, where relevant, action required to improve motivation; explicitly stating whether he is suitable for a community sentence; making 'a clear proposal for sentence designed to protect the public and reduce offending, including for custody where this is necessary'. Where the proposal is for a community rehabilitation order or CPRO, an outline supervision plan should be included, containing a description of the purposes and desired outcomes of the sentence, the anticipated methods, interventions and level of supervision. If a specific additional requirement is proposed, this should be set out as it should be included in the order, together with a likely starting date. Where custody is a likely option, any anticipated effects on family circumstances, current employment or education should be identified.

Offence Seriousness The scope for a PSR to throw light on offence seriousness is illustrated by *R v Salisbury Magistrates' Court, ex parte Gray* (1999) *The Times* 21 July. The interviewing probation officer obtained admissions from a defendant facing sentence for gross indecency with a boy aged 14 that the offence was not 'spontaneous', as previously stated to a psychiatrist who had reported to the Court. Though proposing a probation order, the PSR suggested that as the offence now appeared more serious than had previously been believed, it would seem more appropriate for the magistrates to commit the case to the Crown Court, to reflect concern for such serious offences and to give a message to would-be perpetrators and victims of such crime about how seriously the courts view such instances. After the justices had followed this advice, the offender sought judicial review of their decision, contending that it was wrong for the PSR writer to include in their report details of what had been said in interview if this would expose the offender to a more serious view being taken of their offence. It was also argued that by expressing a view of the seriousness of the offence the PSR writer had failed to conform to the view given in *National Standards* that a PSR should not express a view about the seriousness of an offence.

Dismissing the application, the Divisional Court held that when new material comes to light in the course of PSR inquiries, the reporter is entitled to state this in their report. Sedley LJ stated that 'it was not only permissible ... to investigate the nature of the applicant's offending, it was (his) duty to do so' and to report aspects of the offences and the offender's culpability that would not otherwise be known to the sentencer. Countering the suggestion that a PSR writer should not report what an offender has said in the course of interview where this would indicate that the offending was more serious than might otherwise have been suggested, Collins J held that 'it would be quite wrong if those matters were not available to the court because the court has to sentence an offender with concern for the individual and his circumstances but also with a wider concern as to what is in the public interest'. As for the possible breach of *National Standards*, the Court felt that this was not a material consideration because the issue of seriousness was one on which the magistrates could reach their own conclusion, reading the report 'with their critical faculties intact', and also the applicant had conceded that the report could not be struck out as *ultra vires*.

Risk of Harm and of Re-Offending This element of PSR content is perhaps the most controversial, given that future risk of harm is distinct from offence seriousness and the imprecise nature and unreliability of risk assessment. Among questions which have not received authoritative answers from the higher courts: how valid a consideration is risk of a nature unrelated to the present offence for sentence? What is the relevance of risk posed in the PSR that is simply 'diagnostic without any related proposal as to how this might be addressed? Risk is a critical consideration in limited instances of sexual/violent crime where a longer-than-commensurate custodial term is being considered under PCC(S)A 2000 s80(2)(b) (see page 90) or an extended sentence under PCC(S)A 2000 s85 (see page 86), or in assisting the court in determining whether exceptional circumstances apply that justify not imposing an otherwise automatic life sentence under PCC(S)A 2000 s109 (see page 100). In other instances the more speculative nature of this issue is relevant in considering the offender's suitability for specific community sentencing options or in determining the persuasiveness of certain mitigation being urged upon the court. In a recent survey of 200 PSRs (written prior to the most recent version of *National Standards*), Harris (2000) reports the marked lack of specificity offered by reporters; 57 (28%) contained nothing that could be described as an assessment of risk of harm. Though the expertise of the reporter to weigh risk might be open to challenge, Harris notes barristers' reluctance to test probation risk assessments in court.

PSR Conclusions The significance of PSRs for the sentencing process is illustrated by *R v Brown and Lang* (1997, unreported). A report on a young woman aged 17 convicted of domestic burglary with an adult male had indicated that she was a very unsophisticated offender with a history of disadvantage, being placed in care as a result of violence at home and thereafter experiencing frequent shifts in placement, being described as having a life that was 'empty, uncomfortable and desperately lonely'. The report had proposed a supervision order for one year but the judge imposed sentence of 15 months. Noting that the judge had made no reference in his sentencing remarks to 'a very extensive' PSR and its recommendation and to why the clearly presented issues in mitigation could not be applied in determining sentence, the Court of Appeal stated:

> 'We take the view that it is incumbent upon judges, when faced with material from experienced writers of pre-sentence reports ... to make reference to those matters and to make it clear that they have taken into account mitigating circumstances in deciding the penalty.'

The Court considered that as the PSR had raised only a single proposal 'it is entirely understandable why the judge, faced with that bald recommendation, perhaps thought that this was a girl who needed to be punished rather than helped'. With the benefit of a rather more detailed proposal that included specified activities requirements, the Court substituted a two year supervision order.

It is noteworthy that the Appeal Court referred to 'experienced' PSR writers, the implication being that sentencers need not take the same care when choosing not to take notice of material presented by inexperienced reporters. This begs the question as to the basis on which experience is gauged, other than on the unreliable basis of the sentencer's personal knowledge of the writer, since *National Standards* do not require reporters to state their experience. It is submitted that experience of the reporter should not be a relevant issue but rather the quality, informativeness and insight of the report.

Offender's Co-operation The question may arise (though not as commonly as might be imagined) whether an offender is obliged to submit to the experience of being the subject of a PSR. Statutory provisions make no reference to any scope on the defendant's behalf to opt out of the process and the only related legislation comes under the Bail Act, as detailed at page 51. Refusal of bail to enable a report to be prepared or the granting of bail with a condition of co-operation with the preparation of reports poses the question whether a defendant can decline a report if, for example, they consider a report to be an irrelevance or an unwanted intrusion on their privacy or potentially damaging to their predicament. In some instances a defendant anticipating an inevitable custodial sentence may wish to know their sentence without delay and will thus invite the sentencer to proceed without a report on the basis that a PSR is not necessary (see page 77). The *National Standard for PSRs* (1995 version, para 4) specified that that if an offender withholds consent to the preparation of a report, 'the report writer remains under a duty to produce the most useful report possible using the information available.' As the defendant is the main source of information for most reports, non-co-operation will in many instances make a report a practical impossibility. The 2000 version of *National Standards* makes no reference to the issue. A report is clearly to assist the court, not the offender, but what sanction, if any, attaches to non-cooperation? In *R v Salisbury Magistrates' Court, ex parte Gray* (see above) the point was raised by the applicant that 'if offenders know that they are liable to have what they say to a reporter put in a report, they may be less willing to be frank and honest, and they may even be advised to be careful what they say'. Collins J was not impressed and commented:

'It seems to me that an offender would be very ill-advised not to be fully co-operative with the probation officer because if he is not then that will be noted in the report and the obvious conclusion will be drawn, and it will be a conclusion which does not assist the offender. The probation officer can be trusted to put before the court what is relevant and if, not withstanding that it appears to be something that is adverse to the offender, the probation officer takes the view that there are mitigating factors or matters that should be drawn to the attention of the court which takes the sting from such adverse matters, then the probation officer will no doubt refer to them.'

In reality, refusal to co-operate or giving a clearly guarded account may well mean that the offender cannot be considered suitable for certain community sentences but should not be treated an aggravating feature of their offence, albeit that non-compliance with the court's expectations may diminish the amount of mitigation arising from a guilty plea or any other mitigation such as remorse offered on the defendant's behalf.

Taking Offences into Consideration

Though TIC procedure is not governed by statute and rests simply upon conventional practice, this provides a convenient way for other offences admitted by the defendant to be dealt with without the necessity of being formally the subject of charge. Outstanding matters are thus dealt with at minimum cost to the prosecution and the defendant is able to wipe the slate clean, usually with only marginal effect upon the sentence received. The process can be conveniently summarised as follows:

(i) Offences should not be TICed unless the defendant requests the sentencing court to do so and admits their commission. Though the police normally compile the list of TIC offences on the basis of an accused person's admissions, the defendant is entitled to request for some but not the complete schedule of offences to be taken into consideration. Sometimes the full basis of TIC offences is not resolved when a PSR is requested in respect of the substantive offences and the reporter thus has to be alert to the possibility of TICs without assuming that all potential TIC offences will be finally admitted.

(ii) The court has discretion whether or not to accept the defence invitation to TIC an offence. It is, for example, contrary to good practice to TIC an offence which is more serious than the offence for which the defendant has been convicted or which is of a completely different nature from the substantive offence.

(iii) When taking offences into consideration, the court's powers remain limited to the maximum penalty for the substantive offence and no additional sentencing power arises in respect of a TIC offence. The only exception to this is that the Crown Court (but not a magistrates' court) can order compensation to be paid in respect of a TIC offence. A court should not TIC an offence which carries licence endorsement or disqualification from driving (mandatory or discretionary) if the substantive offence(s) are not endorsable.

(iv) Though the sentencer is entitled to increase the sentence or order for the substantive offence(s) in the light of the TICs, the extent of such increased penalty will almost certainly be less than what the offender would have received had the TIC offences been prosecuted separately.

Previous Convictions and Response to Previous Sentences

A defendant's criminal record has traditionally been an important element in sentencing. It is certainly central to the assessment of risk posed by the offender. But it is less clear how record relates to sentencing based on proportionality. The appropriateness of punishing persistence is a long-standing problem in sentencing theory. For many offenders a sentence that reflects their record appears to punish them twice over for their past wrongdoings. Sentencers may respond that if two offenders appear together charged with, say, burglary where this is the first offence for one and the fifth conviction for the other, it is clear common sense that they should not be treated the same.

The framework for sentencing introduced by CJA 1991 sought to address the issue in s29 by specifying firstly that 'an offence should not be regarded as more serious by reason of any previous convictions or failure to respond to past sentences', but secondly by adding that the court could take account of any aggravating factors of an offence as disclosed by the circumstances of other offences in forming an opinion as to the seriousness of the offence. This section attracted much criticism for inappropriately restricting judicial discretion and a revised version of s29(1), now PCC(S)A 2000 s151(1) was introduced by CJA 1993:

> In considering the seriousness of any offence, the court may take into account any previous convictions of the offender or any failure of his to respond to previous sentences.

Note that for the purposes of this sub-section, a discharge is treated as a conviction and a conditional discharge is treated as a sentence. Similarly, a probation order imposed before 1 October 1992 counts as a conviction and sentence.

The meaning and impact of s151(1) remains unclear, without authoritative interpretation. Ashworth (1995) has suggested that, at worst, the wording has been misunderstood as 'a general licence to aggravate' and, at best, a *laissez-faire* tolerance of discretion, flexibility and plasticity, without wishing to become too driven by the precise technical wording of the provision. The Magistrates' Association *Sentencing Guidelines* (2000) advise somewhat cryptically:

> 'Consider the effect of using previous convictions, or any failure to respond to previous sentencers in assessing seriousness. Courts should identify any convictions relevant for this purpose and then consider to what extent they affect the seriousness of the present offence.'

Progressive Loss of Mitigation

Given this vacuum in judicial guidance, commentators have sought to re-state the theory of 'progressive loss of mitigation' as a rational foundation on which to build. Simply stated, the theory or principle holds that the absence of previous convictions offers clear scope for mitigation and that a repeat offender progressively loses that mitigation until it disappears completely. The current offence nevertheless must be regarded as setting a penalty 'ceiling' beyond which the sentence cannot properly go. There is thus no valid place for cumulative or incremental sentencing whereby the sentence is increased on each occasion of repetition without firm regard to the limits of offence seriousness. The principle is said to reflect a legitimate and intuitive degree of tolerance for the first time offender, a recognition of human weakness or inexperience, together with a correspondingly increasing intolerance for those who fail to respond appropriately to the censure of prosecution (see Wasik and von Hirsch, 1994). This precept is not entirely self-evident or of universal applicability. For example, is the principle valid in the case of a sophisticated and meticulously planned or a very grave first offence? The answer may be that there will be adequate basis for discerning aggravating features that will validly counteract any mitigation arising from previous good record. As the Court of Appeal noted in *R v Billam* [1986] 1 WLR 349, a guideline decision on rape, the offender's previous good character is 'of only minor relevance'.

The Court of Appeal was regarded as giving implicit endorsement to the theory in a number of pre-CJA 1991 decisions such as in *R v Queen* (1981) 3 Cr App R(S) 245 where sentence of 18 months' imprisonment for a cheque deception value £50 was overturned on the basis that:

'...the proper way is to decide on a sentence which is appropriate for the offence. Then in deciding whether that sentence should be imposed or whether the court can properly extend some leniency to the offender, the court must have regard to those matters which tell in his favour; and equally to those matters which tell against him, in particular his record of previous convictions .... He should not be sentenced for the offences which he has committed in the past and for which he has already been punished.'

Speaking for the Government as the revised s29(1) was before Parliament, Home Office Minister Earl Ferrers was dubious of the 'progressive loss' principle, seeking to undermine it by characterising it thus:

'The offender starts off with a certain amount of mitigation "in the bank", because he has never offended. As he repeats the offence, he progresses upwards towards the maximum sentence ... Many sentencers would wish to take the view that repeated offending can indeed make the current offence more serious and does not merely deprive the offender of mitigation.'

Nevertheless, Lord Taylor CJ, in a speech rather than in an appeal judgement (cited in Wasik and von Hirsch, 1994), after the 1993 Act had been passed, commented that 'the court will still approach the question of seriousness by looking primarily at the instant offences which have to be dealt with, but looking at them not in a vacuum or in blinkers but against previous history.' He appeared to support the continued relevance of cases such as *Queen* and thus to affirm the principle of progressive loss of mitigation. There is no basis for regarding s151(1) as conferring unfettered discretion upon courts. As the sub-section clearly states, the seriousness of the current offence is the key consideration. If this offence is of limited seriousness, no amount of previous convictions for offences of that nature should serve to carry the present offence across the 'so serious' threshold and perhaps not even the 'serious enough' threshold either.

Among other points that may be identified in seeking a principled approach to previous convictions and offence seriousness:

- Record may serve to negate any impression that the present offence resulted from inadvertent lapse, mere impulsiveness, one-off opportunism, exceptional or unprecedented loss of self-control, mere coincidence, happenstance of target, a mitigating motive or some other exculpatory possibility.

- Study of the circumstances of past offences may reveal some element that reflects specifically on the offender's culpability in the present offence, e.g. a pattern of racist motivation, or a propensity to violent temper when intoxicated that the offender has failed to heed, that might otherwise not be apparent. *R v Reynolds* [1999] 2 Cr App R(S) 20 illustrates the contribution that a PSR can make to the assessment of a defendant's culpability in the light of previous, seemingly unrelated convictions. A 21 year old man had set fire to a property in which his brother, at that time remanded in custody, had a bed-sit, as revenge because he believed his brother had burgled his home. Though he had no previous convictions for arson or criminal damage, the PSR was able to indicate that at least three of the burglaries on his record that appeared to be property crimes for gain had had been committed out of a grudge against the occupants. The probation officer commented that he 'displays rather rigid thinking in terms of the necessity to settle scores and does not seem able to rise above a perceived slight or injustice'. The Appeal Court cited this assessment in upholding sentence of six years for aggravated arson.

- Record may suggest what the Court of Appeal in *R v Aramagh* (1983, see Stone, 2000: 36) referred to (in the context of possession of cannabis) as 'a persisting flouting of the law'. 'Flouting' suggests more than mere repeated transgression; rather a defiant or mocking attitude to legal regulation, treating a particular legal prohibition with contempt or as of little importance. Such defiance may be perceived in instances suggestive of a cynical, exploitative professionalism in the offending or a clear preparedness to put other priorities before the law, e.g. in pursuing a vendetta against a particular victim or class of victim. 'Defiance' should not be detected too readily. As Wasik and von Hirsch observe: 'people re-offend for all kinds of reasons – economic and social circumstances, lack of personal control, fecklessness, boredom – which have nothing to do with defiance of the court.'

- Can previous offences on the record serve not to aggravate seriousness but to mitigate, for example if the record reveals some persisting vulnerability or weakness that may reduce the offender's culpability?

- It is difficult to state whether a clear distinction can be drawn between past convictions of a similar nature to the present offence and those which are of a very different nature. Does the principle of progressive loss of mitigation apply so readily where the offender varies their mode of criminal behaviour? Can it be argued that there is a failure to learn from past experience if the offender shifts to another kind of crime? Some elements of similarity between the past and present offences would appear necessary if the focus is not to drift from offence seriousness, but the consequence may be to reward criminal versatility. Should defendants with 'all-rounder' records have an advantage denied to those who repeatedly plough a single furrow of deviance?

- How relevant is record if the previous convictions, albeit closely resembling the current offence, arose a long time ago?

Failure to Respond to Previous Sentences

As an initial and perhaps technical point of interpretation, the use of the plural 'sentences' appears to mean that the offender has been sentenced at least twice before and that a single previous sentence, albeit one that has not been responded to, will not count for the purposes of the sub-section. This interpretation was given by the Divisional Court to the phrase 'non-custodial penalties' in CJA 1982 (*R v Southwark Crown Court, ex parte Ager* (1990)12 Cr App R(S) 126).

If the issue of previous convictions is far from clear, that of 'failure to respond' is particularly ambiguous. This phrase is not defined and is open to extremely wide interpretation. For example, is 'response' to be assessed in terms of the avoidance or commission of further offending or on the basis of failure to fulfil other expectations integral to certain sentences? Is the offender's current crime to be viewed as aggravated by their re-offending at any stage after the experience of the earlier sentence or only if the current offence occurred during the life of the earlier sentence? Wasik and von Hirsch argue persuasively for a narrow interpretation, restricting the issue of failure to respond to relevance to the seriousness of the current offence.

Drawing analogy with the commission of an offence whilst on bail (under s151(2), see page 79), since both involve a breach of trust, they suggest that where a penal order has lapsed, later re-offending does not constitute a 'failure to respond'. 'A sentence should not be seen as a directive to behave well, valid indefinitely.' Even in instances where this narrow interpretation applies, they suggest that it is the inherent seriousness of the new offence that should be the driving factor in sentencing and that breach of trust does not make the new offence greatly more serious. A number of unanswered questions arise:

(i) This line of argument would suggest that it is only possible to 'respond' to a penal measure that has a clear form of continuing life, such as a community order or a conditional discharge. It is difficult to maintain that a fine has this quality even if payment is made by instalments over an extended period. What of a custodial sentence? Presumably the response zone arises on release. Is response during a period of conditional release (when expectations of conformity may be higher) to be viewed differently from response following unconditional release or following expiry of licence or post-custody supervision?

(ii) What if the penal measure contains its own built-in consequence for failure to respond, e.g. on breach of conditional discharge, following failure to comply with a community sentence or through revocation and re-sentencing following a further sentence for a fresh offence, through the 'at risk' provisions of PCC(S)A 2000 s116 (see page 89) built into all custodial sentences? If the failure to respond carries its own separate sanctions, how logical or fair is it also to penalise the failure though s15(1)? In the case of a fresh offence committed during the currency of a suspended sentence, for example, the Appeal Court has held that the proper approach is to deal with the new offence on its merits and only then to consider whether the suspended sentence should be activated.

(iii) In regard to a community service order where the penal measure has a variable life span depending on the offender's progress, apparent illogicalities may arise. To illustrate: offender X and Y each receive CSOs of 150 hours for a joint offence of burglary. X has work commitments and health problems and 11 months later commits a further offence while some hours of his CSO remain to be worked. Y is unemployed and fit and completes his hours in three months. He commits another offence four months after the date of his CSO. It would appear to follow from Wasik and von Hirsch's interpretation that a court dealing with X's fresh offence is able to regard this offence as a 'failure to respond' but is not able to take this view when dealing with Y's fresh offence, despite the fact that Y has offended much more quickly.

(iv)   Does a sentence of probation/community rehabilitation carry particularly raised expectations of a good response because of the intrinsic rationale of this measure in preventing crime and promoting the rehabilitation of the offender? If a probationer re-offends at a very early stage of their order, should this be regarded as a clear 'flouting' of the order or an understandable lapse at a point when the benefits of supervision have not begun to manifest themselves?

(v)   Does it matter if the penal order to which the offender has failed to respond was imposed for an offence of an entirely different nature to the offence now being dealt with?

Note that if an offender made subject to a community order fails to comply with that order and as a consequence the order is revoked with a view to re-sentencing for the original offence, the offender's non-compliance with the order cannot be treated as aggravating the offence for the purposes of the re-sentencing exercise: *R v Clarke* [1997] 1 Cr App R(S) 163. The Court of Appeal went on to add:

'The fact that (an) offence is committed while the offender is already subject to a community order is a matter which may obviously be regarded as aggravating the later offence and is to be taken into account when (he) is sentenced for that later offence.'

Provision of Antecedents

The availability of accurate information about an offender's criminal record is always an important issue but especially so where the offender may be subject to minimum sentence provisions outlined in Chapter 4 (see also Wasik, 2001). In a *Practice Direction (Crime: Antecedents)* [1998] 1 Cr App R 213, issued on 9 October 1997, the Lord Chief Justice announced new procedures for the provision of antecedent information in the Crown Court and magistrates' courts, replacing the *Practice Direction* of October 1993. Agreed by the LCD, CPS, ACPO and the Magistrates' Association, the new Standard on the level of information to be provided follows the introduction of computerised information from the Police National Computer.

Magistrates' Courts and the Crown Court Courts will receive (a) personal details of the defendant and a summary of convictions and cautions; (b) previous convictions; (c) recorded cautions.

Crown Court In addition, the Crown Court receives (d) brief details of the last three similar convictions and/or of convictions likely to be of interest to the court, the latter judged on a case by case basis; (e) where the current alleged offence is within the term of an existing community order and it is known that the order is still in force, details of the circumstances of the offence leading to the community order (to enable the court to consider the possibility of revoking the order).

Antecedents for the Crown Court are prepared following committal proceedings and supplied by the police within 21 days. A copy is then supplied by the court to the Probation Service. Where the record is disputed, the onus lies with the defence to challenge its accuracy, wherever possible seven days before the hearing. If a custodial sentence is imposed, a copy is attached to the order sent to the prison. Seven days before the hearing date, the police check the defendant's record and details of any additional convictions should then be provided, along with details of any additional outstanding charges.

Antecedents for magistrates' courts should be submitted to the CPS with the case file. The CPS should provide a copy to the Probation Service 'when appropriate'. Where antecedents are supplied some time before the hearing, the police will check the record of convictions if requested to do so by the CPS, providing details of any additional convictions and outstanding cases.

Antecedent information is formally given to the Crown Court by prosecuting counsel after 'opening' the case and summarising the facts (in the case of a guilty plea) or after the jury's verdict of guilty in a contested case.

If the defendant disputes any previous conviction alleged against them in their antecedents, this must either be proved under the usual rules of evidence or ignored.

Spent Convictions (see Appendix 1) In accordance with *Practice Direction (Crime: Spent Convictions* [1975] 1 WLR 1065, 'no one should refer in open court to a spent conviction without the authority of the judge, which authority should not be given unless the interests of justice so require' (para 6). When passing sentence, 'the judge should make no reference to a spent conviction unless it is necessary to do so for the purpose of explaining the sentence to be passed' (para 7).

Credit for Guilty Plea

The established principle of reducing sentence, or giving a 'discount', from the sentence which would otherwise be imposed following conviction after contested trial, acquired statutory recognition in CJPOA 1994 s48, now governed by PCC(S)A 2000 s152.

PCC(S)A 2000 s152

(1)   In determining what sentence to pass on an offender who has pleaded guilty to an offence in proceedings before that or another court, a court shall take into account—

(a)   the stage in the proceedings for the offence at which the offender indicated his intention to plead guilty, and

(b)   the circumstances in which this indication was given.

(2)   If, as a result of taking into account any matter referred to in s152(1), the court imposes a punishment on the offender which is less severe than the punishment it would otherwise have imposed, it shall state in open court that it has done so.

Whereas the judicial principle had been applied primarily in determining the length of custodial sentences, s152 is clearly applicable across the board, including non-custodial sentencing, requiring the court to take into account not the timing of the defendant's guilty plea but the stage in proceedings when their intention to plead guilty was indicated and the circumstances prompting such an indication. In some instances a guilty plea will be entered late in proceedings but the defendant is still entitled to full advantage of discount because they indicated at an early stage their willingness to plead guilty to the offence for which they are ultimately convicted but the actual plea was delayed for procedural reasons, e.g. the defence was negotiating the nature of the charge or the factual basis of the case with the prosecution. If, however, the defendant simply chooses to wait and see whether prosecution witnesses will turn up before switching their plea, the credit accruing to them will be substantially diminished.

The section does not detail how the court should exercise this judgement and is thus understood simply to confirm and reinforce the judicial guidance already developed in determining the size of any discount and the circumstances in which the discount can be withheld or reduced. Though s152(2) requires the sentencer to state in open court if has imposed a less severe sentence in the light of plea, the omission to do so does not entitle an offender to a (further) reduction on appeal if the appropriate sentence, taking account of plea, has been passed and it is not open to doubt that the sentencer had in reality taken this factor into account: *R v Wharton* (2001) *The Times* 27 March, declaring that the provision is simply procedural and affirming practice prior to the section (*R v Bishop* [2000] 1 Cr App R(S) 432).

The basis for rewarding a guilty plea in this way is sometimes explained in moral or correctional terms, that the plea is indicative of the offender's remorse or contrition and capacity to face up to their wrongdoing, so that a lesser punishment is appropriate for retributive, deterrent or reformative purposes. In reality, the discount is applied routinely, irrespective of whether the defendant is prompted by remorse, self-interested damage-limitation or bowing to the inevitable, and it would be difficult, if not invidious, to seek to distinguish the genuinely penitent from those who are simply calculating that they will gain a lower sentence. The real justification for discount appears actually more pragmatic. The criminal justice system depends heavily on guilty pleas in order to run smoothly and to turn over its workload. Defendants are thus rewarded for saving time, expense, stopping the courts from becoming clogged and, importantly, sparing victims and witnesses (particularly in cases involving sexual crime) the stress of having to attend to give evidence. Note the Court of Appeal's comments in *R v Buffrey* (detailed below). Where an offender who pleads guilty and demonstrates particular remorse or regret, or gives enhanced assistance to the criminal justice system by their unprompted admissions to the police or their willingness to give evidence against an accomplice, the court has further scope to mitigate sentence, as outlined on page 38. Alternatively, if the offender pleads guilty but does not demonstrate remorse, their discount may well be reduced, as *R v Miller* [1998] 2 Cr App R(S) 398 (a case of racially motivated affray) illustrates. As in *Miller* the absence of remorse may come to the sentencer's attention through the PSR.

For a critique of sentence discounts, see Darbyshire (2000) who argues that discounting: undermines suspects' right to silence, because police officers can promise a sentence benefit to secure a confession; induces some innocent persons to plead guilty; ignores justifications for sentencing such as desert, deterrence, incapacitation and treatment; undermines the right to trial and is racially divisive, since ethnic minority defendants are more likely to exercise their right to trial; offends against the European Convention on Human Rights which asserts the privilege against self-incrimination and the right to be treated fairly without discrimination. She points out that many defendants are charged with less serious offences than the facts justify and so such offenders gain an undeserved second benefit. She adds that the Scottish criminal justice system seems to manage without sentence discounts and argues that the resources in the Crown Court could cope with the increase in contested trials that might follow the banning of discounts.

Size of Discount

The extent of discount in most instances will be in a range or scale between one-third and one-fifth, depending on the timeliness of the circumstances and the plea. The Magistrates Association's *Sentencing Guidelines* (2000) suggest:

> '...a timely guilty plea may attract a discount of up to a third (*the earlier 1993 version referred to 'about a third'*) but the precise amount of discount will depend on the facts of each case. A change of plea on the day set down for trial may attract only a minimal reduction in sentence'.

R v Buffrey (1993) 14 Cr App R(S) 511 is often cited as the most recent leading case from the Court of Appeal in support of one-third as the appropriate discount. *Buffrey* involved a serious pensions fund fraud and the Court of Appeal was conscious how complex and costly such cases are if they have to be unravelled in contested trial, causing considerable stress to every participant, including the judge and jury. There was thus a particularly strong basis for positive recognition for a guilty plea. In this particular case, the defendants pleaded guilty at a late stage, just before the start of the trial. Though their sentence was reduced, they were deemed not to deserve full 'praise' from the Court for their 'public spirited acceptance of what they had done'.

Guilty Plea at Last Possible Moment If the defendant has been running a 'not guilty' plea 'up to the wire' and switches their plea to guilty at the last possible moment, their discount will be 'substantially and visibly reduced from that which they would otherwise have earned': *R v Okoe and West* [1998] 2 Cr App R(S) 199, where a discount of 10% was considered ample in such circumstances. In such instances, though witnesses are spared the ordeal of giving evidence, they have to live with the thought that they will need to do so until a late stage in proceedings.

Though s152 requires the court to state that it has given credit for a guilty plea in determining sentence, the sentencer is not required to indicate the size of discount. Defendants who feel that they have failed to receive any or adequate discount to which they believe themselves entitled may seek to appeal against sentence, as illustrated by the following case example, observed by the author, which also shows the complications posed where the offender is facing sentence for a number of summary offences where the justices' maximum powers are limited.

Case Illustration Mark Ford (26) pleaded guilty to two offences of aggravated vehicle taking (AVT) and to one offence of driving whilst disqualified (DWD) arising from one of the AVT incidents. The two vehicle takings were aggravated because of the damage caused to both vehicles but because the damage caused in each instance was less than £1,000, these offences could be dealt with only summarily with a maximum penalty of three months' imprisonment in each instance. The magistrates imposed sentence of two months' imprisonment for each AVT offence and a further two months for the DWD offence, the sentences to be served consecutively, making six months in total. Mr Ford appealed against sentence on the grounds that as the maximum term available in aggregate for the three offences is six months (see page 77), he should have received a shorter sentence in recognition of his guilty pleas. (He happened also to be simultaneously remanded in custody on further unrelated charges and so, irrespective of the outcome of his appeal, he would remain in custody. However, if his appeal was successful, he would be able to revert more quickly from the status of sentenced prisoner to remand prisoner with the accompanying benefits.)

The Crown Court clearly felt reluctant to reduce sentence, given that the appellant had received a third less than the maximum term available for each offence, and asked counsel whether it would not be proper for a magistrates' court to impose the maximum aggregate term as an alternative to committing a defendant to Crown Court for sentence. The court was reminded that the power to commit for sentence was not available in this case as the offences stood to be treated as summary matters, not either way offences (PCC(S)A 2000 s3 does not permit committal for sentence in these circumstances). The court thus felt obliged to reduce sentence, having regard to s152, but restricted itself to cutting sentence for DWD from two months to one month consecutive, making an aggregate term of five months. Mr Ford thus achieved the benefit of only a one-fifth discount overall for his guilty pleas.

Plea Before Venue Under the provisions of MCA 1980 ss17A–17C (see page 41), introduced by CPIA 1996 s49, a defendant may 'plead guilty before venue', i.e. at the magistrates' court prior to committal to Crown Court. *R v Rafferty* [1999] 1 Cr App R 235 clarifies that a defendant entering a plea at this early stage is entitled to a greater discount than an accused person who delays making plea until pleading to the indictment at the Crown Court. The Court of Appeal made clear that the sentencer should give a reduced discount where the plea is entered at that later stage in the absence of a satisfactory explanation for the delay, less than would have been awarded prior to the change in legislation, rather than award an additional discount for the early plea before venue.

Discount and Mandatory Minimum Sentences

As outlined on pages 106-108, a controversial feature of the provisions of PCC(S)A 2000 ss110-11 specifying minimum sentences for repeat drug trafficking and domestic burglary offending is a maximum discount of 20% for guilty pleas (s152(3)).

Loss of Discount

As s152 requires the court to 'take into account' the offender's guilty plea, the legislation preserves the court's discretion to reduce or withhold discount, and case law has identified a number of exceptions to the normal presumption of credit, as acknowledged by the Court of Appeal in *R v Costen* (1989) 11 Cr App R(S) 182. A court is not required by s152 to state or explain its decision to withhold discount.

(i) *Plea Tactics* The defendant persists in indicating a not guilty plea until a very late stage, in circumstances where there is little or no valid basis for a defence, especially where this is done to gain some tactical advantage with which the court finds little sympathy, e.g. to delay the process of trial and sentence, or to ensure that as much time as possible which could count towards sentence will be spent as an unconvicted remand prisoner with the status advantages this can bring. Such tactics can cause delay, extra work and, in some instances of very late change, the disruption of court business and the unnecessary attendance of witnesses.

(ii) *Caught 'Red Handed'* The offender's guilt is so blatantly clear and the evidence so overwhelming that s/he has little choice but to plead guilty and it is thus unnecessary or inappropriate to give credit for such a plea. This exception is not straightforward, suggesting that courts should determine to what extent a defendant's pleading guilty might have had a plausible defence. If the rationale for the discount is to reward the defendant's contribution to the smooth running of the system, this would seem equally applicable even to defendants whose guilt is patently obvious as they could opt perversely to plead not guilty despite the weight of evidence against them, and might feel more inclined to do so if they had nothing to lose. The exception is used sparingly and by no means consistently, and reported instances usually arise in cases featuring episodes of very bad driving in which the offender is detained 'at the wheel', where the sentencer wishes to impose the maximum sentence despite their guilty plea. Recent examples include:

R v Landy (1995) 16 Cr App R(S) 908. The offender took a car, while disqualified from driving, was pursued by the police, drove dangerously and crashed, being arrested while still in the upturned vehicle. His appeal against sentence of two years' imprisonment for aggravated vehicle taking (with six months concurrent for excess alcohol) the maximum term despite his guilty plea, was dismissed.

R v Hastings [1996] 1 Cr App R(S) 167. The offender was involved in a high speed chase by police through city streets. He jumped red lights and collided with another vehicle. He was arrested at the scene, making an immediate admission of responsibility, and pleaded guilty to dangerous driving and excess alcohol, receiving sentence of two years' imprisonment, upheld on appeal.

R v Jackson (2000) (JP 2/12/00) Though the offender had been caught red-handed and had an appalling driving record, thus justifying the maximum term despite guilty plea, the judge had indicated that he was giving some discount for plea and thus sentence for driving whilst disqualified was reduced from six to five months.

(iii) *Specimen Offence* (but now see page 34) Until recent case law clarifying the position regarding 'specimen offences', where the offender pleaded guilty to a single offence but the court viewed the offence as representative of a larger number of offences. In *R v Costen* (1989) 11 Cr App R(S) 182 the female offender pleaded guilty to indecency with a child, a girl aged 11. She had been living with the child's step-father and had been involved in encouraging her to masturbate him. Though the Court of Appeal acknowledged in principle that discount could be withheld in such instances, in the circumstances of the case where the defendant was of low intelligence and her plea had spared the child the distress of giving evidence a limited degree of credit for plea was allowed and sentence was reduced from the maximum term of two years to 21 months, a discount of one-eighth.

(iv) *Giving Evidence for Co-Defendant* If an offender who has pleaded guilty opts to give evidence for a co-defendant who is denying guilt and that co-defendant is nevertheless convicted, this does not justify the sentencer in withholding discount for guilty plea. To refuse discount in such circumstances is in effect improperly to penalise the offender for 'telling lies in the witness box': *R v Lawless* [1998] 2 Cr App R(S) 176.

Maximum Sentence

The discount principle means that a defendant pleading guilty should not normally receive a sentence of the maximum term that the court can impose for that offence. As will be noted in the preceding section, this can occur if the case falls within one of the established exceptions. Very occasionally, a sentence of maximum length may be upheld in the absence of such a factor because of the very serious view taken of the offending episode. This has arisen particularly in the case of young offenders aged under 18 for whom a special maximum term of YOI detention applied (previously 12 months but raised to two years by CJPOA 1994) prior to the introduction under CDA 1998 of the detention and training order. In *R v Winspear* (1987) 9 Cr App R(S) 243 the maximum term of 12 months was upheld for a 16 year old pleading guilty to burglary of a dwelling, entered twice on the day he was released from a previous custodial sentence for domestic burglary. His brazen behaviour immediately upon release was clearly considered to forfeit any discount consideration within the ceiling then applicable on grounds of age. Similarly, in *R v Reay* [1993] RTR 189, sentence of 12 months imposed on a 15 year old pleading guilty to taking without consent and reckless driving was upheld because of the high level of danger he had posed and the prevalence of that kind of offending in the locality. However, in *R v Sharkey and Daniels* (1995) 16 Cr App R(S) 257 maximum terms of 12 months and two years imposed for aggravated vehicle taking (not a 'red handed' exceptional case) on offenders aged 16 and 18 were set aside as wrong in principle in the light of their timely guilty pleas, despite the seriousness of their misconduct. *Reay* was cited with approval in *R v Scarley* [2001] 1 Cr App R(S) 86 where a two year term of imprisonment was upheld for dangerous driving, committed in circumstances that afforded the defendant, a man with a very bad record for driving offences and at the time disqualified from driving, 'no practical defence'. The Appeal Court observed that if he had been given 21 months for his dangerous driving and three months consecutive for DWD, instead of 24 months plus three months concurrent, he could have had no complaint.

If an offender aged under 18 pleads guilty at Crown Court to a 'grave crime' within PCC(S)A 2000 s91 (see page 115) and which in the court's view comes close to meriting such longer term detention, the court may properly impose the maximum detention and training order term without giving credit for guilty plea, for otherwise the offender would gain an unwarranted double advantage. For an example of the application of the discount principle to a DTO sentence for an offence other than a grave crime, thus obliging a reduction of sentence length from 24 months to 18 months (the next longest term available under the permitted lengths for this form of custodial sentence – see page 123), see *R v Kelly* [2001] Crim LR 583.

A magistrates' court dealing with an offender who pleads guilty to repeated summary offences may feel some temptation to impose the maximum custodial term available to the court of six months (see page 77), for otherwise it may appear absurd that an offender who stands to be dealt with on the same occasion for multiple offences of a summary but serious nature will always gain the automatic advantage of discount, irrespective of their persistent criminal activities. Even here the discount principle may hold good in order to ensure the avoidance of contested trials, as illustrated by the case example on page 19. However, in *McCarthy v DPP* [2000] Crim LR 316 the Divisional Court has recently sought to end uncertainty about whether a defendant is entitled to discount in such circumstances. The offender pleaded guilty to interfering with a motor vehicle (maximum term: three months) and driving while disqualified (maximum term: six months). He received consecutive terms of one month and five months. Rejecting his argument that by receiving six months, the maximum available, he had not received credit for his pleas, the Court said that such an interpretation would lead to unacceptable results not intended by Parliament and he had received appropriate discount through the individual sentences passed.

If the magistrates' court is dealing with an either way offence and considers that the offence merits in excess of six months, the appropriate course would be to commit for sentence, not to determine the notional appropriate term (say nine months) and then impose the maximum term of six months on the basis of discount.

Risk to the Public of Serious Harm

The Court of Appeal in *Costen* considered that it would be proper to withhold discount where a longer sentence was appropriate to protect the public from a dangerous offender. This issue should now be addressed within the specific provisions of CJA 1991 s2(2)(b) to allow longer than commensurate sentences for violent or sexual offences in certain instances where necessary for public protection. In *R v Crow and Pennington* (1995) 16 Cr App R(S) 409 the Court of Appeal stated that a plea of guilty should be taken into account in determining length of sentence but that this should be given rather less weight than in commensurate sentencing.

Community Sentencing

The application of the discount principle is less clear in the calculation of community sentences, especially community service orders. If an offence is deemed to merit a custodial sentence but the court considers there is sufficient mitigation or other basis for a community order instead, there can clearly be no basis for disputing an order of maximum length, e.g. 240 hours community service imposed upon a guilty plea. If on the other hand an offence is deemed 'serious enough' to merit a community sentence but not 'so serious' that a custodial sentence is merited, an offender pleading guilty may feel justifiably aggrieved to receive an order of 240 hours.

Plea-Bargaining

Plea-bargaining is an inevitable feature of a system that gives discount for guilty pleas (see Darbyshire, 2000). Though a well-established feature of criminal justice in the United States the fiction has been maintained in this jurisdiction that the practice is alien and to be discouraged. Long-standing Court of Appeal authority has specified the principles applicable to private discussions between the judge and advocates: *R v Turner* [1970] 2 QB 321. Lord Parker CJ stated that though there must be freedom of access between counsel and judge, such access should be sought only where felt to be really necessary and any discussion must be between the judge and counsel for the defence and for the prosecution. The judge should never indicate the sentence which s/he is minded to impose. 'A statement that on a plea of guilty he would impose one sentence but that on conviction he would impose a severer sentence is one that should never be made. This could be taken to be undue pressure on the accused, thus depriving him of that complete freedom of choice which is essential.' It is permissible for the judge to say that, irrespective of plea, the sentence will or will not take a particular form. It is also appropriate for the judge to indicate that, on a guilty plea, 'he will, for instance, make a probation order, something which may be helpful to counsel in advising the accused' but the judge should be careful not to indicate what he would do in the event of conviction following a not guilty plea. When discussion has taken place between counsel and the judge, counsel for the defence should disclose this to the accused and inform him of what took place. In subsequent cases the Court has stated that such discussion in chambers should be recorded by shorthand writer or tape. In a number of instances a breach of the *Turner* principles has led to a quashing of a conviction on a guilty plea and an order of *venire de novo*, in effect a re-trial. In instances where the judge has appeared to go back on an indication to counsel, the Appeal Court has felt it necessary, in the interests of avoiding what may appear an injustice, to quash sentence in favour of a lesser penalty.

Counsel have been faulted for trying to extract from the judge an indication about sentence in order to give their client informed advice on plea. In a recent such instance, *R v Dossetter* [1999] 2 Cr App R(S) 248 the Appeal Court deplored a 'blatant attempt by counsel to engage in plea-bargaining' before the defendant decided on plea. 'Plea-bargaining to extract an exact sentence forms no part of English jurisprudence.' Subsequently, in *R v Ryan* (1999) 163 JP Reports 849, a case involving an indication by a judge to a defendant that he would probably impose a sentence of no more than 18 months on a plea of guilty to possession of heroin with intent to supply, prompting the defendant to change her plea to guilty, resulting in a term of four years from a second judge who had not been informed of the first judge's indication, the Appeal Court reiterated:

- Approaches to a judge seeking an indication of the length of sentence which might be imposed in the event of a guilty plea are to be deprecated.

- Where such an indication is given and conveyed to a defendant, it will normally be binding not only on the judge who gave the indication but on any other judge before whom the defendant might appear.

- Where a defendant has changed their plea in the light of such an indication but has subsequently received a more severe sentence, the Court of Appeal will often but not invariably feel constrained to reduce the sentence to that indicated, even if the indicated sentence is less than the offence merits.

Sentence of four years was thus reduced to 18 months.

In *Attorney-General's Reference No 44 of 2000 (R v Peverett)* [2001] 1 Cr App R(S) 460, an offender facing counts of indecent assault against children who were pupils at the school where he was headteacher had indicated that he was not willing to plead guilty if the consequence was that he would be sent to prison but was otherwise prepared to admit guilt on the limited basis that he had administered punishment in an inappropriate manner. Counsel for the prosecution and defence made a joint approach to the judge saying that the Crown would accept his guilty pleas on that basis. The judge indicated that a suspended sentence would follow and guilty pleas were duly entered. Deploring this practice, the Court of Appeal said that this kind of approach and agreement were an affront to justice. Such a process was only appropriate in 'wholly exceptional cases', for example where a defendant was dying but was not aware of this. Though the Court felt that suspension of sentence was not justified in this case, nevertheless the prosecution was party to an understanding on which the defendant was entitled to rely and which had given rise to a legitimate expectation on his part. It was thus not open to the Attorney-General to seek to have the sentence reviewed as unduly lenient.

Concurrent or Consecutive Sentence?

When an offender is sentenced for more than one offence, the court should impose a separate sentence for each offence (though with scope to make an order for no separate penalty, a recourse usually adopted only for minor, subsidiary offences) and should give a clear indication which sentence relates to which offence and whether sentences are to run concurrently or consecutively or with a mixture of both, a feature which can make the sentencing of a number of offences quite complicated to follow and record. If the court fails to indicate its intent, the ambiguity is resolved in the offender's favour and sentences are presumed to be concurrent. Similarly, if an offender receiving a custodial sentence is already serving such a sentence, the court should indicate whether the fresh sentence is to be served concurrently with or consecutive to the existing term. To ensure that the new sentence is not absorbed into the existing term, the sentencer needs to make it clear that the new sentence is to be 'consecutive to the total period of imprisonment to which you are already subject': *Practice Direction (Sentence)* [1959] 1 WLR 491. Where imposing consecutive sentences, the sentencer will also need to have regard to the 'totality of sentence' (see page 27).

The principles outlined below have emerged in respect of custodial sentencing. The scope for concurrent or consecutive sentencing in respect of community orders is addressed in Chapter 5 but note that a community rehabilitation order commences on the day it is imposed and there is thus no scope for a consecutive order.

As a general rule, where two or more offences form part of the same transaction, concurrent sentences should be imposed. However, as Ashworth (1995) notes:

'It is very difficult to construct a workable definition of a single transaction, especially since it seems to be little more than a pragmatic device for limiting overall sentences rather than a reflection of a sharp category distinction. Indeed, the Court of Appeal has taken advantage of this fuzziness to extend the principle considerably beyond what might be expected. Thus a series of offences of the same or similar type, committed against the same victim, may properly be regarded as parts of the transaction unless they were committed over a fairly lengthy period of time.'

The principle seems best understood in terms of 'proximity in time and proximity in type of offence'.

Consecutive sentences can normally be expected in a number of specific instances where the Court of Appeal has indicated that a distinctive additional dimension of the further offence should be marked by additional punishment to discourage conduct of that nature:

• where the offender commits an assault, usually on a police officer, in attempting to resist arrest for the initial offence or to escape the scene (e.g. assaulting a householder who interrupts a burglary);

• where the offender carries a firearm in the course of committing another offence and falls to be sentenced for a separate offence contrary to the Firearms Act;

• where the offender attempts to pervert the course of justice in respect of their earlier offence, as illustrated by *Attorney-General's Reference No 1 of 1990* (1990) 12 Cr App R(S) 245 where an offender facing prosecution for indecent assault wrote to the victim from prison while on remand awaiting trial, to try to discourage him from giving evidence;

• where the offender commits the further offence while on bail in respect of the earlier offence. Though a long acknowledged basis for a consecutive sentence, this has to be queried in the light of PCC(S)A 2000 s151(2) (see page 79) which makes the commission of a further offence while on bail an aggravating feature of the original offence. Can it be valid both to increase the sentence for the original offence and to penalise the defendant by consecutive sentencing in circumstances where a concurrent sentence would otherwise be appropriate?

In what can be regarded as exceptional circumstances, the Court of Appeal has sometimes upheld the legitimacy of imposing consecutive sentences for offences arising out of the same transaction which are not within the special instances identified above. Reported examples usually concern episodes of bad driving by a defendant with a record of persistent offending of this nature. Though a 'transaction' involving, for example, dangerous driving and driving whilst disqualified will usually attract concurrent sentences, the court may consider that if an offender has broken not one but two significant road traffic laws and the sentence does not signify double disapproval, the impression will be gained that the additional default does not make any significant difference. Thus in *R v Wheatley* (1983) 5 Cr App R(S) 417, a sentence of 12 months imprisonment for DWD, ordered to run consecutively to six months for excess alcohol, was upheld on the basis that concurrent sentences might encourage a persistent offender to believe that s/he could drive with excess alcohol while disqualified without fear of additional penalty. More recently, in *R v Jordan* [1996] 1 Cr App R(S) 181, an intoxicated and banned offender took a car parked at a police station, prompting a police chase in the course of which he collided with another vehicle causing minor injuries to the driver. He then attempted to drive away and struggled when arrested. He had previous convictions for excess alcohol and DWD offences. He was sentenced to 14 months' imprisonment for aggravated vehicle taking with six months for driving while unfit through drink and a further six months for dangerous driving, all to run consecutively, i.e. 26 months in total. The Court of Appeal upheld the validity of consecutive sentencing in cases of persistent offending of this kind, albeit reducing both six month sentences to five to allow credit for a guilty plea. The Court indicated that, despite the common element of driving, the offences were effectively different in substance. In *R v Webb* [2001] 1 Cr App R(S) 112 where the offender had committed racially aggravated common assault and criminal damage, hitting a minicab driver and kicking his car, the Appeal Court held that consecutive sentences were fully justified for 'different dimensions' of her offending, albeit occurring in the same episode. See also *R v Dent* (2001, unreported) where the Court of Appeal approved a sentence of six months consecutive to one of 21 months for dangerous driving, noting that "each case depends on its own facts" and that a 21 month term for the dangerous driving with six months concurrent for DWD would have been fully deserved.

Implications for Early Release

Where a custodial term is imposed on an offender who is already completing a previously imposed custodial term, the sentencing court seeking to add a certain period of 'real time' to the defendant's existing liability to imprisonment or detention will need to have regard to the provision of CJA 1991 s51(2) which requires that the two sentences shall be treated as forming a single term for the purposes of determining whether the prisoner is a 'short term' or 'long term' prisoner for early release purposes. This application is demonstrated in *R v Singh* [1999] 1 Cr App R(S) 445 where a man completing a 12 year term (with nine months to serve before his non-parole date (NPD), i.e. after 8 years) had been further convicted of possession of heroin with intent. The judge wished him to serve an additional two years' actual time and initially imposed a consecutive term of four years until counsel pointed out that his automatic release at his non-parole date would arise after two-thirds of that four year period, i.e. longer than two years. The judge then adjusted sentence length below the four year term (that normally leads to long term status) to 3 years 10 months, overlooking the effect of s51(2). On appeal, the Court of Appeal resolved that to achieve the judge's objective, a consecutive term of three years should be substituted, i.e. making a total term of 15 years (i.e. with an NPD after 10 years). In *R v Brown* [1999] 1 Cr App R(S) 47 where the offender who had been sentenced to 2.5 years appeared for a further offence and was given a further 18 months consecutive, thus rendering him a long-term prisoner. It was unclear whether the judge had been alert to the implications of this for the defendant's early release and as a consequence the Appeal Court reduced the 18 month term to 15 months to give the offender the benefit of the doubt. The Court stated that where circumstances such as this arise, the judge should decide whether the sentence which might otherwise be appropriate should nevertheless be reduced to allow for the fact that the offender would otherwise spend extra time in prison in respect of the first offence (assuming he does not gain parole). Advocates should inform judges of the effect of the additional sentence on the status of an earlier but current sentence: *R v McCarton* (1998, unreported).

Totality of Sentence

Allied to the prospect of consecutive sentencing (see above), a court should have regard to the totality of sentence. The 'totality principle', first coined by Thomas (1979), is given statutory recognition by PCC(S)A 2000 s158(2) (formerly CJA 1991 s28(2)):

> Without prejudice to the generality of s158(1) *(see page 38)*, nothing in *(ss35–36, ss79–82 & s128)* shall prevent a court—
>
> (a)   from mitigating any penalty included in an offender's sentence by taking into account any other penalty included in that sentence; or
>
> (b)   in a case of an offender who is convicted of one or more other offences, from mitigating his sentence by applying any rule of law as to the totality of sentences.

In essence, when finalising the sentence on any sentencing occasion, the sentencer should have regard to the overall weight of the complete sentence, whether in regard to the aggregate of penalties for a single offence, or in combining penalties imposed for a number of offences dealt with on the same occasion, or in combining the penalty to be imposed on that sentencing occasion with any penalty to which the offender is currently subject arising from an earlier sentencing exercise. This principle, dignified now as a 'rule of law', tends to receive greatest attention in respect of custodial sentencing, for obvious reasons, but is also applicable in weighing community and financial penalties. Note that the sub-section does not require the sentencer to pay heed to the principle but simply makes it a discretionary consideration. The calculation or 'arithmetic' of sentencing is clearly of primary concern to sentencers but should be kept in mind by sentencing advisors. The issue is well covered by Ashworth (1995) and the following is simply a brief outline.

Multiple Offences

Thomas (1979) identified as a first sub-principle of 'totality':

> 'The aggregate sentence should not be longer than the upper limit of the normal bracket of sentences for the category of cases in which the most serious offence committed by the offender would be placed.'

If the sentencer was simply to decide the proportionate sentence for each offence separately and reach a total sentence by simple addition, the bottom line of sentence could be very substantial, even if due heed is paid to the principles of concurrent rather than consecutive sentencing (see page 24). It could mean the offender receiving the kind of total sentence for a number of less serious crimes that would normally be considered appropriate for a crime of far greater seriousness. As the Court of Appeal put it in unreported case of *R v Holderness* back in 1974, the sentencer should 'stand back and look at the overall effect of the sentence'. In that case where four years imprisonment was imposed for a variety of offences, primarily motoring matters, the sentencer should have appreciated that 'he was imposing the kind of sentence which is imposed for really serious crime'. This approach to proportionality raises interesting dilemmas that are unlikely to be satisfactorily resolved. While we may agree that multiple instances of driving while disqualified should never result in a sentence akin to the penalty for a single case of rape, can a large number of burglaries justify a sentence of that kind?

As Ashworth comments, 'if the leading principle is to retain some overall proportionality with the seriousness of the type of offence involved, it follows that each extra offence must have a diminishing incremental effect on the overall sentence.' The offender stands to receive a lower total sentence than he would have received if he had been before the court on a number of separate occasions for the same number of offences. This produces what Ashworth characterises as 'a discount for bulk offending' (or perhaps binge offending). The fact that the whole can be considerably less than the sum of the parts is not lost on offenders who can sometimes bemoan that outstanding matters are not brought to court for sentence on the same sentencing occasion, thus depriving them of the benefit of the discount.

The outline so far may suggest that the totality principle operates as a limiting factor; in other words, the sentencer first calculates the appropriate sentence for each individual offence and then reduces the sub-total to arrive at an appropriate final total. In practice, there is evidence that sentencers sometimes start with the totality in mind rather than ending with it, reaching some early sense of the proper sentence overall and then working out individual penalties that are consistent with that conclusion.

Avoiding a 'Crushing Burden'

Thomas suggested a second sub-principle of totality that the total sentence should not be such as to impose a crushing burden on an offender whose prospects are not hopeless. Ashworth concludes that this reflects 'rehabilitative notions', coupled with the principle of restraint in the use of custody, and is of doubtful compatibility with the sentencing framework of the 1991/2000 Acts. However, there appears to be some continuing element of judicial sensitivity to the impactful weight of a sentence, particularly a custodial term that may make it difficult for the offender to keep some grip on their external identity and future prospects, or may risk the atrophy of positive outside attachments and commitments. However, as Ashworth notes, it is difficult to find specific authority for the sub-principle, albeit that it may feature in the thinking of PSR writers.

A version of this sub-principle applies to community sentencing. Though it may not be appropriate to view community order demands as 'crushing burdens', the danger of placing too many obligations on an offender are well recognised and the totality principle may serve alongside considerations of 'suitability' (see page 132) to set a realistic limit upon the aggregate of demands.

Changed Status of Custodial Sentence

Where an offender is receiving a further custodial sentence that will be served consecutively to a custodial term already being served, the result may be that the offender acquires the status of long-term prisoner (see page 86) because he will now be serving an aggregate term of four years or longer. In *R v Brown* (1999, see page 26), the Court of Appeal stated in respect of the latter instance that judges should consider whether the sentence being imposed should be reduced to allow for the additional time that the defendant may spend in prison in respect of the first offence (because of the different early release provisions that will now govern the total term), even though the proposed additional sentence is not manifestly excessive.

Impact of Offence on Victim

In assessing the harm caused by an offence as an essential element in weighing offence-seriousness, it may seem obvious to take adequate account of the impact of the crime upon the victim, particularly if an individual rather than a corporate entity was victimised. The means by which that impact, physical and psychological, should be ascertained and such information should reach the sentencer has been far from clear. Should the sentencer simply rely on assumptions based on popular wisdom, for example by taking account of the adverse psychological effects widely reported to result from domestic burglary, or the belief that crime of that nature impacts more upon older women living alone? This requires little or no information specific to the particular victim. Such assumptions are more controversial in regard to sexual offences. In *R v O'S* (1993) 14 Cr App R(S) 632, however, a judge sentencing for incest and indecent assault felt able to comment that the offences had resulted in serious damage to the child victims who might be marked for the rest of their lives, though there was no specific evidence before the court to justify such comments.

Another possible source of information of a more specific kind might be the prosecution advocate in outlining the facts of the case. Thus in *R v Hobstaff* (1993) 14 Cr App R(S) 605, where the offender had pleaded guilty to three offences of indecent assault against children, prosecution counsel had referred to the effect on the victims, such as nightmares and sleep-walking, though there was no evidence to support these claims in the case papers and statements. The Appeal Court considered that what the prosecution had said 'was wholly improper and still more so when clothed in colourful and emotive language'. The Court indicated that if it was considered necessary to bring such information to the sentencer's attention, the proper approach would be to obtain an expert's report and/or witness statement, serve these on the defence in advance and present them formally to the court. Procedural fairness requires that the defence should not be faced with unsubstantiated allegations and should have proper opportunity to challenge substantiated allegations. Thus in *R v Doe* (1994) 16 Cr App R(S) 719 and *Attorney-General's Reference No 2 of 1995* [1995] Crim LR 835 (both involving sexual crime), it was established that a court may receive evidence of the psychological effects of the effect on the victim. That said, it may be observed that a criminal court may not be a particularly appropriate arena in which to evaluate the subtleties of harm where this is subject of dispute. How should the defence seek to challenge evidence of this nature? By asking for the opportunity to cross-examine the expert assessor, by obtaining an alternative assessment, even by seeking to cross-examine the victim?

The PSR may offer a further source of information. *National Standards* (2000 edition, para B6) instruct that the 'offence analysis' section of a report should include an assessment of 'the consequences of the offence, including what is known of the impact on any victim, either from the CPS papers or from a victim statement where available'. The Home Office is thus not encouraging direct approaches to victims by PSR writers, simply a close reading and interpretation of the case papers that may well be before the court anyway. Should the report writer take the initiative in instances where the victim is known to another agency, such as a Social Services Department dealing with a child who has been sexually abused or a woman who has experienced domestic violence, to obtain additional information without the need to trouble the victim directly? If the writer interviews the victim, as may happen where the victim is also the offender's spouse in a crime of domestic violence, how much attention should be paid to victim impact? PSR authors may understandably feel on securer ground pursuing an assessment of the offender's attitude to the victim and awareness of the consequences of their crime (as also addressed by para B6).

Some of these issues were posed in *R v Perks* [2001] 1 Cr App R(S) 66, a case of street robbery by a heroin user of a woman by seizing her bag, causing her to fall over and sustain comparatively minor injuries. Her husband had sent the CPS a written 'update' on his wife's progress following the attack in which he referred to the 'devastating effect' on her, her tearfulness, sleep disturbance, nervousness and continuing fears that the offender would come after her. He went on to doubt the sincerity of the offender's expressions of regret, labelling him a greedy, self-indulgent thug who should be jailed as an example to others. This had been submitted to the judge with the case papers. In passing sentence, the judge had referred to the offence leaving 'an appalling blot on her memory'. After reviewing the body of relevant case law, the Appeal Court was able to derive the following propositions as general guidance to sentencers:

- A sentencer must not make assumptions, unsupported by evidence, about the effects of an offence on the victim.

- If an offence has had a particularly damaging or distressing effect on a victim, this should be known to and taken into account by the court when passing sentence.

- Evidence of the effects of an offence on the victim must be in a proper form, a Section 9 witness statement, an expert's report or otherwise, duly served upon the defence prior to sentence.

- Evidence of the victim alone should be approached with care, the more so if it relates to matters which the defence cannot realistically be expected to investigate. (For example, in *H* (1999) *The Times* 18 March, five complainants of childhood sexual abuse had made statements indicating that their experience had had a serious impact on their lives, including the way in which they related to their own children, a matter on which they had not been cross-examined.)

- The opinions of the victim and their close relatives on the appropriate level of sentence should not be taken into account. The court must pass what it judges to be the appropriate sentence, having regard to the circumstances of the offence and of the offender, (subject to two exceptions noted below).

A number of jurisdictions provide for the submission of a formal 'victim impact statement' (VIS), either via the PSR (as in South Australia) or the prosecution, or directly to the court (see Ashworth, 1993). This development has led to uncertainty whether VISs inform sentencers or actually serve other purposes, giving victims an expressive 'voice' or helping to 'educate' judges. Victim Support (1994) reported that research shows that none of these purposes are satisfactorily fulfilled. In England and Wales, the *Victim's Charter* (1996) states:

> 'You can expect the chance to explain how the crime has affected you, and your interests to be taken into account ... The police will ask you about your fears about further victimisation and details of your loss, damage or injury. The police, Crown Prosecutor, magistrates and judge will take this information into account when making their decisions.'

A number of pilot projects were established in 1996/97 (in Bedfordshire, Hampshire, Lancashire, London, Merseyside and Sussex) to improve communications between victims and criminal justice agencies. Evaluation of the way in which victim statements (VSs) had been collected and used (Hoyle *et al*, 1998) reported:

- Nearly a third of eligible victims opted to give a VS; 60% having 'expressive' reasons for doing so, while 55% wanted to influence the case outcome.

- Though more victims stated that their participation was satisfactory, 20% regretted making a VS. Some victims believed that their VS would affect sentencing more than was ever likely to happen. Some did not like relaying sensitive feelings and details to police officers, particularly in respect to sexual crime. The timing of VSs was problematic, being made soon after the accused was charged when long-term consequences were not yet known.

- Many prosecutors and judges said that few VSs contained significant material not already on file.

- Around 90% of victims had no idea what happened to their VS, after it was made, many feeling that it had been ignored.

Follow-up research (Morgan and Sanders, 1999) reported that VSs 'rarely influence the sentence. When they do, it is always to increase their severity'.

> 'Information is only likely to influence sentence if it makes the impact unusual. Anything unusual would normally have to be verified if it is to be believed and acted upon. Otherwise, sentencers simply fall back on their experience.'

Challenges to the content of VSs are rare, in part because advocates are reluctant to antagonise sentencers but also because prosecution and defence often reach agreement on what is, and is not, acceptable. While VSs are widely supported by professionals, this is at the level of rhetoric rather than practice, for three main reasons: (a) victims' rights are difficult to operationalise in practice; (b) the scheme in operation collected the wrong information in the wrong form at the wrong time; (c) in most cases the impact revealed is what decision-makers would have expected anyway.

Issues of principle remain. From the victim perspective, the advantages are unclear. As Ashworth (1995, 310) comments:

> 'It is sometimes claimed that making a statement can have a cathartic effect ... but on the other hand it may create or increase the fear of reprisals from the offender's family or associates, and may raise the victim's expectations about the sentence.'

From the stance of sentencing principles, what is the real relevance of such 'after-effects' information? Is it right that sentence should vary according to 'the chance circumstance of whether a particular victim suffers after-effects that are unusually great or unusually small?' (Ashworth, 1995). As Fenwick (1997, 330) observes:

'It appears to offend against the requirements of justice to punish an offender more or less severely because the victim happens to be particularly resilient, particularly forgiving or particularly sensitive, since such factors are not directly related to the culpability of the defendant. It might be pointed out in reply that this argument tends to exaggerate the extent to which the consequences are likely to be unforeseen. If a victim is known to an attacker, the likely effects of the attack may be readily apparent and quite particularised. Where an attack is by a stranger, there may be communication between defendant and victim, perhaps as part of a mercy plea, which might inform the attacker, for example, that the victim is pregnant. In other instances, the defendant might be assumed to have no particularised knowledge of the likely consequences of the offence, but could be assumed to be able to make a common sense estimate of them, depending on its gravity and his/her knowledge of the victim's characteristics – where such knowledge could be assumed from the nature of the offence. It is suggested that a compromise might be reached ... whereby sentencing could be influenced by victim statements only where a reasonable person endowed with the defendant's knowledge of the victim would find that the actual consequences were within the range of probable consequences.'

Fenwick suggests that an exception should be made for defendants with clear intellectual impairment that renders them incapable of foreseeing matters which the average defendant would be likely to foresee.

Sentencing case law has barely begun to tackle such dilemmas. However, in the *Billam* guidelines on sentencing for rape (see Stone, 2000), the Court of Appeal indicated that a high degree of trauma resulting from the offence should be viewed as an aggravating factor. The corollary appears to be that less-than-expected trauma is a relevant consideration that may reduce sentence. This logic was accepted by the Court of Appeal in *R v Hind* (1994) 15 Cr App R(S) 114 where there was evidence that the victim, the offender's former lover, had not experienced as much trauma as might otherwise arise from being raped, thus providing a basis for reduced sentence. This case may be viewed as primarily a matter of 'forgiveness' by a victim and is thus dealt with below.

Victim's Forgiveness or Distress

Though there is no formal provision to allow a victim to give an opinion on prospective sentence, it is not unknown for victims or their families to take the initiative to express forgiveness, seek the court's mercy or to place other factors before the court that may cause the court to take a more lenient view. Summing up case law on these special circumstances, the Appeal Court in *Perks* (see above) identified two exceptions to the general rule that the opinion of victims and their families on the level of sentence should not be taken into account:

(i)   Where the sentence passed on the offender is aggravating the victim's distress, the sentence may be moderated to some degree.

(ii)   Where the victim's forgiveness or unwillingness to press charges provide evidence that his or her psychological suffering must be much less than would normally be the case.

Examples of Distress In *R v Brett D* [1996] 1 Cr App R(S) 196, in reviewing a four year term of imprisonment imposed for rape, incest and indecent assault on a man now aged 22 who from age 12 to 19 had sexually abused his sister (aged two years younger), the Appeal Court was particularly impressed by a letter from the victim stating that he needed help and counselling that was not available to him in prison and that his continuing imprisonment without treatment was having an adverse effect on her. Noting also that there was no evidence that he was a continuing abuser, the Court substituted a probation order.

In *R v Nunn* [1996] 2 Cr App R(S) 136, a case of causing the death of the offender's friend by dangerous driving, the Court on hearing an appeal against a term of four years imprisonment had been shown letters from the deceased's mother and sister that the sentence was having an adverse effect on their ability to come to terms with their loss and grief. The Court stated:

'It is an elementary principle that the damaging and distressing effects of a crime on the victim represent an important factor in the sentencing decision, and those consequences may include the anguish and emotional suffering of the victim or, in the case of death, his surviving close family. The opinions of the victim or surviving family member does not provide any sound basis for re-assessing a sentence. If the victim feels utterly merciful towards the criminal, as some do, the crime has still been committed and must be punished as it deserves. If the victim is obsessed with vengeance, as sometimes happens, the punishment cannot be made longer than would otherwise be appropriate. Otherwise, cases with identical features would be dealt with in widely different ways, leading to improper and unfair disparity. Carried to its logical conclusion, unfair pressures would be imposed on victims or survivors that many would find painful or distasteful. ... In the present case, the Court was concerned not with the judgement of the deceased's mother and sister but with the clear evidence that the sentence was adding to their grief and anxiety.'

As an exercise of mercy, consistent with the Court's duty to sentence appropriately those causing death by driving dangerously under the influence of alcohol, the sentence was reduced to three years.

In *R v Roche* [1999] 2 Cr App R(S) 105 where the deceased victim of dangerous driving was the offender's cousin, their mothers being sisters and their fathers brothers, where the court had received a letter from the family indicating that the sentence imposed (of four years) was delaying their grieving and having an adverse effect on the family, sentence was reduced to three years as an exercise of compassion.

In somewhat similar vein, in *Attorney-General's Reference No 72 of 1998* (noted in JP Vol.163 201) the victim of robbery by the 17 year old offender was his great-grandmother aged 95 who was concerned that his grandmother with whom he lived found life difficult without him. The trial judge had thus opted to impose a probation order. This exercise in tempering justice with mercy was upheld by the Appeal Court, rejecting the A-G's Reference.

Examples of Forgiveness The second exception to the general rule may arise in cases of rape of a former sexual partner, as illustrated by *R v Hind* (see above) and *R v Hutchinson* [1993] Crim LR 718, in both instances the victim taking a forgiving attitude to the perpetrator in the period between the crime and the point of sentence. This allowed the court to conclude that the psychological and mental suffering caused must have been less than in many instances of rape, thus offering some mitigation. In *R v Darvill* (1987) 9 Cr App R(S) 225 the Court of Appeal indicated that the defendant must be sentenced for the offence they have committed but 'forgiveness can in many cases have an effect, albeit an indirect effect ... It may reduce the possibility of re-offending, it may reduce the danger of public outrage ...'

In *A-G's Reference No 18 of 1993* (1994) 15 Cr App R(S) 800 the offender had struck at a pregnant woman, missing her but hitting a child on her lap. The sentencer had been shown a letter from the woman and other members of her family indicating that they forgave the defendant and stating that in their view he had been punished sufficiently by his time on remand in custody. Reviewing the probation order imposed, on reference on grounds of undue leniency, the Court of Appeal, having received a further letter in similar vein, acknowledged the 'very exceptional circumstances' and allowed the sentence to stand.

Sample or Specimen Offences

Where the defendant is understood to have committed a number of similar offences over an extended period, it has been common practice for the prosecution to opt to charge the offender with only a limited number of offences, perhaps only a single instance, and invite the court for sentencing purposes to treat these as specimen or sample offences which should be considered as indicative of a much more substantial episode of offending or a continuing course of misconduct. Other offences which are not formally charged could be identified and listed as TICs (see page 10) but this could generate an unwieldy list not well suited to the formal TIC procedure. It thus became accepted practice, albeit without any statutory power, for the court to sentence on the basis of the full extent of repeated offending, provided that:

- the defendant pleads guilty to the specimen offences(s);

- the defence accept that the charged offences are merely samples. If the defence dispute that similar offences were committed on other occasions, the court should sentence only on the basis of what the defendant admits.

This convenient and economical device typically arose where the offender had fraudulently obtained Social Security Benefit over a long period and is charged with a limited number of deception offences, each involving a relatively small amount but it is clear that the total span of offending had caused a loss of a much more substantial sum. It could also arise in respect of intra-familial child abuse where the defendant is said to have sexually abused a child victim over a period but the child is unable to particularise any specific occasions of abuse.

This practice has been recently reviewed and challenged by the Court of Appeal in *R v Canavan, Kidd and Shaw* [1998] 1 Cr App R 79, in which Lord Bingham CJ stated:

'A defendant is not to be convicted of any offence with which he is charged unless and until his guilt is proved. Such guilt may be proved by his own admission or (on indictment) by the verdict of the jury. He may be sentenced only for an offence proved against him (by admission or verdict) or which he has admitted and asked the court to take into consideration when passing sentence. .... it is not easy to see how a defendant can lawfully be punished for offences for which he has not been indicted and which he has denied or declined to admit.'

As Thomas indicates in his commentary on the judgement ([1997] Crim LR 768), prosecutors will now need to find a balance between including sufficient counts on an indictment (or charges in summary trial) to allow the sentencer to pass an adequate sentence in the event of conviction, and overloading the prosecution. While this challenge is unlikely to present difficulties in respect of episodes of sexual offending, cases of extended fraud can cause problems, as *R v Rosenburg* [1999] Crim LR 94 illustrates. The offender had improperly obtained Income Support over a period exceeding two years while working, totalling around £30,000. On his conviction of nine counts relating to specific weeks and involving £2,500, the Crown Court judge stated that he considered that if other counts relating to the overall period of fraud had been put to the jury the defendant would have been convicted and he thus stood to be sentenced on the basis of the whole sum involved. Appeal against sentence of 30 months' imprisonment was upheld on the basis that this was manifestly excessive for the offences charged and a term of 24 months was substituted.

PSR writers should thus take care to ensure that they understand the basis on which an offender will be sentenced and would be wrong to regard an offence as a sample of an extended episode of unlawful behaviour if the court will be addressing only offences which are admitted or proved. However, it may be important for the reporter to take stock of the full picture in assessing risk to the public of re-offending. *R v Ralf* (1989) 11 Cr App R(S) 121 illustrates the kind of dilemma which can be posed. The defendant pleaded guilty to ABH, admitting that she had lost her temper with the four year old daughter of her male partner on one occasion, punching her in the stomach. On examination, the child was found to have many bruises on the head, neck and body, including bruises on the back consistent with direct blows. The child's grandmother had stated that she had seen bruising on the child on an earlier occasion. Though the Court of Appeal was clear that the offender should only have been sentenced on the basis of the admission made, it could well be appropriate to assess risk and suitability for supervision in the light of the concerns as a whole, while making clear that the PSR writer is not seeking to challenge the factual basis for sentencing.

In a contested case involving allegations of repeated offending, the prosecution will almost certainly proceed on a limited number of counts or 'specimen' charges, with the anomalous result that the defendant convicted on this limited basis can be treated less harshly than a defendant who pleads guilty and confessed to the full extent of the offending episode. This unsatisfactory prospect was acknowledged by the Court of Appeal in *R v Evans* (1999) *The Times* 8 June, a contested case of Housing Benefit fraud in which the defendant was said to have netted some £25,000 but had been found guilty of counts totalling around £2,000. While the trial judge had been wrong to sentence the defendant on the basis of her assumed guilt of fraud involving the total sum the

Court agreed that it was unfair that she should be in a better position, even without credit for a guilty plea, than a defendant who co-operated in admitting responsibility for fraud of the full sum. The Court did not feel able to suggest a remedy, postponing consideration until the issue could be fully argued in a future case.

Equality and Disparity

Co-defendants facing sentence for participating together in the same offence will have a legitimate expectation that they should receive the same sentence unless there is a sound basis for distinguishing between them on the basis either of their different degree of responsibility for the offence or of their different personal circumstances affecting mitigation or suitability for different forms of sentence. PSR writers will thus be alert to the general principle of equality or parity in sentencing and to the possible justifications for disparity.

Valid Basis for Disparity

Co-offenders can be distinguished and sentences can be correspondingly different on the basis of a number of legitimate grounds, of which the following is not an exhaustive list:

Responsibility and Culpability Difference may lie in the respective roles played in the offence or in some distinguishing feature of their offending, e.g. one was acting in breach of trust (as in the case of the burglary of premises where one offender was an employee trusted with keys to that property).

Difference in Personal Circumstances One offender may have the benefit of a mitigating circumstance not available to the other. This may be something very obvious such as a significant difference in age (which may also reflect difference in record or available form of sentence, addressed below) or may be located in some more subtle mitigatory factor. Note that a difference simply of sex is not a valid basis for disparity (*R v Okuya and Nwaobi* (1984) 6 Cr App R(S) 253).

Difference in Plea It is obvious that if one pleads guilty, s/he will have the benefit of a sentence discount unavailable to the other who is convicted after contested trial.

Difference in Criminal Record To the extent that criminal record affects the court's assessment of seriousness (see discussion of s151(1) at page 11), legitimate disparity may distinguish co-offenders with contrasting records.

Difference in Risk to the Public In respect of a sexual or violent offence where one is considered to present a significant risk to the public that a longer-than-commensurate sentence is necessary under s80(2)(b) (see page 90), disparity will be valid if the other is not assessed as a risk to the public (*R v Bestwick and Huddlestone* (1995) 16 Cr App R(S) 168, a case involving two young men in an arson offence where one was assessed as a normal personality but the other was considered a seriously disturbed personality who was obsessed with fire-raising for the excitement offered).

Different Forms of Sentence

Valid differentiation may arise from the nature of sentences available, one co-offender being eligible for a particular penalty for which the other is not. For example, on grounds of age, one offender may be 21 or over and thus able to receive a suspended term of imprisonment while his 20 year old co-offender can be sentenced only to an immediate custodial term. Similarly, if the court's power of sentence is restricted in the case of one co-offender by reason of age (e.g. in the length of YOI detention that may be imposed on a defendant aged under 18), a longer term may properly be imposed on the older co-offender (*R v Harper* (1995) 16 Cr App R(S) 639).

Where one offender is properly sentenced to a term of four years' imprisonment and the co-offender to a lower custodial term, the difference arising from the first being a long-term prisoner and thus eligible only for discretionary early release while the second gains automatic early release at the same point of sentence is not a basis for claiming unjustified disparity: *R v Ensley* [1996] 1 Cr App R(S) 294.

Where one co-offender is suitable and motivated towards a particular form of community sentence but the other is not, there is no basis to claim unjustified disparity if the other co-offender is sentenced to imprisonment. This point is illustrated very graphically by *R v Bowles* [1996] 1 Cr App R(S) 248. The appellant claiming unjustified disparity had received 18 months' imprisonment for an offence of burglary and another of handling a stolen car used in the commission of the burglary. His co-defendant, sentenced for two burglaries and two handlings of stolen cars, received a two year probation order with a requirement of participation in a therapeutic programme, despite being regarded as the active force behind their offences, having been in possession of the stolen vehicle for a longer period and having a significantly worse criminal record. Though the Court of Appeal acknowledged that ordinarily the aggrieved appellant could have expected to receive a less severe sentence than his more culpable colleague, the judge had properly felt able to take an exceptional course with the co-offender, having heard that he 'had reached the point at which he had sufficient motivation to change his ways' and it might thus be possible 'to break his cycle of offending once and for all'. It could not be said that the appellant was in the same position; his sentence was appropriate and fair for his level of participation and his appeal was dismissed.

Different Judges

Though offenders involved in the same offence should be sentenced by the same judge or Bench, wherever practicable, in the event that a different sentencer deals with one offender after another co-offender has already been sentenced the second judge should pass the sentence considered appropriate and should not feel obliged to achieve parity of sentence. However, *R v Cummings* (1998, unreported), where one co-defendant received six months at one Crown Court centre while the other defendant facing the same indictment and an additional indictment received 18 months on the matters for which responsibility was shared, illustrates that the Court of Appeal will reduce sentence on grounds of disparity, here cutting sentence by 12 months to achieve parity of outcome.

Disparity as Ground of Appeal

Where an offender has received a sentence which is not open to criticism as excessive if considered in isolation, but which is significantly more severe than the sentence imposed upon their co-offender without any valid basis for differentiation, the appeal court may reduce their sentence, but only if the disparity is serious. The test proposed in *R v Fawsett* (1983) 5 Cr App R(S) 158 is to ask: 'would right-thinking members of the public, with full knowledge of the relevant facts and circumstances, learning of this sentence, consider that something had gone wrong with the administration of justice?' In *R v Ware* (1998, unreported), where the two defendants were sentenced separately for overlapping but not identical sets of offences, one receiving a community sentence from a magistrates' court and the other a custodial sentence at Crown Court, the Court of Appeal, though finding no disparity about which the appellant could complain, stated that it was unfortunate that they were dealt with in different court levels. The magistrates should have committed the other defendant for sentence so that the Crown Court could have considered the overall culpability of both men.

Personal Mitigation

PCC(S)A 2000 s158(1) specifies:

Nothing in–

(a) sections 35 and 36 above (imposing community sentences),

(b) sections 79 to 82 above (imposing custodial sentences), or

(c) section 128 above (fixing of fines),

shall prevent a court from mitigating an offender's sentence by taking into account any such matters as, in the opinion of the court, are relevant in mitigation of sentence.

This important discretionary and open-ended scope to mitigate sentence on grounds other than the circumstances of the offence, formerly specified by CJA 1991 s28(1), is explored in Stone (2000).

2
PROCEDURAL ISSUES

This chapter seeks to bring together a disparate range of subsidiary issues and processes that can precede, inform or accompany the business of sentencing, particularly those that may concern the practice of pre-sentence report writers.

Change of Plea

Instances may arise, particularly in magistrates' court proceedings involving an unrepresented person, where a defendant has pleaded guilty but doubt arises in the course of PSR enquiries about the status or validity of their plea.

Equivocal Plea

Ambiguous pleas (typically, a person accused of shoplifting who says 'I took it but I didn't intend to steal it') are usually obvious at the point when the plea is entered. The court will then be under a duty to ascertain whether the plea is sound and should not proceed to sentence on the basis of such ambiguity, even if the defendant is anxious to be dealt with to get the case over and done with. This equivocation may not become apparent until the defendant is interviewed for their report (though in some instances the defendant, particularly where a custodial sentence is a real possibility, may seek legal advice and representation, probably on the advice of the court, between conviction and sentence, and their solicitor identifies the difficulty). Where the defendant remains unrepresented, the report writer should encourage the accused to seek legal advice. If the defendant has a solicitor, the reporter will almost certainly consult that legal representative. If it appears to the reporter that a change of plea will be necessary, the basis for the PSR is thrown in obvious doubt pending resolution of the issue of guilt and instead a note should be submitted to the court indicating this unexpected development. It may be helpful to consult the Clerk to the Justices (if the case is proceeding summarily) before a final decision is made. If the issue remains ambiguous, it may well be appropriate to complete a report, including a reference to the issue of ambiguity, in case the question is resolved in favour of guilt at the next hearing and the case can thus proceed to sentencing without further delay. In such instances it may be difficult to address important aspects of the report fully, including risk of re-offending and proposals for a suitable community sentence. A court faced with a plea judged to be ambiguous must set the plea aside and allow a fresh not guilty plea to be entered. A reporter may properly conclude that the defendant's denial of guilt makes the preparation of a useful report an impossibility and in this event should inform the court in writing accordingly.

Unequivocal Plea

The court has discretion but not the obligation to allow the defendant to withdraw their unequivocal plea of guilty at any stage prior to sentence. Discretion is exercised sparingly. In *R v South Tameside Magistrates' Court, ex parte Rowland* [1983] 3 All ER 689 the Divisional Court upheld the magistrates' decision not to allow a change of plea. An unrepresented defendant had unequivocally pleaded guilty to theft of a handbag and asked for a similar offence to be taken into consideration. The court adjourned to allow the defendant to obtain legal representation, having indicated that a custodial sentence was being considered. The defendant instructed her solicitor that her co-defendant had taken the handbag, unbeknown to her. The Divisional Court concluded that the magistrates were entitled to reach the conclusion that the defendant's motive for changing her account was her fear of imprisonment. The Divisional Court indicated that the discretion to allow a change of plea 'should be exercised judicially, very sparingly and only in very clear cases'.

Plea on Legal Advice

If the defendant was legally represented at the point of their plea, the court will be far less minded to exercise discretion to allow change of plea. However, a plea of guilty must be the defendant's voluntary personal choice. If at the time of plea the defendant experienced such pressure that s/he did not exercise genuine choice then their plea is a nullity and should be set aside. A reluctant guilty plea is not necessarily involuntary; a plea is involuntary only if legal advice was so forceful that it took away free choice. The dividing line between firm and over-forceful advice on the strength of the prosecution evidence and the advantages of a guilty plea can appear narrow. The Bar Council's *Code of Conduct* (7th edition, 2000) indicates that, in advising a client about plea, a barrister 'may, if necessary, express his advice in strong terms' but 'must make it clear that the client has complete freedom of choice and that responsibility for the plea is the client's' (*Written Standards for the Conduct of Professional Work*, para. 12.3). A PSR writer faced with doubt in this respect should consult the defence and if this does not resolve the matter to the writer's satisfaction, should also consult the Clerk to the Justices (in summary cases). For issues of 'plea-bargaining', see page 23.

Where a defendant insists on pleading guilty, despite telling their barrister that s/he is in fact innocent, the *Code* (para. 12.5.1(a)) specifies:

> 'Counsel must continue to represent him but only after he has advised what the consequences will be and that what can be submitted in mitigation can only be on the basis that the client is guilty.'

For instance, 'counsel will not be able to assert that the defendant has shown remorse through his guilty plea' (para. 12.5.2(b)). Defence solicitors are likely to follow this guidance on professional conduct. There is obvious scope for tension between the defence account and the defendant's account as relayed in the PSR, and uncertainties may need to be clarified with the defence before the court can proceed to sentence.

Mental Disorder

In rare instances the defendant may be unable to make an informed choice about their plea because of their state of mind. This is likely to be apparent at the time of plea and may thus raise the issue of their fitness to plead. In highly unusual cases, however, this may become apparent only in the course of PSR enquiries. *R v Swain* [1986] Crim LR 480, where the defendant, unknown to their legal representative, was under the influence of LSD at the time of plea, provides an illustration of the kind of case which might arise. It was subsequently established that use of this hallucinogenic drug could cause delusions and irrationality rendering plea unreliable and a nullity.

Plea Before Venue

CPIA 1996 s49 amended MCA 1980 s17, adding ss17A–17C, implemented on 1 October 1997. Section 17A provides that a defendant aged 18 or older, accused of an either way offence, shall have the opportunity to indicate his or her intended plea before the magistrates decide on mode of trial. Previously, the magistrates had made this decision without knowing the accused's intentions in respect of plea. The purpose is to ensure that cases that can properly be dealt with at magistrates' court remain there, thus avoiding unnecessary committals to Crown Court for trial. It also allows the defendant an opportunity to gain additional credit for an early guilty plea under PCC(S)A 2000 s152 (see pages 16 and 19).

The opportunity presents the defendant with three options:

(i)   If the accused indicates that he will plead not guilty, the court proceeds to a mode of trial decision under MCA 1980 s18 in the normal way: s17A(7).

(ii)   If the accused fails to indicate how s/he intends to plead, s/he shall be taken to indicate a not guilty plea and (i) above applies: s17A(8).

(iii)   If the accused indicates an intention to plead guilty, the mode of trial decision is side-stepped and the court must proceed as if the proceedings constituted a summary trial from the beginning (s17A(6)). However, the magistrates still retain the discretion to commit for sentence under PCC(S)A 2000 s3, if they consider their powers of sentence to be inadequate, even taking account of discount under s152. The court must explain this possibility when giving the defendant the opportunity to indicate plea: s17A(4)(b). As Thomas has put it (in his commentary [1998] Crim LR 687), the mode of trial hearing has been replaced by a 'mode of sentence' hearing.

In considering whether or not to commit for sentence, the court should adopt the following approach, specified by the Divisional Court in *R v Warley Magistrates' Court, ex parte DPP* [1998] Crim LR 684.

(a)   In considering whether its sentencing powers are adequate, the court must have regard to the discount for guilty plea to be granted, having regard to each offence separately. If, after discount, any offence ought to attract a sentence in excess of six months, committal to Crown Court for sentence should follow. (The Divisional Court indicated that the *National Mode of Trial Guidelines* are likely to be of great assistance in determining whether to use s3 at this stage.) Sentences should be made consecutive only if it is right in principle to do so.

(b)   Where the court concludes that an appropriate sentence can be imposed only by using its sentencing powers to the full, it should adopt that course and indicate that it has been able to retain jurisdiction only because of the credit given for guilty plea (and for other relevant mitigation).

(c)   Where the court decides that it has insufficient powers, even after allowance for plea, it should be prepared to commit for sentence without seeking a PSR or hearing mitigation in full. The defendant should be informed of the course proposed and given an opportunity to make a brief submission against it. If the court is persuaded by such a submission to change its mind, the prosecution should be invited to make representations in reply. For example, the prosecutor may be able to draw the court's attention to any relevant guideline judgement or to the existence of a power of sentence available only to the Crown Court (such as a confiscation order under DTA 1994).

(d)   Where the court considers its powers of sentence to be adequate, it should not commit for sentence simply because the case is of a type which it considers ought to be dealt with at a higher level.

(e)   If the court determines that it is possible to deal with the case within its own powers but wishes to keep open the possibility of a committal for sentence when it adjourns for a PSR or for some other reason, 'care should be taken to ensure that nothing is said or done which may indicate to the accused that that option has been ruled out'. If, for example, the court stated that it was satisfied that the case was not one in which it would be necessary to commit for sentence, this would tie the hands of a differently constituted bench considering a PSR (or other new information).

(f)   If there are disputes as to fact, the procedure to be followed regarding the need for a *Newton* hearing is as stated at page 47. If a magistrates' court conducts a *Newton* hearing and then decides to commit to Crown Court, it should record its findings for the benefit of the Crown Court. The Crown Court should not allow the defence to challenge those findings at Crown Court unless the defence can point to some 'significant development' such as the discovery of important further evidence.

(g)   The Divisional Court will only interfere with sentences imposed by a magistrates' court in exercise of this process if sentences are 'truly astonishing', showing a failure to have regard to a material consideration.

In his commentary, Thomas identifies a number of consequences of the 'plea before venue' process, suggesting that the committal for sentence process was not designed for such regular usage in respect of complex and serious (albeit either way) offences, being more of an occasional 'escape route' for magistrates who had accepted jurisdiction without knowing all the relevant facts. The s38 process will now be used routinely to deal with cases but lacks the flexibility of committal for trial.

Among the implications of these provisions:

(i)   The Crown Court receiving such committals must consist of a judge sitting with two justices, often dealing with issues with which magistrates are not trained nor equipped by experience to handle.

(ii)   There is no scope to vary or amend the charges when the case reaches Crown Court, even if these seem inept or inadequate on reaching the higher level.

(iii)   If the offender seeks other matters to be TICed at Crown Court but that Court declines to accept this proposal, new charges cannot be added at the Crown Court and fresh proceedings will be necessary before the magistrates' court.

(iv)   The role of the prosecution is weakened in that, under the mode of trial procedure, the prosecution takes the initiative in making full representations, whereas under 'plea before venue' procedure, the prosecution has merely a 'right of reply'.

(v)   The Divisional Court's interpretation in *ex parte DPP* of the Crown Court's scope to conduct a *Newton* hearing following such a hearing at summary level appears contrary to the power of the Crown Court under PCC(S)A 2000 s5 (see page 66) in dealing with committals for sentence to 'inquire into the circumstances of the case'.

Remand Status Following Committal for Sentence

In *R v Rafferty* [1999] 1 Cr App R 235 the Appeal Court indicated that in most cases where a plea of guilty is made at the plea before venue stage it will not be usual to alter the defendant's position as regards bail or custody. If the defendant has been on bail up to that point this should continue, even if it is anticipated that a custodial sentence will be imposed by the Crown Court.

Factual Basis for Sentencing

Any sentence passed by the court must be consistent with the facts of the offence, as established by verdict or guilty plea, as the following seeks to amplify, with obvious implications for PSR preparation and offence analysis:

(a)   In a contested case, if the offender is acquitted of a more serious charge but convicted of a less serious charge arising from the same incident, the sentence must be passed on the basis of the latter offence. Thus in *R v Gillespie* [1998] 2 Cr App R(S) 61 the defendant, a door-to-door salesman, accused of attempting to have non-consensual intercourse with a 14 year old girl home alone at a house at which he had called, his version being that she had consented to kissing and fondling, was acquitted of attempted rape but pleaded guilty to indecent assault. Setting aside sentence of four years' imprisonment and substituting six months, the Court of Appeal indicated that the sentencer could pass sentence on a basis of fact which was different from that advanced by the defendant only if the factual basis was consistent with the verdict, and did not include facts found as a result of accepting evidence which the jury had not accepted. Here the sentencer appeared to have accepted the whole of the victim's evidence but if she was to be believed then the defendant was guilty of attempted rape, contrary to the verdict. The Appeal Court stated that if there is any possible inconsistency, the sentencer should explain the factual basis of sentence so that it is clear to the defendant and to the public that sentence was being passed on a permissible basis. This situation may cause a PSR writer some difficulty if, for example, in a case like *Gillespie* the defendant were to tell the reporter that the victim's version was actually true. It is clearly not the role of the PSR to challenge or re-write the verdict.

(b)   If the prosecution accepts a guilty plea to a less serious offence where the defendant was charged with a more serious crime, sentence must be passed on the basis of the more limited offence. Thus in *R v Stubbs* (1988) 89 Cr App

R 53 where the prosecution accepted a plea of guilty to s20 wounding by stabbing and did not proceed with the initial charge of s18 wounding with intent, sentence was reduced by the Court of Appeal on the basis that the original sentence was justifiable only if the offender could be regarded as having used the knife 'purposefully', i.e. within the ambit of s18. Alternatively, if the defendant's plea of guilt is offered on a specified limited basis and accepted on that basis by the prosecution, the offender should be sentenced on that basis. The Court of Appeal has indicated that the basis on which plea is accepted should be placed in writing to avoid later uncertainties: *R v Myers* [1996] Crim LR 62 where the offender admitted possession of Ecstasy with intent to supply but on the basis that he was intending to supply to friends on a 'social' transaction. There was later dispute as to the number of friends involved. Because as a matter of sentencing principle a sentencer is required to seek to sentence on a basis that is true, the prosecution should not lend itself to any agreement that will cause the case to be presented to the court on a basis of an unreal or untrue set of facts about the offence.

(c) Sentence should not be passed on the basis that the defendant has committed similar offences on other occasions, if these have not been the subject of TICs (see also pages 10 and 34). In *R v Burfoot* (1990) 12 Cr App R(S) 252 the defendant had pleaded guilty to six counts of burglary but unexpectedly declined to admit a schedule of 600 further offences which it was believed could be taken into consideration. The prosecution then added a further 19 offences from that list to the indictment. He was convicted of the additional matters but did not now ask for the further 581 offences to be TICed. The Court of Appeal held that the sentencer was wrong to proceed on the basis that the offender had committed all the outstanding offences and his sentenced was reduced accordingly.

(d) The offender stands to be sentenced for the offence(s) of which s/he has been convicted, not for another offence that s/he appears to have committed on the basis of the facts of the conviction offence. Thus in *R v O'Prey* [1999] Crim LR 233 the defendant had pleaded guilty to driving while disqualified, driving while unfit through drugs and possession of cannabis. When apprehended he had a piece of cannabis in his mouth. The sentencer appeared to take the view that he had driven dangerously as a result of having the drug in his mouth and imposed a term of three years' imprisonment for possession of cannabis to reflect this fact, a sentence in excess of the maximum for dangerous driving. Substituting a term of one month's imprisonment for the possession offence, the Appeal Court indicated that he should have been sentenced on the basis that the criminality relating to the use of cannabis as related to his driving lay in the offence of driving while unfit, for which six months was the proper term. The prosecution should always consider whether the matters charged or contained in the indictment properly reflect the gravity of the case and, if the Crown appears to have overlooked to do so, in the Crown Court it is open to the judge at a plea and directions hearing to question the prosecution on this point.

As Thomas points out in his commentary on *O'Prey* [1999] Crim LR 234, this principle has clear implications for offences such as wounding, ABH and criminal damage which under CDA 1998 can be charged as 'racially aggravated' versions of the crime (see page 79). If the offence is charged in its unaggravated version (or the defendant is acquitted of the aggravated version), s/he cannot be sentenced more heavily on the basis of racial aggravation perceived in the circumstances of the 'simple' offence.

Conspiracy Cases

In cases of conspiracy it is particularly important for the court to clarify the basis of a guilty plea – whether, for example, the basis of plea is guilty to the overall conspiracy but with limited active participation in any crimes committed pursuant to it, or on the basis of limited involvement in the conspiracy itself, for example by joining late or by leaving early: *R v McFeeley* [1998] 2 Cr App R(S) 26.

Written Basis of Plea

As indicated above (page 44), the Court of Appeal has encouraged the practice of clarifying the basis of a guilty plea in writing when the offender is admitting only a limited version of the alleged offence. That version may detail preceding, relevant events, such as a history of tension where the complainant in respect of an offence of violence had acted provocatively. The Court of Appeal has indicated that it will not accept a particular version of the facts favoured by the defence unless this has been placed in writing or otherwise expressly accepted by the trial judge. In *R v Kesler* [2001] Crim LR 582, involving a man observed standing for a prolonged period outside a public house where he was approached by a number of people before being found in possession of 40 Ecstasy tablets, the offender pleaded guilty to possession with intent to supply MDMA. In police interview he said he was selling the drug to pay off a debt. He later told his PSR writer that he would never sell to persons unknown to him. On his appeal against a term of four years, he claimed that the judge had dealt with him as a commercial dealer whereas he had pleaded guilty on the basis that he was intending to supply only to friends prior to their group going to a club. The court dismissed his appeal, noting that there was no written basis of plea and that the judge had not accepted such a version of events. Any written basis of plea should preferably be signed by counsel for both the prosecution and defence, particularly where the factual basis claimed by the defendant is 'inherently improbable' as here.

A sentencer is, of course, not bound by such an agreed version of events and can direct a *Newton* hearing (see below) if this departs too far from the weight of the evidence. If the written basis of plea is not accepted by the prosecution, it will not normally be correct for this to be accepted by the sentencer. Thus in *Attorney-General's Reference No. 81 of 2000* [2001] 2 Cr App R(S) 16, a case of s18 GBH against a neighbour, the offender claimed that he reacted excessively in self-defence when faced by what he had believed to be an intruder. His initial statement on arrest had not referred to such factors and the claim was in contrast to the victim's statement. The Court of Appeal disapproved of the judge's decision to accept the defence version, stating that the complainant 'had a right to be heard before his evidence was rejected', there being no special circumstances that might have justified the judge's decision, such as that the victim was no longer prepared to give evidence in accordance with his statement.

Similarly, in *Attorney-General's Reference No. 58 of 2000* [2001] 2 Cr App R(S) 19, a case of causing death by dangerous driving, the Appeal Court disapproved of the judge's decision to accept a basis of plea that included the assertion that consumption of alcohol did not play any part in the offender's manner of driving.

Newton Hearings

In many instances where the factual details of an offence are not readily agreed between prosecution and defence, disputes will be resolved between the two sides prior to plea, perhaps after negotiations sometimes referred to as 'fact bargaining' (sometimes also linked to 'charge bargaining') in which the defence trades a guilty plea in return for the prosecution agreeing a version of the facts which places the defendant in a less culpable light (see above point (b)).

If agreement is not achieved but the defendant pleads guilty, the version of the facts which the court accepts may make a significant difference to the assessment of seriousness. The defence may, for example, ask the court to pass sentence on a basis that is different from the prosecution's case. Further, irrespective of any agreement between prosecution and defence, the court's obligation to sentence on a 'true' basis means that the court is entitled to seek to resolve the proper factual basis for sentence within the offence to which a guilty plea has been entered. The agreement is thus not binding upon the court which should view the agreed account sceptically, taking account also of the position of any other defendant. The offence analysis within the PSR may provide the basis on which the court is prompted to seek to establish the 'truth' of a case (though see *R v Tolera* described below). It is unfair to the defendant if s/he does not learn that their version of the facts has been rejected until sentence is passed. The court should make its views known at an earlier stage.

One option, particularly where the dispute concerns a relatively insignificant detail, is for the court to hear submissions from both sides but to follow the normal convention of accepting 'so far as possible' the version offered by the defence as correct. The court is not obliged to do so if it concludes that the defence account is 'wholly incredible' or, as it is sometimes phrased, is 'manifestly absurd'. Thus in *R v Hawkins* (1985) 7 Cr App R(S) 351 the defendant, who had pleaded guilty to burglary having acted as get-away driver in a joint offence committed with two others, claimed that he had been unaware of the break-in until they emerged from the building, having simply agreed to drive his co-defendants to certain premises and pick them up an hour later. The judge disbelieved this and sentenced the defendant on the basis put by the prosecution that he had been a knowing participant throughout. The defendant's appeal was dismissed on the basis that his claim to ignorance was an 'incredible assertion' and the judge was thus 'fully entitled ... to reject the submission put forward in mitigation'. The court's rejection of the defence claim must, however, be in accordance with the facts and not simply on the basis of judicial hunch or assumption. Thus in *R v Costley* (1989) 11 Cr App R(S) 357, where the defendant claimed that he had inflicted GBH because the victim had made a homosexual approach and had dripped blood on him, claiming to be suffering from AIDS, and the judge rejected this explanation as 'wholly incredible' on the basis only of the prosecution opening and defence mitigation, the Court of Appeal held that it was not open to the judge to come to this conclusion without further inquiry through a *Newton* hearing, a procedure that will now be outlined.

If there is clear divergence or substantial conflict on important factual aspects of the offence, the court can conduct a *Newton* hearing, considering evidence presented by both sides and reaching a conclusion about the disputed issue. This procedure was approved by the Court of Appeal in *R v Newton* (1982) 77 Cr App R 13 where the defendant had pleaded guilty to buggery of his wife, claiming that she had consented, while the prosecution alleged that it was against her will (at the time, consensual anal intercourse was an offence). The trial judge improperly sentenced him on the basis that the offence was non-consensual without hearing any evidence. To reiterate, the purpose of a *Newton* hearing is to determine a disputed issue of fact within the limits set by the terms of the conviction. An obvious instance of circumstances in which a *Newton* hearing should be conducted would be in a case of assault admitted by the defendant where the prosecution claim racial motivation denied by the defendant: *R v Earley and Bailey* [1998] 2 Cr App R(S) 158.

The decision whether to hold a *Newton* hearing is a matter for the court and does not depend on the view or consent of the prosecution or defence, but the parties have the opportunity to call such evidence as they wish and to cross-examine witnesses called by the other side. If the hearing is at the court's instigation, despite an agreement between prosecution and defence and/or a defence version that the prosecution does not feel able to challenge, the court is nevertheless entitled to expect assistance from the prosecution in the presentation of prosecution evidence and the testing of defence evidence. As the Court of Appeal clarified in *R v Beswick* [1996] 1 Cr App R(S) 343, in so far as any agreement may hamper the process of establishing the truth, it must be considered as being conditional upon the approval of the court. Without that approval, the defence cannot hold the prosecution to it. The prosecution's prior willingness to agree a basis of plea should not hamper the sentencer's task of ascertaining the truth. The issues to be tried should be clearly identified in advance of the hearing. The burden of proof rests with the prosecution to satisfy the court beyond reasonable doubt that their version of events is correct. The sentencer should, so far as possible, leave the conduct of the hearing to the advocates and should not intervene unduly in the examination of witnesses: *R v Myers* [1996] Crim LR 62. If the court decides the issue against the defence, the defendant may lose some (but not all) of the credit which would normally accrue for a guilty plea (see page 16). The court's decision to hold a hearing does not create a ground upon which the defendant should be allowed to vacate his or her guilty plea, even if the defence basis of plea is found to be unreal.

A *Newton* hearing should not serve to allow the court to find the defendant guilty in effect of an offence more serious than that with which s/he was charged. Thus in *R v Druce* [1993] Crim LR 469, where the prosecution had accepted a guilty plea to USI and indecent assault in place of an initial allegation of rape, from a man who had allowed a girl aged 14 on the run from a residential unit to stay with him. In the course of the *Newton* hearing the prosecution had alleged that the victim had not consented to intercourse but if that was the allegation, the rape allegation should not have been abandoned. Though a hearing might have been pertinent in resolving an issue within the offence for sentence, such as whether sexual activity had been at the instigation of the offender or the victim, it could not be right to ask the judge, in effect, to conclude that the defendant was guilty of a crime other than that for which he stood to be sentenced.

The defence may not seek to dispute any part of the prosecution case but instead seek to claim the benefit of extraneous mitigation that is within the exclusive knowledge of the defence, for example that the offender had been subject to threats in acting as a drug courier. It has been generally assumed that such matters are not appropriately the subject of a *Newton* hearing but rather for the defence to seek to persuade the court of. However, in *R v Tolera* (see below), the Court of Appeal suggested that such a mitigatory claim should be tested in a hearing in which the prosecution should seek to rebut the explanation.

Though the issue to be resolved will usually be quite central to the pre-sentence report writer's potential exploration and analysis of the offence, the sentencing court may nevertheless seek to speed progress by ordering a PSR prior to the *Newton* hearing. The court may anticipate that a further adjournment may be necessary beyond the hearing date to allow the report preparation to be concluded in the light of the hearing outcome. If, however, the court wishes the report to be ready so that sentencing can proceed at the conclusion of the hearing, the writer may clearly have some difficulty in addressing the offence and judging an appropriate proposal and may face a choice between completing the report on a note of uncertainty or requesting further time. Of course, if the court reaches conclusions contrary to the defendant's version the offence analysis is likely to be correspondingly limited in much the same way as after a full trial following a not guilty plea.

Alternative Version of Facts in PSR

A pre-sentence report may give an account of the offence which is substantially different from the account on which the prosecution relies. This is more likely to occur where the defendant has given the report writer an exculpatory version of events which would reduce the offender's culpability if accepted by the court. Reporters will obviously seek to compare the version offered with the witness statements and the police summary, if available, as well as the information to hand regarding any previous convictions for similar offences recorded against the defendant, probing the offender's account accordingly. If the issue at stake concerns subjective issues such as motive it may be more difficult to test the account offered in interview. *R v Oakley* [1998] 1 Cr App R(S) 100 illustrates the problem well and specifies how the court should deal with the dilemma.

The offender aged 17 of previous good character had pleaded guilty to burglary of a family of deaf persons. Three days before the offence, he had called at the victims' home with his adult uncle, aggrieved that the victims had allegedly been making offensive remarks about the defendant's mother and the recent death of her baby twins. There was an acrimonious exchange (in sign language) which failed to resolve the grievance. The basic facts of the offence were that two males in stocking masks entered the victims' home in the early hours of the morning and confronted the father of the family, terrifying him, threatening him with knives, assaulting him by punching, cutting his face with one of the knives and leaving him tied up. The prosecution alleged that the men had demanded money (the victim indicating that he did not have any). The account in the PSR indicated that the offender went to the home on the second occasion to question the victim further about what he was believed to have said regarding the offender's mother's loss, that a struggle had ensued and that he had punched the victim out of anger as he had gained no satisfaction and thought that the victim was going to hit either him or his uncle. The encounter had got out of hand. The judge did not accept the version offered to the PSR writer, stating in remarks at point of sentencing that if the motive had been to remonstrate with the victim about the grievance, there would have been no point in wearing masks to prevent identification or taking knives. In his view, the motive was financial gain and the offender was sentenced accordingly, receiving three years YOI detention (in itself an unlawful sentence, the maximum for a 17 year old being two years).

On the offender's appeal, the Court of Appeal stated that the divergence between the two versions was such that a *Newton* hearing was called for. The judge had been in error in two respects. He had not taken the initiative to order a *Newton* inquiry nor had he given any indication to the defence during mitigation that he did not accept the PSR version so that counsel might have requested a *Newton* hearing. The court should have either ordered a *Newton* hearing or sentenced on the basis of the PSR version upon which the plea of guilty was tendered. The Appeal Court considered that justice demanded a reduction of sentence (see page 241) and substituted 18 months' YOI.

R v Tolera [1999] 1 Cr App R(S) 25 provides a further illustration of the issues as they may be shaped by the contents of a PSR. The defendant had pleaded guilty to possession of heroin with intent to supply, having been stopped in his mini-cab carrying 55.8 grams at 51% purity. The pre-trial PSR reported that he had described being threatened with violence by persons to whom he owed money if he did not act as courier. The Crown Court sentencer had indicated that he did not accept this account and directed a *Newton* hearing, deciding at the conclusion that the offender was more than a mere courier and also rejected the claim that the defendant had been under a degree of compulsion short of duress. Reviewing the case on his appeal, the Court of Appeal stated:

> 'It often happens that when a defendant describes the facts of an offence to a probation officer for purposes of a PSR, he gives an account which differs from that which emerges from the prosecution case, usually by glossing over, omitting or misdescribing the more incriminating features of the offence. While the sentencer will read this part of the report, s/he will not in the ordinary way pay attention for purposes of sentence to any account of the crime given by the defendant to the probation officer where it conflicts with the prosecution case. If the defendant wants to rely on such an account by asking the court to treat it as the basis for sentence, it is necessary that the defendant should draw the relevant paragraphs to the attention of the court and ask that it be treated as the basis of sentence. It is also very desirable that the prosecution should be forewarned of this request, even though the prosecution now ordinarily see the PSR. The issue can then be resolved, if necessary by calling evidence.'

In similar vein, in *R v Welby* [2000] Crim LR 59 an offender aged 18 pleading guilty to robbery at knife-point of a wallet at the 45 year old victim's home told the probation officer preparing the PSR that the victim had raped him, causing him to retaliate with such ferocity that the victim had offered him his cash cards to persuade him to desist. The victim had claimed that he had been attacked from behind with a knife held to his throat. The Crown indicated that they would not pursue a *Newton* hearing. The judge heard both accounts and determined that the defendant's version was simply not credible.

On his appeal against sentence of 12 months' YOI detention, the Appeal Court was critical of the judge's failure to give indication that he was rejecting the offender's basis of plea and reaching his conclusion without any inquiry or evidence. However, the Court did not reduce sentence, stating that, even if a sexual approach had been made, a term of 12 months was the irreducible minimum term that could have been passed, as a knife had been used and considerable brutality shown.

The PSR may present a more serious version of the offence from that presented by the prosecution, as illustrated by *R v Cunnah* [1996] 1 Cr App R(S) 393. The defendant had pleaded guilty to various counts of indecent assault of two girls. They had described serious assaults involving oral sex and digital penetration. He had entered his plea on the basis that he had touched the victims in various less serious, non-penetrative ways. The PSR prepared after plea stated that he now admitted the truth of most of the girls' accounts. In criticising the lack of attention to the version of facts offered in the PSR in court prior to sentencing, the Court of Appeal stated that where fresh and relevant material appears in a PSR, the content of the report should be raised with the advocates in court so that the basis on which sentencing should proceed can be clearly established. It seems clear that if the defence is unable to accept the more serious version of the facts, either the defence should request a *Newton* hearing or the sentencer must decide to hold such an inquiry to determine the proper factual basis for sentence or should proceed on the basis of the defence version upon which plea has been tendered. In his commentary on *Cunnah*, Thomas suggests that one reason why a *Newton* hearing need not be necessary would be if the PSR relies on information that would not be admissible as evidence. Addressing the question of admissions made by the defendant in interview which s/he is later not willing to acknowledge or own in court, Thomas speculates that these 'would clearly be vulnerable to an application for exclusion under PACE 1984 s78', the provision allowing the court to refuse to allow admission of evidence where, having regard to all the circumstances, including the circumstances in which the evidence was obtained, admission 'would have such an adverse effect on the fairness of proceedings that the court ought not to admit it.'

It will normally be good practice for PSR writers to discuss with the defence solicitor ahead of the sentencing occasion any serious divergence between the prosecution version or the defence's basis of plea and the defendant's account in interview.

Plea Before Venue and Committal for Sentence: Dispute as to Facts

Where a magistrates' court is determining whether to commit for sentence following a guilty plea under MCA 1980 s17A (see page 41) and there is a dispute as to the facts, the Divisional Court in *R v Warley Magistrates' Court, ex parte DPP* [1998] Crim LR 684 (see page 41) indicated that the following procedure should apply in regard to whether a *Newton* hearing should be held:

(1) Where the court would have adequate sentencing powers whatever the outcome of a hearing, the court should conduct a hearing.

(2) If the case would have to be committed to the Crown Court for sentence, whatever the outcome of a hearing, the Crown Court should be left to conduct the hearing.

(3)   If the decision whether or not to commit for sentence depends on which version of the facts the court decides to accept, the court must conduct a hearing.

(4)   If the court conducts a hearing and then commits the defendant to the Crown Court, it should record its findings for the benefit of the Crown Court.

Adjournment for Reports

Magistrates' power to adjourn for a PSR to be prepared or for other inquiries/assessments to be made, and the length of an adjournment is provided by MCA 1980 s10(3):

> A magistrates' court may, for the purpose of enabling inquiries to be made or of determining the most suitable method of dealing with the case, exercise its power to adjourn after convicting the accused and before sentencing him or otherwise dealing with him; but if it does so, the adjournment shall not be for more than four weeks at a time unless the court remands the accused in custody and, where it so remands him, the adjournment shall not be for more than three weeks at a time.

The court is, of course, at liberty to further adjourn beyond the initial period if the report is not available or inquiries are still continuing, subject to the time limits as before. In a youth court, s10(3) is qualified by CYPA 1933 s48(3) which specifies that any adjournment must be such that the child or young person appears before a court or a justice 'at least once every 21 days'.

Provisions Regarding Bail

The 'general right to bail' under BA 1976 s4, subject to the exceptions specified in Sch 1 of the Act, is specifically extended by s4(4) to:

> a person who has been convicted of an offence and whose case is adjourned by the court for the purpose of enabling inquiries or a report to be made to assist the court in dealing with him for the offence.

Among exceptions contained in Sch 1, para 7 specifies:

> Where his case is adjourned for inquiries or a report, the defendant need not be granted bail if it appears to the court that it would be impracticable to complete the inquiries or make the report without keeping the defendant in custody.

Bail Condition to Co-operate with Inquiries Among requirements that may be imposed as a condition of bail, BA 1976 s3(6)(d) specifies that the bailee may be required to comply with:

> such requirements as appear to the court to be necessary to secure that he make himself available for the purpose of enabling inquiries or a report to be made to assist the court in dealing with him for the offence.

This provision may seem to give quite broad scope to impose a degree of discipline on defendants who have been lax in co-operating with PSR or related inquiries or are considered unlikely to comply with inquiries and preparation of a report. It is qualified somewhat by the provision of Sch 1 para 8(1A):

No condition shall be imposed under s3(6)(d) unless it appears necessary to do so for the purpose of enabling inquiries or a report to be made.

An additional condition of this nature should thus not be imposed gratuitously or unless there is some specific need or justification.

Where a bailee is required to reside at a bail or probation hostel, whether during any period of inquiries, bail assessment or otherwise, BA 1976 s3(6ZA) specifies that 'he may also be required to comply with the rules of the hostel'.

If a defendant fails to comply with a condition under s3(6)(d) (or any other bail condition), their non-compliance renders them liable to arrest without warrant under the provisions of BA 1976 s7(3)(b) and (4), to be brought before a court or magistrate acting for the PSA in which arrested (unless arrest is effected within 24 hours of the time when the defendant is required to surrender to custody in which case s/he should be brought before the relevant court: s7(4)(b)). The PSR reporter thus has the clear discretion to report the non-compliance to the police with a view to arrest, rather than await the adjourned hearing date when it would be necessary to report lack of progress. However, the reporter may wish first to consider offering the defendant a further opportunity to keep an interview appointment.

PSR Requests, Indications by Sentencers and Legitimate Expectations

A series of judgements prior to CJA 1991 developed the principle that if a court adjourns for a pre-sentence report in circumstances that create a legitimate expectation in the defendant's mind that a non-custodial sentence will result if the assessment proves favourable, it is contrary to natural justice for the sentencer receiving that report to impose a custodial sentence. As stated by Watkins LJ in the leading case of *R v Gillam* (1980) 2 Cr App R(S) 267 where the sentencer had asked that the offender's suitability for community service should be assessed, in language couched in the old thinking about 'alternatives to custody':

'When a judge ... purposely postpones sentence so that an alternative to prison can be examined and that alternative is found to be a satisfactory one in all respects, the court ought to adopt the alternative. A feeling of injustice is otherwise aroused.'

The *Gillam* principle depends on 'there having been something in the nature of a promise, express or implied, that if a particular proposal is recommended, it will be adopted' by the sentencer: *R v Moss* (1983) 5 Cr App R(S) 279.

Subsequent cases illustrated the principle in respect of assessment for a requirement of residence in a probation hostel (*R v Ward* (1982) 4 Cr App R(S) 103) and a probation centre placement (*R v McMurray* (1987) 9 Cr App R(S) 101). Further, the Crown Court has been held bound by the implied promise by a magistrates' court where the lower court has committed the case for sentence (*R v Rennes* (1985) 7 Cr App R(S) 343) or if the offender appeals against sentence (*R v Isleworth Crown Court, ex parte Irwin* (1992) 156 JP Reports 453).

The principle required re-consideration in the light of CJA 1991 and the statutory role now played by a PSR in assisting the court to form a view on the level of offence seriousness. At the same time, PSR writers have valued some indication from the court as to its preliminary thinking about the level of seriousness and any specific reasons why the report is being sought beyond the core procedural requirement for a PSR to be obtained. It is clear from a number of reported cases that the *Gillam* principle still holds good where the court in adjourning for a report gives a positive indication or uses words that create a justifiable expectation that a favourable report will result in a particular non-custodial sentence. Thus the Court of Appeal in *R v Chamberlain* (1994) 16 Cr App R(S) 473 stated:

> 'Defendants should invariably be told in clear terms that they must not assume from the fact that the court is ordering a further adjournment for further assessment or investigation that s/he is likely to receive any particular form of sentence or that a custodial sentence is ruled out.'

However, it is also clear that where a court simply adjourns for a report, it is under no obligation to give a specific warning that a custodial sentence remains a possibility. While giving such a warning may be regarded as good practice, mere failure to warn, even if the defendant is granted bail for the adjournment period, does not of itself justify any expectation in the defendant's mind. As the Court of Appeal made clear in *R v Rennan* [1994] Crim LR 379: 'Silence by a judge ... should never be taken as an indication that a non-custodial sentence will be considered appropriate.' The Court indicated that the defence advocate should ensure that the defendant understands the position.

In a more recent application of the *Gillam* principle, *R v Jackson* [1996] Crim LR 355, a custodial sentence was imposed for unlawful wounding after the judge had asked counsel to consider what level of compensation would be appropriate for the victim's injury, adjourning the case over the lunch interval. On resuming the hearing, counsel had indicated a sum of £5,000 which the defendant was able to pay from his earnings. The Court of Appeal agreed with the defence submission that the sentencer had created an expectation of a non-custodial sentence if compensation could be paid. In a critical commentary on this decision, Thomas suggests that *Jackson* takes the *Gillam* principle too far: 'It is one thing to leave the defendant waiting for several weeks in a reasonably clear expectation of a non-custodial sentence, another to seize on a possible inference from the sentencer's interest in the possibility of a compensation order and allow that to be a bar to the passing of a custodial sentence only two hours later'. The implication appears to be that 'if any hint is given, even obliquely, that the sentencer is prepared to contemplate the possibility of a non-custodial sentence, s/he will be caught by the principle and prevented from passing a custodial sentence, even though at the end of the day that is the appropriate sentence'.

Many magistrates resort to stating when requesting a report that 'all sentencing options are being kept open', even if specifying that a particular form of sentence is under consideration. The Magistrates' Association (1994) suggested that justices should give some guidance as to why they are asking for a report, that these observations should be recorded by the clerk and that the following form of words should be adopted in announcing the report request:

> 'On what we have heard so far, we are considering a community sentence/custodial sentence. We must point out that the magistrates who deal with your case will not be bound by our view or any suggestion in the report about how your case should be dealt with.'

Disclosure of PSRs

PCC(S)A 2000 s156 makes provision for the disclosure of PSRs to both defence and prosecution. Under s156(2), the court shall give a copy of the PSR:

(a)   to the offender or his counsel or solicitor; and

(b)   to the prosecutor, that is to say, the person having the conduct of the proceedings in respect of the offence.

This provision is qualified in two respects:

(i)   In respect of s156(2)(a), if the offender is under 17 and is not legally represented, the court has discretion to give a copy instead to the juvenile's parent or guardian, if present in court.

(ii)   In respect of s156(2)(b), if the prosecutor is not one who is approved for this purpose by order of the Home Secretary, the court has discretion not to supply a copy if of the view that it would be inappropriate to do so. By the *Pre-Sentence Reports (Prescription of Prosecutors) Order* (SI 1998/191) the Home Secretary has approved the following prosecutors for disclosure purposes: crown prosecutors; any other person acting on behalf of the CPS; a person acting on behalf of Customs and Excise, the Department of Social Security, the Inland Revenue or the Serious Fraud Office.

The purpose of s1526(2)(b) is to enable the prosecution to fulfil its proper responsibility to correct any misleading or inaccurate information from reaching the court. Safeguards regarding the prosecutor's use of the PSR are provided by s156(5):

No information obtained by virtue of s156(2)(b) shall be used or disclosed otherwise than for the purpose of—

(a)   determining whether representations as to matters contained in the report need to be made to the court; or

(b)   making such representations to the court.

Other Reports

In respect of reports made by a probation officer or YOT member to assist the court in determining the most suitable method of dealing with the offender but not falling within the definition of a PSR, s157 specifies that the court shall give a copy to the offender or his counsel or solicitor (not to the prosecutor). If the offender is aged under 17, a copy need not be given to him but to his parent/guardian if present in court: s157(3).

Age Boundaries and Sentencing

PSR writers may face uncertainty in contemplating sentencing prospects when the defendant attains their birthday in the course of proceedings and their age has significance for particular disposals for which they may now be eligible or, alternatively, may cease to be eligible. This issue arises in respect of young offenders as they cross a variety of thresholds prior to age 21. In some instances the statutory provisions empowering the use of a particular disposal make the issue clear; in other cases the ambiguity has been resolved by judicial interpretation. The basic principle is that the relevant age for determining eligibility is nearly always the offender's age at date of their *conviction,* i.e. the date on which they pleaded guilty or were found guilty in the case of a contested trial.

Probation/Community Rehabilitation Order, Community Service/Punishment Order, Combination/CPR Order: eligible if aged 16 at date of conviction.

Attendance Centre Order exceeding 24 hours: the statutory provision allowing an order beyond the usual ceiling up to 36 hours is not completely explicit but appears to indicate that the determining factor is being aged 16 at date of *sentence.*

Detention and Training Order: PCC(S)A 2000 s100 specifies that this sentence applies where 'a child or young person (that is to say, any person aged under 18) is convicted of an offence ... punishable with imprisonment'. Applying *R v Danga* [1992] QB 476, the relevant age is date of *conviction*, not sentence. Similarly, a youth aged 14 at date of conviction but 15 when before the court for sentence will not be eligible for a detention and training order if he does not satisfy the 'persistent offender' criterion in respect of offenders aged under 15.

Note that if a young offender is initially sentenced to a community order regulated by PCC(S)A 2000 Sch 3 which is subsequently revoked, allowing the court to re-sentence for the original offence, the court's powers are not governed by the offender's age at conviction for that offence. The court revoking the order may deal with the offender 'in any manner in which it could deal with him if he had just been convicted by the court of the offence' (Sch 3 paras 4(1)(d), 5(1)(d), 10(3)(b)(ii) and 11(2)(b)(ii)). There could be scope for uncertainty if the offender reaches a critical birthday between date of revocation and date of re-sentencing. The wording of the relevant sub-paragraphs suggest that the date of revocation determines the court's powers. In respect of community orders regulated by PCC(S)A 2000 Sch 7 and Sch 8, the relevant wording is different and the court revoking the order may deal with the offender 'in any way in which he could have been dealt with for that offence by the court which made the order if the order had not been made' (Sch 7 para 2(2)(b) and Sch 8 para 2(2)(b)). In other words, the court shall exercise powers available to it in respect of the offender's age at date of original sentence even if he would not eligible for such disposal if now freshly convicted of the offence.

Detention under PCC(S)A 2000 s91: the relevant date for the purpose of determining a young offender's eligibility for this form of detention for grave crimes is date of conviction (*R v Robinson* [1993] 1 WLR 168).

Adult Co-Defendant The Court of Appeal (e.g. in *R v Saleh* [2000] Crim LR 57) has often indicated that it is usually undesirable for a magistrates' court to deal with a juvenile offender while their adult co-accused is dealt with by the Crown Court, it being preferable for both offenders to be sentenced on the same occasion by the same court. However, as Thomas points out in his Commentary on *Saleh*, given the abolition of committal for sentence in respect of those aged under 18, it is not possible to secure that both the accused are dealt with at Crown Court unless the adult concerned is committed for trial for an indictable offence and the younger defendant appears before the magistrates jointly charged with the adult on the same occasion.

Staggered Sentencing

The issue may arise whether it is appropriate for the court dealing with a case to deal on different occasions with different elements in its disposal. In *R v Talgarth Justices, ex parte Bithell* [1973] 1 WLR 1327 the Divisional Court held that a magistrates' court had no power to adjourn part of a sentence and stated that such a course is in any event bad sentencing practice. This decision was considered in *R v Annesley* [1976] 1 All ER 589 where an offender had received a prison term for TWOC and excess alcohol but the issue of disqualification was held over for later consideration because the offender's driving licence and record was not available. The Court of Appeal held:

'The Crown Court enjoys the common law jurisdiction to put off passing the whole or part of a sentence, if the circumstances make it necessary. While accepting the proposition that to take two bites at the sentencing cherry is bad practice, there may be circumstances in which it is very desirable, when all the material necessary to complete all elements of a sentencing problem is not immediately available, to deal with the substance at once and postpone what may have to be done in addition, rather than postpone the whole of the sentence until all the material is to hand.'

In this instance the Court felt that it would have been 'unnecessarily cruel' to keep the offender in the dark as to whether and for how long he would go to prison and the decision to stagger sentencing was thus correct.

Sentencing in the Defendant's Absence

Crown Court Trial on Indictment

An accused person must be present at the commencement of trial so that he may plead. However, if he subsequently absents himself voluntarily, for example by failing to surrender or by escaping from custody, the judge has discretion to complete the trial in his absence, also proceeding to pass sentence: *R v Jones (No.2)* [1972] 1 WLR 887. If the accused misbehaves in such a disruptive manner that it is impracticable for the hearing to continue in his presence, the judge may order that he be removed from the court and the trial will then proceed without him. This can include passing of sentence, though the defendant may be allowed to return to the court if he gives an undertaking to behave appropriately. Misconduct may attract a sentence for contempt in the face of the court. If the defendant is absent for reasons beyond his control, namely ill-health, the trial may not proceed in his absence unless he gives consent.

In a Magistrates' Court

MCA 1980 s11(1) empowers a court to proceed in an accused person's absence and this extends to passing sentence if the court finds the case proved. However, s11(3) qualifies this power by specifying that the court may not sentence him to imprisonment or make an order that an existing suspended sentence shall take effect. In like vein, s11(4) prevents a court from imposing a disqualification except where the case has been adjourned post-conviction under MCA 1980 s10(3) (see page 51). Where the case is adjourned to enable the defendant to be present, the court may then impose disqualification in his absence if he has been given notice of the reason for the adjournment. Any sentence imposed in contravention of s11(3) or (4) will be a nullity. A court wishing to impose a penalty governed by s11(3) or (4) or requiring the offender to be present even in respect of another kind of disposal is likely to consider issuing a warrant for his arrest under MCA 1980 s13(1).

Counts to Lie on File

Where a defendant at Crown Court pleads not guilty to some of the allegations against him, one option under CJA 1967 s17 is for the prosecution to offer no evidence, with the consequence that the court may order that a verdict of not guilty be recorded against him without requiring a verdict from a jury. This outcome is appropriate where the case against the defendant proves weaker than anticipated. An alternative course at the discretion of the judge is for the court to order that an indictment or counts within an indictment shall 'lie on the file', marked 'not to be proceeded with without leave of the court or of the Court of Appeal'. This course avoids the demands of a trial without giving the defendant the benefit of an acquittal in cases where the evidence is considered to be strong enough to be put to a jury. It is thus advantageous in instances where the defendant has pleaded guilty to substantial allegations and the result in respect of the contested matter(s) is not likely to make a significant difference to the sentencing outcome. The matters so left on file are likely to be given leave to be tried only if the defendant's convictions in respect of the matters to which he pleaded guilty or was found guilty are quashed on appeal. In other instances, the intention of the court is that he should never have to stand trial. Even in the event of a successful appeal, the court may regard an application for leave to be 'so oppressive to have a trial that leave to proceed would inevitably be refused': *R v Central Criminal Court, ex parte Raymond* [1986] 1 WLR 710.

Extradited Persons Sentenced to Imprisonment

In the case of a person who has been extradited to the United Kingdom to face criminal proceedings and who was kept in custody in the foreign jurisdiction prior to extradition, CJA 1991 s47(2) specifies that, if he receives a term of imprisonment, the sentencer may make an order that a period not exceeding the total period spent in custody outside the UK shall count towards the period of time spent on custodial remand which is taken into account in the computation of his sentence. The period shall be such as the court considers 'just in all the circumstances': s47(3). There is thus no need for the term of sentence to be adjusted to reflect time in custody abroad. If there is evidence that the offender has caused the period in custody abroad to be extended beyond what would otherwise have been necessary, by resisting extradition or by otherwise seeking to play the system, it is proper that he should not receive maximum credit. In *R v Andre and Burton* [2001] Crim LR 660, where the offenders had deliberately left the UK to avoid apprehension, the Court of Appeal upheld the judge's decision to order that only six months should count of 11 months when they were detained abroad.

Where an offender absconds from the jurisdiction after conviction in the UK and subsequently spends time in prison in another country prior to being returned to the UK, he is not an extradited person under s47. Thus in *R v Lodde and Lodde* (2000) *The Times*, 8 March, the offenders absconded after their conviction, being sentenced in their absence. They were subsequently arrested in Holland where they were detained for nearly eight months. The Appeal Court noted that they had brought their Dutch imprisonment on themselves in a bid to cheat justice and had also prolonged their time in a Dutch prison by resisting extradition. The court nevertheless allowed three months of that period to count towards computation of sentence.

3
ALTERNATIVES TO IMMEDIATE SENTENCING

This chapter aims to cover the scope for a court to do other than deal with the defendant forthwith, either by purposeful delay of sentence by deferment or by transferring the defendant, upwards or sideways, to another, more appropriate court for sentence.

Deferment of Sentence

Power to defer or postpone sentence, provided by PCC(S)A 2000 s1 (formerly PCCA 1973 s1) and available to a youth court, a magistrates' court or the Crown Court, is specifically designed to allow the court the opportunity to 'have regard ... to (a) (the defendant's) conduct after conviction (including, where appropriate, the making by him of reparation for his offence) or (b) any change in his circumstances': (s1(1)). Deferment should be a purposeful exercise and not simply a means of ducking a difficult sentencing decision. It may allow the court space to see whether constructive developments anticipated in the defendant's life actually occur or it may serve to positively encourage the defendant to make progress in their life or to demonstrate capacity for good conduct or a changed attitude. In effect the offender is given additional time to earn personal mitigation (under PCC(S)A 2000 s158(1)) – see page 38). The following factors apply:

(i)   The court must be satisfied that, having regard to the nature of the offence and the offender's character and circumstances, deferment would be in the interests of justice: s1(2)(b).

(ii)   The defendant must consent in open court to deferment: s1(2)(a).

(iii)   The court must make it clear to the offender the particular purposes that it has in mind and the conduct that is expected of the defendant during the deferment period (*R v George* [1984] 1 WLR 1082).

(iv)   The deferring court should make a careful note of what has been said to the defendant and, ideally, the defendant should be given notice in writing of the court expectations of what s/he should do or refrain from doing, so that there can be no doubt or misunderstanding in the defendant's mind which might subsequently lead to a sense of injustice (*George*, as above).

(v)   The defendant should understand that sentence has been deferred and that keeping to the expectations of the court is not in itself a sentence.

Deferment should thus be reserved for cases where the objectives of the exercise cannot be readily achieved by an immediate sentencing disposal. In particular, it should not be used to promote behaviour which could more appropriately be included as a requirement of a probation/community rehabilitation order. As Lord Lane CJ put it in *George*:

'Deferment of sentence will be more appropriate where the conduct required of the defendant is not sufficiently specific to be made the subject of a condition imposed as part of a probation order without creating uncertainty in the mind of the probation officer and the defendant as to whether there has been a breach of the order.'

Thus in *R v Skelton* [1983] Crim LR 686 the Court of Appeal criticised use of deferment with the expectation that the offender should fulfil his undertaking to receive voluntary in-patient treatment at a psychiatric hospital, an objective which clearly could have been achieved by a probation order with a mental treatment requirement. The Court observed that the purpose of deferment is to see if the offender is capable of behaving himself, not to impose some form of discipline, residence or treatment, but this should not be taken to mean that all expectations of this nature are an improper use of deferment. It would, for example, seem legitimate to give a drug dependent offender the opportunity to seek or sustain assistance from a specialist agency.

Youth Justice

Deferment is not readily compatible with current policy to speed the disposal of prosecutions of young offenders. In a speech to the Magistrates' Association (28 October 2000) the Lord Chancellor reminded his audience that 'it is vitally important for the youth court's disposal to follow swiftly on the heels of the offence' and urged sentencers to 'consider most critically whether it is ever in the interests of the young person to defer a final disposal'.

Length of Deferment Period

The period of deferment should not exceed six months after the date on which deferment is announced (s1(3)) but can be for such shorter period as allows realistic space for expectations to be addressed. The date to which sentence is deferred and upon which the defendant should return to court must be fixed at the time of deferment. Note that the defendant is not remanded on bail for the purposes of deferment (s1(4)) but if he fails to appear on the deferment date the court may issue either a summons requiring appearance or a warrant for his arrest (s2(4)).

Role of Probation Service/YOT During Deferment

Despite the instance of *Smith* (1979) (detailed on page 61), it would not seem appropriate for the Court to specify a deferment expectation that the offender should maintain contact with a probation officer or YOT member. This is precisely the kind of objective which could be appropriately met by a community rehabilitation order and the spirit of deferment of sentence is to give the offender the opportunity to demonstrate their ability to make efforts under their own initiative. However, some practitioners take the view that it is appropriate to maintain or at least of offer contact with the offender during the deferment period to encourage and monitor effort. Further, in some instances the person subject to deferment of sentence will already be subject to statutory oversight under an existing community order. In such instances the deferring court may make it an expectation of deferment that the defendant complies with their community order, even though this is a matter which the offender is already under a legal requirement, backed by sanctions, to fulfil and despite Lord Lane's advice in *George* that expectations should not be included which are precise enough to be the subject of a specific sentence.

In any event, the court reviewing the offender's progress at the end of deferment will probably wish to consider a pre-sentence report, either as an update of the PSR considered prior to deferment or as a fresh exercise if a PSR was not prepared for the benefit of the deferring court. Any request for a PSR should be sought at the time of deferment to avoid unnecessary delay at the end of the deferment period. If the reporter decides to prepare simply an update on the earlier PSR, the original report should be submitted with the new report.

Sentencing After Deferment

Every effort should be made to sentence the offender on the date to which sentence was deferred. In exceptional circumstances, however, it may be necessary to adjourn until a later date, even if this takes proceedings beyond the six month maximum postponement, and this delay does not deprive the court of its jurisdiction to sentence. Where possible, the same sentencer(s) who made the original deferment decision should sit to reconsider the case. The power of the court to deal with the offender in a case where sentence has been deferred is defined by s1(5) as:

(a)   power to deal with him, in respect of the offence for which passing of sentence has been deferred, in any way in which it could have dealt with him if it had not deferred passing sentence; and

(b)   without prejudice to the generality of para. (a), in the case of a magistrates' court, includes the power under s3 to commit to the Crown Court for sentence.

The task of the court on dealing with an offender at expiration of the deferment period was spelt out by Lane CJ in *George*, with particular emphasis on the defendant's legitimate expectations if s/he has fulfilled the deferring court's expectations:

'First the purpose of the deferment and any requirement imposed by the deferring court must be ascertained. Secondly, the court must determine if the defendant has substantially conformed or attempted to conform with the proper expectations of the deferring court, whether with regard to finding a job or as the case may be. If he has, then the defendant may legitimately expect that an immediate custodial sentence will not be imposed. If he has not, then the court should be careful to state with precision in what respects he has failed. If the court does not set out its reasons in this way, there is a danger, particularly where the sentencing court is differently constituted from the deferring court, that it may appear that the former is saying that the defendant should have been sentenced to immediate custody by the latter.'

Deferment has thus been characterised as an agreement or bargain between the court and the defendant in which the offender trades compliance for a non-custodial sentence. The court may be reliant on the pre-sentence report, either as an addendum to the earlier PSR or as a fresh exercise, to assess the extent of compliance. Uncertainty will arise where compliance has been only partial. Though there are few Court of Appeal judgements on the issue, it seems clear that the mere avoidance of further offending will not ensure a non-custodial sentence if the offender has failed to comply with other expectations. Thus in *R v Smith* (1976) 64 Cr App R 116, a defendant convicted of burglary had been expected to work regularly and reduce his alcohol consumption during deferment. Subsequent sentence of 18 months' imprisonment was upheld by the Court of Appeal because he had failed to achieve either target, despite his avoidance of further offending. However, substantial compliance with expectations should ensure a non-custodial outcome even if the offender has failed to meet expectations in minor ways. Thus in *R v Smith* (1979) 1 Cr App R(S) 339 an offender convicted of social security fraud had been expected to stay in employment, behave sensibly, see a probation officer and try to repay the sum dishonestly obtained. He had failed only in the final expectation and had a good excuse for his default. The Court of Appeal quashed his subsequent sentence of imprisonment.

Deferment of Sentence: Case Illustration

To give some practical illustration of the use of deferment, the following case concerns a defendant (who has never held a full driving licence) convicted of driving whilst disqualified, an offence occurring halfway through a six month period of disqualification. At time of conviction that earlier ban had nearly expired. A further period of disqualification was likely but discretionary. A custodial sentence was also a very real possibility. As an alternative to immediate sentence, the PSR proposed deferment with the following expectations upon the offender:

(a) to obtain a provisional driving licence;

(b) to drive only in accordance with driving licence regulations;

(c) to undertake a driving course provided by a qualified driving instructor;

(d) to take an MOT driving test;

(e) to commit no further offences;

(f) to keep interview appointments with the Probation Service as requested.

The final expectation would allow the offender to be re-interviewed at the end of his current driving ban to consider with him what steps he would be taking to pursue objectives (a) to (d), to interview him again prior to his return to court to take stock of his efforts to fulfil the expectations, and perhaps to see him in the interim to check on his progress if this would be helpful in keeping him to task.

Unresolved Criminal Charges Following deferment, an offender may be charged with a further offence allegedly committed during the deferment period, but is not convicted by the end of the deferment period. Such unresolved matters should not influence the sentencing court in any way (*R v Aquilina* [1990] Crim LR 134) and power to postpone sentencing to await the outcome of the further proceedings should not be exercised 'save where there are strong reasons which make it necessary for the judge, before deciding what to do, to know the result of the trial of the other outstanding charges' (*R v Ingle* (1974) 59 Cr App R 306). Note that there is no power to re-defer sentence (s1(2)), the only exception being that if a magistrates' court ultimately opts to commit the offender to Crown Court for sentence (see page 66), the Crown Court has power to further defer sentence (s1(8A)).

Sentencing Prior to Expiry of Deferment

Though deferment will normally run until the end of the period specified, specific provisions of PCCA s2 allow the offender to be dealt with earlier following conviction of another offence, even if that offence was committed prior to deferment. These provisions can be summarised as follows:

(i)   The deferring court may sentence forthwith for the deferment offence(s) following the defendant's conviction in Great Britain of any offence (s2(1)).

(ii)   Any court in England or Wales sentencing the offender for any offence for which the offender is convicted during the deferment period may also sentence for the deferment offence(s), if this has not already been done, but a magistrates' court may not sentence for an offence for which sentence was deferred by the Crown Court (s2(3)(a)). (In such instances the magistrates' court should give notice of the further conviction to the Crown Court which can then deal with the offender under s2(1)). Where the court dealing with the further offence is the Crown Court and the deferment court was a magistrates' court, the Crown Court may deal with the deferment offence but may exercise only the powers available to a magistrates' court (s2(3)(b)).

Committal for Sentence

PCC(S)A 2000 s3 (formerly MCA 1980 s38) gives a magistrates' court a general power to commit an offender to the Crown Court for sentence, provided that the following criteria are satisfied:

(i)   *Age* The defendant is 'aged 18 or over', the relevant statutory point of time being date of conviction. *Blackstone's* suggests that in practice the defendant should have been at least 18 at the point where mode of trial was determined because, if the defendant had no right to elect trial at Crown Court at that point because s/he was still a 'youth', it would seem unfair to expose them to the greater sentencing powers of the Crown Court even if s/he has reached their 18th birthday by the date of conviction. Power to commit juveniles for sentence (under MCA 1980 s37) was repealed by CDA 1998 to coincide with power to make a detention and training order.

(ii)   *Offence* The defendant has been convicted on summary trial of an either way offence.

(iii)   *Grounds* Section 3(2) specifies that the court must be of the opinion either:

(a)   'that the offence or the combination of the offence and one or more offences associated with it was so serious that greater punishment should be inflicted for the offence than the court has power to impose; or

(b)   'in the case of a violent or sexual offence, that a custodial sentence for a term longer than the court has power to impose is necessary to protect the public from serious harm from him'.

These grounds (a) and (b) are a familiar echo of the provisions of s79(2) and s80(2) justifying a custodial sentence and determining the length of such a sentence (see Chapter 4). However, under s3(2)(a) it is not essential that the court has custody in mind. If the court considers that the offence merits a fine of greater amount than it has power to impose committal under s3 is quite proper: *R v North Essex Justices, ex parte Lloyd* [2001] 2 Cr App R(S) 86.

As one of the factors which magistrates must have regard to in determining mode of trial for an either way offence is 'whether the punishment which a magistrates' court would have power to inflict for it would be adequate', it is likely that offences which satisfy ground (a) will reach the Crown Court for trial because the justices decline summary jurisdiction. Committal for sentence has thus been an unusual course, likely to arise in only limited circumstances where new information has come to the court's attention since the mode of trial decision, as follows (though committal for sentence has become more prominent since introduction of 'plea before venue' procedures addressed below):

(i)   The defendant's record of previous convictions, presented to the court only after conviction, or 'failure to respond to previous sentences', cause the court to take a more serious view of the offence(s) for sentence, within the provisions of s151(1) (see page 11).

(ii)   Hitherto undisclosed aggravating features of the offence(s) for sentence cause the court to view the offence(s) more seriously.

(iii) The defendant asks for further offences to be taken into consideration which the court considers to be of sufficient significance to transform its view of offence seriousness.

New information about the offence or a fuller impression of the offender's culpability can reach the court most readily through the prosecution but may be disclosed in the offence analysis section of pre-sentence report. The PSR may also be a potent source of information about the defendant's response to previous sentences.

Where an offender has been given a legitimate expectation that he will not be committed for sentence, he should not be committed if he subsequently appears before a differently constituted Bench: *R v Nottingham Magistrates' Court, ex parte Davidson* [2000] 1 Cr App R(S) 167 and *R v Norwich Magistrates' Court, ex parte Elliott* [2000] 1 Cr App R(S) 152. Whether such an expectation has been raised may raise a dispute about what was said (as illustrated by *R v Sheffield Magistrates' Court, ex parte Ojo* [2001] Crim LR 43 – Thomas' Commentary advises all concerned to make a full verbatim note of anything said pertaining to the possibility of committal so that in the event of later uncertainty the necessary evidence will be available).

Though the decision to commit for sentence will normally arise in the light of information received by the court *after* the mode of trial decision or conviction, this is not a statutory requirement of s3. After a conflict of opinion in the Divisional Court, it has been regarded as settled that a court can commit for sentence even if no information emerges after the mode of trial decision which casts the offence in a more serious light than originally perceived: *R v North Sefton Magistrates' Court, ex parte Marsh* (1994) 16 Cr App R(S) 401. In other words, magistrates could reconsider their initial decision and may conclude that they made a mistake in accepting jurisdiction. That said, the Divisional Court in *ex parte Marsh* cautioned that, despite this freedom, a magistrates' court should continue to think carefully before accepting jurisdiction in the first instance ' because normally a defendant should be able to conclude that once jurisdiction has been accepted, he would not on the same facts be committed to the Crown Court'. More recently, the issue has been thrown back into uncertainty by *R v Wirral Magistrates' Court, ex parte Jermyn* [2001] 1 Cr App R(S) 485 which appears to suggest that committal is only available if pertinent new information emerges after the mode of trial decision, even where the defendant has been warned of the court's power to commit.

The importance of fairness to the defendant was also emphasised in *R v Dover Magistrates' Court, ex parte Pamment* (1994) 15 Cr App R(S) 778. Note that it is not appropriate to commit for sentence simply because the case is of a type which the court considers ought to be dealt with at a higher level, even though it considers its powers to be adequate: *R v Warley Magistrates' Court, ex parte DPP* [1998] Crim LR 684 (detailed at page 41).

Where a magistrates' court adjourns for a pre-sentence report, it should make explicit that the defendant may still be committed to Crown Court, otherwise the court will have raised a legitimate expectation that this course will not follow: *R (on the application of Rees) v Feltham Justices* [2001] 2 Cr App R(S) 1, where the Divisional Court considered that a simple statement by the magistrates that they were leaving 'all options open' was not sufficient to counteract such expectation. Use of that phrase had to be considered in the context in which it was used. The Bench in this instance had heard defence submissions that the case (possession of cannabis with intent to supply a prisoner) could be dealt with within their sentencing powers and general mitigation. They had then retired before announcing that they could not pass sentence that day as they required further information from a PSR. They could readily have stated that their options included committal for sentence but did not do so. Their decision to commit was thus quashed.

The PSR writer's assessment may serve to influence the magistrates' judgement towards committal for sentence, as strikingly illustrated by *R v Salisbury Magistrates' Court, ex parte Gray* (1999) *The Times* 21 July (see page 7). Though proposing a probation order, the PSR suggested that as the offence now appeared more serious than had previously been believed, it would seem more appropriate for the magistrates to commit the case to the Crown Court, to reflect concern for such serious offences and to give a message to would-be perpetrators and victims of such crime about how seriously the courts view such instances. Though dismissing the application, the Divisional Court agreed that this suggestion was 'arguably misplaced'.

Plea Before Venue

Under MCA 1980 ss17A–17C, introduced by CPIA 1996, the defendant has the opportunity to indicate plea to an either way offence prior to any mode of trial decision. If the defendant indicates their intention to plead guilty, the court shall proceed with the case as a summary trial, while retaining the option to commit for sentence under s3. This new procedure will thus increase the use of s3 committals and the process is detailed at page 41. For the procedure to be followed in regard to the need to hold a *Newton* hearing in such circumstances, see page 41 *et seq*. For the principles and procedure applicable to the court's decision whether to commit or not, see page 50.

Related Offences

Where a court convicts an offender of an either way offence following indication of willingness to plead guilty if the case were to proceed to summary trial but the court has committed the offender to the Crown Court for trial in respect of one or more 'related offences', it may commit him in respect of the either way offence: s4. If he is then convicted of the related offence(s), the Crown Court has scope to deal with him for the either way offence under s5(1) (below) but if he is not convicted at Crown Court of a related offence, the Crown Court shall deal with him for the either way offence in any way that the magistrates' court could deal with him if it had just convicted him. Offences are 'related' 'if, were they both to be prosecuted on indictment, the charges for them could be joined in the same indictment': s4(7).

Other Offences

When a magistrates' court opts to commit for sentence where it is considered that an either way offence warrants a sentence in excess of the court's powers, it is obviously convenient if the Crown Court can also deal with other offences for sentence of which the defendant stands convicted, even if the magistrates' sentencing powers for these additional offences would otherwise be adequate. Scope is provided by s6. Where a court commits an offender to be sentenced or otherwise dealt with for an offence (known as 'the relevant offence') under:

(i)   s3 or s4, or

(ii)   s13(5) (conditionally discharged person convicted of a further offence: see page 229), or

(iii) s116(3)(b) (conviction during currency of original sentence: see page 89), or

(iv)   s120(2) (conviction during operational period of suspended sentence),

then if the 'relevant offence' is indictable the offender may also be committed in respect of any other offence whatsoever in respect of which the committing court has power to deal with him: s6(2). If the 'relevant offence' is a summary offence (as will not be the case under ss3–4) the committing court may also commit the offender in respect of any other imprisonable offence of which that court has convicted him or any offence which carries power of disqualification from driving under RTA 1988 ss34–36 or any offence subject to suspended sentence which that court has power to bring into effect: s6(3).

Custody or Bail?

Section 3(1) provides that the defendant may be committed to the Crown Court in custody or on bail. The usual presumption in favour of bail under the Bail Act 1976 does not apply at this stage of proceedings and the Court of Appeal (*R v Coe* [1968] 1 WLR 195) had indicated that committal in custody should usually be adopted, on the basis that it is hardly logical for a magistrates' court to conclude that an offender should receive a custodial sentence in excess of six months but then grant bail. However, in *R v Rafferty* [1998] Crim LR 433 the Appeal Court indicated that where a plea of guilty is made at magistrates' court, it will not be usual to alter the defendant's remand status. Defendants who have been on bail until that point should normally remain on bail, even if it is anticipated that a custodial sentence will be imposed, unless there are good reasons for remanding in custody. If the defendant has been in custody up until that point, it will unusual to alter that position if the reasons for RIC remain unchanged.

Power of the Crown Court

PCC(S)A 2000 s5(1)

Where an offender is committed by a magistrates' court for sentence under ss3 or 4 above, the Crown Court shall inquire into the circumstances of the case and shall have power to deal with the offender in any manner in which it could deal with him if he had just been convicted of the offence on indictment before the court.

Committal will be to the 'most convenient' Crown Court location, in accordance with normal local practice. In dealing with committal for sentence, the Crown Court must consist of a judge (or recorder) sitting with between two and four lay justices (SCA 1981 s74(1)). If the defendant is appealing against conviction in respect of the offence now awaiting sentence, sentencing should be adjourned pending the outcome of that appeal.

As made clear by s5(1), the Crown Court has discretion to deal with the defendant committed under s3 as if he had just been convicted on indictment. This means that for the purposes of determining eligibility for a particular sentence by age, the relevant point is the defendant's age at the moment of sentence by the Crown Court. The Crown Court is certainly not bound by the magistrates' court view of the seriousness of the offence and is thus able to exercise powers within the lower court's range of disposals. The Crown Court can also defer sentence, even if the magistrates' court had previously deferred sentence before deciding to commit for sentence. In respect of offences committed under s6, s7(1) gives the Crown Court power to deal with the offender 'in any way in which the magistrates' court could deal with him as if it had just convicted him of the offence', because the purpose of this provision is to allow all matters to be dealt with conveniently by a single court, not to expose the offender to the possibility of greater punishment.

When the magistrates' court had adjourned for reports in the manner which gave rise to the defendant's legitimate expectation that a non-custodial outcome would follow if reports proved favourable, the Crown Court is equally bound under the *Gillam* principle (see page 52) not to impose a custodial sentence, in the same way as the lower court would have been (*R v Rennes* (1985) 7 Cr App R(S) 343). It is, however, unlikely that committal for sentence will arise in such circumstances as cases of this kind should not result in committal (see the *Feltham Justices* judgement, above).

Revocation of a Community Order

Where a magistrates' court revokes a community order and 'deals with' the offender for the original offence 'in any manner in which it could deal with him if he had just been convicted by the court of the offence' (now PCC(S)A 2000 Sch 3 para 4(1)(d)), the court must deal with the offender itself and does not have the option to commit to the Crown Court for sentence: *R v Jordan* [1998] Crim LR 353. By the same logic, committal for sentence will not be an option following revocation in revocation proceedings under Sch 3 para 10(3)(b).

Recent Use of Committal for Sentence

The following Table demonstrates the drop in the committal rate following introduction of CJA 1991, together with a more recent increase, doubtless arising from the Divisional Court's more expansive interpretation of what was then s38 (see page 63). It is also clear that a sentence of immediate custody is not the inevitable outcome of committal for sentence, albeit that this is the outcome in approximately six cases in ten. The statistics do not indicate the percentage of custodial sentences imposed by the Crown Court which were of a length within the maximum powers of a magistrates' court.

	Number of Persons	Immediate Custody	Community Sentence	Fine/ Discharge	Otherwise Dealt With
1992	5,561	47%	27%	9%	17%
1994	2,852	57%	22%	6%	13%
1996	4,218	65%	17%	4%	12%
1998	17,632	66%	24%	3%	4%
1999	19,048	67%	24%	2%	4%

The *Supplementary Criminal Statistics* for 1998 and 1999 yield the following details of the number of defendants committed for sentence for indictable offences (including motoring) by age and sex and as a percentage (in brackets) of the total number found guilty:

	15 < 18		18 < 21		21 +	
	M	F	M	F	M	F
1998	897 (3%)	44 (1%)	3,588 (8%)	249 (4%)	12,068 (8%)	1,420 (5%)
1999	861 (3%)	47 (1%)	3,999 (9%)	275 (4%)	12,756 (8%)	1,460 (5%)

Remitting to Another Magistrates' Court

A magistrates' court with jurisdiction to sentence an offender has discretionary power under PCC(S)A 2000 s10 to remit the offender to another magistrates' court so that the matters before each court can be dealt with together, thus allowing outstanding matters to be resolved in a single sentencing exercise. This power is exercisable in the following circumstances:

(i)   the defendant has attained age 18 (separate powers apply to youths under s8);

(ii)   the remitting court has convicted the defendant of the offence(s) which it is proposed to remit;

(iii)   the offence(s) before the remitting court is punishable with imprisonment or disqualification from driving;

(iv)   the court to which it is proposed to remit the defendant ('the other court') has convicted him/her of an imprisonable/disqualifiable offence but has not yet dealt with the defendant for that offence by sentence or otherwise;

(v)   the other court has given consent to the matter being remitted.

The offender may be remanded in custody or on bail for this purpose. Appeal is not possible against a decision to remit. Exercise of this power does not preclude the remitting court from first making a restitution order under PCC(S)A 2000 s148 (see page 205). The procedure to be followed between the two courts is specified by MCR 1981 r19. The other court is thus empowered to deal with the offender as it sees fit, including the power to remit the case on to a third court under s10: s10(4).

4
CUSTODIAL SENTENCES

This chapter combines together measures that share the designation and status of custodial sentence, either for adults or juveniles, together with the applicable generic procedural or ancillary provisions, save that the complexities of life sentences are dealt with in a separate text (Stone, 1997), though the new power to impose an 'automatic life sentence' is outlined here because it post-dates that text. Further, the scope to add a 'hospital direction' to a custodial sentence is addressed in Stone (forthcoming).

General Provisions and Imprisonment

The introductory part of this Chapter aims to sketch the generic provisions governing custodial sentences of whatever nature in so far as these are regulated in common by PCC(S)A 2000 ss76–83 (formerly contained in Part One of CJA 1991) and to detail the power to impose adult imprisonment in particular. The 2000 Act (s76(1)) defines a 'custodial sentence' as:

(a)   in relation to an offender of or over the age of 21 years, a sentence of imprisonment;

(b)   a sentence of detention for a grave crime under PCC(S)A 2000 ss90 and 91 (formerly under CYPA 1933 s53);

(c)   a detention and training order under PCC(S)A 2000 s100 (formerly CDA 1998 s73).

Sentences of detention in a YOI (under PCC(S)A 2000 s96) and of custody for life (under PCC(S)A ss93 and 94) also were custodial sentences but both forms of sentence have been repealed by CJCSA 2000 which specifies that offenders aged 18–20 shall cease to receive a distinct young adult form of custody but shall be eligible for imprisonment in common with other adults, subject to certain differentiating provisions, as outlined at page 127.

The seminal 1991 Act did not attempt to provide any rationale for custodial sentencing but the statute was viewed as an initiative, if not wholeheartedly to make imprisonment a 'sanction of last resort' (as proposed by the United Nations, 1990), then at least to ensure that custodial sentences should be reserved for more serious cases for which there is no alternative. The White Paper *Crime, Justice and Protecting the Public* (1990) was interpreted as promoting restraint in the use of custody as regards both meeting the threshold criterion justifying custody and determining the length of any such sentence. Two short extracts from the White Paper suggest the tenor of its thinking. First, it suggests that prison 'can be an expensive way of making bad people worse', reflecting grave doubts about the rehabilitative worth of imprisonment. Second, 'most crimes are not violent and for many of those who commit them, punishment in the community is likely to be better for the victim, the public and the offender than a custodial sentence.' The letter and spirit of the 1991 Act had been amended markedly since implementation.

Threshold Criteria

PCC(S)A 2000 s79(2) (formerly CJA 1991 s1(2)) specifies two alternative justifications for a custodial sentence:

> Subject to s79(3) (*see page 82*), the court shall not pass a custodial sentence on the offender unless it is of the opinion:
>
> (a) that the offence, or the combination of the offence and one or more offences associated with it was so serious that only such a sentence can be justified for the offence; or
>
> (b) where the offence is a violent or sexual offence, that only such a sentence would be adequate to protect the public from serious harm from him.

The criterion of s79(2)(b) will not be pursued here. Instead, protective sentencing will be outlined at page 90 in regard to longer-than-proportionate sentence lengths for violent and sexual offences under s80(2)(b), which receives far more attention in practice. Section 79(2)(b) has proved of little practical significance because any sexual or violent offence that raises serious consideration of public protection needs will inevitably satisfy the 'so serious' test under s79(2)(a).

In respect of a detention and training order, the minimum length of sentence being four months (see page 123), the custody threshold is higher since the court must determine not only that the offence is 'so serious' but also that it demands a sentence of at least that length: *R v Inner London Crown Court, ex p. N and S* [2001] 1 Cr App R(S) 343.

Note that though an offence may satisfy the test under s79(2)(a), it does not automatically dictate that a custodial sentence must follow. As Lord Taylor CJ stated in *R v Cox* [1993] 1 WLR 188: 'the court is still required to consider whether such a sentence is appropriate having regard to the mitigating factors available and relevant to the offender, as opposed to such factors as are relevant to the offence.' Although concluding that only a custodial sentence could be justified for the offence of reckless driving in the course of a police pursuit, the Appeal Court set aside a YOI term in favour of a probation order in the light of the offender's age, personal mitigation and proposals contained in the pre-sentence report.

Interpreting 'So Serious' Criterion

In endeavouring to offer some guidance on the interpretation of s1(2)(a), the Court of Appeal in *R v Cox* [1993] 1 WLR 188 adopted the test proposed for this criterion under earlier legislation gatekeeping the use of custody for the under-21s in *R v Bradbourne* (1985) 7 Cr App R(S) 180:

> 'The kind of offence which ... would make all right-thinking members of the public, knowing all the facts, feel that justice had not been done by the passing of any sentence other than a custodial one.'

In formulating this test, Lawton LJ expressed confidence that 'courts can recognise an elephant when they see one, but may not find it necessary to define it'. In other post-1991 Act cases, appeal judges have referred to 'the present climate of opinion' about certain kinds of behaviour as a factor in weighing seriousness (e.g. in *R v Keogh* (1994), a case of relatively less serious dishonesty, see below) and to behaviour considered to be 'a blight on our society' (*R v Costello* (1994), involving theft from and damage to public phone boxes, see below). These various tests have been subjected to critical scrutiny by Ashworth and von Hirsch (1997): (a) Taken literally, they appear to substitute the test of popular opinion in place of seriousness as the determining factor; (b) Judges are not well placed to identify public opinion; (c) Reasonable lay persons are not well placed to make this kind of judgement as imprisoning people falls outside the ambit of everyday experience. They thus regard the 'right-thinking person' test as conceptually flawed and empirically unsupported.

As regards the interpretation that certain misbehaviour may cause considerable knock-on consequences (e.g. a damaged phone can result not just in inconvenience but may result in tragedy if the phone is required for a life-and-death emergency before being repaired), Ashworth and von Hirsch argue that this relies unfairly on the 'worst case scenario' in assessing seriousness without regard to the extent to which such a consequence was reasonably foreseeable in the particular case: 'It is wrong to assess seriousness by reference to a merely possible consequence.' Similarly, the argument that hostile encounters between drivers 'can easily develop into quite serious incidents of violence' (*R v Fenton* (1994), see below) seems to suggest that the seriousness of an encounter should be judged on the basis of what might have happened rather than on the basis of what did happen. As Ashworth and von Hirsch put it: 'it is wrong in principle to sentence one offender simply on the basis of what others might have done if the situation had been different.'

Finally, as regards the argument sometimes promoted by the Appeal Court that an offence merits custody because of prevalence or, put more crudely, 'there's a lot of it about', Ashworth and von Hirsch suggest that this simplistic approach is also flawed. Taken at face value the idea that an offence merits custody because it is common behaviour is a nonsense that would lead to imprisonment for a host of minor offences. If the Appeal Court is trying to reflect a growing fear of certain kinds of anti-social behaviour, 'fear is a phenomenon that is not necessarily related to culpability ... Should a seemingly minor assault be treated as more serious because it fuels or generates a climate of fear?' And would it be right to impose differing sentences in different localities according to prevalence rates?

Given these criticisms of the level of judicial guidance, Ashworth and von Hirsch seek to outline a more principled approach to seriousness, as discussed at page 1. Here it is possible to note only some of the appellate decisions on the interpretation of s1(2)(a), demonstrating that the Appeal Court has adopted a less than restrictive approach to the threshold. It has to be remembered that these should not be regarded as guideline cases and are perhaps atypical instances where the Appeal Court has been asked to review a Crown Court sentence considered excessive by the defence. This selection is classified according to the broad category of crime.

Theft and Deception (a) Making off without paying a taxi fare of £50 held 'so serious': *R v Foster* (1993); (b) Taking item value £35 from DIY store and exchanging it for other goods of the same value held 'so serious': *R v Keogh* (1994) 15 Cr App R(S) 279; (c) Ticket clerk re-issuing four used £1 ferry tickets and in possession of 13 more tickets held 'so serious': *R v McCormick* (1995) 16 Cr App R(S) 134; (d) Stealing from public telephone boxes held 'so serious': *R v Arslan* (1994) 15 Cr App R(S) 40 (drilling into cash box and stealing £82); *R v Costello* (1994) 15 Cr App R(S) 240 (aiding attempt to drill into cash box). Compare *R v Bond* (1994) 15 Cr App R(S) 430 where theft of gammon value £3.50 from a supermarket was held not 'so serious', a term of imprisonment being replaced by 12 months' probation in the light of the offender's personal problems.

'Road Rage' Violence Getting out of his car, approaching other driver and pushing him in chest (common assault) held 'so serious' though 14 days reduced to 7 days' imprisonment: *R v Fenton* (1994) 15 Cr App R(S) 682 .

Indecent Assault Grabbing female traffic warden's bottom held 'so serious': *R v Goodway* [1996] 1 Cr App R(S) 16. Compare *R v Orriss* (1993) 15 Cr App R(S) 185 where a 19 year old touching a 12 year old boy's thigh over his clothing, having masturbated in front of the victim, was not held 'so serious'. A number of recent cases have considered instances of rubbing against women on crowded public transport so that the victim could feel the offender's erect penis. Though in *R v Chagan* (1995)16 Cr App R(S) 15 this was held not 'so serious', this kind of behaviour was regarded as 'so serious' in *R v Townsend* (1995) as it is 'thoroughly degrading' and could make the victim apprehensive of using public transport in future. The stance taken in *Townsend* has since been followed in *R v Tanyildiz* [1998] 1 Cr App R(S) 362, albeit that for a first-time offender a short sentence of three rather than six months was deemed sufficient.

Without seeking to examine any particular view of the Appeal Court, Lord Bingham CJ (1997) commented that he was not surprised that sentencers have had 'more ready resort to custody' (and increased the length of sentence) in the preceding five years:

> 'The tenor of political rhetoric has strongly favoured the imposition of severe sentences; this rhetoric has been faithfully reflected in certain elements of the media, and judges accused of passing lenient sentences have found themselves routinely castigated in some newspapers. Against this background, judges have, understandably, sought to avoid the unwelcome experience of passing sentences which *(are referred to the Court of Appeal as unduly lenient – see page 245).'*

Lord Bingham went on to warn of the volatility of public opinion and cautioned sentencers not to 'be blown hither and thither by every wind of political and penal fashion'.

The Criterion Re-Interpreted The Court of Appeal has recently re-examined the justification for a custodial sentence under s1(2)(a), recognising that the issue whether an offence is 'so serious' is 'one of the most elusive problems of sentencing'. In *R v Howells and others* [1999] 1 Cr App R(S) 335, Lord Bingham CJ (who had already expressed his doubts about the *Bradbourne* interpretation – see Bingham, 1997) stated that there is no 'bright line' separating offences for which only a custodial sentence could be justified and those which were not 'so serious'. But it could not be said that the 'right-thinking member of the public' test is helpful because the sentencing court has no means of ascertaining the views of such persons and inevitably attributed to them its own views and reflected its own opinion. In place of that test, it would be wrong to lay down prescriptive rules governing the exercise of judgement and any guidance must be subject to exceptions and qualifications. However, in approaching cases which are on or near the threshold, the Appeal Court suggested the following considerations:

- It will usually be helpful to begin by considering the nature and extent of the defendant's criminal intention and of any injury or damage caused to the victim.

- Other things being equal, an offence which was deliberate or premeditated will usually be more serious than one which was spontaneous and unpremeditated or which involved an excessive response to provocation.

- An offence which inflicted personal injury or mental trauma, particularly if permanent, will usually be more serious than one which inflicted financial loss only.

Having provided these three unsurprising pointers in the assessment of offence seriousness in terms of the offence itself, Lord Bingham switched to focus on familiar, statutory factors pertaining to the offender pre-offence:

- The court might take into account any previous convictions or any failure to respond to previous sentences (s29(1)) and had to have regard to s29(2) (offending while on bail).

Lord Bingham then proceeded to give greatest attention to well-recognised matters that relate to the *offender* rather than to the offence and to post-offence issues:

- A court would ordinarily heed an admission of responsibility for the offence, particularly if reflected by a guilty plea at the earliest opportunity (PCC(S)A 2000 s152) and accompanied by hard evidence of remorse (e.g. by an expression of regret to the victim and an offer of compensation).

- Where offending had been fuelled by addiction to drugs or drink, a court would be inclined to look more favourably on an offender who has already demonstrated, by practical steps, a genuine, self-motivated determination to address their addiction.

- Youth and immaturity will often justify a less rigorous penalty than appropriate for an adult.

- Some measure of leniency will ordinarily be extended to offenders of previous good character, the more so if there is evidence of positive good character as opposed to merely the absence of previous convictions.

- It will sometimes be appropriate to take account of family responsibilities, or physical or mental disability.

- While a court should never impose a custodial sentence unless satisfied that it is necessary to do so, there is even greater reluctance to do so where the offender has never before served such a sentence.

In conclusion, the Lord Chief Justice mentioned: (i) sentencing is intended in almost every case to protect the public, whether by punishment, reform or deterrence, or all of those things; (ii) courts should not be unmindful of the need to maintain public confidence in sentencing; (iii) if a custodial sentence is imposed, it should be for no longer than is necessary to meet the penal purpose that the court has in mind (Lord Bingham here drew attention to the 'important' observations of the Court in *R v Ollerenshaw* – see page 76).

The Court proceeded to deal with the various unrelated appeals before it, all relating to relatively short custodial terms of up to 12 months. Of the seven cases reviewed shorter custodial terms were substituted in four cases, leave to appeal was refused in one case and in the two remaining cases conditional discharges were imposed in place of the original custodial terms (though the Court indicated that the correct initial sentence would have been community service). These cases are noted where appropriate in Part 1 of this text (Stone, 2000) in the context of specific offences. As a flavour of the Appeal Court's approach, it is worth noting *R v Hussain* (unreported, 2000) where a custodial term was upheld as correct in principle for a first-time offender pleading guilty to possession of herbal cannabis valued at £245 which he had bought in bulk for his own use but admitted also supplying to close friends.

'So Serious' Criterion: 'Associated' Offences

The court's capacity to assess the aggregate seriousness of associated offences is clarified by PCC(S)A 2000 s161(1) (formerly CJA 1991 s31(2)) which specifies that an offence is associated with another if:

(a)   the offender is convicted of it in the proceedings in which he is convicted of the offence or (although convicted of it in earlier proceedings) is sentenced for it at the same time as he is sentenced for that offence; or

(b)   the offender admits the commission of it in the proceedings in which he is sentenced for the other offence and requests the court to take it into consideration in sentencing him for that offence.

In other words, 'associated' does not mean that the offences were committed as part of the same criminal episode but simply that the offender stands to be dealt with for the offences on the same sentencing occasion. This includes any offences which the defendant asks the court to take into consideration (TICs). By this generous definition an offence which was previously made the subject of a conditional discharge and which now stands to be dealt with afresh because of the commission of a further offence during the discharge period is associated with that further offence, provided that the offender is dealt with for that original offence, but not if the court takes no action in respect of it: *R v Godfrey* (1993) 14 Cr App R(S) 804. If the court opts to activate a suspended term of imprisonment, the offence in respect of which the suspended sentence was passed is not associated with a further offence, because sentence for the earlier offence has already been passed and activation does not count as being sentenced: *R v Crawford* [1993] Crim LR 539.

Length of Sentence

Issues of appropriate length of sentence are primarily addressed in judicial guidance in respect of specific offences. As a general rule under the 1991 Act, if the offence(s) satisfy the 'so serious' criterion and the court determines to pass a custodial sentence, s80(2)(a) specifies that:

The custodial sentence shall be for such term (not exceeding the permitted maximum) as in the opinion of the court is commensurate with the seriousness of the offence, or the combination of the offence and other offences associated with it.

The subsection has not been the subject of extended consideration by the Appeal Court, perhaps because its clear and mandatory requirement to make the length of a custodial sentence proportional to offence seriousness was given early authoritative interpretation (which commentators such as Ashworth (1995: 83) have regarded as a 'flagrant misreading' of the statute), allowing sentencers 'to continue largely with "business as usual", the different sentence lengths for crimes reflecting not the relative seriousness of offences but rather an ad hoc mixture of considerations.' In *R v Cunningham* [1993] 1 WLR 183 the judge in sentencing the offender to four years' imprisonment for robbery had said that 'others who might be tempted to follow your example must realise that a long deterrent sentence will follow.' Rejecting the defence argument that deterrence was not a legitimate consideration under the 1991 Act, Lord Taylor CJ stated that 'commensurate with the seriousness of the offence' 'must mean commensurate with the punishment and deterrence which the seriousness of the offence requires.' However, though deterrence has thus been approved as a permissible consideration in setting sentence levels, Lord Taylor acknowledged that s2(2)(a) prevents the court from increasing the length of sentence to make a special example of the defendant.

Prevalence of Offence The Court in *Cunningham* also stated that prevalence is a legitimate consideration within s2(2)(a). Lord Taylor commented:

'The seriousness of an offence is clearly affected by how many people it harms and to what extent. For example, a violent sexual attack on a woman in a public place gravely harms her. But if such attacks are prevalent in a neighbourhood, each offence affects not only the immediate victim but women generally in that area, putting them in fear and limiting their freedom of movement. Accordingly in such circumstances, the sentence commensurate with the seriousness of the offence may need to be higher there than elsewhere.'

This reasoning has a clear appeal and addresses the secondary or indirect harm that an offence can inflict. The difficulty lies in establishing on what basis a court can determine (i) that an offence has become more prevalent and (ii) the level of fear and restriction of choice that it has generated. As Ashworth (1995: 88–89) indicates, what may be assumed intuitively to represent a local crime wave may be a phenomenon explicable on other grounds and fear of crime does not necessarily reflect objective risk. It may say more about media manipulation or personal sensitivities. 'There may be more constructive ways of responding to fear of crime than through sentencing.' In a recent judgement, *R v Law* [1998] 2 Cr App R(S) 365 concerning serious robbery committed by a young adult, the Court of Appeal has shown its continuing adherence to issues of prevalence linked to its belief in deterrence:

'If the offence is more prevalent and if it is believed that deterrent sentences should be passed to protect the public interest, then longer sentences than presently passed may be justified. Similarly, if the crime is increasingly committed in a particular area, sentences longer than those passed before may be appropriate, even having regard to the age of the offender.'

Clearly, an offence may be 'so serious' but may nevertheless attract a very short custodial term. Prior to the 1991 Act the Court of Appeal had periodically indicated that in some cases 'any prison sentence, however short, may be an adequate punishment and deterrent' (Lord Lane CJ in *R v Bibi* [1980] 1 WLR 1193). Lord Lane had particularly (but not exclusively) in mind offenders convicted of comparatively less serious offences who were either first time offenders or were comparatively lightly convicted and now facing their first custodial sentence. Judges sometimes claimed to identify the merits of what became characterised as the 'clang of prison gates' theory, as expressed by Lawton LJ in *R v Sargeant* (1974) 60 Cr App R 74:

> '... he has had the humiliation of hearing prison gates closing behind him. We take the view that for men of good character the very fact that prison gates have closed is the main punishment.'

And in *R v Doland and Cormack* [1981] Crim LR 657 the Appeal Court stated with regard to middle-aged first-time offenders, 'there is no doubt that the effect of imprisonment is felt in the first month or the first two months. After that, people get inured to it'.

This 'theory' that pre-acclimatisation exposure to custody in the early days of sentence is particularly salutary may owe more to common sense intuition and anecdote than to clear penological evidence. Further, under the 1991/2000 Act framework, the offender of previous good character has the benefit of mitigation that may limit their term on desert grounds without the need to theorise the likely psychological impact.

Another thread of the Appeal Court's reasoning has reflected concern about overcrowding within the penal estate and the consequent impact on quality of life for those imprisoned in shorter term accommodation. Thus in *R v Upton* (1980) 71 Cr App R 102 Lord Lane CJ, referring to the use of custody for less serious non-violent offenders, commented that sentencers 'should appreciate that overcrowding in many of the penal establishments in this country is such that a prison sentence, however short, is a very unpleasant experience indeed for the inmates' and urged that if there is no choice other than custody, the term should be as short as possible. Again, it may be considered that length of term should be determined according to commensurability and mitigation, not the sentencer's imperfect knowledge of the varying state of the prison system. However, echoes of *Upton*, *Sargeant* and *Bibi* still resonate in the Appeal Court's thinking, as expressed recently in *R v Ollerenshaw* [1999] 1 Cr App R(S) 65. Though the case concerned fraudulent excise duty evasion (by bootlegging trips to France to bring back alcoholic drinks and tobacco), Rose LJ expressed the following principles for general guidance:

> 'Where a court is considering a comparatively short custodial sentence, of about 12 months or less, it should generally ask itself, particularly where the defendant has not previously been in prison, whether custody for an even shorter period might be equally effective in protecting the interests of the public and deterring criminal behaviour. For example, six months may be as effective as nine months and two months as four months. Such an approach is no less valid in the light of today's prison overcrowding as it was in the case of *Bibi*.'

Among recent examples of the application of *Ollerenshaw,* see *R v Busby* [2000] 1 Cr App R(S) 279 where sentence of nine months for possession of 14 Ecstasy tablets to share with two friends was reduced to six months, and *R v McNally* [2000] 1 Cr App R(S) 535 where sentence of 12 months was reduced to six months for assault of a hospital doctor by a father of previous good character when highly anxious about his infant son's lack of response to treatment. Note that the scope to impose very short custodial terms upon young offenders is restricted by statute (see page 123).

Invalid Motive for Extending Term In keeping with the principle of proportionality, it is clearly invalid to impose a longer-than-commensurate term to seek to achieve a desirable custodial outcome, such as to allow the offender to receive treatment for addiction or psychiatric needs or a form of therapy (such as the sex offender treatment programme, or the therapeutic community at HMP Grendon) that is only available for those serving terms of a certain minimum length, e.g. *R v Bassett* (1985) 7 Cr App R(S) 75.

Use of Maximum Term Where the offence carries a maximum determinate term of imprisonment (e.g. 10 years for non-dwelling burglary), it is well established that a sentence of that length should not be imposed unless the offence in question is one of the worst examples of that kind of crime as encountered in practice and where there is no personal mitigation. Thus a maximum term will generally not be legitimate where a guilty plea is entered (see page 16). In most instances, this principle will not restrict the sentencer's discretion as the maximum is usually high enough to allow plenty of scope for substantial terms short of that ceiling. Problems can occasionally arise where the maximum is low and changed sensitivities suggest terms close to that limit.

Minimum/Maximum Terms in Magistrates' Courts General limits upon the custodial sentencing powers of a magistrates' court apply. Under MCA 1980 s132 the minimum term of imprisonment that may be imposed is five days (though see the power to detain for the day of sentence only, page 226). The maximum term of custody for any offence is six months (subject to any shorter maximum for the offence): PCC(S)A 2000 s78(1). The maximum aggregate term for more than one offence is also six months except in respect of two or more either way offences, for which the maximum aggregate sentence is 12 months: MCA 1980 s133. These limits apply also to the Crown Court where it is exercising the powers of a magistrates' court. Note, however, that different provisions apply to detention and training orders (see page 124).

Threshold and Length: Procedural Requirements

1. Pre-Sentence Report Before forming any opinion that the offence(s) satisfy the 'so serious' criterion and/or regarding the length of sentence commensurate with seriousness, PCC(S)A 2000 s81(1) specifies that 'the court shall obtain and consider a pre-sentence report', subject to the caveat in s81(2) that this otherwise mandatory requirement 'does not apply if in the circumstances of the case the court is of the opinion that it is unnecessary to obtain a PSR'. Note that the court has to make a considered decision to dispense with a PSR and it does not satisfy the 'opt out' provision of s81(2) simply to overlook the requirement and proceed to sentence without benefit of a PSR. However, s81(5) provides that 'no custodial sentence shall be invalidated by the failure of a court to obtain and consider a PSR' under s81(1), but any court on an appeal against such a sentence shall obtain a PSR if none was obtained by the court below. Here too a 'let out' provision allows the appeal court to dispense with a PSR if of the opinion either (a) that the court below was justified in concluding that a PSR was not needed or (b) that even if the lower court was not justified in this forming that opinion, it is now unnecessary to obtain a report: s81(6).

Home Office research (Charles *et al*, 1997) on sentencing without a report following the relaxation in CJPOA 1994 of the requirement to consider a PSR found that in both the Crown Court and magistrates' courts 15% of cases in which a custodial sentence was imposed were sentenced without a report. Judges were more likely to dispense with a report in the most serious cases where custody was virtually inevitable. At summary level, stipendiary magistrates (now district judges) were much more likely to dispense with a report than lay colleagues (24% compared with 10%), citing instances where Appeal Court guidance indicated that a custodial sentence was appropriate (for example, in instances of 'road rage') and also instances where the time that would be spent remanded in custody while the report was prepared equated with the term of the proposed custodial sentence. Some 35% of those sentenced to a term of less than two months were dealt with without a PSR. In interview, magistrates indicated that they would consider dispensing with a report most frequently where an earlier PSR was available to the court, checking with the defendant whether the information thus given was still correct or sometimes asking a probation officer to undertake a 'stand-down' inquiry so that the old report could be updated verbally. In youth courts 6% of custody cases were sentenced without a report but there were significant differences between courts, with a range from nil such cases in two areas studied to 17% in a third area. The Magistrates' Association had earlier issued guidance (1995) that as few cases suitable for summary trial are so serious that a custodial sentence would be the only conclusion drawn by magistrates a PSR will be useful to sentencers in most instances.

Recent Appeal Court guidance throws some light on the exercise of s81(1) following conviction after a contested trial hearing. In *R v Gillette* (1999) *The Times* 3 December, where a man aged 72, in poor health, convicted after trial of indecent assault had been sentenced to 12 months' immediate imprisonment without a PSR. On his appeal the Court stated that 'in all cases where a court is contemplating sentencing any defendant to prison for the first time, other than for a very short period, it should be the inevitable practice to obtain a PSR before passing such a sentence'. The only possible exception to this rule that the Court could anticipate would be if the court had been specifically asked by the defence to sentence immediately, as might be the case if the defendant wished to know their punishment without further delay. However, the Court qualified its view in *R v Armsaramah* [2001] 1 Cr App R(S) 467, where the offender had been convicted after trial of conspiracy to kidnap, robbery and possession of an imitation firearm with intent to kidnap and was sentenced to five years without a PSR. In this instance, the Court noted that the defence had not requested an adjournment for a PSR (unlike *Gillette* where the judge had turned down such a request). Additionally, defence counsel had put forward all matters which could be said in the offender's favour and the judge had had the advantage of conducting the trial and had indicated her preparedness to make every possible assumption in the defendant's favour. In the Court's view there was nothing in respect of which a PSR could have aided the sentencer. Her decision that a report was unnecessary was thus upheld.

Armsaramah should not be read as indicating that a PSR can always be validly dispensed with where there has been a contested trial. In *R v Stephenson* (2001, unreported) the offender who had previous convictions for violence but none involving immediate imprisonment had been sentenced to three years without a report for s20 wounding and ABH in a pub lavatory. The Appeal Court agreed that a PSR should have been sought. A report was available on appeal, indicating that the offender was now admitting his guilt and his difficulty in containing his aggression and assessing him as highly motivated to address his violence. That said, the court concluded that the sentence, though severe, was not manifestly excessive or wrong in principle.

Special Provision for Under 18s Where the offender is aged under 18, a court is not empowered to form the opinion under s81(2) that a PSR is unnecessary unless either (i) the offence (or an associated offence) is triable only on indictment or (ii) the court has the benefit of a previous PSR prepared about the offender: s81(3). If there is more than one such report prepared in earlier proceedings against the young offender, the court must have regard to the most recent.

Function of PSR Note that a court is required to consider a PSR *prior to* forming any opinion about (i) whether the offence(s) meet the criterion in s79(2)(a) and (ii) the proportionate length of a custodial term. The PSR is thus central to the determination of offence seriousness in custodial sentencing, though this does not apply in respect of community sentencing (see page 133).

2. *Circumstances of the Offence* In forming the opinion that the offence(s) satisfy the 'so serious' criterion and in determining the commensurate sentence, s81(4)(a) specifies that a court:

> shall take into account all such information as is available to it about the circumstances of the offence or (as the case may be) of the offence and the offence or offences associated with it, including any aggravating or mitigating factors.

Two aspects of offending are identified by statute as aggravating factors which the court must heed:

(i) *Offence Committed on Bail* PCC(S)A 2000 s151(2) (formerly CJA 1991 s29(2)) specifies that offending on bail is always an aggravating feature in assessing offence seriousness:

> In considering the seriousness of any offence committed while the offender was on bail, the court shall treat the fact that it was committed in those circumstances as an aggravating factor.

Note that it matters not if the accused had been bailed by the police or by a court, whether the allegation in respect of which bail was given was of an entirely different nature to the offence the seriousness of which is now being assessed or if the allegation in respect of which bail was given was subsequently dropped against the offender. The provision thus has very wide ambit and such considerations may only be taken into account to mitigate the weight of s151(2).

(ii) *Racially Aggravated Offence* PCC(S)A 2000 s153 (formerly CDA 1998 s82) requires a court that is considering the seriousness of any offence committed on or after 30 September 1998 (other than an offence specifically defined as racially aggravated under CDA 1998 ss29–32 – i.e. assault, criminal damage, public order or harassment) that is 'racially aggravated' to treat that element of the offence as an aggravating factor increasing seriousness. The court is required to state in open court that the offence was so aggravated. An offence is 'racially aggravated' if it meets the definition given by CDA 1998 s28:

(a)   at the time of committing the offence, or immediately before or after doing so, the offender demonstrates towards the victim of the offence hostility based on the victim's membership of a racial group; or

(b)   the offence is motivated (wholly or partly) by hostility towards members of a racial group based on their membership of that group.

'Racial group' means 'a group of persons defined by reference to race, colour, nationality (including citizenship) or ethnic or national origins': s28(4). It is immaterial whether or not the offender's hostility is also based to any extent on the fact or presumption that any person or group of persons belongs to any religious group: s28(3)(a). The Appeal Court has held that an offence can be racially aggravated even though the offender and the victim share the same ethnicity and that 'racial group' should be given a broad, non-technical meaning: *R v White* [2001] Crim LR 576 (where calling a woman bus conductor a 'stupid African bitch' racially aggravated a POA 1986 s4 offence).

In *R v Saunders* [2000] 2 Cr App R(S) 71, the Court of Appeal indicated that it will often be appropriate if the sentencer first considers what would be the proper sentence for the offence in the absence of racial aggravation, before adding a further term for the racial element. The Court indicated that even if the basic offence does not cross the 'so serious' threshold, the aggravating element may well result in that criterion being satisfied. When passing sentence, the court should have regard to the circumstances of the individual case, including: the nature of hostility demonstrated, whether by language, gestures or weapons; the location of the offence, the same behaviour being likely to attract a heavier penalty if it occurs in a crowded church, mosque or synagogue than in an empty public house. *Saunders* involved racially aggravated assault occasioning actual bodily harm, which is now a distinct offence carrying a maximum sentence two years higher than that pertaining to that offence in its unaggravated form. The Court of Appeal in *R v Morrison* [2001] 1 Cr App R(S) 12, a case of racially aggravated burglary under the generic provisions of s153(2), clarified that *Saunders* should not be regarded as authority for the proposition that the maximum additional term intended to reflect racial aggravation, applicable in any instance, ABH or otherwise, is limited to two years. Each case will depend on its own circumstances. In assessing the extent of racial aggravation, sentencers should distinguish between a racially motivated offence and an offence where racist language is used in the course of commission of the offence: *R v Foster* [2000] Crim LR 1030. The Court has made it clear that police officers and other public service personnel are as entitled to protection from racial abuse as anyone else: *R v Jacobs* [2000] 2 Cr App R(S) 174, a case in which an offender under arrest at a police station had used racist abuse against an Asian officer conducting PACE procedures. In *R v Kelly and Donnelly* [2001] Crim LR 411 the Court clarified, in light of advice from the Sentencing Advisory Panel (see Stone, 2000: xii), that the sentencer should first identify the sentence considered appropriate for the basic offence without the racial element and then identify the sentence that reflects the racial aggravation. This approach of identifying the enhancement arising from the racial element serves the interests of transparency in sentencing. *Kelly and Donnelly* involved an attack on two Asian men amounting to ABH, accompanied by racist abuse. The Appeal Court considered that the use of a bottle and a ballpoint pen as weapons and the persistence with which the incident was sustained justified a sentence of 18 months, to which it added a further nine months to reflect the racial aggravation which, while serious and central to the conduct of the offenders, was not at the top end of the scale.

In its advice, the Advisory Panel (2000) identified the following features as seriously aggravating an offence on racial grounds: planning; being part of a pattern of racist offending by the offender; membership of or association with a group promoting racist activities; deliberately setting up the incident to be offensive or humiliating to the victim or to the victim's ethnic group; timing and/or location of offence being calculated to maximise the harm or distress; expressions of hostility repeated or prolonged; offence at or in close proximity to the victim's home; particularly vulnerable victim; victim providing a service to the public; particular distress caused to victim or his family; offence causing fear and distress throughout a local ethnic community or more widely. The Panel advised that at the lower end of the scale, the racial element might be considered as a less seriously aggravating factor if: the racist element of the offence was limited in scope or duration; the motivation for the offence was not racial, and the element of racial hostility or abuse was minor or incidental.

3. *Absence of Legal Representation* PCC(S)A 2000 s83 seeks to ensure that custodial sentences should not be imposed upon two classes of defendants who are not legally represented before the sentencing court unless the defendant has refused or failed to apply for legal aid or, having applied, has been refused legal aid on grounds of means:

(a) *First Time Imprisonment* Section 83(1) specifies that a court shall not pass a sentence of imprisonment without this opportunity or safeguard on a person who has not previously been sentenced to punishment by imprisonment by a court in any part of the United Kingdom.

(b) *Under 21s* Section 83(2), as amended by CJCSA 2000, specifies that a court may not impose any of the following custodial sentences without this opportunity or safeguard: (i) detention under PCC(S)A 2000 ss90 and 91; (ii) imprisonment on a person who, when convicted, was aged at least 18 but under 21; (iii) a detention and training order.

4. *Stating Reasons for Custody* PCC(S)A 2000 s79(4) requires that where a court passes a custodial sentence under s79(2), it shall state in open court that it is of the opinion that either or both s79(2)(a) or s79(2)(b) apply and why it is of that opinion. The court must also 'explain to the offender in open court and in ordinary language why it is passing a custodial sentence on him.' Further, a magistrates' court shall cause a reason so stated to be specified in the warrant of commitment and to be entered in the court register: s79(5). As indicated in *R v Baverstock* [1993] 1 WLR 202, the requirements of s79(4) should not normally demand a two-stage process and the two tasks should usually be possible at one and the same time.

5. *Explaining Effect of Sentence* Because statutory provisions governing the practical effect of custodial sentences, such as the actual period to be served and the conditions

applicable on release, have not been widely understood, the Lord Chief Justice issued a *Practice Direction (Custodial Sentences: Explanations)* [1998] 1 Cr App R 397 in January 1998 specifying that in future a sentencer in the Crown Court passing an immediate custodial sentence should, in addition to complying with relevant statutory requirements, give an explanation of that sentence so that this should be understood by the offender, the victim and any member of the public who was present in court or who read the transcript of proceedings. 'Sentencers should give the explanation in terms of their own choosing, taking care to ensure that the explanation is clear and accurate.' No form of words is prescribed but the Direction included short statements as models for adoption and adaptation. The Direction made clear that an explanation is not to constitute the sentence of the court which remains as pronounced by the court. There is clearly the possibility that the judge may misrepresent the effect of the sentence and the Lord Chief Justice was doubtless anxious to avoid his colleagues unwittingly generating perceived grounds for appeal because of misunderstandings, mistakes or slips of the tongue. Different forms of words are suggested according to whether the total term is:

(i)   less than 12 months;

(ii)   12 months or longer but less than four years;

(iii)   four years or longer;

(iv)   a discretionary life sentence.

Each 'model' explanation covers: early release; time on licence (if applicable); the relevance of time on remand in custody; the 'at risk' period under PCC(S)A 2000 s116 (formerly CJA 1991 s40) (see page 89); extension of sentence under PCC(S)A 2000 s85) (formerly CJA 1991 s44) (see page 86). No model form of words is offered in respect of terms of imprisonment on offenders aged under 21 attracting statutory supervision under CJA 1991 s65 (see page 127).

Custody Following Refusal to Consent to Community Sentence

In the original form of PCC(S)A 2000 s79(3) (CJA s1(3)) an important exception was created to the restrictions in imposing custodial sentences by specifying that nothing in that sub-section 'shall prevent the court from passing a custodial sentence on the offender if he refuses to give his consent to a community sentence which is proposed by the court and requires his consent'. On occasion a defendant might tactically decline consent to a community sentence offered, not because of any resistance to such a possibility in principle but from a wish to benefit from time already spent in custody on remand through receiving a short custodial term.

The significance of s1(3) had declined as a result of the changes introduced by C(S)A 1997 s38 abolishing the requirements for consent in the making of most community orders. The surviving exceptions where the offender's expression of willingness is still necessary are in imposing additional requirements in a probation/community rehabilitation order (or supervision order, where the young offender is aged 14 or older) of treatment for mental condition or for drug or alcohol dependency. To these CDA 1998 added the imposition of a drug treatment and testing order. The current version in s79(3) states that nothing shall prevent the court from passing a custodial sentence if the offender fails to express willingness to comply with a requirement proposed by the court that requires such expression. The changes of C(S)A 1997 s38 apply to offences committed on or after 1 October 1997 and so for the shrinking number of cases involving crimes pre-dating implementation of the section the original version of s1(3) will continue to apply in instances where the court seeks to make a community service order, a curfew order, or a probation order of any kind.

Because s79(3) is designed to allow a custodial sentence to be imposed in cases that would not necessarily satisfy the 'so serious' criterion but the court's view of the appropriate commensurate punishment is frustrated by the defendant's unco-operative stance, it follows that the procedural prerequisites are also different. The court is not required to consider a PSR under s3(1) since that provision applies to forming an opinion under s79(2). However, the court is obliged to comply with the provisions of s79(4) in giving reasons for imposing custody.

The 1991/2000 Acts make no specific reference to the calculation of length of a custodial term imposed under s79(3), though the provisions of s80(2)(a) apply requiring a commensurate term. If the offence, considered without issues of personal mitigation, is 'so serious', there is no problem. If, however, the offence does not satisfy the 'so serious' criterion, the court faces the challenge of determining an appropriate term for a crime that in principle does not fall within the custodial range.

Restriction on Consecutive Sentences for Released Prisoners

PCC(S)A 2000 s84(1) specifies a restriction first introduced by CDA 1998 s102(1), that a court sentencing a person to a term of imprisonment 'shall not order or direct that the term shall commence on the expiry of any other sentence of imprisonment from which he has been released under CJA 1991 Part II'. This has created knotty problems for sentencers faced with offenders who have been released on licence and have been recalled under CJA 1991 s39 following a further offence committed while on licence. In *R v Laurent* [2001] 1 Cr App R(S) 224 a judge dealing with such a situation had sought to order that the new term of imprisonment for the fresh offence should be consecutive to the offender's period of recall. This was clearly in breach of ss102/84 but the Appeal Court ruled that the proper course in such circumstances is to make an order for the offender's return to prison under CJA 1991 s40 (now PCC(S)A 2000 s116 – see page 89). Provided the period of the s116 return order does not end on the day that the licence period (and thus recall liability) terminates, the s84 rule will not be violated.

Mentally Disordered Offenders

Certain safeguards are built into the legislative framework against the inappropriate use of custodial sentences for mentally disordered offenders, defined by PCC(S)A 2000 s82(5) as 'suffering from a mental disorder within the meaning of MHA 1983'. These provisions are detailed in Stone (2002), including power to impose custodial sentence with a 'hospital direction', but in summary:

Duty to Obtain a Medical Report PCC(S)A 2000 s82(1) specifies that in any case where the offender is or appears to be mentally disordered, the court shall obtain and consider a medical report before passing a custodial sentence. However, s82(2) modifies this requirement somewhat by specifying that s82(1) does not apply if the court is of the opinion that it is unnecessary to obtain a report.

Duty to Consider Effect of Custody on Condition and Treatment Before passing a custodial sentence on an offender who is or appears to be mentally disordered, a court shall consider:

(a)   any information before it which relates to the offender's mental condition (whether in a medical report, PSR or otherwise); and

(b)   the likely effect of such a sentence on that condition and on any treatment which may be available for it: s82(3).

Any custodial sentence passed without compliance with s82(3) is nevertheless valid but any court on appeal against such sentence shall obtain and consider a medical report: s82(4).

Scope to Sentence in Most Appropriate Manner To make clear that the relevant provisions of PCC(S)A 2000 should not be interpreted to require a custodial sentence to be imposed even though there may be more suitable means of disposal, s158(3) clarifies that 'nothing ... shall be taken (a) as requiring a court to pass a custodial sentence, or any particular custodial sentence, on a mentally disordered offender; or (b) as restricting any power (whether under MHA 1983 or otherwise) which enables a court to deal with such an offender in the manner it considers to be the most appropriate in all the circumstances'.

Early Release

Scope for the early release, remission or parole at a stage prior to the expiry of the full term of a custodial sentence is a familiar penal devise. This can be viewed as a means of rewarding co-operation in custody, as a way of reducing the penal population, as a means of containing or reducing the risk of re-offending posed by released persons and as an exercise in compulsory benevolence through advice and support to those who may need help in achieving successful resettlement back in the community. Just how and when to stage this in a way that is congruent with the sentence of the court, is fair to prisoners by avoiding undue reliance on opaque executive discretion, targets those presenting greatest risk or need and is realistic within the constraints of available resources, has been the subject of much recent re-thinking. For the most prominent review of the issues, leading to proposals on which the scheme under the 1991 Act was based, see the Carlisle Report (1988). C(S)A 1997 was intended to introduce an entirely new scheme, aiming to achieve greater 'honesty in sentencing'. The incoming Government decided not to implement this part of the 1997 Act and has instead opted to modify the 1991 scheme through provisions in CDA 1998. For the purposes of sentencing law, only a brief outline of the evolving provisions can be provided, having particular regard to the elements of the scheme that give discretion to the sentencer. This outline may assist court duty officers who interview newly sentenced prisoners who may be seeking early information about their early release prospects. For enforcement of licence issues, see Stone (1999).

Short-Term Prisoners

A 'short-term prisoner' (STP) is a person serving a sentence of imprisonment, or YOI or s91 detention for a term of less than four years: CJA 1991 s33(5). STPs are released *automatically* after serving one-half of their sentence. Whether an STP is released *conditionally* or *unconditionally* depends on the length of their sentence. Under the original 1991 Act scheme, STPs aged 18 or over serving terms of less than 12 months have been released unconditionally, subject only to the 'at risk' provisions of s40 (now s116, page 89), until their sentence expiry date (SED) and to special supervisory requirements under CJA 1991 s65 for those aged under 21 at time of sentence. Those serving terms of 12 months or longer have been released on licence. Licence has remained in force until the three-quarters point of sentence (i.e. covering 25% of the sentence period), requiring the licensee to comply with standard conditions relating to supervision and any additional conditions felt necessary. Upon expiry of licence, the released STP has remained subject to the provisions of s40 until SED. Special provisions have allowed early release of any STP on compassionate grounds in exceptional circumstances ahead of the half-way point of sentence (CJA 1991 s36) but this power has been exercised very sparingly. STPs on automatic conditional release licence who fail to comply with licence conditions have been subject to prosecution for an offence under CJA 1991 s38. This form of enforcement has been replaced under CDA 1998 by making STPs liable to recall to custody under s39(1) and (2) in the same way as long-term prisoners.

This relatively straightforward system becomes more complicated under the provisions of CDA 1998 s83 which introduces a new s34A(3) into CJA 1991, giving the Home Secretary a new discretionary power to allow release on licence of any STP serving three months or longer ahead of the half-way point of sentence, once the STP has served 'the requisite period'. The requisite period varies according to the length of full sentence, as follows (s34A(4)):

(a)   3 months to less than 4 months – 30 days;

(b)   4 months to less than 8 months – 'a period equal to one-quarter of the term';

(c)   8 months or more – 'a period that is 60 days less than one-half of the term'.

Overall, put simply, a STP stands to gain early release up to two months earlier than would otherwise be the case.

Release on licence under s34A(3) must include a curfew condition under CJA s37A, requiring the released person to remain for specified periods (totalling not less than 9 hours in any day) at a specified place or places (which may be an approved probation hostel). Further, the curfew must be electronically monitored. A curfew condition remains in force until the STP would otherwise have been released at the half-way point of their sentence. Breach of curfew conditions renders the licensee liable to revocation of licence and recall to custody by the Home Office. As regards whether the s34A(3) licence will also contain a condition of supervision, CJA 1991 s37(4A) (inserted by CDA Sch 7 para 54(5)) specifies that this will depend on the length of full sentence. If sentence is for 12 months or longer, the licence *shall* include conditions as to supervision by a probation officer or (in the case of a licensee aged under 18) a YOT member. If sentence is shorter than 12 months, the licence *may* include supervision conditions. Note that if an STP is serving a term of 12 months or longer, he will remain on licence and subject to supervision to the usual three-quarters point of sentence, albeit that the curfew condition ceases at the half-way point.

Long-Term Prisoners

A 'long-term prisoner' (LTP) is a person serving a sentence of imprisonment, or YOI or s53(2) detention, for a term of four years or more: CJA 1991 s33(5). A LTP is eligible to be released on licence at the discretion of the Home Secretary, on the recommendation of the Parole Board, after serving one-half of sentence. If not paroled, the LTP shall be released on licence at the two-thirds point of sentence. The parole process is detailed further in Stone (1999, chapter 15).

Sexual and Violent Offenders: Extended Sentences

Under the original provisions of CJA 1991 s44, where the whole or any part of a sentence is imposed for a sexual offence (as defined then by CJA 1991 s31(1); see page 92) and the defendant is liable to early release on licence, whether as a STP or LTP, the court has power to order that licence shall remain in force until SED, instead of the three-quarters point of sentence. In making this discretionary order, the sentencer should have regard to (a) the need to protect the public from serious harm from the offender and (b) the desirability of preventing the commission of further offences and of securing the offender's rehabilitation. This measure was thus not intended to be a gratuitous additional punishment. In *Attorney-General's Reference No 7 of 1996* [1997] Crim LR 64, Lord Bingham CJ observed that s44 provided a helpful resource to enhance the protection of the public and expressed concern that it had been insufficiently applied in some court areas. In *R v Geary* [1998] 2 Cr App R(S) 434 where defence counsel had argued in an appeal against sentence of 14 years imposed for an 'appalling catalogue' of sexual offences against girls aged 12 to 15 that the offender's liability to s44 made his sentence more onerous, the Appeal Court dismissed the appeal, stating: 'we do not regard those powers as affecting significantly the appropriateness of the total period of imprisonment imposed'. This appears to leave open to argument the extent to which exercise of s44 (and, now, use of the power of 'extended sentence' – see below) may make any marginal difference to the custodial period set or whether liability to extended supervision on release is irrelevant in determining that term.

CDA 1998 s58 introduced a new sentencing power applicable where a court: (i) proposes to impose a custodial sentence for a sexual or violent offence; and (ii) considers that any period (if any) for which the offender would otherwise be subject to licence would not be adequate for the purpose of preventing further offences and securing his or her rehabilitation. In these circumstances the court has discretionary power to pass an 'extended sentence'. These provisions are now contained in PCC(S)A 2000 s85. An 'extended sentence' (a term which should not be confused with an earlier sentencing measure of this name, abolished by CJA 1991) is defined as the aggregate of (a) 'the custodial term', i.e. the term of custody that the court would otherwise have imposed; and (b) 'the extension period', i.e. the period of licence that the court considers necessary for the purposes of (ii) above. An extended sentence may be imposed for a sexual offence where the custodial term is of a length that would not ordinarily attract licence liabilities: *R v Ajaib* [2001] 1 Cr App R(S) 105, where a 15 month extension period was added to a custodial term of nine months for indecent assault.

The power is subject to three main restrictions:

(i) In the case of a violent offence, the custodial term must be for not less than four years: s85(3). This means that if the offence does not attract a sentence of that length then normal licence obligations will apply. The qualifying term of four years must be imposed for a single offence and a judge cannot treat two shorter consecutive sentences for violent offences as an aggregate term of four years for this purpose: *R v Langstone* [2001] Crim LR 409 (where the judge erroneously sought to extend sentence on the basis of imposing three years for s20 wounding and an order returning the offender for committing that offence during the unexpired 'at risk' period (see page 89) of an earlier sentence for s18 wounding). In other words, the Act intends use of extended sentence powers to be used only where a violent offence is sufficiently serious to justify at least four years custody.

(ii)   The term of an extended sentence shall not exceed the maximum term permitted for the offence: s85(5). This means that if the offence carries a maximum sentence of, say, two years, it would not be lawful to sentence the offender to an extended sentence consisting of a custodial term of 18 months with an extension period of 12 months, since the total sentence would exceed the permitted maximum by six months.

(iii) The extension period may not exceed the following maxima (s85(4)): sexual offence – 10 years; violent offence – 5 years. This has the somewhat anomalous effect that the shorter the custodial term passed the longer the scope for an extension period and, conversely, the longer the custodial term, a factor that may well be indicative of risk posed, the shorter the extension period available to the court.

Note that as regards sexual offences, the extended sentence is not restricted to LTPs nor even to STPs who would otherwise be liable to ACR licence requirements. It is thus possible for a sexual offender who would otherwise receive a term of less than 12 months to be the subject of an extended sentence. This is unlikely to be common in practice but if the court is dealing with an offender whose offence merits a commensurate sentence of, say, nine months' imprisonment but they are considered to need supervisory oversight on release, an extended sentence may be imposed. The power is available, in theory at least, to a magistrates' court as well as the Crown Court.

Implementation This provision was implemented on 30 September 1998 but without retrospective effect so that it is applicable only in respect of offences committed on or after that date. In consequence, in respect of sexual offences committed before that date, the court may order that an offender who is liable on release to supervision on licence shall remain on licence until the expiry of the full term of sentence under the original provisions of CJA 1991 s44.

Pre-Sentence Reports Under *National Standards* (Home Office, 2000, para B9), where the report relates to a 'serious' sexual or violent offence, it must provide 'advice on the appropriateness of extended supervision'.

Sentencing Guidance A number of early Appeal Court judgements have helped to indicate the ambit of use of this sentencing measure. In *R v Gould* [2000] Crim LR 311, the offender pleaded guilty to s18 wounding, having glassed his companion in a pub quarrel.

He had several previous convictions for violence and a history of substance misuse. While upholding a custodial term of five years, the Appeal Court reduced the extension period from the permissible maximum of five years to two years, as the period set was longer than the purpose of imposing it justified and could result in the offender, if recalled to prison, serving custodial time totalling nearly nine years. The implication is that the court should have regard to the potential period in custody which may ensue and not simply weigh the extension period in terms of risk management and rehabilitation. In *R v Barros* [2000] Crim LR 601 the offender had met the victim, a girl aged under 16, in a pub and began kissing her, eventually putting his hand up her skirt and indecently assaulting her by digital penetration. Quashing imposition of an extension period of three years, the Appeal Court stated that this was not an appropriate case for extension of licence and the judge appeared to have had regard only to the circumstances of the offence. In *R v Cridge* [2000] 2 Cr App R(S) 477, a case of indecent assault and dangerous driving where the judge had sought to impose a five year custodial period and a four year extension for the sexual offence together with an additional 12 months for the driving offence, the Appeal Court stated that it is 'generally inappropriate' to impose a custodial sentence to run consecutively in such circumstances, given the practical problems that can result in calculating the consequences for licence length purposes. Subsequently, in *R v Barker* [2001] 1 Cr App R(S) 514, where the offender faced sentence for various sexual offences, the judge had imposed custodial terms totalling 10 years (passed as a longer than commensurate length) together with what he stated to be two consecutive extension periods each of five years, thus amounting to a total extension of 10 years. The Court of Appeal found it to be lawful, strictly speaking, to pass consecutive extended sentences but in the circumstances reduced sentence to a total custodial term of eight years together with concurrent extension periods of five years. In his commentary on this case, Thomas points out that it is far from clear how consecutive extension periods would operate and that 'it is arguable that they would both begin at the end of the normal licence period and thus take effect concurrently in any event', thus defeating the presumed intention of making these consecutive.

The Court of Appeal has informed the Sentencing Advisory Panel of its intention to issue guidance on the use of extended sentences and the Panel has, in turn, issued a consultation paper (June 2001) recommending that such guidance should begin with a general view of enhanced powers available to the courts in dealing with sexual and violent offences, including a longer than commensurate custodial term (see page 90) – when it is more appropriate to impose one of the available measures or both in combination. The Panel also conclude that consecutive extended sentences should be avoided as a matter of good sentencing practice.

Early Release and 'At Risk' Provisions As a consequence of s58 (now s85), CDA 1998 s59 introduces an entirely revised version of CJA 1991 s44 regulating the offender's release. The interplay of these provisions with the usual early release provisions of CJA 1991 is quite complex. A prisoner subject to an extended sentence will be released on licence at the point of their custodial term that a prisoner serving a sentence of that length would be released under the normal early release provisions. The 'extension period' comes into effect at the point when licence would otherwise expire. For example, if X receives an extended sentence with a custodial term of six years and an extension period of five years, and is released on parole licence after three years (i.e. at the halfway point of the custodial term), he will be on licence for 18 months (as in the case of a person sentenced to a standard term of imprisonment for six years who is released after serving half of their sentence) followed by the extension period, making a total period of licence of $6^1/_2$ years. Licence remains in force until the end of the extension period. The 'at risk' provisions of PCC(S)A 2000 s116 (see below) (and CJA 1991 s40A) apply to the full period of the extended sentence, not just to the length of the custodial term: PCC(S)A 2000 s117(5). Where an extended sentence is passed in respect of a sexual offence and the custodial term would not otherwise attract any licence liability, as in *Ajaib* (see page 86), the Appeal Court there declared that the offender would be subject to licence for $19^1/_2$ months from date of release at the halfway point of sentence, comprising the unserved part of nine month custodial term together with the 15 month extension period. With respect, that interpretation is incorrect. CDA 1998 s44(5)(a) states that the extension period shall begin on the date on which the prisoner would otherwise have been released unconditionally, licence to remain in force until the end of the extension period.

Further Offence During the 'At Risk' Period

The provisions of PCC(S)A 2000 s116 (formerly CJA 1991 s40) are detailed in Stone (1999, chapter 16) but clearly are a significant dimension of custodial sentencing where it is important to note whether the offence being freshly sentenced was committed prior to the SED of any previous custodial sentence imposed upon the defendant. It is thus necessary to have details of SED and often the court will look to the Probation Service to trace this information. If the offender has been on licence, the SED will normally be stated in the licence. Otherwise, the information is obtainable from the Discipline Office of the releasing prison. This information may conveniently be included in a PSR.

In essence, s116 gives the court discretionary power to return the offender to custody for the part of their previous sentence which remained unexpired at the date of the further offence. The critical date is the date that the new offence was committed, not the date of their conviction for the new offence. Even if the offender's previous sentence has expired by the date of their new conviction, liability under s116 still arises. In the case of re-offending during the unexpired term of an extended sentence under PCC(S)A 2000 s85, s117(5) clarifies that the 'at risk' provisions shall have effect 'as if the term of the extended sentence included the extension period'.

Other points worth noting:

- Section 116 applies only if the new offence is imprisonable.

- The court must first determine what is the appropriate sentence for the new offence, so that it receives the sentence that it merits on its own terms. In next considering whether a s40 order should be made, the court should normally have regard to the nature and extent of any progress made since release (*R v Taylor* (1998) 161 JP 797).

- Any period ordered under s116 shall be served before any custodial sentence for the new offence or concurrently with that sentence, not consecutively to that new sentence: s116(6)(b). The court should have regard to the totality of sentence. It follows that a magistrates' court cannot impose a term of immediate imprisonment for the new offence while committing the offender to the Crown Court for the s116 issue to be considered there. The justices should either deal with sentence and return to custody themselves or commit both matters to the Crown Court: *Bone (R on the application of) v Worthing Magistrates' Court* (2001, unreported).

• A s116 order counts as a sentence of imprisonment for the purposes of early release provisions of CJA 1991: s116(6)(a). This means that the offender will be released after serving the appropriate fraction of that period. Also, the return period must be aggregated with any new sentence imposed in determining the total sentence to be served and its status, i.e. whether it attracts conditional release on licence and whether it is a long- or short-term sentence.

• CDA 1998 s105 inserts s40A into CJA 1991, applicable where a court passes a sentence of imprisonment which includes or consists of an order under s40 and is for a term of 12 months or less. On the offender's release at the halfway point of sentence, s/he is released subject to licence of three months duration. The intention is to ensure that those who re-offend in this way shall be subject to supervision even if their term of imprisonment is of such a length that would not otherwise command licence liability. This measure came into effect on 30 September 1998 but without retrospective effect. It thus applies only in respect of offences committed on or after that date. Breach of licence renders the offender liable to prosecution for a summary offence punishable by a Level 3 fine or to a term of imprisonment not exceeding the period of licence still remaining at the date of the failure to comply.

Protection of Public: Longer Than Commensurate Sentence

Though clearly related to the 'public protection' criterion justifying custody in PCC(S)A 2000 s79(2)(b) (see page 70), the practical importance of protective sentencing lies with the provisions of s80(2)(b) (formerly governed by CJA 1991 s2(2)(b)) which specifies that where the offence is a 'violent or sexual offence', a custodial sentence may exceed the term that is commensurate with the seriousness of the offence and be 'for such longer term (not exceeding the permitted maximum) as in the opinion of the court is necessary to protect the public from serious harm from the offender.' As a measure that departs from the central principle of proportionality and allows a 'longer than normal' custodial sentence on the basis not of past harm and culpability but of prediction and assumed dangerousness, s80(2)(b) is exceptional and controversial. The likelihood of over-predicting dangerousness is well known and this exercise in 'social defence' should be and is exercised sparingly. The provision has attracted criticism for its looseness in defining risk, its lack of fair safeguards for the exposed defendant and for its failure to follow through with special early release provisions. Given also that the sentencer is required to bear commensurablity in mind in setting the protective term, it can be questioned how substantially the public is protected by provisions that keep the dangerous individual in custody for what may in effect be a comparatively brief additional period. As Thomas ([1997] Crim LR 139) has commented, many longer-than-normal sentences will be the result of a compromise between two competing purposes and thus achieve neither, being too long to be just to the offender and too short to afford adequate protection to the public. Yet the need for a protective measure of some kind is generally accepted and although this is territory where psychiatric opinion is likely to carry more importance, there is a clear role for social inquiry and risk assessment through the PSR, using skills in analysing past offending patterns and seeking to interpret the offender's current pre-occupations, fantasies, remorse, victim empathy, etc.

The circumstances in which this provision can apply may also prompt consideration of either a discretionary life sentence (if the offence carries that maximum) or, in the case of a mentally disordered offender, a hospital order, with or without a restriction, or a hospital direction. For discretionary life sentences see Stone (1997) though note that a longer than commensurate determinate sentence may be imposed in circumstances that do not justify an indeterminate term, for which the justifying criteria are stricter. For hospital orders and directions, see Stone (2002).

Eligible Offences

Violent Offence As defined descriptively by PCC(S)A 2000 s161(3):

> An offence which leads, or is intended or likely to lead, to a person's death or to physical injury to a person, and includes an offence which is required to be charged as arson (whether or not it would other wise fall within this definition).

The definition is quite comprehensive, covering instances where death or physical injury was caused, even though not intended or even likely, and occasions where no physical harm was actually caused but was nevertheless risked by the offender. The physical injury need not have been serious. There are, nevertheless gaps in the ambit of the definition, as illustrated by *R v Richart* (1995) 16 Cr App R(S) 977 where the offender made several telephone threats to the victim, including threats to kill her, and posted her a bullet with her name on it. As there was no physical injury nor any evidence that the threats were intended or likely to lead to physical injury, the Court of Appeal regretfully concluded that this was not a 'violent' offence, despite the adverse psychological impact and the victim's reasonable apprehension of violence.

While in many instances the 'violent' nature of the offence is obvious, in some instances, particularly in cases of robbery and also threatening to kill, the issue has to be resolved with regard to the particular facts of the crime. Among reported cases on this point:

- Where a knife is used to threaten a robbery victim, albeit with no intention to injure but merely to intimidate or to frighten, the offence is 'violent' as it is likely that injury could be caused if the victim tries to escape or puts up resistance or a struggle otherwise ensues: *R v Cochrane* (1994) 15 Cr App R(S) 708, recently reiterated in *R v Grady* [2000] 2 Cr App R(S) 468, even though the off-licence assistant had managed to escape unharmed.

- Where an imitation firearm or an unloaded firearm is used to threaten the victim, the offence is not *per se* 'violent': *R v Khan* (1995) 16 Cr App R(S) 180; *R v Palin* (1995) 16 Cr App R(S) 888.

- A threat to kill is not normally likely to lead to the death or physical injury of the person at risk unless that person is in an immediately vulnerable position (such as standing in a position such as a high ledge that exposes them to danger in reaction to the threat or if they suffer a health disability that could be adversely triggered by the threat, even if the offender intends to carry out the threat). However, in less unusual circumstances, where the defendant had told both a psychiatrist seen as an out-patient, his keyworker and others of his intention to kill his wife, causing them to believe that he posed a real and serious threat to her (he was a trained butcher and had put knives aside for the specific purpose of mutilating her; he was assessed as having an untreatable abnormal personality), the threats were considered enough to constitute a 'violent' offence: *R v Wilson* [1998] 1 Cr App R(S) 341. Compare *R v Tucknott* [2001] 1 Cr App R(S) 318 where the Appeal Court urged that the offence of threatening to kill should be specifically included by statute within the definition of a 'violent offence'.

Sexual Offence This kind of offence is defined by s161(2), not descriptively but by reference to a list of statutory offences:

(a)   an offence under Sexual Offences Act 1956 (other than under ss30, 31 or 33–36);

(b)   an offence under Mental Health Act 1959 s128 (sexual intercourse with mentally disordered woman patient);

(c)   an offence under Indecency with Children Act 1960;

(d)   an offence under Theft Act 1978 s9 of burglary with intent to rape;

(e)   an offence under Criminal Law Act 1977 s54 (inciting a female to commit incest with the offender);

(f)   an offence under Protection of Children 1978;

(g)   an offence under Criminal Law Act 1977 s1 of conspiracy to commit any of the above;

(h)   an offence under Criminal Attempts Act 1981 of attempting to commit any of the above;

(i)   an offence of inciting another to commit any of the above.

Accordingly, an offence of abducting a child under the Child Abduction Act 1984 does not qualify for this purpose, even when committed by an offender with a record of sexual offending in circumstances suggestive of a sexual motive: *R v Hutchinson* (1998, unreported). Nor is the common law offence of outraging public decency: *R v Gaynor* [2000] Crim LR 397. Note that an offence can be both a 'violent' and a 'sexual' offence. The categories are not intended to be mutually exclusive. The kind of offence most likely to be the subject of a s80(2)(b) sentence, if the reported appeal cases are any reflection of usage, is most likely to involve sexual violence or fixated paedophile abuse, though the reports also show consideration in cases of violent robbery (e.g. motivated by addiction to drugs), arson and serious violence against domestic partners or ex-partners.

Nature of Risk

Broadly put, 'risk' has two obvious dimensions: the degree of likelihood of future harmful behaviour and the level of harmfulness of anticipated behaviour. As von Hirsch and Ashworth (1996) have identified (in the context of CJA 1991 s2(2)(b)) s80(2)(b) does not explicitly address the first issue, other than indicating that a longer term should be considered 'necessary'. The authors argue that:

> 'to qualify for a s2(2)(b) sentence, the offender must present not just the possibility of future offending but a substantial risk of further offending. A less demanding standard would allow the exception to swallow the rule.'

They draw support for this restrictive interpretation from the Court of Appeal in two cases: *R v Danso* (1995) 16 Cr App R(S) 12 where the Court spoke of 'a significant risk', and *R v Crow and Pennington* (1995) 16 Cr App R(S) 409 where Lord Taylor CJ referred to 'a substantial risk'.

'Serious Harm' Though unhelpfully drafted as regards the seriousness of risk, s80(2)(b) is explicit as regards the seriousness of prospective harm, permitting a protective sentence only where 'serious harm' can be anticipated. 'Serious harm' is defined by s161(4) to mean: 'death or serious personal injury, whether physical or psychological, occasioned by further such offences committed by' the offender.

Accordingly, a serious risk of some harm is an insufficient basis for a protective sentence, as illustrated by *R v Creasey* (1994) 15 Cr App R(S) 671 where the offender had followed a boy aged 13 home from school and had attempted to masturbate him through his trousers. Though the Court acknowledged a real risk that the offender would commit further such offences against teenage boys, it was not convinced that offending of this nature would cause 'serious harm', suggesting that this kind of indecent assault was 'unpleasant and distressing' rather than seriously harmful. This view of such predatory behaviour may be considered by some to be somewhat complacent and the decision should not be regarded as a precedent in regard to offending of this nature. However, in *R v T* [2001] 1 Cr App R(S) 205, the Appeal Court concluded that the 'serious harm' test was not satisfied in a case involving a man aged 78 with a long record of sexual offences and a serious but untreatable psychosexual abnormality. He was visited by young people in his home and had placed his hand on the leg of a boy aged 15, offering to masturbate him, had touched the bottom of a girl aged 12 and had exposed himself to several girls. The sentencer appeared to have been over-influenced by reference in the pre-sentence report to the 'high risk of harm' posed by the offender. Note that to satisfy the test for a protective sentence, it is not necessary that the offender has already caused serious harm, either by the current offence or by some past offence (*R v Bowler*, discussed below), though the absence of seriously harmful consequences arising from the offender's conduct to date will obviously make it harder to establish that he poses this level of risk in the future. In *R v Cochrane* (1994) 15 Cr App R(S) 708, the Court of Appeal spoke of acts 'likely to lead to serious injury', a view since approved by the Court in *R v Harper and Sabin* (1998) *The Times* 11 October 1998.

Psychological Harm Though this kind of harm does not feature in the definition of a 'violent' offence, it comes within the ambit of future 'serious harm' and is clearly a potential consequence of non-violent sexual crime. The question arises as to what degree of psychological impact is sufficient to satisfy the test as opposed to being merely upsetting. The decision in *Creasey* (above) illustrates the difficulty in reaching this decision. *Creasey* can be compared with *R v Bowler* (1994) 15 Cr App R(S) 78. The offender had indecently assaulted a girl aged six by briefly touching her genitals through her knickers. He had six previous convictions for similar assaults upon adult women, none being prolonged or involving any attempt at penetration. His sexual fetish was for touching his victims' underwear. He was assessed as likely to continue to commit such offences. The Court of Appeal considered that there were adequate grounds entitling the sentencer to conclude that members of the public could suffer serious psychological injury. An indecent assault of this nature on a young girl could well cause such injury because of the victim's inherent vulnerability. Moreover, some women might be seriously disturbed by such conduct, even though many women could shrug off such unwelcome attention. Sections 2/80(2)(b) should protect those 'less robust than average' who are vulnerable to this kind of behaviour.

As von Hirsch and Ashworth point out, a weakness of the Court's reasoning in *Bowler* is the absence of evidence that the offender was likely to re-offend against children who are *per se* vulnerable or that he would target adult victims who lacked robustness and were thus particularly vulnerable. They question whether the mere possibility that a victim may have particular sensibility to this kind of intrusion should be an adequate basis for protective sentencing. Can the risk be regarded as substantial enough? They refer to victims with 'unusual or "eggshell" sensibilities'. However, a traumatised reaction to indecent assault of this nature does not seem fairly characterised as an 'eggshell' sensibility but one that may quite reasonably be anticipated. Psychological injury as a result of a knicker fetishist's attentions would seem a very real possibility rather than a remote prospect. However, there may be other kinds of behaviour where the likelihood of psychological trauma is remote and thus outside the ambit of 'substantial risk'.

Ambit of Risk Though s80(2)(b) refers to protection of 'the public', it is not necessary for the offender to pose risk to the public at large. In *R v Hashi* (1995) 16 Cr App R(S) 121, a longer than commensurate term was upheld for wounding with intent where the offender had stabbed in the chest a man he had seen drinking with his former partner. The ambit of risk was the offender's ex-partner and any man associating with her, given the offender's possessive jealousy, but this was sufficient to justify a protective sentence. It is uncertain whether s80(2)(b) is applicable if the risk is posed to a single person. In *R v Nicholas* (1994) 15 Cr App R(S) 381 the offender had assaulted his ex-wife on numerous occasions during their marriage and in the aftermath when he would not accept her decision to cease their relationship. A protective sentence was not justified because the court was informed that the victim now had the benefit of a court order restraining the offender from molesting her and the offender had now accepted that their marriage was over. The same principle has been applied in cases where the offender has repeatedly sexually abused his step-children but his offending has been confined to children of the family and the court has accepted that there will be no future contact with the victims and child protection procedures will prevent further opportunities for abuse arising. In such circumstances, protective sentencing is not appropriate: *R v L* (1994) 15 Cr App R(S) 501; *R v S* (1995) 16 Cr App R(S) 303. If the ambit is very narrow, perhaps confined to a single prospective victim, where the risk remains a live issue, it is submitted that s80(2)(b) will be applicable.

Basis for Forming s80(2)(b) Opinion

As suggested above, the statute does not include any procedural safeguards in the application of s80(2)(b). PCC(S)A 2000 s81(4)(a) applies, as to all custodial sentencing, requiring the court to 'take account of all such information about the circumstances of the offence or (as the case may be) of the offence and the offence or offences associated with it (including any aggravating or mitigating features) as is available to it'. In addition, s81(4)(b) allows the court to 'take into account any information about the offender which is before it.' The exercise of protective sentencing has thus had to develop judicial ground rules regarding the evidential basis for assessing risk and related procedural demands, as can be distilled as follows. In summary, the court should have regard to: previous convictions; the facts of the present offence(s); the background of the defendant; risk assessment and predictions of future offending in the reports before the court.

- Though the court has no statutory duty to give notice that that it is considering a longer than commensurate term, the Court of Appeal has indicated that the sentencer should give express indication to the defence so that appropriate representations may be made: *R v Baverstock* [1993] 1 WLR 202.

- The court should take account of the circumstances of the current offence(s), the nature and circumstances of previous offences, medical and other evidence about the offender. If the offence is an isolated instance or there is no reason to fear a substantial risk of further seriously harmful violence or sexual offending, a protective sentence will not be appropriate. A protective sentence is not justified simply because of the repugnant nature of the offender's behaviour in the current offence and the wish to express clear disapproval of that kind of offending, nor because of the worrying prevalence of that kind of behaviour. In emphasising that proper account should be taken of the offender's background, the Appeal Court in *R v Harper and Sabin* (1998) *The Times* 12 October upheld terms of 18 and 15 years on offenders who had both been convicted of manslaughter by knife for which they were detained at Broadmoor on ss37/41 hospital orders and on release had committed four offences of robbery armed with a shotgun and an unsheathed knife. The first defendant had also committed unlawful wounding.

- In assessing whether the offender is likely to commit further violent or sexual offences, the court may need to examine the circumstances of the present offence in greater detail than would be necessary if determining a commensurate sentence. The importance of having accurate information may make it necessary to conduct a *Newton* hearing to inquire into any important issue that throws light on risk: *R v Oudkerk* (1995) 16 Cr App R(S) 172.

- If the assessment of risk draws substantially upon any previous conviction or convictions, the circumstances of the earlier offence(s) may need to be investigated in detail: *R v Samuels* (1995) 16 Cr App R(S) 856. In *Oudkerk* (above) the Appeal Court found that details relating to the offender's record were insufficient to justify the judge's conclusion that a longer-than-commensurate sentence was justified and emphasised the importance of accurate information about such convictions.

- Though previous convictions will usually be a key indicator of the danger posed by the offender, a protective sentence may be justified even though the offender has no previous convictions akin to the current offences. In *R v Thomas* (1995) 16 Cr App R(S) 616 (see also below) the defendant (29) had committed s18 wounding by attacking a shop assistant with a stone causing injuries to her face and head. His only relevant previous convictions were possession of an offensive weapon as a juvenile and assault of a police officer 10 years previously. The Court of Appeal disagreed with the defence argument that there had to be a history of violent offending to justify a s2(2)(b) term; there could be a number of matters before the court which, individually or in combination, justified this course. However, in this case, though the offence involved gratuitous violence and a total lack of contrition, it was an isolated instance and the medical evidence did not clearly portray the offender as likely to be a risk to the public. The sentencer appeared to have been influenced unduly by the manner of the offence and the accused's indifference to the victim's injuries. A longer-than-commensurate sentence was thus overturned.

- If the danger posed appears 'due to a mental or personality problem, the sentencer should always call for a medical report': *R v Fawcett* (1995) 16 Cr App R(S) 55. This not only assists the assessment of risk but also affords the court advice whether a mental health disposal is appropriate. *R v Thomas* (1995) 16 Cr App R(S) 616 (see also above) illustrates the importance of medical evidence in determining whether a protective sentence is justified. The offender had no history of offending of this nature and the medical evidence was equivocal. The judge had been wrong to attach as so much importance to the manner in which the current offences had been committed.

- It is not necessary for the court to obtain a psychiatric report if the court is satisfied of the need to protect the public in the light of all the circumstances of the case: *R v Hashi* (1995) 16 Cr App R(S) 121 (outlined above). Cases of this nature are likely to be somewhat rare.

- In dealing with co-offenders, they should be assessed individually. It may be justified to impose a longer than commensurate term upon one and a commensurate sentence upon the other: *R v Bestwick and Huddlestone* (1995) 16 Cr App R(S) 168, where two young men had joined in arson offences. The younger was assessed as of normal personality. He enjoyed the excitement of fires but had no urge to light fires to experience that excitement. The other man was considered a seriously disturbed personality, obsessed with lighting fires and likely to continue to raise fires to gain excitement.

- Proper account must be taken of the offender's age. With younger offenders, protection of the public must be balanced against the possible added risk that may be presented on release from a crushingly long sentence.

How Much Longer Than Commensurate?

The obvious question arises as to the discretion of the sentencer to impose an incapacitative sentence that has no relationship to the seriousness of the current offence. In *R v Mansell* (1994) 15 Cr App R(S) 771 and *R v Crow* (1995) 16 Cr App R(S) 409 Lord Taylor indicated that as a general principle the sentencer should balance the need to protect the public with the need to look at the totality of the sentence to ensure that the sentence is not out of all proportion to the nature of the offending. A s80(2)(b) sentence should bear a 'reasonable relationship' to the offence for which it is imposed. Thus the sentencer cannot adopt an entirely incapacitative stance and offence seriousness remains a balancing consideration. That said, *R v Keenan* [1995] Crim LR 578 illustrates circumstances where the court imposed a term 75% greater than the commensurate sentence. And in *R v Fisher* [1995] Crim LR 173 sentence for a brief and comparatively less serious indecent assault was reduced from eight to six years, prompting Thomas to comment that the '"reasonable relationship" principle is less important in relation to relatively minor offences than in relationship to more serious offences'. In contrast, *R v Gabbidon and Bramble* [1997] 2 Cr App R(S) 19 illustrates that where the offence(s) would attract a lengthy commensurate sentence, the enhancement for public protection should represent a smaller proportion of the commensurate sentence than would be appropriate if the commensurate sentence were shorter. In that case the commensurate sentence for several armed robberies was considered to be 15 years and the proper s2(2)(b) term was set at 20 years, an enhancement of a third. In *R v Williams* [1999] 1 Cr App R(S) 105, a case of kidnapping a girl aged 8 in fulfilment of sexual fantasy, for which the proper determinate term was assessed as six years, the public protection term was reduced from 14 to nine years, again an enhancement of a third.

The Court of Appeal remains in flux on this point, as illustrated by more recent cases. In *R v Chapman* [2000] 1 Cr App R(S) 277 where a hostel resident had committed arson being reckless whether life would be endangered by setting fire to bedding, a term of ten years was imposed, seven being added to the three years felt commensurate with seriousness. *Chapman* was followed in *R v Wilson* [2000] Crim LR 503 for an almost identical offence committed by a serving prisoner setting fire to his cell. However, in *R v De Silva* [2000] 2 Cr App R(S) 408, where two years was considered the proportionate term for indecent assault of children, together with taking indecent photographs of them, the Court (comprising the Lord Chief Justice and another of the judges who had sat in *Chapman*) deemed an additional three years for public protection to be 'manifestly excessive', despite the offender's record of sexual offending including eight years for rape committed in similar circumstances (purporting to be a professional photographer who could help advance the victim's modelling aspirations), and reduced the s2(2)(b) sentence from five years to three years to be more proportionate to the gravity of the offences. As the effect was to keep the offender in prison for an additional six months, the extent of public protection thus gained was rather marginal. *Chapman* and *Wilson* had in common that a life sentence had initially been imposed in each case and, in ruling that the strict criteria pertaining to a discretionary life sentence had not been satisfied, the Appeal Court nevertheless sought to extend a substantial degree of incapacitation in the interests of public protection.

However, *Chapman* was cited by the Court of Appeal in *R v Smith* [2001] 2 Cr App R(S)

160 when upholding a term of four years for ABH, an unprovoked attack on a woman aged 85 standing in a bus queue who had commented that he had pushed to the front of the queue. He had spat in her face, then punched her to the ground when she remonstrated with him. Agreeing with the sentencing judge that the appropriate commensurate sentence was one of 18 months, the court noted psychiatric opinion that the offender posed a high risk of further violence and showed no remorse, believing that he was justified in his conduct. Though the extension to over twice the commensurate term was 'unusually high', it concluded that there was nothing wrong in principle with this sentence.

This issue may depend on the nature of the offence for which a public protection sentence is deemed appropriate. As Taylor CJ stated in *Crow and Pennington*, 'each case turns on its facts and different offences committed in different ways may require different responses from the court'. Such scope for differentiation was developed by the Court in *Gabbidon and Bramble* where Henry LJ spoke of ensuring 'that the final sentence is not disproportionate (as it would likely to be if there was any significant degree of double counting in that sentencing process)'. In *R v Winfield* (1998, unreported) the Court (in dealing with a case of robbery where a term of eight years was reduced to six, five as the proportionate term plus an additional year) explained this reference to 'double counting' as:

> 'a reference to the track which exists in certain categories of offence. That track is the deterrent factor which is built into the sentencing guidelines for such offences. The deterrent factor caters not merely for the seriousness of the offence, but for the necessity to protect the public from the offender and from offenders with like proclivity.'

Thus if the offence is of a nature where a commensurate sentence should include an element of deterrence, any additional period added for public protection should not be such as to, in effect, penalise the offender twice over.

Though the primary purpose is public protection, some allowance should be made, even in the worst cases, for a guilty plea: *R v Crow* (see above). However, in *R v Bowler* (see above) the Court of Appeal said that matters of personal mitigation, such as a guilty plea, the impulsive nature of the offence and the offender's limited intelligence should carry less weight than in the fixing of a commensurate sentence. As to how credit for plea should apply, uncertainty continues. Logic might suggest that a discount should be reflected in the part of the overall sentence that is intended to be commensurate, not in the added public protection period. However, the possibility then arises that the additional period may simply be extended to compensate for the reduction given for plea.

Consecutive Sentences Where the court is dealing with more than one offence, one or some of which are considered to justify a longer-than-commensurate term, the Appeal Court has indicated that it is not appropriate to make the s80(2)(b) period consecutive to the commensurate term imposed for an offence outside the ambit of this provision, e.g. *R v Ellis* [2001] 1 Cr App R(S) 148, setting aside sentence of six months for shop theft and three years consecutive for administering a noxious substance (spraying staff with CS gas when they sought to intervene) in favour of a three year term. However, in *R v Blades* [2000] 1 Cr App R(S) 463 the Court had endorsed a longer-than-commensurate term consecutive to an order that the offender should return to prison under s116 (then CJA 1991 s40) (see page 89). More recently, in *R v Everleigh* (2001) *The Times* 16 May, the Court has reaffirmed that it is not appropriate to pass a s80(2)(b) sentence consecutive to another sentence imposed on the same occasion, because the former is intended to protect the public without the need for any additional penalty for conduct punishable at the same time. However, the Court recognised that it may be desirable without being illogical to impose a s80(2)(b) sentence consecutive to a sentence imposed on an earlier occasion or to a s116 order. In such cases the sentencer should make plain the reasons for making the s80(2)(b) sentence consecutive.

Giving Reasons for Protective Sentencing

In addition to the procedural requirements of PCC(S)A 2000 s79(4) (see page 81), s80(3) specifies that where a court passes a longer than commensurate sentence, it shall:

(a) state in open court that it is of the opinion that s80(2)(b) applies and why it is of that opinion; and

(b) explain to the offender in open court and in ordinary language why the sentence is for such a term.

However, failure to fulfil this requirement does not invalidate the sentence.

Early Release

Offenders sentenced to longer than commensurate determinate terms are in the same position as those receiving commensurate terms for the purposes of early release eligibility. For those receiving terms of four years or longer, as the clear majority of those receiving protective sentences will be, eligibility for release on parole arises at the half-way point of sentence, with automatic release on non-parole licence at the two-thirds point. There are no special provisions to reflect the protective nature of sentence, either to safeguard individual liberty or to reflect continuing danger to the public. There is no provision for the prisoner to be reviewed at the point where they have completed what would otherwise have been the proper commensurate term to assess if they continue to present a serious risk to the public. Equally, there is no power to detain the prisoner beyond the two-thirds point, even if they are assessed as presenting a continuing, even heightened risk to the public.

Public Protection Sentence or Extended Sentence?

Since the introduction of the extended sentence (see page 86), courts now have to consider parallel provisions designed to protect the public from the risk posed by sexual/violent offenders, as illustrated by *R v Thornton* [2000] Crim LR 312. Dealing with a man for indecent assault (by grabbing the woman victim in the street at night and attempting to pull down her tights), and in the light of his five previous convictions for offences of this nature, a Crown Court judge imposed a term of five years under s2(2)(b) as a longer-than-commensurate sentence. The Court of Appeal agreed that s2(2)(b) was applicable in these circumstances but felt that the sentencer had paid insufficient regard to the fact that the offender, who suffered Asperger's Syndrome, had made a voluntary confession of guilt to staff at the hostel where he lived, without which he would not have been detected for this assault. In the circumstances, the Court concluded that it was more appropriate to deal with him by a two year commensurate custodial period backed by a three year extension period.

This case indicates the choice that faces courts when dealing with sexual or violent offenders who pose continuing risk to the public, while seeking to reflect factors of culpability and mitigation. Under the proposed s2(2)(b) sentence, this offender would have been eligible for discretionary release after serving 30 months, with automatic release after 40 months, licence running for either 15 or five months until the 45 month point. The alternative course of an extended sentence had the effect of affording him automatic release after 12 months, followed by a total licence liability of 42 months (six months ordinary licence plus the three year extension). Given the mitigating factors, the Appeal Court felt it more just to impose less immediate custodial liability but with the assurance of statutory oversight for, at maximum, 27 months longer than would otherwise have been the case. Of course, it is possible in appropriate circumstances for a court to seek the 'best of both worlds' in the interests of public protection, by imposing a longer-than-commensurate custodial period as part of an extended sentence. Such a substantial combination would not have been justified in this instance and the course adopted has obvious attractions as the preferable option in the circumstances. See also *R v T* [2001] 1 Cr App R(S) 205 (noted at page 93) where the provisions of s80(2)(b) were not satisfied but an extension period of six years felt appropriate. As Thomas notes in his Commentary on *T* (at [2000] Crim LR 867), an extension period has potentially far more onerous consequences than the difference between a commensurate and a longer than commensurate sentence.

Mandatory Life Sentence: Second Serious Offence

Though life sentences generally are detailed in Stone (1997), this more recent provision, introduced by C(S)A 1997 s2 and now contained in PCC(S)A 2000 s109, is outlined conveniently here. In essence, the court is required to impose an automatic life sentence on a defendant convicted of a second 'serious offence' unless there are exceptional circumstances justifying the avoidance of this course.

This measure has been criticised as a blunt instrument, 'arbitrary and capricious' (Thomas, 1997), that will not target dangerousness with any accuracy. To illustrate the clumsy anomalies it may generate, Thomas posed three case examples:

1. X tries to rob a sub-post office, employing a cucumber concealed in a plastic bag to make the staff think he is armed. He has a previous conviction for a similar offence.

2. Y breaks into a house in the small hours knowing that it is occupied by a woman and her small children. He enters her bedroom intending to rape her but she wakes up, screams and disturbs the children and he leaves. He has a previous conviction for rape in almost identical circumstances.

3. Z commits an undetected series of sexual attacks on women over several years, including rape using potentially lethal violence. Finally caught for such a crime, he is assessed as an aggressive but untreatable psychopath who is likely to offend again. He has no previous convictions.

Only X qualifies for an automatic life sentence under s109, despite being the least dangerous in public protection terms. Defendant Y is not eligible because his offence of burglary with intent to rape is not a 'serious' offence for the purposes of s109 (and he cannot receive a discretionary life sentence as this offence carries a maximum of 14 years). Defendant Z has not committed any of his offences after a prior conviction for such a crime. In introducing the measure, the Government made much of the statistic that in 1994 of 217 offenders convicted of a second serious violent or sexual offence, only 10 received a discretionary life sentence. However, in only two cases did the Attorney-General feel it appropriate to refer the sentence to the Court of Appeal as unduly lenient (see page 245).

Among other concerns: (i) offenders facing an automatic life sentence will be much more likely to plead 'not guilty' as there is nothing to lose, thus exposing victims, and women in particular, to the ordeal of trial; (ii) there may be more incentive to plea bargain downwards, e.g. from s18 GBH to s20, thus underplaying the seriousness of the crime; (iii) where GBH with intent has arisen in circumstances of domestic violence, family members may be less willing to press charges where a life sentence is at stake; (iv) s18 encompasses a wide range of behaviour and it may be out of proportion to both seriousness and risk to impose an indeterminate sentence on every repeater, irrespective of the circumstances and level of harm.

Eligible Offenders

An offender stands to be dealt with in this way if (s109(1)):

(a)   convicted of a qualifying 'serious' offence committed after the commencement date (30 September 1997); and

(b)   at the time the offence was committed was (i) aged 18 or over and (ii) had been convicted in any part of the UK of another qualifying offence.

Qualifying Offences

The offences which count as a 'serious offence' for the purposes of s109 are (s109(5)):

(a)   attempted murder, conspiracy to murder, incitement to murder;

(b)   soliciting murder;

(c)   manslaughter;

(d)   wounding or GBH with intent (OPA s18);

(e)   rape, attempted rape;

(f)   USI with girl under 13 (SOA 1956 s5);

(g)   possession of firearm with intent to injure, use of firearm to resist arrest, carrying firearm with criminal intent (FA 1968 ss16–18);

(h)   robbery involving possession of firearm or imitation firearm 'at some time during the commission of the offence'.

The list above refers to offences under the law of England and Wales. The equivalent offences under Scottish and Northern Ireland legislation are specified by s109(6) and

(7). Note that an attempted offence does not qualify unless explicitly stated to do so (i.e. attempted murder or rape), nor do conspiracy or incitement, save as indicated in (a).

Any previous conviction counts as a qualifying offence, irrespective of the offender's age when it was incurred, whether it is 'spent' under ROA 1974, and whether it pre-dated the commencement of s2. The previous conviction need not concern an offence of the same type as the qualifying offence of which the defendant now stands convicted. However, a conviction resulting in discharge, absolute or conditional, does not count (unless the conditional discharge was breached and the offender thus sentenced – see Chapter 7), nor does a previous finding of unfitness to plead, acquittal by reason of insanity or committal by a magistrates' court to hospital detention under MHA 1983 s37 without first convicting the defendant. A conviction resulting in a care order (under CYPA 1969 s7(7), repealed by CA 1989) does count, as does a binding over following conviction. As a further illustration of the complex nature of questions whether disposals count for this purpose, *R v Frost* [2001] 2 Cr App R(S) 124 clarified that a qualifying offence for which an offender was convicted and received a probation order prior to 1 October 1992 (date of implementation of CJA 1991) does not count for the purposes of s109. Although that outcome counts as a conviction for the purposes of s151(1) (see page 11), it is not stated in any statutory provision to count for this purpose and is thus subject to the old statutory rule that a conviction leading to a probation order as conceived before the 1991 Act should not count as a conviction for any purpose other than the proceedings in which it was made. However, by an anomaly identified in *Frost*, where a juvenile offender received a supervision order prior to 1 October 1992 it does count as a conviction for the purposes of s109 because there is no equivalent provision restricting the status of an offence resulting in such a disposal. As the Appeal Court recognised in *Frost*, this could result in 'injustice of some magnitude' for an offender to be penalised simply by reason of their age at point of their earlier conviction and thus the Court chose to regard this as 'exceptional circumstances' (see below) allowing the automatic life sentence to be quashed, even though it could not be said that the offender posed no significant risk to the public.

'Exceptional Circumstances'

Section 109 affords the court narrow scope not to impose a life sentence if 'of the opinion that there are exceptional circumstances relating to either of the offences or to the offender which justify its not doing so': s109(2). If the court finds exceptional circumstances which justify not imposing the otherwise mandatory sentence, 'it shall state in open court that it is of that opinion and what the exceptional circumstances are': s109(3). This provision was considered by the Court of Appeal in *R v Kelly* [2000] QB 198 in an appeal against a s2 life sentence imposed for a s18 wounding where the offender had a previous conviction in 1980 for three robberies committed when he was 19 for which he had received 14 years. It was argued that his youth at the time of the earlier offences, the 18 year gap prior to the current offence, his intervening good record and the dissimilarity between the past and present crimes amounted to exceptional circumstances. The Court dismissed the appeal, despite agreeing that in the absence of C(S)A 1997 s2 a life sentence would not have been given serious consideration. Lord Bingham CJ stated:

'To be exceptional a circumstance need not be unique, or unprecedented, or very rare; but it cannot be one that is regularly, or routinely, or normally encountered. To relieve the court of its duty to impose a life sentence under (s109), however, circumstances must not only be exceptional but such as, in the opinion of the court, justify it in not imposing a life sentence, and in forming that opinion, the court must have regard to the purpose of Parliament in enacting the section... Parliament intended life sentences to be imposed in cases in which, under the existing law, they were not being imposed, whether because of the conditions which the courts had laid down to govern the exercise of the power to impose such sentences or because the courts were reluctant to exercise it. Otherwise, there would have been no need to enact s2.'

This decision suggested that exceptionality would be found very sparingly. However, in *R v Buckland* [2000] 1 WLR 1202 the Court of Appeal demonstrated a more flexible approach in a case involving attempted robbery of a bank in which the offender, having a plastic imitation handgun in his pocket, queued at a customer services desk and handed over a note demanding money written on an envelope bearing his name and address. He waited quietly as instructed and did not resist arrest. He had an earlier conviction for an imitation firearm offence. On his appeal against an automatic life sentence, the Appeal Court agreed that his incompetence, lack of aggression and non-use of the imitation gun were 'exceptional' and as he presented no serious and continuing danger to public safety, the life sentence should be quashed.

This provision has been comprehensively reviewed by the Court of Appeal in the light of the European Convention of Human Rights in *R v Offen and Others* [2001] 2 Cr App R(S) 44. Revising the interpretation given in *Kelly* without reliance on HRA 1998, Lord Woolf CJ felt that the rationale of the provision was relevant not just when the court had concluded that there are exceptional circumstances but in deciding whether exceptional circumstances exist. 'The question of whether circumstances are appropriately regarded as exceptional must surely be influenced by the context in which the question is being asked.' Lord Woolf went on to explain:

'The policy and intention of Parliament was to protect the public against a person who had committed two serious offences. It therefore can be assumed the section was not intended to apply to someone in relation to whom it was established there would be no need for protection in the future. In other words, if the facts showed the statutory assumption was misplaced, then this, in the statutory context was not the normal situation and in consequence, for the purposes of the section, the position was exceptional. The time that elapsed between the two serious offences could, but would not necessarily, reflect on whether, after the second serious offence was committed, there was any danger against which the public would need protection. The same is true of two differing offences, and the age of the offender. These are all circumstances which could give rise to the conclusion that what could be normal and not exceptional in a different context was exceptional in this context.'

The Court of Appeal concluded by indicating that it was approaching the application of the provision as though it is no different from the imposition of a discretionary life sentence. A judge is 'obliged to pass a life sentence (under s109) unless the offender poses no significant risk to the public'. If the offender is a significant risk, a life sentence imposed under s109 will not contravene the European Convention. [Note, however, that 'exceptional circumstances' can exist even though it cannot be said that the offender presents no significant risk to the public, as illustrated by *Frost* (above).]

In demonstrating the proper approach to the application of s109, the Court in *Offen* considered five separate cases:

Offen: The offender robbed a building society branch using a toy gun. He apologised to staff and did not resist when a security officer grabbed the bag containing the stolen money from him outside. He had an earlier conviction for robbery using an imitation gun committed 10 years earlier. A psychiatric report stated that he was suffering a depressive illness and was not a danger to society. Life sentence quashed.

McKeown: The offender approached a man with whom he had been earlier in dispute and demanded an apology. When this was refused he punched the man to the ground and kicked him in the face (s18 GBH). He had a previous conviction for s18 wounding at age 16. He had not gone out that night with violence in mind, had inflicted a single kick and had desisted and left the scene through his own choice. There was no evidence that he presented a significant risk to the public and the life sentence was quashed.

McGilliard: The offender pleaded guilty to s18 wounding by stabbing in the course of a public house argument, having a previous conviction at age 17 for manslaughter. He had a record of repeated offences of violence and substance misuse, was assessed as presenting a high risk of further offending and had limited motivation to address his problems. Life sentence upheld.

Okwuegbunam: The offender pleaded guilty to the manslaughter of the mother of his children, having inflicted blows on her in the context of bullying and humiliating her, then forcing her to take a cold bath which activated a subdural haemorrhage. He had a conviction for rape of a girl aged 13 a decade before and a previous conviction for ABH upon the deceased victim. Though considered 'close to the borderline', the Court concluded that the case came within the rationale of the automatic life sentence which was thus upheld.

Stephen S: The offender was convicted of numerous sexual offences against his daughters, including rape. He had a previous conviction for s18 GBH (an attack with a pool cue in a pub). The difference between the two sets of offences did not amount to exceptional circumstances. He had other offences of violence and his offending against his children had involved physical abuse and threats of violence. The case fell within the rationale of the provision and a life sentence was correct.

Subsequently, in *R v Wallace* [2001] Crim LR 407, where a woman aged 19 had pleaded guilty to s18 wounding (attacking a man with a bottle in a nightclub because he had not, in her view, assisted her boyfriend after he had collapsed), having been made subject of a probation order in 1998 for a s18 offence. The PSR reported that she had posed a high risk because of her explosive temper, that the risk had diminished during the course of her probation order but that she still posed a continuing risk of harm. The risk was also identified in a psychiatric report which diagnosed an anti-social personality disorder. Given this evidence and the short interval between the two s18 convictions, the Court could not say that she did not constitute a significant risk to the public and the automatic life term was upheld, despite the fact that the first conviction was dealt with by a community sentence.

A further illustration of the new approach to exceptionality is provided by *R v Close* [2001] Crim LR 586, where an offender convicted of s18 GBH in 1992 and sentenced to 16 months YOI was further convicted of s18 wounding in 1998 for stabbing a woman with whom he had had a relationship, through resentment that she had befriended another man. Quashing his life sentence in favour of a sentence of $4\frac{1}{2}$ years, the Court of Appeal noted that he had incurred no further convictions since 1992 until now, had given himself up to the police and had expressed remorse and recognition that he had acted out of possessive jealousy. A psychiatrist considered that he did not have a personality disorder or morbid jealousy. He had since reconciled with the victim. It was thus proper to conclude that he did not represent a significant risk to the public.

The *Offen* judgement leaves to be resolved definitively whether the test of what constitutes a 'significant risk to the public' for this purpose is the same as applies when a court considers imposing a discretionary life sentence (see Stone, 1997) or whether a less stringent criterion of dangerousness applies.

A judge's finding of exceptionality can properly prompt a Reference by the Attorney-General on grounds of undue lenience, as in *Stephen S.* above. In *Attorney-General's Reference No 71 of 1998* (1999, unreported) the Court held that the fact that imposition of a s2/s109 life sentence would result in wide disparity of sentence between two co-offenders, only one of whom is subject to this provision, does not constitute exceptionality

Setting 'The Relevant Part'

As in the case of discretionary life sentences, the sentencing judge shall specify the determinate period (usually referred to as the 'tariff' or the penal term) to be served by the lifer before being eligible for release on life licence. This term shall be that 'part' considered appropriate, 'taking into account the seriousness of the offence or the combination of the offence and other offences associated with it': s28(3).

In *R v Errington* [1999] Crim LR 91, a case involving an offender with a record of serious offending including rape, s18 wounding and robbery, now convicted of further offences including two robberies while in possession of an imitation firearm, the sentencer ordered a specified period or 'part' of 12 years. On appeal, the Appeal Court determined that a court considering what period to specify should first decide the determinate term that would have been appropriate if the offender had not fallen to be dealt with by automatic life sentence and then fix as the relevant part a half of that notional determinate term, unless there are particular circumstances making a longer proportion appropriate. In this instance, the determinate term would have been 12 years and the appropriate specified period was thus reduced to six years. (As Thomas points out in his case commentary, the limitations of the automatic life sentence are shown up by the fact that if the offender had committed the fresh robberies armed with a knife or even a live hand grenade, the provisions requiring automatic life would not have been met, though this particular offender was probably eligible for a discretionary life sentence.)

Regard to Special Experience of Indeterminate Sentence The Court of Appeal has suggested that in arriving at the determinate part in the exercise of s109 it is relevant to have regard to the feelings of 'uncertainty and hopelessness experienced by a prisoner who has been made subject to a life sentence': *R v Adams and Harding* [2000] 2 Cr App R(S) 274, cited in *R v Banks* [2001] 1 Cr App R(S) 39. However, the Court has also indicated that it is inappropriate to set the determinate part 'a little on the low side' 'to encourage good behaviour during imprisonment': *Attorney-General's Reference No 6 of 2000* [2001] 1 Cr App R(S) 72.

Minimum Sentences

As anticipated in the White Paper *Protecting the Public: The Government's Strategy on Crime in England and Wales* (1996), C(S)A 1997 ss3–4 introduced the novel sentencing concept of mandatory minimum sentencing in the Crown Court for the repeated commission of offences felt to present a special threat to the social fabric: drug trafficking and domestic burglary. This approach to punishment is clearly controversial. It departed from the 1991 Act's central principle of proportionality. It significantly restricts the scope for judicial discretion and may, in particular, prevent sentencers from passing the sentence most likely to prevent offending. It may also have a counter-productive impact upon other aspects of criminal justice policy. The force of the proposal was substantially reduced in the course of the Bill's passage through Parliament so that there is now only what may be regarded as a presumption that a term of minimum length will be imposed, with greater scope for judicial discretion to depart from that presumption. The measures are now incorporated in PCC(S)A 2000.

Class A Drug Trafficking

As envisaged by the White Paper, the measure is intended to ensure 'that when persistent dealers in hard drugs are caught and convicted, they will automatically go to prison for a very long time.' In essence, PCC(S)A 2000 s110 imposes a minimum seven year term for a third offence of this nature.

Eligible Offenders To be eligible for a minimum sentence, an offender must (s110(1)):

(a)   be convicted of a Class A drug trafficking offence committed after the commencement of the provision (30 September 1997); and

(b)   at the time that the offence was committed—

   (i)   have been aged 18 or over, and

   (ii)   been convicted in any part of the UK of two other Class A drug trafficking offences, where one of those other offences was committed after he had been convicted for the other.

It is thus necessary for the offender to have incurred the two earlier convictions not only on separate occasions but the second offence must have followed conviction for the first. The earlier convictions can be in respect of offences committed before the commencement date and those convictions may predate commencement. The age at which the offender acquired their earlier convictions is not material and may thus have been incurred when the offender was a juvenile. Convictions for which the offender received a conditional or absolute discharge do not count as convictions for the purposes of s110 (see discussion at page 102).

Eligible Offences A 'drug trafficking offence' means a trafficking offence under DTA 1994, or the Proceeds of Crime (Scotland) Act 1995, or the Proceeds of Crime (Northern Ireland) Order 1996: s110(5). Among offences thus included: production, supply and possession with intent to supply controlled drugs; improper importation of controlled drugs; conspiracy, attempt or incitement to commit any of the preceding offences. If the current offence is ordinarily triable either way, s110(4) specifies that it shall be triable only on indictment for the purpose of this provision.

Minimum Sentence The court shall impose a custodial sentence for a term of at least seven years: s110(2). Note that seven years is a merely the minimum term, not the mandatory term to be imposed.

Exception to Minimum Term Section 110(2) allows the sentencer to depart from the obligation to impose seven years or longer by adding: 'except where the court is of the opinion that there are particular circumstances which:

(a)   relate to any of the offences or to the offender; and

(b)   would make it unjust to do so in all the circumstances'.

Where the court does not impose a term of seven years or longer, 'it shall state in open court that it is of that opinion and what the particular circumstances are': s110(3).

The original wording in the Crime (Sentencing) Bill, prior to amendment, permitted departure from a term of minimum length only where there were 'exceptional circumstances'. The Conservative Government had to accept the diluted version in order to ensure that the Bill was passed before the General Election, though clearly dismayed that the original strength of the measure had been fatally weakened. The Minister of State Baroness Blatch commented in the House of Lords that 'any judge could exercise any judgement whatever that (the minimum) was unjust, and against no test at all'. One frequently expressed fear in regard to the measure as originally proposed was that it would ensnare small-time addicts selling small quantities primarily to support their own addiction. The provision now allows sentencers far greater scope to distinguish the persistent large scale trafficker, presumably the main target of the measure.

In *R v Stenhouse* [2000] 2 Cr App R(S) 386, a case illustrating the exercise of judicial discretion, the offender pleaded guilty to supplying an undercover police officer making test purchases on four occasions. His last Class A conviction, in 1997, had concerned supply of a single tablet or ampoule of methadone, for which he was placed on probation. Given that such a sentence indicated that this was viewed as a less serious instance of this kind of offence and also noting his 'determined and considerable efforts', as reported in the PSR, to conquer his drug habit, the Court of Appeal considered that the combination of factors relating both to the offender and one of his previous convictions made it unjust to require him to serve the statutory minimum term. Sentence of seven years was thus reduced to three years to encourage the offender to continue his efforts.

Mentally Disordered Offenders The provisions of s110 do not in any way interfere with the sentencer's powers to make a hospital order under MHA 1983 s37 instead in appropriate cases. If imprisonment is imposed under s110, the sentencer is nevertheless able to make a hospital direction under MHA 1983 s45A (as included by C(S)A 1997 s46: see Stone, 2001).

Discount for Guilty Plea One common criticism of the minimum sentence policy has been that defendants facing such a term would have no incentive to plead guilty, irrespective of the strength of the evidence against them. C(S)A 1997 Sch 4 para 17 thus introduced an amendment to CJPOA 1994 s48, now contained in PCC(S)A 2000 s152(3) (see page 19) to the effect that a court imposing a minimum sentence under s110 may nevertheless reflect a guilty plea by a limited discount. The court may impose 'any sentence which is not less than 80% of that specified in' s110(2). This means that if a not guilty plea would have attracted seven years, the lowest sentence for a guilty plea is 67.2 months. A maximum discount of 20% is clearly lower than the 'going rate' in sentencing generally.

Where a court imposes a sentence of longer than the prescribed minimum following a guilty plea, the sentencer should indicate how the sentence has been calculated in the light of credit given for plea. In *R v Brown* [2000] 2 Cr App R(S) 435 the offender had pleaded guilty to selling crack and heroin to under-cover police officers. He received the minimum of seven years, 78 months for supply and six month consecutive on revocation of the CSO to which he was then subject. As the judge had not identified the application of credit for plea, the appellant argued that either he should have received a term of 5 years $7^{1}/_{2}$ months (i.e. 80% of seven years) or, alternatively, the judge must have had in mind a starting point of over eight years from which he had deducted 20% to reach the actual term imposed, in which case the sentence was too long. The Appeal Court agreed, reducing the term of 78 months to 68 months, with six months concurrent.

Domestic Burglary

This measure was included in the 1997 Act in the light of statistical evidence that the average sentence imposed by the Crown Court on third or subsequent conviction in 1993-94 was only 18.9 months. In essence, C(S)A 1997 s4 required a mandatory minimum sentence of three years for a third conviction. After postponing implementation of this measure, the Government announced in January 1999 that it would be brought into effect in December that year in the light of a stabilisation of the prison population, thus making resources available to absorb the increase anticipated from this measure. The provision is now contained in PCC(S)A 2000 s111.

Eligible Offenders To attract a minimum sentence, the offender must (s111(1)):

(a)   be convicted of a domestic burglary committed after 30 November 1999; and

(b)   when that burglary was committed, have been (i) aged 18 or over and (ii) been convicted in England and Wales of two other domestic burglaries.

One of those other burglaries must have been committed after the offender had been convicted of the other and *both* of them must have been committed *after* the commencement date: s111(1)(c). All three convictions must thus arise from separate court appearances and each must be in respect of an offence committed after the previous conviction. Note that offences of attempted burglary do not count for this purpose nor do convictions resulting in discharge (see page 106). Because all the offences that count for the purposes of this provision must occur after commencement, this measure has a somewhat delayed impact, probably beginning to show its weight only two years or more after commencement. It is anticipated that the first recipient of minimum sentencing will be sentenced under s111 around June 2001.

Eligible Offences Domestic burglary is defined as 'a burglary committed in respect of a building or part of a building which is a dwelling' (s111(5)) and includes aggravated burglary of a dwelling. If the current offence would otherwise be triable either way, s111(4) specifies that it shall be triable only on indictment for the purposes of this provision, to ensure that the Crown Court gains jurisdiction.

Minimum Sentence and Discretion for Exception The term shall be for 'at least three years', subject to the sentencer's discretion to reach the opinion not to follow this presumption in the light of 'particular circumstances' relating to 'any of the offences or the offender' which 'would make it unjust (to impose a minimum term) in all the circumstances': s111(2). Scope for this exception is in exactly the same terms as for Class A drug trafficking (see above). The same limited scope for discount to reflect a guilty plea applies as under s110. As regards mentally disordered offenders, the same alternatives as mentioned above apply.

Suspended Sentence of Imprisonment

Introduced by CJA 1967 as a measure to divert less serious offenders from custody by requiring courts to suspend virtually all prison terms of six months or less, the suspended sentence was clearly meant to be a custodial measure but was clearly also perceived by sentencers as a non-custodial deterrent in cases that were not serious enough to justify custody. As a result, the benefits gained by its diversionary impact were eroded by the activation of suspended sentences that had been unjustifiably imposed in the first instance, sometimes for disproportionately long terms. There was also evidence that the measure disproportionately benefited 'white collar' offenders, such as those convicted of 'breach of trust' dishonesty. It is thus not surprising that the White Paper *Crime, Justice and Protecting the Public* (1990) took the view that although courts have found the measure useful, the suspended sentence 'does not fit easily into the proposed new sentencing arrangements'. It noted that many offenders see a suspended sentence as a 'let off' (or 'a walk out'), 'since it places no restrictions other than the obligation not to offend again'. The 1991 Act nevertheless resisted the logic of abolition (there already being no scope to suspend a YOI term or any custodial sentence upon an offender aged under 21, prompting some young offenders to complain of discrimination). Instead, the Act amended the relevant provisions of PCCA 1973, curtailing its use by narrowing the basis on which a prison sentence can be suspended. That provision has now been incorporated in PCC(S)A 2000.

The Criterion for Imposing a Suspended Sentence

PCC(S)A s118(4) specifies that 'a court shall not deal with an offender by means of a suspended sentence unless it is of the opinion:

(a)   that the case is one in which a sentence of imprisonment would have been appropriate even without the power to suspend a sentence of imprisonment; and

(b)   that the exercise of that power can be justified by the exceptional circumstances of the case'.

In other words, the offence must be imprisonable and the 'so serious' criterion set by PCC(S)A s79(2)(a) must be satisfied. In the words of Lord Parker CJ in *R v O'Keefe*

[1969] 2 QB 29: 'before one gets to a suspended sentence at all, the court must go through the process of eliminating other possible courses such as conditional discharge, probation order, fines and then say to itself: this is a case for imprisonment'. *R v Smith* (1990) 12 Cr App R(S) 85 illustrated the improper use of a suspended sentence to achieve a tangential aim. The offender obtained employment as a supply teacher by using the name and qualifications of a friend without her knowledge. A suspended term was imposed to try to ensure that the defendant would be prevented from obtaining further work as a teacher.

Length A sentence of imprisonment for an offence may only be suspended if it is for a term of not more than two years: s118(1). This maximum is subject to the usual limit upon a magistrates' court's powers to pass a custodial sentence (see page 77). Thus the court which concludes that a custodial sentence is appropriate must next consider the appropriate length, applying PCC(S)A 2000 s80(2)(a). If the offence justifies a term in excess of two years, suspension is not lawful or appropriate. A court should not set a suspended term that is longer than the term it would have imposed to take immediate effect. In other words, the length should be fixed before the decision to suspend is made. When determining the length of the suspended term, a court should take account of any period spent by the offender in custody in respect of the offence.

'Exceptional Circumstances' This is explored at more length below.

The Operational Period The 'operational period' is 'the period specified in the order', which must be 'not less than one year or more than two years beginning with the date of the order': s118(2). The consequence is that 'the sentence shall not take effect unless ... the offender commits in Great Britain another offence punishable with imprisonment' during that period 'and thereafter a court having power to do so orders that the original sentence shall take effect': s118(1). For activation of suspended sentences under s119, see page 232. On passing a suspended sentence, the court must explain to the offender in ordinary language his liability under s119 if he commits an imprisonable offence during the operational period: s118(7).

Addition of Financial Penalty PCC(S)A 2000 s118(5) requires a court passing a suspended sentence to 'consider whether the circumstances of the case are such as to warrant in addition the imposition of a fine or the making of a compensation order'. Note that it would be wrong in principle (and not 'exceptional circumstances') for a sentence to be suspended simply to allow a defendant who has the means to pay to make compensation to the victim.

Concurrent or Consecutive Where a court imposes two or more suspended sentences on the offender on the same sentencing occasion, it should state whether, if activated, these are to run concurrently of consecutively. But where a suspended sentence is imposed upon an offender who is already subject to a suspended sentence imposed on an earlier occasion, the sentencer on the second occasion should not specify whether, in the event of activation, these should be served concurrently or consecutively, since that is a decision for the activating sentencer.

Incompatibility of Community Sentence on Same Sentencing Occasion A court which passes a suspended sentence for an offence 'shall not impose a community sentence in his case in respect of that offence or any other offence of which he is convicted by or before the court or for which he is dealt with by the court': s118(6). Sentencing principles also indicate that a suspended sentence should not imposed on the same occasion as an immediate term of imprisonment for another offence, nor should a suspended term be imposed on a defendant currently serving an immediate custodial term.

'Exceptional Circumstances'

The introduction of this 'test', intended to ensure that the suspended sentence should be used far more sparingly, has been the main cause of its striking decline since the 1991 Act (see figures below). Sentencers have clearly adopted a strict and more disciplined approach to the exercise of discretion in finding exceptionality, receiving little encouragement from the Court of Appeal to adopt an expansive interpretation. In the early guideline case of *R v Okinikan* [1993] 1 WLR 173, Lord Taylor CJ indicated that 'taken on their own, or in combination, good character, youth and an early plea' do not constitute exceptional circumstances, as they are commonplace features. It seems clear that other common mitigatory circumstances such as a degree of domestic or financial stress, or routine ill-health, will also not suffice. In *Okinikan* the Court declined to define exceptionality, stating that this will depend on the special facts of each individual case. Lord Taylor amplified this view in *R v Thomas* (unreported, 1995), saying that 'the circumstances which could produce a justification for suspension may not be any one particular matter but a combination of matters. It must be left open to individual judges to decide ...'.

Perhaps the best known illustration of the Court's restrictive stance on suspension and its unwillingness to be swayed by the kind of adverse consequences that can be expected to flow from prosecution, especially for white collar crime, is *R v Lowery* (1993) 14 Cr App R(S) 485. A serving police officer had pleaded guilty to false accounting, retaining moneys received as fines payments to pay for adaptations to the home to assist his wife who had severe disabilities. He had lost his job and the home that went with it, his pension rights were frozen, his wife's health had suffered and he had twice attempted suicide. Despite this considerable clustering of adversity, described by the Court as 'catastrophic consequences', suspension was declined. Doubtless, other defendants with lesser burdens to bear have benefited from suspension despite this marker case.

The scope for the Court of Appeal to oversee sentencers' discretion in this respect is, of course, somewhat limited, being limited to instances where the defence appeal against immediate terms of imprisonment and, less frequently, where the Attorney-General refers to a suspended sentence as unduly lenient (see Chapter 8). The reported cases thus do not provide an accurate reflection of contemporary use of the suspended sentence. (For an early look at the reality of suspension, see Stone, 1994.) In so far as any principles or pattern emerge from the law reports, the following points may be gleaned. There nevertheless remain doubts about both the consistency of the Court's approach and about the logic of exceptionality as a justification for suspension. If the circumstances of the case are unusual, why is suspension the correct approach rather than either (a) use of a community sentence or (b) the imposition of a shorter term of immediate imprisonment? The answer appears to be that in some instances the sentencer wishes to spare the defendant any actual experience of imprisonment but feels nevertheless that their offence must be seen to attract, symbolically at least, the mark of a custodial sanction. Deserts tempered with mercy. The suspended term will thus continue to find a niche in the space between mainstream imprisonment and community sentencing.

Offence or Offender? Though exceptionality appears more likely to arise from mitigation personal to the offender, the facts of the offence can present exceptional circumstances. For example, in *R v Kondal* (1995) 16 Cr App R(S) 845 a sub-postmistress, described as a woman of 'admirable character', had stolen some £27,000 from the Post Office. Her previous positively good character and her background of domestic and financial problems were not 'exceptional' but the Court of Appeal suspended sentence because she took the money in the reasonable expectation that she could replace it within a very short time as she had applied for a loan. Though clearly a serious breach of trust, her culpability was clearly less substantial.

Provocation The mitigating feature of provocation has sometimes been viewed as a valid basis for exceptionality. In *R v Brookin* (1994) 16 Cr App R(S) 78, the offender, who had received news by telephone that his girlfriend had been attacked, went to the scene with a hammer hidden in his sleeve. Her assailant, by now under arrest in the back of a police car, pulled a face at him. The offender struck him on the head with the hammer through the open car window, causing minor injuries. The Court assessed there to be sufficient provocation both in the period prior to the assault and at the time to justify suspension. Compare, however, *R v Sanderson* (1993) 14 Cr App R(S) 361 where the offender struck the victim on the head with a chisel. The Court upheld six months immediate imprisonment for s20 wounding, indicating that the combination of good character, family circumstances and some measure of provocation were relevant only to the length of sentence and did not justify suspension.

The Graver the Offence, the Greater the Exceptionality Unsurprisingly, the Court has indicated that the more serious the crime, the more exceptional the circumstances will need to be to justify suspension. In *R v Armstrong* [1997] 1 Cr App R(S) 255 Simon Brown LJ said that if the offence was grave, the circumstances must be more than exceptional, they 'must truly be unique'. Mr Armstrong nevertheless met this test. He had been involved in a conspiracy to smuggle a handgun into a prison to assist prisoners to escape. He had subsequently offered valuable assistance to the police and had given evidence against his co-defendants, thus placing his life in considerable danger. Though the Crown Court judge imposed an immediate prison sentence, feeling that he could not suspend sentence, he had invited the defence to appeal. Suspending sentence, the Court of Appeal commented that the judge 'should have had the courage of his convictions'. In a number of cases, the Court has overturned suspended sentences imposed for crimes of significant violence, at the invitation of the Attorney-General, e.g. *Attorney-General's Reference No 45 of 1996* [1997] 1 Cr App R(S) 429 where the offender had used extensive violence against his victim, including banging his head on the pavement and kicking him, fracturing his skull. His previous clean record, the out-of-character nature of his behaviour, his remorse and a degree of provocation did not prevail.

Offender's Ill-Health As a reflection of reported Court of Appeal cases , this is the most likely circumstance to justify suspension, where there is clear medical evidence of the offender's serious mental and/or physical health problems, whether of significance to the offender's state of mind at the time of the offence and/or on the basis of their present health problems, including their capacity to cope with imprisonment. (For the approach generally to ill-health, see Stone, 2000.) Examples include:

R v French (1994) 15 Cr App R(S) 194: a psychiatric report indicated that the offender would become 'significantly depressed' if sent to prison, 'substantially undermining her ability to succeed on release'.

R v Khan (1994) 15 Cr App R(S) 320: a solicitor aged 69, convicted of mortgage fraud, medical reports indicating his paranoid psychosis that had affected his judgement and was a continuing problem.

R v Morrish [1996] 1 Cr App R(S) 215: offender suffering clinical depression at time of VAT fraud and on a continuing basis.

R v Weston [1996] 1 Cr App R(S) 297: man aged 60, of previous good character, convicted of indecent assault of girl aged 13, where he and his wife were suffering 'pitiable' ill-health.

R v Oliver [1997] 1 Cr App R(S) 125: the offender was involved in a shooting incident while awaiting trial for possession of amphetamine with intent to supply. His life was still in danger from a bullet that could not be removed. The Court felt that the case fell 'just on the right side of the dividing line' allowing suspension.

Compare *R v Bradley* (1994) 15 Cr App R(S) 597 where the offender had a history of mental ill-health, and had been suffering severe depression at the time of stealing from her employer. Sentence was reduced but not suspended.

In *R v Murti* [1996] 2 Cr App R(S) 152, a Post Office counter assistant, a mother of two young children who had been suffering post-natal depression at the time of her offending, had allowed other women to cash Benefit giros that she knew to be stolen. She had co-operated fully with the investigation. Her husband had left her, taking their children, and she had tried to commit suicide in prison. Though indicating that suspension was not appropriate, the Court substituted a probation order in place of her immediate prison sentence.

Ill-Health of Third Party Exceptionality may more unusually arise not from the offender's ill-health but from the health needs of someone dependent upon the offender. In *R v Bellikli* [1998] 1 Cr App R(S) 135, the Court suspended sentence imposed for facilitating illegal immigration because the offender's child was very ill and would probably require major surgery in the near future. The offender would be needed to assist medical staff in communicating with the child. In *R v Webb* [2001] 1 Cr App R(S) 112, the Appeal Court was persuaded by a letter from a GP stating that since the offence the offender's grandmother had died, leaving her with responsibility for caring for her grandfather who suffered a chronic lung disease and was also experiencing a severe bereavement reaction. Her care was assessed to offer the only hope of preventing his potentially irreversible deterioration.

Post-Offence Initiatives Taking Priority Exceptionality may arise where the offender has embarked upon some constructive rehabilitative initiative since their offence that is considered to be a legitimate priority. In *R v Cameron* [1993] Crim LR 721 the offender was convicted of physical assault (ABH) of his child aged five (slapping the boy hard enough to cause bruising to his face, arms and buttocks). Social Services indicated that rehabilitative work was underway in what appeared a promising initiative eventually to reunite the children of the family with him. This was considered to meet the children's best interests and the offender was co-operating in a sincere and constructive manner. In *R v Absolam* (unreported, 1994) the offender had pleaded guilty to supplying crack cocaine but by the time of his arrest he had sought and successfully completed treatment for his addiction and was now helping to educate young people about the dangers of drug misuse.

Serious Injury To Offender Resulting from Crime Instances of such 'natural punishment' incurred by the offender as a consequence of their offending (see Stone, 2000: 143) may provide exceptionality. In *R v Snelling* [1996] 2 Cr App R(S) 56 the offender had agreed to help a physically disabled friend who wished to be re-housed to another area, by setting fire to her house. She was trapped in the fire, suffering burns to her back and legs. Given the selfless motive for this arson and the personal consequences for the offender, the Court said that the case fell 'four square' within the power to suspend. This stance is unlikely to be taken readily in cases where it is not uncommon for the offender to be injured as a consequence of their dangerous or reckless misconduct, i.e. in the course of an episode of illegal driving. For example, in *R v Frow* (1995) 16 Cr App R(S) 609 suspension was declined where the offender had incurred serious leg injuries in an episode of dangerous driving.

Recent Use of Suspended Sentences

In the Home Office's recent Crown Court survey (1998), of 1,361 offenders aged 21 or over sentenced in 18 Crown Court centres, 43 (3%) received suspended terms of imprisonment. First offenders were twice as likely to receive this measure as offenders with a prior criminal record (4% as compared with 2%, though the numbers were to small to be statistically significant). Cases involving breach of trust by the offender were three times as likely to receive a suspended sentence, bearing out earlier research by Moxon (1988). The most common reasons given by judges for suspension were:

(a)   defendant's physical or mental illness or addiction;

(b)   defendant's care for dependent relative (two-thirds of those where such responsibility was mentioned being women. In two cases the women were mothers of dependent children and co-defendants of partners who were sent to prison);

(c)   previous good character.

In the parallel Magistrates' Court study, a suspended sentence was the principal sentence in 0.3% of cases in the sample. In interview, justices stated that 'exceptional circumstances' would include: 'family or business reasons', a 'change of attitude' demonstrated by the defendant, and a war veteran suffering from post-traumatic stress syndrome. Mothers of dependent children where immediate imprisonment would cause hardship to their children were the most frequent beneficiaries of suspension. Magistrates were divided in their views of the suspended sentence, some seeing it advantageously as an 'extra strong' and deterrent conditional discharge while others felt that use of suspended sentence, particularly when imposed for want of a more appropriate sentence, created significant difficulties when sentencing the offender on a subsequent occasion.

Suspended Sentence Supervision Order

When passing a suspended sentence for a term of more than six months for a single offence, the court may make a supervision order (SSSO) placing the offender under the supervision of a supervising officer for a period specified in the order, being a period not exceeding the operational period of the sentence: s122(1). Because of the six month minimum term eligible for this additional measure, the effect is that only the Crown Court has power to impose a SSSO. The supervision order must specify the PSA in which the offender resides or will reside and supervision is exercised by a probation officer assigned to that PSA: s122(2).

Obligation An offender subject to a SSSO 'shall keep in touch with the supervising officer in accordance with such instructions as he may from time to time be given by that officer and shall notify him of any change of address': s122(3). Note that the court is not empowered to add additional requirements to a SSSO, whether of a kind that may be included in a probation order or otherwise.

Sentencing Guidance The Court of Appeal has made little comment on the appropriate use of the SSSO but in the pre-CJA 1991 case of *R v Terry* (1992) *The Times* 20 March, the Court indicated that a sentencer should not opt to impose a suspended sentence backed with a supervision order as a means of achieving a 'probation order with teeth'. Firstly, a probation order has teeth of its own and secondly, if the offence does not attract a custodial sentence but can be dealt with by means of a probation order, it would be wrong in principle to impose a suspended sentence, with or without supervision.

Recent Use In the six years 1993–98 since implementation of the 1991 Act, the numbers of persons commencing SSSO supervision have been low but showing a tentative growth in usage: from 322 in 1994 to 562 in 1997, though falling back to 493 in 1999. On 31 December 1999, a total of 755 persons were being supervised (compare 3,249 in 1991).

Detention for Grave Crimes

Though the standard custodial sentence for defendants aged under 18 is the detention and training order (see page 120), intended to avoid prolonged loss of liberty at this stage in young persons' lives, PCC(S)A 2000 ss90 and 91, replacing CYPA 1933 s53, gives a special alternative power to the Crown Court to impose terms of detention for longer periods and upon a wider age range of young offenders where their crime is of a particularly serious nature. Power to detain indefinitely at Her Majesty's pleasure under s90 (formerly s53(1)) on conviction of murder is detailed in Stone (1997) and the following outlines the provisions of s91 (formerly s53(3)). For more detailed consideration, including use of discretionary indeterminate terms of detention, see Ball *et al* (2001).

As the Court of Appeal stated in the leading guideline case of *R v Fairhurst* [1986] 1 WLR 1374, endorsed more recently in *R v Mills* [1998] S Cr App R(S) 128:

115

'On the one hand there exists the desirability of keeping youths under 17 (now 18) out of long terms of custody .... On the other hand it is necessary that serious offences committed by youths of this age should be met with sentences sufficiently substantial to provide both the appropriate punishment and also the necessary deterrent effect, and in certain cases to provide a measure of protection to the public. A balance has to be struck between these objectives.'

The courts have long been anxious to exercise restraint imposing lengthy terms of custody upon youths, conscious 'that it would seem to the young men involved, particularly if they are not outstanding intellectually, that the far end of it is out of sight ... The sentencer should take care to select a duration on which the offender can fix his eye with a view to emerging in the foreseeable future': *R v Storey* (1984) 6 Cr App R(S) 104. That said, the Court of Appeal has been prepared to endorse substantial terms for seriously violent or sexually predatory offences by adolescents. As Macpherson J commented in *R v Powell* (1994) 15 Cr App R(S) 611 in respect of a 16 year old sentenced for rape who had a previous conviction for indecent assault, the offender 'must be able to see light at the end of the tunnel but in these circumstances the tunnel should be a long one so that as much attention can be given to this man as is possible during his teens.' However, a s91 term should not be longer than would be appropriate in the case of imprisonment for an adult convicted of the same offence. On the contrary, mitigation on grounds of youth should ensure that in the clear majority of cases, the term should be of shorter duration. Note that s91 detention may be imposed as a longer than commensurate sentence under PCC(S)A 2000 s80(2)(b) (see page 90) though this will be warranted within this age group only in a small number of exceptional cases.

Eligible Offences

Child or Young Person 10 to under 18: On conviction on indictment of (s91(1)):

(a) 'an offence punishable in the case of a person aged 18 or over with imprisonment for 14 years or more', except where the sentence is fixed by law; or

(b) indecent assault on a woman (SOA 1956 s14: maximum term 10 years); or

(c) indecent assault on a man (SOA 1956 s15).

The most common offences that can attract detention under s91(1) are: robbery, wounding/GBH with intent, burglary of dwelling, aggravated burglary, rape. Thomas (in his commentary on *R v Walsh* [1997] Crim LR 362) has described the determining of sentence availability on the basis of maximum sentence length for an offence as 'bizarre' and leading to 'anomalies, which change as maxima are increased and decreased'. Thus non-residential burglary ceased to be an eligible offence when the maximum penalty was reduced by CJA 1991 from 14 to 10 years. Additionally, it may seem perverse that a s20 offence of wounding by stabbing cannot attract a s91 term but that of handling a stolen knife used for the stabbing is eligible for s91 detention. Note that common law offences such as false imprisonment are not subject to a set maximum sentence and are thus eligible for a s53 term.

Young Person 14 to under 18: On conviction on indictment of (s91(2)):

(a) causing death by dangerous driving (RTA 1988 s1); or

(b)   causing death by careless driving while under the influence of drink or drugs (RTA 1988 s3A).

Note that detention under s91 may only be ordered where the offender has been convicted by the Crown Court on indictment. The Court of Appeal has thus encouraged youth courts to commit appropriate cases to the Crown Court and not to opt to try offences that may merit a s91 term: *R v Learmonth* (1988) 10 Cr App R(S) 229; *R v Mills* [1998] 2 Cr App R(S) 128.

Determining Criterion

The court must be of the opinion 'that none of the other methods in which the case may legally be dealt with is suitable': s91(3).

Statutory Minimum and Maximum Terms

Detention under s91 is subject to no statutory minimum term or any maximum other than that the period shall not exceed the maximum available for the offence.

Section 91: Sentencing Principles

The broad statutory ambit of s91 has been the subject of still evolving case law interpretation, principally in *R v Fairhurst* [1986] 1 WLR 1374, updated by *R v Mills* [1998] 2 Cr App R(S) 128. Much of what follows has concerned the appropriate use of s53 instead of the alternative of YOI detention and will doubtless receive further examination in the light of the new detention and training order. This summary seeks to adapt existing case law to the new sentencing provisions.

(1)   It is not necessary for the crime to be of exceptional gravity (such as attempted murder, manslaughter, wounding with intent, armed robbery).

(2)   In the case of an offender eligible for a DTO, a s91 sentence for a longer period than 24 months available as a DTO should not be imposed 'unless the offence is clearly one calling for a longer sentence': *R v Mills*.

(3)   Though the court should not exceed the 24 month limit without much careful thought, if it concludes that that a longer sentence is required, even if not a much longer sentence, then the court should impose whatever detention period it considers appropriate: *R v Mills*. This view supersedes the previous rule of interpretation that it was generally inappropriate to pass a s53 sentence on a 15–17 year old of less than three years: *R v Wainfur* [1997] 1 Cr App R(S) 43. This rule was based on the belief that it was desirable to have a sentencing 'no-man's-land' of around 12 months to distinguish between the kind of 'ordinary' case attracting YOI and the more unusual case attracting a s53 response. If the case called for a longer sentence than the maximum YOI term but not by a clear margin of difference in length, it was considered preferable for the offender to receive the YOI maximum. So if the sentencer felt that the case deserved more than 24 but less that 36 months, the rule required sentence to be within the YOI ceiling. The problem with this approach was that it created a dilemma for judges faced with an offence deserving, say, four years s53 but with mitigation that justified a reduction of sentence to 30 months. Was it

right for the sentencer to be obliged to drop to 24 months, which could be an inadequate term, or be forced to impose 36 months which could be excessive? In *Mills* the Court of Appeal concluded that 'the result in practice may have been to lead sentencers to pass a higher sentence than they think strictly justified rather than a lower'. The two forms of detention were thus viewed as a continuum and the principle should remain the same now that DTOs have replaced YOI detention.

(4)   Where more than one offence is involved for which s91 detention is possible but the offences vary in seriousness, then provided that at least one offence is sufficiently serious to merit s91 detention, s91 sentences of under two years duration, whether concurrent or consecutive, may properly be imposed in respect of the other offences.

(5)   Where more than one offence is involved and one offence is eligible for s91 detention and another offence is not, yet the latter offence is the more serious offence, *Fairhurst* established that it is not open to the sentencer to get round the lack of availability of s91 power for the more serious offence by imposing s91 detention for the less serious offence unless the more serious offence was 'part and parcel' of the events giving rise to the less serious offence. *R v Brown* (1995) 16 Cr App R(S) 932 illustrated the problem. The offender aged 16 had committed two domestic burglaries and handling (offences eligible for s53 detention) and three burglaries of shops by ram raiding, the latter being the more serious offences yet not eligible for s53. (He had been caught trying to sell stolen items to a second-hand shop being staffed by undercover police officers.) The judge opted to take a 'broad view' of the seriousness of the offences overall and sought to overcome the 12 month ceiling that then operated in respect of the commercial burglaries by imposing three years s53 for the less serious offences, with 'no separate penalty' (see page 228) for the ram raiding. The Court of Appeal appreciated the judge's difficulty but, applying *Fairhurst*, ruled that as the less serious offences on the basis of their gravity could not be said to attract three years or even two years and the ram raiding could not be said to be 'part and parcel' of those offences, they could not be dealt with by a s53 term but only by 12 months YOI. It followed that the ram raiding could be dealt with by a maximum of 12 months YOI.

The defence may suggest that the offence carrying s53 eligibility is the less serious but the court may, of course, view the facts otherwise. Thus in *R v Walsh* [1997] Crim LR 362 where the victim was subjected to a prolonged episode of abuse and degradation leading to prosecution for false imprisonment and s20 wounding, the defence claim that it was wrong to impose s53 detention for false imprisonment because the real gravity lay with the wounding offence was rejected, since the real seriousness lay in holding the victim against her will in terrifying circumstances rather than in her relatively minor injuries. The issue at stake is whether s91 detention can be justified for the offence for which it is imposed. Revisiting the issue in *R v Mills*, the Court of Appeal suggested that the problem has been eased by the provisions of CJA 1991 allowing the sentencer to weigh seriousness in the light of 'associated offences' (see page 74) even if an associated offence is not part and parcel of the main offence and is not eligible for s91 detention.

(6) If one or more offences fell within s53 and merited s53 detention and other offences do not fall within s53 but merited YOI detention, the *Fairhurst* approach was that it is better to impose no separate penalty for the latter matters, the reason being that s53 detention and YOI detention were subject to different provisions regarding early release and credit for time spent in custody before sentence. This approach appears to remain valid under the provisions of s91 juxtaposed with DTO powers, as the two sentences have separate provisions in respect of crediting time spent in custody and eligibility for release. [In *R v Lang* [2001] 2 Cr App R(S) 175 the Appeal Court (in the light of *Hayward and Hayward* – see page 124) ruled that a term of s91 detention may not be imposed to run consecutively to a detention and training order that the young offender is currently serving in custody, since there is no statutory provision permitting this sequence. Any s91 term must thus take immediate effect.]

(7) If the appropriate custodial term for an offender aged 15 or over is 24 months or less, it may still be open to the judge in exceptional circumstances to impose a s91 sentence for that term if there is clear evidence that the kind of detention provision that will be made under a DTO is clearly unsuitable and that there is a place available at another kind of institution willing to receive the defendant if he is subject to a s91 sentence. Such circumstances satisfy the determining criterion or pre-condition of s91(3) (above) that no other method of dealing with the offender is 'suitable', having regard to the welfare principle of CYPA 1933 s44(1): *R v Brown* [1999] 1 WLR 61. This case involved a girl aged 15 convicted of robbery and assault with intent to rob, for whom a place was available at a secure unit and where there was evidence that YOI detention would be detrimental to her development. This principle is likely to apply primarily to 15 year olds as older young offenders are less likely to be placed in alternative accommodation. However, under the new powers of DTOs, recourse to s91 will not generally be necessary in such circumstances because the new sentence allows greater placement flexibility and the Youth Justice Board are seeking to adopt a common approach to the needs of young offenders irrespective of the statutory basis of their sentence.

(8) *Offenders aged under 15*: Where an offender aged under 15 is ineligible for a DTO sentence because he does not meet the eligibility criterion of being a 'persistent offender' (see page 121), a s91 sentence for less than 24 months may be justified for an eligible offence. For example, in *R v McHugh* (1994) 15 Cr App R(S) 192 sentence of 10 months s53 detention was upheld for a boy aged 14 with no previous convictions who had committed two night-time residential burglaries involving aggravating features such as sophisticated means of entry, ransacking, soiling and targeting of an older woman victim. See also *R v Jenkins-Rowe and Glover* [2001] 1 Cr App R(S) 377 where a s91 sentence of 15 months for robbery was imposed on a boy aged 14 of previous good character.

(9) Instances may arise where the offender is eligible for a DTO sentence but the

Crown Court may consider that the proper term is for a period less than 24 months which is not one permitted under the provisions of s101(1) (see page 123). If the court feels unable to reduce the term to fit with that provision, it would appear open to the sentencer to impose s91 detention instead where the offence is within the ambit of s91. In *R v T and F* [2001] 1 Cr App R(S) 294 the Court of Appeal reduced sentence of a girl aged 13 from 30 months to 18 months but retained as a s109 term rather than a DTO as they were informed that a change of sentence status would mean that she could not remain at the secure unit where she was making good progress.

Announcing Sentence

A series of appeal cases established that sentencers must make it explicitly clear that their intention was to impose detention under s53(3): e.g. *R v Venison* (1994) 15 Cr App R(S) 624. In a recent instance, *R v Read* [1999] Crim LR 169, the judge had announced sentence on a 17 year old for aggravated burglary as 'three years YOI', clearly an unintended error. It was not sufficient to pass sentence of, say, three years 'detention', even though a three year term of YOI was not then a lawful sentence for an offender aged under 18. If there was any ambiguity in the sentencer's intent, or error as in *Read*, the defendant was entitled to the benefit and the sentence would be treated as a YOI term, any excess being remitted under CJA 1982 s1B(5). Since implementation of DTO sentencing and the consequent greater differentiation between the names of the alternative sentences the scope for ambiguity or mistake should be much reduced, if not eliminated. A sentence of 'three years DTO' will still be open to challenge as above and the application of s101(5) (see page 123) to remit the excess. In the event of such a mistake, the Crown Court has a time-limited opportunity to re-list the case to allow the incorrect sentence to be altered (see page 236).

Accommodation

Detainees are detained 'in such place and under such conditions as the Secretary of State may direct or may arrange with any person': s92(1). This flexibility in principle allows allocation between residential child care establishments, secure training centres and Prison Service provision for young persons, according to the best interests of the offender, in the light of their vulnerability, balanced against the protection of the public, subject inevitably to available resources. Generally speaking, accommodation outside Prison Service facilities should be made available for boys aged under 15 and girls aged under 16.

Recent Use of s53(3)

In 1999 a total of 607 young offenders received terms under s53(3), down from 724 in 1997. Of these, 258 received their sentence for robbery, by far the most common offence to attract such a sentence, followed by 111 for violence and 101 for burglary. The clear majority of sentences attracted terms either of over two years up to three years (266) or over three years and up to four years (128).

Detention and Training Orders

Introduced by CDA 1998 ss73–79 to replace what the 1997 White Paper *No More Excuses* viewed as a 'chaotic and dysfunctional' approach to custodial sentences for young offenders, the detention and training order, now incorporated in PCC(S)A 2000 ss100-106, is the new generic custodial sentence for offenders aged under 18. It replaces the YOI sentence for this age group and also the secure training order for 12–14 year olds. However, detention under CYPA s53, now PCC(S)A 2000 s91, is not affected. The sentence is characterised by (a) its availability across the full age range of young offenders; (b) the flexibility it affords regarding the kind of institution and accommodation in which sentence is served, so that allocation can reflect needs rather than the nature of the sentence imposed; (c) discretion in determining the point of release; (d) the greater emphasis given to supervision after release as an integral part of sentence rather than a subsidiary postscript to the 'real' sanction. Though the statutory provisions apply also to young offenders aged 10–11, such application is being held in reserve and will be extended to that age group 'only if should prove necessary or desirable'. Such extension will require an affirmative resolution by Parliament, not simply the Home Secretary's discretion.

Definition and Status A DTO 'is an order that the offender .... shall be subject, for the term specified in the order, to a period of detention and training followed by a period of supervision': s100(3). The DTO is a 'custodial sentence' for the purposes of the threshold and procedural provisions of PCC(S)A 2000 ss79–83: s76(1)(e).

Power to Impose a DTO

Courts to which available The Crown Court, youth courts.

Offence for which available Any offence punishable with imprisonment in the case of a person aged 18 or over: s100(1)(a).

Criteria to be satisfied The court must be of the opinion that the offence is 'so serious that only such a sentence can be justified' and/or in the case of a violent or sexual offence 'that only such a sentence would be adequate to protect the public from serious harm' from the offender: PCC(S)A s79(2)(a) and (b). Alternatively (and rarely), the provisions of s79(3) (allowing use of a custodial sentence where the offender does not express willingness to comply with a proposed community sentence that requires such consent) must be satisfied.

In addition, further gate-keeping criteria apply in respect of offenders aged under 15 at time of *conviction* (note, not the time of committing the offence) to try to ensure that sentencers do not make inappropriate use of custody for younger juveniles.

Offender under 15 at time of conviction: A DTO shall not be imposed unless the court 'is of the opinion that he is a persistent offender' (s100(2)(a)). The statute does not provide a definition of 'persistent' (for example, by replicating the criteria under CJPOA 1994 justifying imposition of a secure training order: conviction of three or more imprisonable offences and breach of a supervision order). There is no requirement that the offender should have been previously convicted, as instanced in *R v C* [2001] 1 Cr App R(S) 415, in respect of a 14 year old who had been bailed for a burglary and being carried in a vehicle taken without consent. He went on to commit two further burglaries and an aggravated vehicle taking. Though he had not been convicted before, the Court of Appeal had no difficulty in concluding that he satisfied the criterion and was thus properly sentenced to detention and training. The Court ruled that the definition of 'persistence' adopted in a 1998 Home Office Circular on *Tackling Delays in the Youth Justice System* (*i.e.* having been sentenced on three or more separate occasions) is not pertinent in this different context and it is for a court to decide the issue on the basis of the facts of each individual case. In *R v S* [2001] 1 Cr App R(S) 62 (reported as *R v Smith* [2000] Crim LR 613) the Appeal Court was satisfied that a 14 year old boy without previous convictions was a persistent offender on the basis of an episode of offending committed over a period of 24 hours, involving the robbery of other boys, one of whom was detained, bullied and subjected to indignities, offences that could have attracted 'grave crimes' detention.

A court is able to have regard to offences for which the offender has been cautioned (and, by implication, reprimanded or warned under CDA 1998) in forming the opinion that he is a persistent offender: *R v D* [2001] 1 Cr App R(S) 202, where a boy aged 14 was held to be properly sentenced to a DTO for a domestic burglary and handling goods stolen in a similar offence, having been cautioned three times prior to this first-time prosecution. The sentencer can also have regard to offences committed after the offence for which a DTO is being considered: *R v B.* [2001] 1 Cr App R(S) 389, where a boy without previous convictions, aged 12 at time of committing a domestic burglary, had since been cautioned for being carried in a vehicle taken without consent and for possessing cannabis, both matters committed since the burglary, thus providing basis for finding 'persistence'. The Appeal Court stated that to qualify as a persistent offender it is not necessary that the juvenile 'should have been committing a string of offences either of the same or similar character, or that his failure to address his offending arises by his failure to comply with previous orders of the court.

Some sense of the limits to which the term 'persistent' can be stretched is given by *R v D* (not yet reported but noted in *Justice of the Peace* (2000) vol 164 at 870). Convicted of affray, the offender had a previous conviction and a caution, both for handling. He was also awaiting sentence in another court for riding a motorcycle taken without consent. The Court of Appeal held that though the term 'persistent' could apply to defendants without previous convictions who had committed a number of offences within a short period of time, here the notion of 'persistence' had been stretched too far, given the different nature of his previous criminal conduct from his present offence.

Offender under 12 at time of conviction In addition to the 'persistence' criterion (above), the court must also be of the opinion 'that only a custodial sentence would be adequate to protect the public from further offending by him' (s100(2)(b)(i)).This criterion replicates the ground justifying custody in PCC(S)A 2000 s79(2)(b) but without being tied to sexual or violent offending. Additionally, an offender aged under 12 shall not receive a DTO sentence unless the offence was committed on or after the date appointed by the Home Secretary: s100(2)(b)(ii). This is intended to delay the exercise of this power for this age group unless and until adequate accommodation is available for such young children.

On making a DTO in respect of an offender aged under 15, the court has a duty under s100(4) to state in open court that it is of the opinion mentioned in s100(2)(a) or (in the case of a child under 12) both in s100(2)(a) and (2)(b)(i). This is to ensure that sentencers have actively fulfilled the obligation to assess that the respective criteria are satisfied.

Length The minimum term of DTO is 4 months and the maximum term (for a single offence or in aggregate) is 24 months.

A court cannot impose a term of less than four months for an offence, even though the aggregate sentence amounts to four months or longer, since the minimum applies to a single offence. In consequence, a DTO is not permissible for offences carrying a maximum sentence of less than four months, e.g. being found on enclosed premises.

The permitted maximum is qualified by s101(2) which specifies that the term of a DTO 'may not exceed the maximum term of imprisonment that the Crown Court could (in the case of an offender aged 18 or over) impose for the offence'. Note that this provision increases the sentencing powers of youth courts, giving them the same powers to impose DTOs as the Crown Court: *R v Medway Youth Court, ex parte A* [2000] 1 Cr App R(S) 191. As a consequence, the former power to commit under 18s for sentence under MCA 1980 s37 has been repealed. This provision may be challenged as in conflict with the Human Rights Act 1998 on the basis that juvenile offenders are at a disadvantage in comparison with offenders aged 18 or older who cannot be sentenced for a single offence to longer than six months by a magistrates' court and may thus feel that their right to a 'fair trial' under Article Six of the European Convention has been compromised.

Terms of intermediate length must be for a period permitted by s101(1), i.e. 6, 8, 12 or 18 months. This unusual and somewhat inflexible specification of permissible sentence lengths may cause difficulties 'where a court has to deal with a number of defendants and wishes to distinguish between them according to their culpability, or wishes to give credit for an early guilty plea' (Thomas, 1998).

Consecutive Sentences A court making a DTO 'may order that its term shall commence on the expiry of the term of any other DTO made by that court or any other court': s101(3). However, 'a court shall not make ... a DTO the effect of which would be that the offender would be subject to DTOs for a term which exceeds 24 months': s101(4). If the court imposes in error an aggregate term exceeding 24 months, 'the excess shall be treated as remitted': s101(5). (This means that a Crown Court sentencer seeking to impose a term exceeding 24 months for an eligible offence under PCC(S)A 2000 s91 should be explicit and unambiguous in announcing sentence, otherwise the offender may be entitled to the benefit of the doubt and remission of the excess (see page 120). Further, a court making a DTO may not order that its term shall commence on the expiry of an existing DTO in respect of which the period of supervision in the community has commenced: s101(6).

It is now clear that in imposing consecutive terms of DTO a court is able to impose a total term of a length not permitted by s101(1). In *R v Norris* [2001] 1 Cr App R(S) 401 an offender aged 16 serving a term of 10 months faced further sentence for an additional offence. The judge had felt constrained to impose an additional eight months in order to comply with the sub-section (the alternative would have been an additional two months). However, the Court of Appeal resolved the matter pragmatically, declaring that the unfairness this caused the offender was a greater injustice than any disruption to the modular concept of s101(1). A term of six months was substituted, thus making an aggregate term of 16 months.

A court dealing with two or more summary offences is able to impose DTOs totalling longer than six months in aggregate, even though this is not possible in the case of an adult (see page 77). This was held lawful by the Divisional Court in *C v DPP* [2001] Crim LR 671, in an appeal by case stated against a decision of a youth court to impose DTO terms of four months and six months consecutive for two offences of driving while disqualified. Though the court appreciated that a young offender aged under 18 can end up with a custodial sentence longer than an adult co-defendant can receive either from a magistrates' court or the Crown Court, it attributed this differentiation to 'the very special nature and objectives of a DTO ... which are very distinct from those of imprisonment in the case of an adult'.

Where the offender is already serving a sentence of detention under s91 and remains in custody under that sentence, it is not open to a court to make a detention and training order, to be served concurrently with or consecutively to the earlier sentence. This was confirmed in *R v Hayward and Hayward* [2001] 2 Cr App R(S) 149, where two brothers had committed an affray while the younger was on bail for s18 GBH for which he was subsequently sentenced to five years' detention. The Court of Appeal considered the consecutive term of 10 months' DTO entirely justified for the affray but not a lawful option because of a lacuna or gap in the law. There was thus no alternative but to quash the DTO sentence and make no separate penalty, with the result that the offender would be treated for the purposes of punishment as if he had not committed the affray. The court acknowledged that this would create a sense of injustice not only for the victim and the public but for the young offender's older brother (who had been sentenced to 18 months' YOI – then available to the sentencer – so that his term was reduced to nine months to reflect that injustice).

Relevance of Time in Custody In determining the term of a DTO, the court 'shall take account of any period for which the offender has been remanded in custody', including time held in police detention, in secure accommodation under CYPA 1969 s23, or detained in hospital under MHA 1983 ss35, 36, 38 or 48, 'in connection with the offence or any other offence the charge for which was founded on the same facts or evidence': s101(8)–(11). In other words, such time should be reflected in the sentence passed rather than being left to be taken into account in calculating the time actually to be served. The reason for this is to ensure that the young offender spends a period of training in detention prior to the supervisory element. If time on remand took effect in the same way as applies to other custodial sentences, the offender might be eligible for immediate release, contrary to the intention behind this measure. Though this aim is understandable, the provision creates practical difficulties when courts take account of time in custody while determining a sentence length that accords with the permitted terms of DTO specified by s101(1). The Divisional Court in *R v Inner London Youth Court, ex parte I* (2000) *The Times* 12 May, approved by the Court of Appeal in *R v B*. [2001] 1 Cr App R(S) 303, has indicated that 'taking account' does not require a court to reflect the time spent in custody in a precise way or to give mathematically accurate 'one-for-one' discount, let alone a 'two-for-one' reduction. In *R v Fieldhouse and Watts* [2001] 1 Cr App R(S) 361, where the defendants had spent a weekend in custody on remand prior to them receiving DTOs of 24 and 12 months, the Appeal Court stated that such short periods of remand can be ignored, particularly where the proper term is one of the longer periods permitted for a DTO, 18 or 24 months. If a significant time has been spent on custodial remand, the proper approach is to reduce if possible the sentence otherwise appropriate. It will depend on all the circumstances of the particular case, including the apparent impact if any on the offender of the period in custody. If the appropriate term was one of four months, it might be right to conclude that a non-custodial sentence is justified. If 18 or 24 months is appropriate, a court may well conclude that no reduction can properly be made. As Thomas suggests in his Commentary ([2000] Crim LR 1021), the implication seems to be that 'if the time to be taken into account is approximately equal to the interval between two of the permissible terms (in terms of the time to be served), then the lower of the two terms should be chosen', whereas if that time is substantially less than the interval, then it should be ignored.

Detention and Training Period

Accommodation The detention phase of sentence is served 'in such secure accommodation' as may be determined by the Secretary of State or other authorised person: s102(1). Accommodation is approved and allocated by the Youth Justice Board which operates a clearing house to ensure expedited allocation of resources.

Detention as Proportion of Order The offender's detention and training period 'shall be one-half of the term of the order': s102(2), subject to the Home Secretary's power to authorise earlier release on compassionate grounds (s102(3)). However, some degree of variation is allowed.

Release Prior to Half-way Point The Home Secretary is empowered by s102(4) to allow release prior to the half-way point (as a mark of good progress, though this is not spelt out in the statute), depending on the length of the DTO: (a) terms of 8 months or more but less than 18 months, one month before the half-way point; (b) terms of 18 months or more, two months before the half-way point.

Release After the Half-way Point This power of delay is not at the Home Secretary's discretion but s102(5) empowers the youth court, on an application by the Home Secretary, to order the offender's release at a later point of sentence (to reflect poor progress, though this is not spelt out by the statute), depending on the length of the DTO: (a) terms of 8 months or more but less than 18 months, one month after the half-way point; (b) terms of 18 months or more, one month or two months after the half-way point. This provision does not identify which youth court(s) have jurisdiction to hear such applications or specify any procedural rules. The court is not obliged to accede to the Home Secretary's application and the offender will have the opportunity to be heard if he opposes the application.

Supervision Period

Supervision commences at the offender's release and normally ends when the term of the order ends (s103(1)), though supervision may cease at an earlier point if the Home Secretary authorises this: s103(2).

Supervising Agency Supervision shall be undertaken by either a probation officer, a local authority social services social worker or a YOT member, as shall be determined by the Home Secretary: s103(3). If a probation officer is designated, the officer shall be one assigned to the PSA in which the offender resides for the time being: s103(4). If a YOT member or social worker is responsible, this shall be one appointed by the local authority within whose area the offender resides for the time being: s76(5). In practice, supervision will almost invariably be exercised by YOTs.

Supervision Requirements Prior to commencement of the supervision period, the offender shall be given a notice specifying (a) the category of their supervisor and (b) any requirements with which he must for the time being comply: s103(6) and (7). In the event of any subsequent alterations to (a) or (b), the offender shall be given a notice accordingly before any alteration comes into effect: s76(7)(b). Standard Notice of Supervision requirements are as specified in the joint Home Office/LCD/Youth Justice Board Circular of 30 March 2000:

'While under supervision, you must:

(a)   keep in touch with your supervisor in accordance with any reasonable instructions which he may give you;

(b)   receive visits from your supervisor in your home in accordance with any reasonable instructions which he may give you;

(c)   reside at [address] and tell your supervisor if you are going to move;

(d)   only take a job if your supervisor says you can and not change jobs unless your supervisor says you can;

(e)   not travel outside the UK without telling your supervisor;

(f)   not commit any further offences;

(g)   comply with any additional requirements (as attached).'

Enforcement Breach of supervision requirements is regulated by s104 which provides that an allegation of failure to comply shall be initiated by information. Jurisdiction lies with a court acting for the PSA in which the offender resides and also, in the case of a youth court order, with a court acting for the same PSA: s77(2). If breach is established, the court has power either to order the offender's detention in secure accommodation as determined by the Home Secretary, 'for such period, not exceeding the shorter of three months or the remainder of the DTO term', or to impose a fine not exceeding £1,000. Enforcement issues are outlined in detail in Stone (1999).

Detention in Young Offender Institution

Detention in a young offender institution has been the primary custodial sentence for young offenders aged under 21 since its introduction under CJA 1988, amending CJA 1982. CDA 1998 amended the legislation, replacing YOI detention for the under-18s by the detention and training order, as outlined at page 120, leaving YOI as the only form of custodial sentence for those aged 18 to under 21, with the sole exception of custody for life under CJA 1982 s8 (later replaced by PCC(S)A 2000 s94). Power to impose YOI detention was incorporated in PCC(S)A 2000 s96 but, following a Home Office Consultation Paper (1999), the 2000 Act has been rapidly amended by CJCSA 2000 to abolish both YOI detention and custody for life as distinct custodial sentences for young adults, so that those in this age group are subject to imprisonment in the same way as other adults. The Paper argued that to retain the distinctive YOI sentence meant also retention of a division of the prison estate catering for young adults, making it difficult to locate this age group near their homes and to gain best value from regime activities and programmes. The duplication of facilities and resources demanded by a separate sentence did not make economic sense. It was proposed that as adult status is attained at age 18 in the community this should be reflected in prison arrangements. It was recognised that some 18–20 year olds are still quite vulnerable but it was pointed out that some adults have similar problems and a more flexible scheme would allow the development of appropriate regimes to cater for individuals by need rather than by age. The consequence of this step can be summarised thus:

Minimum Term The provision of PCC(S)A 2000 s97(2) specifying a minimum term of YOI detention of 21 days ceases to apply.

Suspension of Sentence Whereas a sentence of YOI detention could not be suspended, the provisions of PCC(S)A 2000 s118 (see page 109) apply to imprisonment imposed on offenders aged under-21.

Liability to Supervision on Release A continuing differentiation for this age group is that those serving terms of imprisonment remain liable to supervision requirements under CJA 1991 s65 (see Stone, 1999 Chapter 14) which is amended by CJCSA 2000 Sch 6 para 98 to apply to imprisonment where the offender is released while under the age of 22, subject to any liability to early release licence.

Victim Contact Duties

Under CJCSA 2000 s69, where an offender is convicted of a sexual or violent offence and receives a custodial sentence of 12 months or longer (including a detention and training order or detention under PCC(S)A 2000 s91) the local probation board for the area in which the offender is sentenced must 'take all reasonable steps to ascertain whether any appropriate person' (defined as 'any person who appears to be, or to act for, the victim of the offence') wishes to:

(a)   make representations about whether the offender should be subject to any conditions or requirements on his release and, if so, what conditions or requirements; or

(b)   receive information about any conditions or requirements to which the offender is to be subject on his release.

Any representations must be forwarded to the person responsible for determining release conditions/requirements.

A 'sexual or violent offence' in this context includes those within the definitions given on pages 91-92, an offence in respect of which an offender is subject to notification requirements under SOA 1997 and also 'an offence against a child', as designated by CJCSA 2000 Sch 4.

This victim contact service must be offered from 1 April 2001 and has been the subject of *Victim Contact Work: Guidance for Probation Areas* (National Probation Service, 2001).

5
COMMUNITY SENTENCES

This chapter combines together non-custodial measures that share the designation and status of community orders, for juveniles only, for adults or for offenders across the age range, together with the applicable generic provisions.

General Provisions

A 'community sentence' is defined simply as 'a sentence which consists of or includes one or more community orders': PCC(S)A 2000 s33(1). In the years immediately preceding CJA 1991, a number of academic commentators (e.g. Wasik and von Hirsch, 1988; Bottoms, 1989) had tried to promote the concept of 'intermediate sanctions' within a 'deserts' framework of sentencing, exploring ways in which non-custodial measures could be posed in terms of their 'intrusiveness' (into the offender's time, choice or autonomy) or their quality of 'compromising' the offender's freedom, physical integrity, psychological well-being or reputation. Other writers (e.g. Raynor, 1997) have sought a more purposeful rationale for community punishment beyond a rather sterile notion of the graduated infliction of harm or pain, emphasising instead the positive scope for reducing the risk of re-offending, for reparation (direct and indirect), reintegration and reattachment to consensus values. (For a recent review of the complexities of locating community sanctions within a hierarchy of sanctions that reflects not only deserts but also denunciation, humanity, efficacy and appropriateness, see Lovegrove (2001) and a response to Lovegrove by Wasik and von Hirsch.)

The 1991 Act had sought to give a new, generic status to a number of already familiar non-custodial measures (and one new one – the curfew order) as a distinctive second tier of punishment in the framework of sentencing. It did not attempt to characterise the measures that were thus corralled but it was clear from the preceding White Paper *Crime, Justice and Protecting the Public* (1990) what unifying features were intended:

(a) partial but nevertheless substantial restriction of liberty;

(b) discipline demanded of offenders, usually extending over a number of months, requiring a real measure of responsibility for fulfilling sentence requirements;

(c) consistent enforcement and 'holding to account'.

The White Paper indicated (para 4.4) that 'it is the loss of liberty involved in carrying out the terms of the order, rather than the activities carried out during the order which is the punishment'. Much effort had previously been expended to promote some of these measures (particularly CS) as credible 'alternatives to custody' but the White Paper concluded that this was confusing, unhelpful and futile because (a) it implied that custody was 'the true benchmark of punishment', and (b) it was 'an unpersuasive fiction to pretend that the equivalent of custody could be achieved in the community'. Community punishment was therefore to be promoted and valued in its own right, allowing more offenders, 'particularly those convicted of property crime and less serious offences of violence', to be dealt with credibly but non-custodially.

In a later Green Paper *Strengthening Punishment in the Community* (1995), the Home Office proposed that all community orders to be subsumed within a single sanction, 'the community sentence', giving courts the discretion to decide on the ingredients of sentence on a bespoke basis in each case, to reflect the threefold aims of restriction of liberty, reparation and prevention of offending. This proposal was comprehensively criticised (see Ashworth *et al*, 1995) and was not pursued, though some of this thinking re-emerged under the Labour Government in the action plan order for young offenders (see page 183).

More recently, the distinctive nature of community sentencing as a restriction of liberty imposed for offences of a certain minimum level of seriousness has been somewhat eroded by the introduction under C(S)A 1997 of power to impose community service and curfew orders as an alternative to a fine for 'petty persistent offenders' (see page 193) and the creation of two new measures for juveniles, the reparation order and the referral order, making active demands on the time and energies of young offenders outside of the framework of community sentencing.

The provisions pertaining to the individual orders are outlined separately later in this chapter but the following seeks to provide the generic legal foundation applicable to all community orders/sentences.

Designated Community Orders

An order has the status of community order by designation as such in the list given in PCC(S)A 2000 s33(1). The list is not static and the cartel was expanded from six to eight orders by CDA 1998, as follows: (a) curfew order; (b) community rehabilitation order; (c) community punishment order; (d) community punishment and rehabilitation order; (e) drug treatment and testing order; (f) attendance centre order; (g) supervision order; (h) action plan order. CJCSA 2000 adds: (aa) exclusion order; (ee) drug abstinence order. Not all offenders are eligible for all ten orders; only 16–17 year olds are eligible for any community order (save a drug abstinence order).

As s33(2) makes clear, there is a distinction between a 'community order' and a 'community sentence'. A community sentence may consist of a single community order but may also consist of more than one order, albeit imposed for a single offence. The only restrictions explicitly imposed upon combining orders in a sentence are specified as follows:

Community Punishment and Rehabilitation Orders Under PCC(S)A 2000 s35(2): '... a community sentence shall not consist of or include both a community rehabilitation order and a community punishment order'. This exception is 'in consequence of the provision made by s51 with respect to community punishment and rehabilitation orders.'

Action Plan Orders Under PCC(S)A 2000 s69(5): 'The court shall not make an action plan order ... if it proposes to make in respect of him a community rehabilitation order, community punishment order, community punishment and rehabilitation order, supervision order or attendance centre order.'

With regard to any other combinations of measures, the sentencer is obliged to consider issues of commensurability and suitability (see below) and also to fall back on the general sentencing principle that 'courts should avoid mixing sentences which fall into well established and different categories': *R v McElhorne* (1983) 5 Cr App R(S) 53. Suggestions are made in respect of the different orders about the merits of various tandem measures, but it is worth noting here a general difficulty that s33 appears to overlook that if more than one order is imposed for a single offence and subsequently one of the orders is revoked with a view to re-sentencing, for example following non-compliance, the re-sentencing court is faced with certain conceptual difficulties if another order remains in force, particularly if the court now proposes to impose a custodial term. For example, if X is sentenced to a community service order of 120 hours and a curfew order of ten hours daily for three months, and the former order is revoked but the latter is proceeding satisfactorily, what proportion of the offence's seriousness should be assumed to have been reflected in the CSO? Such dilemmas suggest that liberal mixing of orders in single sentences is not to be encouraged and sentencers appear to have had little enthusiasm for this facility. However, the increasing availability of the curfew order, the most obvious pairing partner for both community rehabilitation and community punishment orders, may muddy the waters somewhat.

The Threshold Criterion: 'Serious Enough'

PCC(S)A 2000 s35(1) specifies:

> A court shall not pass on an offender a community sentence ... unless it is of the opinion that the offence, or a combination of the offence and one or more offences associated with it, was serious enough to warrant such a sentence.

In forming such opinion, the court 'shall take into account all such information as is available to it about the circumstances of the offence or (as the case may be) of the offence or offences associated with it, including any aggravating or mitigating factors': s36(1). For the mandatory requirement under PCC(S)A 2000 s151(2) to regard offending while on bail as an aggravating factor, see page 79. For the mandatory requirement under PCC(S)A 2000 s153 to regard a racially aggravated offence as more serious, see page 79.

The concept of a distinctive 'community' tier of sentencing is only as strong as the respect and attention paid by sentencers in gate-keeping the threshold. While attention at appeal court level has focused, understandably, upon the custody threshold (see page 70), little or no effort has been made to regulate this boundary – no community sentence version of the 'right-thinking person' test has been forthcoming. In part this reflects the comparative infrequency of appeals against community sentences – the defendant is glad to be at liberty and will usually lack the appetite for further encounters with the judiciary, even if retaining a residual feeling that their penalty was on the high side. But it also appears to reflect a judicial tendency to regard non-custodial measures in an unduly flexible and elastic way, perhaps prompted by the hope or belief that the measure imposed will do some good. *R v Bond* (1994) 15 Cr App R(S) 430 is a case in point. The Court of Appeal had no difficulty in setting aside the term of imprisonment imposed for theft of bacon value £3.50 on the basis that such petty crime came nowhere near satisfying the 'so serious' threshold, but proceeded to impose a sentence of 12 months probation, apparently prompted by the offender's personal problems and anxieties. *R v Cordner* (1992) 13 Cr App R(S) 570 gave a pre-CJA 1991 flavour of the appeal court's reluctance to regulate the threshold for community order sentences, appeal against a 100 hour CSO for theft of 50 pence from a ticket machine being dismissed.

Two more recent cases throw some light on the tenuousness of the 'serious enough' boundary. *R v T and Others* [1999] 2 Cr App R(S) 304 concerned consensual homosexual offences between several adult men occurring in a private home, for which the appellants had been made subject to community sentences, against which they appealed, arguing that they should have received either absolute or conditional discharges. These offences had come to light when amateur videotape of their activities had been found in a police raid. Though the Appeal Court considered that videoed sex acts involving groups of men, sometimes between 'virtual strangers', amounting to what the court considered to be 'orgies', were 'serious enough' to warrant community sentences, the particular community sentences imposed were viewed as 'too onerous' in terms of restriction of liberty, given that none of the appellants had previous convictions for sexual offences. The Court determined that 'the more punitive element of community service was unnecessary' and so the CSOs were quashed and (by implication less punitive) probation orders substituted. In the case of one appellant considered unsuitable for probation, a conditional discharge was substituted. This dubious differentiation between different kinds of orders is considered further at page 133. In *R v Hughes* [1999] 2 Cr App R(S) 329, a man aged 22 of previous good character appealed against imposition of a community service order of 80 hours for possession of 1.3 grams of cannabis, arguing that an offence of this nature usually attracted a fine. The Court upheld the use of a community sentence, asserting that the 'serious enough' test was satisfied, but reducing his sentence to 40 hours. On the basis of these two cases the threshold appears to be low to the point where it may be doubted whether it offers any distinctive discriminative meaning.

The issue is thrown into greater relief by the power introduced by C(S)A 1997 for courts to impose CSOs and curfew orders upon 'petty persistent offenders' for offences that would otherwise attract fines (see page 193). On the one hand this may appear to weaken the currency of two major community orders but, on the other, it obliges magistrates to think harder about the boundary between the fine and the community sentence and to become more conscious of cases that do not meet the 'serious enough' criterion.

Note that s35(1) does not require the court to impose a community sentence if the offence(s) are 'serious enough' to warrant such a sentence. The court still retains discretion to opt instead for a lesser sentence or alternative order, for example in the light of mitigation not related to the offence in the light of s158(1) (see page 38). Similarly, the offence(s) may be of sufficient seriousness to pass the custody threshold under s79(2)(a) (see page 70) but 'there is sufficient mitigation to lead the court to impose a community sentence': *R v Oliver* [1993] 1 WLR 177. However, in a number of instances where the Attorney-General has referred community sentences to the Court of Appeal on grounds of undue leniency (see page 245), the Court has held that it is impossible to justify any other sentence than custody for certain very serious crimes, despite the existence of personal mitigation.

Determining the Nature and Extent of a Community Sentence

If the court is of the opinion that the offence(s) are 'serious enough' to warrant a community sentence, it must determine the nature and extent of that sentence with reference to two considerations specified by s35(3): (i) 'commensurability', to determine the extent of restriction of the offender's liberty; (ii) 'suitability', to determine the particular order appropriate for the offender. As Rex (1998) puts it, desert determines the size of the penalty; suitability then dictates its form. The thought process asked of the sentencer appears logically to focus first on resolving the appropriate restrictiveness justified by offence seriousness, moving on to assessing the kind of order of that level of restrictiveness that is most appropriate to match the individual offender. In fact, s35(3) places suitability (s35(3)(a)) sequentially before commensurability (s35(3)(b)), though this sequence need not be regarded conclusively as of purposeful or determining significance.

Commensurability: '... the restrictions on liberty imposed by the order or orders shall be such as in the opinion of the court are commensurate with the seriousness of the offence, or the combination of the offence and one or more offences associated with it': s35(3)(b). In forming this opinion the court *shall*, once again, 'take into account all such information as is available to it about the circumstances of the offence or (as the case may be) of the offence and the offence or offences associated with it, including any aggravating or mitigating factors': s36(1).

Suitability: '... the particular order or orders comprising or forming part of the sentence shall be such as in the opinion of the court is, or taken together are, the most suitable for the offender': s35(3)(a). In forming such opinion, a court *'may* take into account any information about the offender which is before it': s36(2).

As the Act does not specify which objective should take priority, Wasik and Taylor (1991), writing prior to date of implementation, suggested that the most coherent way of tackling any conflict between the two would be:

'... to say that the most suitable community order should be selected for the offender but only imposed if this does not impose a more onerous burden upon the offender than is justified by the seriousness of the offence. This would be to treat "seriousness" as a limiting factor and would be in accord with the underlying principle of desert. It must be conceded, however, that sentencers will be faced with major problems in satisfying the requirements of s6(2), particularly where a mixture of different community orders is proposed. It seems that sentencers will be left very much on their own to resolve these problems and ... there is no existing framework of Court of Appeal decisions on community sentencing to guide them.'

In other words, 'seriousness' should determine the ceiling of restrictiveness but 'suitability' (or appropriateness) may suggest a less restrictive sentence.

Several years on, no clearer framework has emerged and sentencers are left to exercise their common-sense without undue concern about the fine tuning of community orders. As Rex (1998) commented, 'desert constraints have tended to be confined to the somewhat elastic upper and lower limits to the community sentence band', leaving sentencers to pursue crime preventative aims between those limits. She adds:

'The failure, both by the Act and by the courts, to give priority to the requirements of proportionality has contributed to a tendency for community orders to slip back into the role of "alternatives to custody", in which the need to prove their effectiveness has become more important than their restrictiveness.'

It is difficult to see how the 'principle of desert' can readily be applied as a limiting factor in practice. For a start, the Act does not offer any gradated scale of community orders according to their degree of restrictiveness and it is very difficult to weigh 240 hours CS work against a curfew order requiring the offender to remain at home at night for ten hours daily for three months (a total of 910 hours) or a probation requirement to live in a probation hostel for the first three months of a 12 month order (2,184 hours). All sentences impinge differently upon offenders, subjectively speaking, but this is particularly true of community measures. A night-time curfew sanction for a middle aged and middle class offender who normally remains indoors in the evenings with their family will be received as a very different experience than the same penalty for a 21 year old living alone in a bedsit. The impact of the very individual demand posed by a standard probation order will be very hard to conceive in comparative terms of 'desert' and restriction, with or without the aid of the minimum contact rate set by *National Standards*. And if the sentencer is invited to consider an offender's suitability for a probation group work programme, the sanction will need to be set in terms of the design and integrity of the programme, not by some precise judgement about proportionality and commensurability. One is left only with some very broad notions of appropriate interpretation, such as Raynor's (1997) suggestion: 'no proportional sentence should be artificially inflated simply to make even a possibly effective programme available, since this would conflict both with the empirically-based principle of targeting high-risk offenders and with the moral principle of fairness or treating like cases alike'. For an attempt by the Court of Appeal to place community service above probation supervision on a scale of punitiveness, see *R v T* (above).

Role for Pre-Sentence Report

Whereas the court is required to obtain and consider a PSR (for the statutory definition of and other provisions relating to PSRs, see page 6) in forming an opinion of the seriousness of the offence in relation to the 'so serious' threshold of s79(2) and the length of custodial term that is commensurate with offence seriousness (see page 77), the equivalent provisions for community sentencing ascribe a less prominent role to the PSR. Consideration of a report is not required in forming either a s35(1) opinion or a s35(3)(b) opinion. However, a court *shall* obtain and consider a PSR 'before forming an opinion as to the suitability for the offender of one or more of the following orders' (s36(4)): a community rehabilitation order with an additional requirement under PCC(S)A 2000 Sch 2; a drug treatment and testing order; a CPO; a CPR order; a supervision order with an additional requirement under PCC(S)A 2000 Sch 6. This provision is qualified by s36(5) which provides that 's36(4) does not apply if, in the circumstances of the case, the court is of the opinion that it is unnecessary to obtain a PSR'. This is then further qualified by s36(6) that in the case of an offender aged under 18, save where the offence or any of the associated offences is triable only on indictment, the court shall not reach the opinion that a PSR is unnecessary 'unless there exists a previous PSR obtained in respect of the offender and the court has had regard to the information contained in that report, or, if there is more than one such report, the most recent report'.

Note that in cases where a PSR is required (unless the court considers a report to be unnecessary) the court must make an active decision to proceed without a report. Mere oversight of the requirement does not suffice. However, a community sentence imposed without either a report or this opinion is not invalid. PCC(S)A 2000 s36(7) specifies that 'no community sentence which consists of or includes such an order as is mentioned in s36(3) shall be invalidated by the failure of a court to obtain and consider a PSR', but any court on an appeal against that sentence shall obtain and consider such a report. This obligation upon the appeal court is qualified by s36(8) which allows the appellate court to dispense with a report if of the opinion:

(a)   that the court below was justified in forming an opinion that it was unnecessary to obtain a PSR; or

(b)   that, although the court below was not justified in forming that opinion, in the circumstances of the case at the time it is before the court, it is unnecessary to obtain a PSR.

Home Office research (Charles *et al*, 1997) on the exercise of sentencing without a report reported that both magistrates and judges rarely passed a community sentence without first considering a PSR, dispensing with this facility in only 3% and 2% of cases respectively.

Specific Sentence Reports As a means of providing advice to sentencers which satisfy PCC(S)A 2000 s81(1) (see page 77) and s36(4) (above). Without the full demands of normal PSR inquiries or a formal court adjournment, some Probation Services had developed a new, speedier form of assessment of suitability, the 'specific sentence inquiry', normally completed on day of request. This practice was recognised and promoted by *Probation Circular 85/1999* which suggested that SSRs can reduce delay and make better use of resources and asked Probation Services 'vigorously to promote' their use and to establish protocols with courts on their use. It reported monitoring by West Yorkshire Probation Service that indicated that 'SSRs are no less favourable than full PSRs in terms of successful completion of resulting orders'.

The Circular, echoed later by *National Standards* (2000), indicated that 'as a rough guide, SSRs are most likely to be suitable where the court envisages a CS/CPO of up to 100 hours or a probation/CR order without additional requirements'. (In one Service, Hampshire, agreement had been reached with local magistrates that SSRs would be prepared in instances of less serious offences committed by lower risk offenders, where the court had in mind a short probation order with a requirement to undertake an alcohol-impaired drivers' programme.) 'When requesting an SSR, the court may wish to make it clear to the offender that the sentence it has asked the Probation Service to consider will not necessarily be the sentence imposed. The offender should be aware that an SSR might indicate that the sentence the court has in mind is unsuitable and that a full PSR may consequently be required.' If the reporter has concerns that a risk assessment in an SSR may not be adequate, or there are other issues that need to be explored, the court should be invited to adjourn for a full PSR. Alternatively, the court may consider an alternative sentence that does not require further information or assessment.

A 'specific sentence report' should follow an approved format set out in *National Standards*, following the usual specified PSR headings, largely featuring 'yes/no' responses but with space for comment, based on an initial assessment of risk of serious harm and likelihood of reoffending.

Consent

C(S)A 1997 s38 abolished the previous requirement that an offender must consent before a court could impose: a probation order; a CSO; a combination order; a curfew order; a supervision order with s12A requirements. The old consent provisions apply only in respect of offences committed before the section's implementation date of 1 October 1997. This consideration is thus of rapidly shrinking importance, though there may be a few old matters still in the pipeline, raising the possibility of instances where a court is dealing with a number of offences, some falling before the critical date and some on or after that date, and will thus need to seek consent in respect of some of the matters before it, if proposing one of the above orders. Where a court sentences for an offence committed on or after the critical date, the issue of the offender's stance remains pertinent to considerations of 'suitability', particularly where the sentencer is considering imposing an order that requires the offender's active engagement to be meaningful.

A court must continue to seek an offender's willingness to comply before imposing an additional requirement of treatment (for mental condition or for drug/alcohol dependency) in a community rehabilitation (or CPR) order, or before imposing a drug treatment and testing order (see page 162) (or making a 'psychiatric' supervision order, where the offender is aged 14 or older). As a safeguard against the withholding of consent with the potential to leave the court in a sentencing limbo, PCC(S)A s79(3) specifies:

> Nothing in s79(2) shall prevent the court from passing a custodial sentence on the offender if he fails to express his willingness to comply with—
>
> (a) a requirement which is proposed by the court to be included in a probation order or supervision order and which requires an expression of willingness; or
>
> (b) a requirement that is proposed by the court to be included in a DTTO or an order under s52(4) (order to provide samples).

If an offender is made subject to an order that does not require any expression of willingness to comply, and subsequently fails to comply, the enforcement provisions of PCC(S)A 2000 Sch 3 allow a court that revokes the order in breach proceedings to impose a custodial sentence if the offender has 'wilfully and persistently failed to comply', notwithstanding that the offence does not otherwise meet the criteria of s79(2) (see Stone, 1999 and page 70).

General Sentencing Provisions

In imposing a community sentence, a court may or shall have regard to the provisions relating to plea, totality of sentence, previous convictions and mitigation unrelated to the offence, as outlined in Chapter One.

Pre-Sentence Drug Testing

Where a person aged 18 or over is convicted of an offence and the court is considering passing a community sentence, it may make an order requiring the offender to provide samples of any description specified in the order for the purpose of ascertaining whether the offender has any specified Class A drug in his body: PCC(S)A 2000 s36A. If it is proved to the satisfaction of the court that the offender has, without reasonable excuse, failed to comply with the order, it may impose on him a fine of an amount not exceeding level 4 (see page 189). This power has particular value where a court is considering making a DTTO (see page 163) but is not restricted to such instances.

Electronic Monitoring Requirement

Power to include a requirement of electronic monitoring has become a familiar feature of curfew orders and this was originally included in that context by PCC(S)A 2000 s38. However, CJCSA 2000 s52 amended that Act, extending scope to impose such a requirement to any community order. Under PCC(S)A 2000 s36B(1) 'a community order may include requirements for securing the electronic monitoring of the offender's compliance with any other requirements imposed by the order'. An order which includes such requirements 'shall include provision for making a person responsible for the monitoring; and a person who is made so responsible shall be of a description specified in an order made by the Secretary of State': s36B(5). The court must be satisfied that the necessary provision can be made under available monitoring arrangements: s36B(2). The section includes specific provisions relating to certain kinds of community order (see page 155 in respect of a community rehabilitation order or a CPRO and page 175 in respect of an exclusion order).

Community Sentence Demonstration Project

Established as a joint initiative involving the Home Office, the LCD, the Magistrates' Association, the Justices' Clerks' Society, the Central Probation Council and ACOP, and initiated in Teesside and Shrewsbury courts for a year from April 1997, the Project was intended to establish how far changes in approach, within the present legislative framework, could increase sentencer and public confidence in community sentences (Hedderman *et al*, 1999).

As a result of this initiative, sentencers felt better informed about the content of probation programmes and reported greater confidence in their ability to tailor sentences to individual offenders' needs and problems. There was a significant increase in the proportion of magistrates who saw probation with additional requirements as primarily concerned with the prevention of re-offending. The number who thought prison had a deterrent effect declined. Interviews with Crown Court sentencers revealed that they viewed the use of community penalties as 'taking a risk' and they were inclined to accept the proposals only of PSR writers whose opinion they respected. As regards impact on sentencing, the effect of the project was limited. The overall proportion of offenders receiving community penalties was unchanged at Teesside Crown Court and in Shropshire magistrates' courts. The use of community penalties declined in Teesside magistrates' courts. Only in the Crown Court in Shropshire (involving small numbers) was there an increase in use of fines/community orders and a decrease in custodial sentences. The one sentencing change common to both areas was a rise in the proportion of cases receiving a probation order with additional requirements, which might reflect greater confidence in this kind of disposal.

COMMUNITY REHABILITATION ORDERS

For many years an order of the court made 'instead of sentencing' the defendant (PCCA 1973 s2(1) as originally worded), the probation order assumed a new identity under CJA 1991 among the new range of community orders. Now incorporated within PCC(S)A 2000, ss41–45, the order was renamed by amendments introduced by CJCSA 2000 s41, to become the community rehabilitation order.

Power to Impose a Community Rehabilitation (Probation) Order: PCC(S)A 2000 s41(1)

Courts to which Available Crown Court, magistrates' courts, youth courts.

Minimum Age Offenders aged 16 or older.

Nature of Offence Any offence, imprisonable or not (other than one for which sentence is fixed by law).

Agency Responsible for Supervision Though supervision was previously the exclusive responsibility of the Probation Service, s41(5) provides that in respect of an offender aged under 18, responsibility for supervision may be exercised by a member of a youth offending team established by the local authority within whose area it appears to the court that the offender resides or will reside. Whether, probation officer or YOT member, the supervisor is the 'responsible officer': s41(6).

Criterion The court must be 'of the opinion that (the offender's) supervision is desirable in the interests of:

(a)   securing his rehabilitation; or

(b)   protecting the public from harm from him or preventing the commission by him of further offences': (s41(1)).

The court is not required to identify which of (a) or (b) it considers to apply, nor does the section identify on what basis the court should reach this opinion, beyond the procedural requirements for community orders generally (see page 132). However, the requirement to consider that the proposed order will meet one or other of the two heads of the statutory rationale for community rehabilitation means that it is not appropriate to impose a community rehabilitation order simply as a punishment that restricts liberty if, for example, the offence is considered serious enough to attract a community sentence but the offender is not considered suitable for another kind of community order.

Length and Duration Such period specified in the order, being 'not less than six months nor more than three years': s41(1). It is not lawful for the court to impose an order without specifying the intended length. The length of the order may be varied subsequently by amendment and revoked ahead of termination as a mark of good progress (see Stone: 1999).

Procedural Requirements

(i) Before making a community rehabilitation order, 'the court shall explain to the offender in ordinary language the effect of the order, the consequences which may follow ... if s/he fails to comply with any of the requirements of the order, and that the court has power ... to review the order on the application of either the offender or the supervising officer': s41(7). The previous requirement that the offender should 'express his willingness to comply' was removed by C(S)A 1997 s38(2), implemented on 1 October 1997 in respect of offences committed on or after that date. Consent remains a requirement only in respect of additional requirements for treatment for mental condition or for drug/alcohol dependency (see pages 151-152).

(ii) The order 'shall specify the PSA in which the offender resides or will reside': s41(3). Though this is usually a straightforward matter, complications can arise in respect of defendants of uncertain future location and it may be preferable in case of uncertainty to specify the PSA for the court that imposes the order or within which the offender has been residing. It is important for the order to be checked to ensure that the correct PSA is specified in order to avoid complications in the event that enforcement proceedings are necessary.

(iii) The court imposing the order 'shall forthwith give copies of the order to a probation officer assigned to the court' who shall give a copy to the offender, to the probation officer (or YOT member) responsible for supervision of the order and (in relevant cases) to the person in charge of any institution in which the probationer is required to reside: s41(9). In practice, there can often be a frustrating delay in the preparation and distribution of the paper order. The order is in force as soon as it is imposed (*Walsh v Barlow* 1985, see page 157) and so instructions can be validly given on or from the day of sentence and enforcement proceedings initiated, even though the order has yet to be received from the court or the probation officer initially receiving copies.

(iv) *'Affected Person'* The status of 'affected person' arises in two instances, as specified by s41(12) (inserted by CJCSA 2000 Sch 6 para 147). Where either:

   (a) an electronic monitoring requirement is included in a community rehabilitation order under s36B (see page 136) and that requirement could only be made with the prior consent of a person other than the offender whose co-operation is needed for the requirement to be feasible; or

   (b) an exclusion requirement is included under Sch 2 para 8 (see page 154) to protect a person from being approached by the offender,

   that person is designated as an affected person, with procedural consequences, as follows:

   • The affected person may apply to the court having jurisdiction in enforcement proceedings under Sch 3 for the amendment of the order, and this right should be included in the explanation of the order given to the offender under s41(7) before the order is made.

- When the order is made, the court shall give the affected person 'any information relating to the order which the court considers it appropriate for him to have': s41(9A).

Commencement

As the life of a community rehabilitation order is determined by the passage of time set by the specified period, is predicated upon the current circumstances and needs of the defendant and has been intended to afford the offender 'conditional freedom', it has long been a sentencing principle that an order commences forthwith and thus it is improper to sentence the offender simultaneously to a custodial sentence: *R v Evans* [1959] 1 WLR 26 (see below). It has never been open to a court to order that a probation order shall have delayed effect and come into existence at a later date. This means that it is not possible to impose a community rehabilitation order to run *consecutively* to an order imposed either on the same occasion or on an earlier occasion and thus already in existence. This does not, of course, preclude the imposition of a community rehabilitation order on a defendant already subject to a community rehabilitation order which will be continuing beyond the present sentencing occasion. It simply means that the additional order will commence forthwith and thus overlap with the existing order. This principle may on occasion seem restrictive, e.g. if the defendant is being sentenced for more than one offence, one of which is considered so serious that only a custodial sentence is justified, albeit of short duration, say 28 days. Another offence being dealt with may be considered serious enough to attract a community sentence and the offender may be considered suitable for probation supervision.

Two recent cases have explored the scope for imposing a probation order while the offender is subject to a custodial sentence. In *R v Carr-Thompson* [2000] 2 Cr App R(S) 335, a young offender in breach of a community service order was remitted back to the Crown Court in enforcement proceedings. While awaiting this hearing, she appeared before a youth court for fresh offences and was sentenced to a term of two months YOI detention. When she appeared at Crown Court shortly afterwards, while still a serving prisoner, the Court revoked the community service order and made a probation order for the original offence, at the same time dismissing her appeal against her custodial sentence. The Court of Appeal determined that in dismissing her appeal, the Crown Court was, in effect, passing that sentence upon her and had thus acted contrary to the *Evans* principle. The order was thus quashed and no separate penalty ordered for the offence originally attracting the CSO. However, in *Fonteneau v DPP* [2001] 1 Cr App R(S) 54, where the offender had had his appeal against a short custodial sentence dismissed during the period when another matter against him had been adjourned so that a PSR could be prepared for a magistrates' court, the Divisional Court upheld the imposition of a combination order for the further offence, notwithstanding that the offender was still completing his custodial sentence. While affirming that it will normally be 'futile and thoroughly undesirable' to impose these different forms of sentence on the same occasion, the court determined that as the delay before the combination order could be supervised was minimal (he had 17 days left to serve in prison), the order was lawful. Of course, if sentencing for different offences on the same occasion the court can, when imposing a custodial sentence for one offence, reflect the seriousness of all 'associated' offences, looking at the matter 'in the round', whereas in *Fonteneau* neither court could take this perspective. It might therefore be argued that to seek to impose a custodial and a community sentence on the same occasion is wrong under current statute law. The court in *Fonteneau* did not rule on this point and thus the issue whether a court may make a community sentence which will take early but not immediate practical effect while at the same time imposing a short custodial sentence that will attract no statutory supervision on release remains to be resolved. In *Fonteneau*, the court would not have been able to impose a custodial sentence for the further offence unless that offence satisfied the 'so serious' threshold criterion. If the court had not been able to impose a community sentence, or the earlier custodial sentence had been of significantly greater length, the court would probably have been left with little option but to impose a conditional discharge. The court in *Fonteneau* did not offer any sense of how much longer than 17 days a delay period would need to be before it could no longer be viewed as 'minimal' and would become an obstacle to community sentencing.

It is, of course, common experience for a probationer to be sentenced to custody in mid-order, resuming supervision after serving his sentence. It is also both conceivable (and lawful) for a court to impose a community rehabilitation order and at the same time review the offender's outstanding fines and commit them to prison for non-payment, thus inhibiting the start of supervision in the same way as would a custodial sentence. It would be right, of course, to seek to persuade the court to resist the inclination to send the probationer to prison at the very point that a fresh opportunity has been presented to address their offending and allied problems in the community. It is also the case where the order contains an additional requirement of a very specific kind (e.g. to receive in-patient psychiatric treatment) that that initiative must take absolute priority over any other disposal or order. However, now that the probation/community rehabilitation order is conceptually a punishment there may be some basis for re-thinking the logic of the *Evans* principle to allow a greater degree of flexibility, either by allowing a delayed formal start to the order or by tolerating a late start in practice. Walker & Padfield (1996) suggest that an important argument against postponement of the effect of a community rehabilitation order is that while the offender may be willing to be on probation at the time of sentence, their attitude may have changed by the time the order takes effect. This argument appears to have less merit now that the consent requirement has been abolished.

Tandem Measures

Incompatible Measures The following cannot be imposed simultaneously (i.e. on the same sentencing occasion) with a community rehabilitation order, even for different offences:

    (i)   a suspended term of imprisonment: PCC(S)A 2000 s118(6);

    (ii)   an immediate term of custody (but see discussion above);

    (iii)   an action plan order: PCC(S)A 2000 s69(5)(b).

PCC(S)A 2000 s35(2) specifies that 'a community sentence shall not consist of or include both a community rehabilitation order and a community punishment order', because of the provisions of s51 empowering the imposition of a combination order. It was commonly assumed that although probation and CS could not be imposed for a single offence, it would be lawful to impose both sanctions on the same occasion for different offences, albeit that the court might prefer to deal with the separate offences by concurrent combination orders. However, in *Gilding v DPP* (1998) *The Times* 20 May, the Divisional Court ruled that this is not a lawful option, rejecting the prosecution argument that the restriction then contained in CJA 1991 s6(3) (the predecessor of s35(2)) applied only to the combination referred to in s51 (CJA 1991 s11, as then applied), i.e. probation and community service for 'an offence'. See also page 159.

Compatible Measures As a feature of its revised status as a sentence, a community rehabilitation order can ostensibly be combined with another community order (other than a CSO) for the same offence, the most obvious pairing being with a curfew order, or possibly with an attendance centre order. Such a double-headed disposal will cause certain difficulties in the event that one order is revoked and the court proposes to re-sentence, bearing in mind that the other order, a separate penalty for the same offence, is still in force. How can the re-sentencing court determine what portion of the offence's seriousness to attribute to the revoked order? The challenge appears a conceptual nonsense and this form of combination appears best avoided. This potentially thorny issue will now be less likely to arise, given the introduction of power to include curfew requirements in a community rehabilitation order (see page 154). The same problem may arise in regard to imposing a fine and community rehabilitation for the same offence; in theory perfectly acceptable but less than satisfactory in the event of revocation and re-sentence. Fortunately, sentencers have not readily embraced exotic blends of probation and other primary penalties since implementation of the 1991 Act gave them this possibility, preferring to impose stand-alone probation orders for single offences, adding only ancillary measures such as: compensation order; disqualification from driving; exclusion order (from licensed premises or football grounds); restitution order etc.

Core Requirements

The essential requirements of any community rehabilitation order are specified by PCC(S)A 2000 s41(11):

> An offender in respect of whom a community rehabilitation order is made shall keep in touch with the responsible officer in accordance with such instructions as he may from time to time be given by that officer and shall notify him of any change of address.

This affords the supervisor considerable discretion in giving instructions both as to the frequency and location of contact and as to the manner in which contact shall be pursued, subject to the limitation of 'reasonableness' and guided, of course, by the rubric of *National Standards*. Note that there is no longer any specific requirement that the probationer shall receive visits from their supervisor at home, though this does not preclude an instruction to 'keep in touch' through a home visit, subject to the possible challenge that such an instruction is unreasonable.

Supervisory Responsibility

The offender is 'required to be under the supervision of' their responsible officer (s41(4), as defined by s41(5), either a probation officer or YOT member, determined according to their age. It has been the duty of probation officers 'to supervise the probationers

141

and other persons placed under their supervision and to advise, assist and befriend them': PSA 1993 s14(1)(a) (repealed by CJCSA 2000), reiterated by PR 1984 r33. In *R v Teesside Probation Committee, ex parte National Association of Probation Officers* (1998, unreported) the issue was raised whether it is lawful for a Probation Area to employ non-probation officer staff, designated 'community offender supervisors', overseen by senior probation officers, to assume supervisory responsibilities in respect of probationers assessed as of lesser risk, or contrary to the relevant statutory provisions, as the National Association of Probation Officers claimed. Dismissing the Association's application, Collins J stated that 'supervision' does not require each and every task to be carried out by a probation officer. 'He must make a plan and assess the risk, but he can leave it to others to carry out the plan or any part of it so long as he is kept informed.' (The statutory provisions) do not require—

> 'that there should be personal contact between the probation officer and the offender. I think it is generally recognised that probation officers could not carry out their duties properly without personal contact, at least in the early stages, and that at all times the offender must be able to contact his supervising officer. ... But this does not mean that at all stages personal contact must continue... supervision involves more than mere oversight. It is necessary that the officer receives the necessary information and it cannot be left to the discretion of others to decide what he needs to know. But he can decide that for any particular offender certain tasks can be undertaken by others. I am satisfied that the new scheme is lawful since it will ensure that the offender supervisor will only be involved if a senior officer and the then supervising officer decide that he should and there is in place a requirement that relevant information be provided to the senior officer.'

It is therefore clear that a responsible officer's power to give instructions to the offender in respect of 'keeping in touch', under s41(11) extends to instructing the offender to see another member of that officer's agency on the responsible officer's behalf or under his or her oversight.

Additional Requirements

General Power to Impose

In addition to the detailed schedule of 'off-the-peg' specific additional requirements, now contained in PCC(S)A 2000 Sch 2, outlined below, s42(1) gives a court scope to devise ad hoc extra requirements:

> Subject to s42(3), a community rehabilitation order may in addition require the offender to comply during the whole or any part of the community rehabilitation period with such requirements as the court, having regard to the circumstances of the case, considers desirable in the interests of:
>
> (a)   securing the rehabilitation of the offender; or
>
> (b)   protecting the public from harm or preventing the commission by him of further offences.

Section 42(3) specifies that this power shall not be applied to require 'the payment of sums by way of damages for injury or compensation for loss'. The court has scope to impose this kind of measure through a compensation order.

Section 42(2) adds that without prejudice to the generality of s42(1), the additional requirements which may be included shall include the requirements authorised by Sch 2. Courts have not been encouraged to make widespread use of their general discretion and most kinds of additional requirement that the Probation Service seeks to promote can be accommodated within the provisions of Sch 2 (formerly PCCA 1973 Sch 1A). The following principles can be drawn:

- Schedule 2 is the primary source of additional requirements, providing a clear framework and setting explicit boundaries for the commitments to which the probationer is subject. If it is proposed to include a requirement of a kind regulated by Sch 2, the requirement should be drafted within the terms of the relevant paragraph of that schedule. It is wrong to resort to the general power under s42(1) to seek to evade or side-step the structure and limits of a specific power: *Rogers v Cullen* [1982] 1 WLR 729. It would thus be unlawful to require an offender to attend a probation centre throughout the length of their order in excess of the 60 day limit set by Sch 2 para 3.

- The existence of s42(1) clearly allows the insertion of additional requirements not covered by the schedule, but this should be done with considerable caution, having regard to four particular factors:

  (i)   Does the proposed requirement seek to impose a form of demand for which there is an alternative, explicit statutory provision? For example, it would not be lawful to purport to require the offender under the terms of their probation order to undertake unpaid work akin to community service (see Lord Bridge in *Rogers v Cullen* (above)).

  (ii) Is the proposed requirement enforceable, in the sense that it can be realistically policed? If it requires conduct (or the avoidance of conduct) that cannot be validly overseen by the supervising officer, it would not be appropriate to include in an order, e.g. a requirement that the offender takes a weekly bath (a requirement of this nature has reportedly been attempted).

  (iii) Does the proposed requirement give undue discretionary power to the supervising officer? *Rogers v Cullen* (above) indicated that it would be wrong to allow open-ended interventive powers or control to the probation officer which would unacceptably erode the basic liberty of the individual. Lord Bridge stated: 'Any discretion conferred on the probation officer pursuant to the terms of the order to regulate a probationer's activities must itself be confined within well-defined limits'. Admittedly, that principle was declared before the probation order became a sentence but it is submitted that it still holds good that the offender should know the extent of the powers of the supervising officer unless the law explicitly provides for wide discretion to be exercised, such as a requirement to receive psychiatric treatment under the direction of a doctor (Sch 2 para 5), a matter that the court could not be expected to determine at point of sentence. Thus a requirement that the probationer should not go out between specified hours of night without the prior permission of their supervising officer would be open to challenge as unlawful (the curfew order now offers a specific means to achieve this form of regulation, and thus see (i) above).

(iv)   Is the meaning of the proposed requirement sufficiently clear to be enforceable? For example, a requirement that the probationer 'should not go out with any person without the prior approval of their supervising officer' would be open to challenge on the grounds that 'go out' is too vague or imprecise to be enforceable (quite apart from the question whether such a requirement meets the criteria of (i) and (ii) above, or perhaps violates Article 8 of the European Convention on Human Rights).

The only recent case law on the exercise of PCCA 1973 s3(1) (the predecessor of s42(1)) is *R v Peacock* (1994) 158 JP 115 where the Court of Appeal held that it was lawful for the Crown Court to impose a requirement that the offender 'shall not commit any further offence during the currency of the order', on the basis that non-compliance could be dealt with under the powers of revocation contained then in CJA 1991 Sch 2 para 8. The reasoning of the Court is far from persuasive, appearing to confuse issues of breach and revocation, and it is submitted that this kind of additional requirement adds nothing to the powers of the court already available in the event of the commission of a further offence while a community rehabilitation order is in force.

More appropriate use of s42(1) may be made to incorporate within the order a requirement akin to the extra conditions that can be included in a parole or ACR licence, for which provision is not found in Sch 1A, for example:

- not to approach or communicate with the victim of the offence (or the offender's former partner) without the prior approval of the supervising officer;

- not reside in the same household as any child under a specified age;

- not engage in any work or other organised activity involving a person under a specified age, either on a professional or voluntary basis.

The list of permitted extra licence conditions should not be regarded as a definitive source but merely as illustrative. In one case known to the author involving a defendant who had repeatedly held jobs where they had behaved fraudulently, an additional requirement was proposed that the offender 'inform the supervising officer in advance of any paid employment that s/he proposes to commence'. This would not give the supervising officer power to determine whether the offender should take the job but would allow the officer greater scope to monitor the risk of re-offending. It might be suggested that requirements of this nature should be imposed more appropriately under the specific provisions of Sch 2 para 2 requiring the probationer to refrain from a specified activity. This is discussed at page 149.

Drug Abstinence Requirement Section 42(2) is amended by CJCSA 2000 s49 to require a court to include a drug abstinence requirement in a community rehabilitation order, where specified conditions are satisfied. This new provision is detailed below at page 155.

Electronic Monitoring Requirement The scope for a court to include electronic monitoring requirements for securing the offender's compliance with other requirements in an order, under s36B, is detailed at page 136.

Powers under PCC(S)A 2000 Sch 2

The schedule offers six categories of additional requirements, augmented by a further two forms of requirement introduced by CJCSA 2000 ss47–48 which amend Sch 2 by including curfew and exclusion requirements.

1. Residence Requirements

Schedule 2 para 1(1) gives broad power to the court to 'include requirements as to the residence of the offender'.

Procedural Prerequisite 'The court shall consider the home surroundings of the offender': para 1(2). This will normally be satisfied by reference to a PSR but this is not an essential route and the court has discretion in fulfilling this expectation.

Length The court's powers to impose this kind of requirement are generous in that the requirement can apply throughout the length of the order and the court is not required to specify any period during which the offender is bound, except in one important respect (para 1(3)):

> Where a community rehabilitation order requires the offender to reside in an approved community rehabilitation hostel or any other institution, the period for which he is required to reside shall be specified in the order.

Regard should be given to this mandatory provision in advising the sentencer of the period of residence considered appropriate, either in the PSR or orally at the sentencing hearing. Hostels tend to prefer the period of residence to be comparatively short and purposeful, serving as a bridge to more permanent accommodation while there is a substantial period of the order still to run, so that the offender's transition into the wider community can be supervised closely.

It is open to doubt whether a form of wording specifying residence 'for a period of up to *x* months' satisfies the provisions of para 1(3). Note that approved probation hostels are subject to the *Approved Probation and Bail Hostel Rules* (Statutory Instrument 1995/302). Rule 11(a) specifies that except with the consent of the Chief Probation Officer, no person under the supervision of a probation officer shall reside in a hostel for any longer than the period specified in the probation order. Further, a resident shall not be required to cease to reside at the hostel before the expiry of the term of residence specified in the probation order, except in an emergency: r12(2). These provisions strongly indicate that the period of residence should be specified and not merely be subject to a ceiling limit.

Ancillary Requirements The power to 'include requirements' extends beyond specifying where the offender shall reside to include associated provisions as to residence, the most obvious being that the offender (where subject to a requirement to reside at a hostel) 'shall abide by the rules of the hostel'. This can be of key importance if it is later proposed to allege breach of the order on grounds of failing to comply with the rules, as the defence may seek to argue that if the order does not add this associated specification, the offender is, technically at least, not in breach of the order simply by breaking the rules, since they were not legally so bound. It could be argued in reply that a residence requirement implicitly incorporates a requirement as to how the offender shall behave (see *Caton v Community Service Office* (1995) 159 JP Reports 444 where the Divisional Court held that a requirement to undertake CS work must incorporate a requirement to work in a reasonable manner). However, such difficulties are circumvented if the sentencing court is advised to incorporate in the order an explicit requirement as to compliance with the rules.

Sentencing Practice This power is most frequently exercised to require a period of residence at either a community rehabilitation hostel or another kind of residential unit in the independent sector (though note that if the 'institution' provides treatment for drug or alcohol dependency, the additional requirement should more appropriately set within the ambit of Sch 1A para 6 (below)). In the case of a probation hostel, the defendant is very likely to have spent a period at the establishment for assessment as a condition of bail. Some independent sector establishments may prefer or require residents to stay on a voluntary basis rather than as a legal requirement of a probation order. Where residence at such an establishment is proposed, the basis on which the institution is willing to accept residency should be checked carefully.

A requirement to reside at a hostel or comparable establishment, where the offender will be expected to comply with a programme of activities and other demands of the regime is a substantial restriction of liberty, as well as a valuable rehabilitative opportunity. The Court of Appeal has not given any general guidance on the use of this sentencing measure but *Attorney-General's Reference No 15 of 1994* [1995] 16 Cr App R(S) 619 indicates the scope for certain orders of this nature as a appropriate sentence even for very serious offences. The offender aged 17 had attacked a 60 year old man with a piece of wood, fracturing his skull (GBH with intent). Reviewing sentence of probation with a requirement of residence at a semi-secure children's centre, the Court of Appeal accepted that the sentence was unduly lenient but the order was allowed to continue in the light (among other factors, including the offender's age, guilty plea and experience of disadvantage) of his progress and increased self-discipline at the centre during his time there on remand and since sentence, given also the centre's 'very stiff regime' (residents were not allowed out unaccompanied and were allowed only one accompanied outing per week).

The other main basis for seeking a residence requirement is to afford the supervising officer some control over where the offender will reside beyond the standard right to be informed of change of address. This has led to orders specifying that the offender 'shall reside as directed by the supervising officer' (i.e. akin to a condition frequently included in an early release licence). Such a requirement purports to give very open-ended authority to the supervisor and may appear to be a useful resort if it is proposed that the probationer shall reside at an establishment that opts not to receive residents subject to a specific requirement to reside there, and it is felt to be insufficient to propose a standard order that leaves the matter of residence entirely to the discretion of the probationer. Alternatively, this requirement formula may be proposed in respect of an offender who it is proposed will reside at a community rehabilitation hostel in the first instance but it is wished to have control over where s/he will move on to when their hostel stay ends (e.g. 'shall reside at the XYZ probation hostel for four months and thereafter as directed by the supervising officer'). Though frequently employed, the legality of such a formula is open to doubt on the grounds that it confers undue discretion upon the supervisor, contrary to the dictum of Lord Bridge in *Rogers v Cullen* (see page 143). This point has yet to be tested for authoritative determination. An alternative formula, 'to reside where approved by the supervising officer', appears more sound in law, albeit that it affords the supervisor less control and could, in breach proceedings be open to the defence that the supervising officer's approval was unreasonably withheld in the particular circumstances in which the offender found themselves.

In 1999, out of 55,570 persons commencing probation order supervision, 714 (1.3%) were subject to requirements of residence in probation hostels and only 45 to residence in other institutions. A further 318 were made subject to another form of residence requirement (*Probation Statistics*).

2. Participation in Specified Activities or Attendance at Specified Place

The most frequently adopted form of additional requirement, for the offender to undertake some experience beyond the standard demands of 'keeping in touch' with their supervisor, is empowered by Sch 2 para 2(1) and offers two alternative frameworks within which the necessary instructions can be given:

(a) a requirement 'to present himself to a person or persons specified in the order at a place or places so specified'; or

(b) a requirement 'to participate in activities specified in the order'.

For a 'place' to be specifiable in an order, it 'shall have been approved by the Probation Committee for the area in which the premises are situated as providing facilities suitable for persons subject to probation orders' (para 2(5)). In other words, courts and probation officers do not have free creative expression to propose or specify 'places' at whim. Prior authoritative approval is essential.

The choice between (a) and (b) will depend on whether it is intended to centre the requirement on the *activities* to be undertaken, with flexibility as to the location(s) where such activities will occur (option (b) above), or on the identity of the *person* and location of what is to be undertaken (option (a) above). In many instances, this choice may not make any significant difference to the undertaking of the proposed experience, so long as the court, supervisor and offender know which of the two options will apply and the additional requirement is worded accordingly. In other instances, the proposed experience will be more appropriately grounded in one of the options. For example, if it proposed that the probationer shall attend at a particular independent partnership agency for some form of work to be negotiated flexibly, option (a) will probably be the clear preference. If it is proposed that the offender will undertake a probation run programme with a clear theme or focus, e.g. an anger management programme or an alcohol awareness course, then option (b) would seem more appropriate, especially if the venue will vary.

Prerequisite In respect of both options, para 2(2) requires the sentencing court:

(a)　to consult a probation officer; and

(b)　be 'satisfied that it is feasible to secure compliance with the requirement'.

Further, where the proposed requirement of either kind would 'involve the co-operation of a person other than the offender and the probation officer responsible for his supervision', that other person must consent to the inclusion of the requirement (para 2(3), i.e. where the co-operation of any third person is essential for the requirement to be viable, their agreement must be secured. This provision does not specify how consent should be communicated to the court. Personal attendance is not required but it would certainly aid the fulfilment of the legal prerequisite if the probation officer proposing this course secures agreement in writing to supply to the sentencer.

Length In respect of a specified activities requirement, para 2(1)(b)(i) and (ii) states that the obligation will apply 'on a day or days so specified, or during the probation period or such portion of it as may be so specified'. In both instances the requirement shall operate 'for not more than 60 days in the aggregate': para 2(4) and (6). The statutory wording ('shall operate to ...') indicates that the requirement need not articulate a specific length, nor is it necessary to state the actual number of days which it is intended that the offender will complete, if less than 60. In respect of an activities requirement, it appears necessary for the court to identify either the actual dates on which the obligation will arise (though this is a very unlikely choice) or alternatively to indicate whether the requirement shall operate at any stage during the whole length of the order or during a stated part of the order. To give greatest flexibility, the requirement should specify the full probation period, though the court may wish to build in to the order its wish that the additional demand will apply in the first part of the order, e.g. within the first six months. As regards the number of days, the requirement is probably best phrased exactly as the sub-paragraph states it, i.e. 'for not more than 60 days', as this sets an explicit limit to what will follow while providing discretion as to the actual time that the experience will occupy. The PSR or the proposing probation officer should be able to indicate to the court the anticipated time span of the experience so that the court can gauge the extent of restriction of liberty entailed, without expressing this too precisely in the formal wording of the requirement. There is some need for flexibility in regard to length because it may prove desirable to instruct the offender to repeat some of the sessions of the experience or to re-start the experience in the event of absences. In respect of an offender convicted of a 'sexual offence' (as defined by PCC(S)A 2000 s161(2), see page 92), Sch 2 para 4 makes special provision that either option (a) or (b) requirements may apply beyond 60 days, 'for such greater number of days as may be specified'. Note that the sentencing court must decide to adopt this option and specify the replacement maximum number of days (which can be simply specified as 'for the duration of the order'). If the court does not adopt this course, the normal 60 day maximum will apply. In 1998, 45 orders included such an extension (in respect of both para 2 and para 3 – see below).

Nature of Obligation A person/place requirement (option (a) above) operates to require the offender (i) to attend at the specified place(s) on dates and times specified by the supervising officer (para 2(4)(a)) and (ii) while at the place(s), 'to comply with instructions given by, or under the authority of, the person in charge of that place' (para 2(4)(b)). An activities requirement (option (b) above) operates to require the offender (i) to participate in activities, in accordance with instructions given by the supervising probation officer (para 2(6)(a)), and (ii) 'while participating, to comply with instructions given by or under the authority of, the person in charge of the activities' (para 2(6)(b)). In other words, the supervising officer gives the instruction to attend at a specified time and date and take part, and the person responsible for the activity gives the instructions as to the nature of the activities and manner in which those activities shall be undertaken.

Instructions given by a probation officer under either option 'shall, as far as practicable, be such as to avoid any interference with the times, if any, at which the offender normally works or attends a school or other educational establishment and any conflict with the offender's religious beliefs or with the requirements of any other community order': para 2(7).

In 1999, of 55,570 persons sentenced to a probation order, 10,863 (19.5%) were made subject to specified activities requirements while 853 (1.5%) received a person/place requirement.

3. Requirement to Refrain from Activities

This is a little-used third option within Sch 2 para 2, empowering the sentencer to require the offender to 'refrain from participating in activities specified in the order' (para 2(1)(b)). The statute gives no indication of the kind of activities that can be proscribed by this means, though 'activities' clearly has a different meaning in this context than in requirements to undertake some positive or constructive experience. It may be suggested that the kind of requirements discussed in regard to the general power to impose additional requirements (see page 142) e.g. 'not seek to approach or communicate with' the victim of the crime, could be included under this provision rather than under s42(1), but is approaching or communicating with someone or residing in a household with children an 'activity'? Note too that the para 2(1)(b) provision does not identify that the requirement to 'refrain' may be qualified by specific permission from the supervising officer to undertake the prohibited activity, whereas such authority may be a helpful way of allowing regulated exceptions to the prohibition. Clear questions arise too regarding the enforceability of this kind of requirement. A court is unlikely to favour a prohibition that the offender can ignore with impunity. Walker and Padfield (1996) suggested that a so-called 'negative' requirement could serve to prohibit the offender from entering a public house or frequenting football grounds, but such a measure would be better imposed through an exclusion order or requirement (see page 154). They also suggest: refraining from associating with a person or type of person, or visiting a certain city area. In similar vein *HOC 34/2000* giving *Home Office Guidance on Football-Related Legislation* (see page 211) suggests (para 4.10) that courts may make it a requirement of an order that an offender does not travel abroad to or in connection with or at the time when regulated football matches involving teams from England and Wales are played outside England and Wales. Though not citing para 2 as the source for its exhortation, the Circular adds: 'Where probation services consider that offenders are charged with or convicted of football-related offences, they should remind the courts of their powers and request that they consider a condition (*sic*) of probation that the person should not travel to a regulated football match.' This kind of requirement seems more appropriately dealt with and is likely now to be eclipsed by the new power to impose an exclusion or curfew requirement (see page 154).

Prerequisite Exactly as applies in respect of a person/place or specified activities requirement under para 2(2) (see page 147), except that there is no provision regarding the consent of any third person.

Length The requirement shall apply either on a day or days specified, or during the whole probation period or such portion of it as may be specified. Note that the ceiling or maximum of 60 days governing activities requirements does not apply in this context and so the probationer can be bound for the full length of the order.

Use In 1999 only 32 probation orders commenced containing a refraining requirement, albeit the highest number in any year since the 1991 Act was implemented.

4. Community Rehabilitation Centre Attendance

The second most widely used of additional requirements, Sch 2 para 3(1) empowers a court to 'require the offender during the probation period to attend a community rehabilitation centre specified in the order'. A 'community rehabilitation centre' means 'premises at which non-residential facilities are provided for use in connection with the rehabilitation of offenders', approved by the Secretary of State: para 3(7).

Prerequisite Before including a requirement of this kind, the court must (para 3(2)):

(a)   consult a probation officer; and

(b)   be satisfied (i) that arrangements can be made for the offender's attendance at the centre, and (ii) that the person in charge of the centre consents to the inclusion of the requirement.

The means of consultation and being satisfied of the two necessary factors is left to the court's discretion. In almost all instances the court will have the benefit of a PSR and the writer will be able to offer the court the necessary assurances that attendance is feasible (this may include issues not only of a place being available but of the availability of transport for the offender to attend at a centre at a distance from their home) and that the centre manager has authorised the offender's attendance. In other words, the PSR writer cannot take it upon themselves to propose this kind of requirement without prior reference to the centre.

Length The offender can be instructed to attend the specified centre 'on not more than 60 days': para 3(3)(a). The order should not identify a smaller number of days for attendance as this maximum applies to all such orders. The wording of the order should thus echo the provision as stated. An offender convicted of a sexual offence (as defined by CJA 1991 s31(1)) may be required to attend the centre for 'such greater number of days as may be specified in the order': Sch 1A para 4. Such an extension of the maximum (which may apply for the full duration of the order) must be specifically stated by the sentencer, otherwise the normal maximum length will apply.

Obligation The offender is required (a) to attend the centre in accordance with instructions given by the supervising officer, and (b) 'while attending there, to comply with instructions given by, or under the authority of, the person in charge of the centre': para 3(3)(a) and (b). Attendance at the centre includes attendance elsewhere in accordance with instructions by or under the authority of the person in charge: para 3(5).

Use In 1999, 2,639 orders were imposed containing a requirement of this nature, nearly 5% of the total number of probation order commencements.

5. Treatment for Mental Condition

The so-called 'psychiatric probation order', an additional requirement may be imposed under Sch 2 para 5(2) requiring that the offender:

> shall submit, during the whole of the community rehabilitation period or during such part or parts of that period as may be specified in the order to treatment by or under the direction of a duly registered medical practitioner or a chartered psychologist (or both, for different parts) with a view to the improvement of the offender's mental condition.

The relevant provisions are summarised below but are dealt with in greater detail in Stone (2002).

Criterion The court must be 'satisfied, on the evidence of a duly registered medical practitioner that the mental condition of the offender:

(a)   is such as requires and may be susceptible to treatment; and

(b)   is not such as to warrant the making of a hospital order or guardianship order' (MHA 1983 s37).

The medical practitioner does not have to be a psychiatrist but has to be 'approved for the purpose under MHA 1983 s12' and thus normally will be. The evidence does not have to be given orally and the court will normally be satisfied on the basis of a written report from the doctor. Even if the proposed requirement is for treatment by a chartered psychologist rather than a doctor, the evidence must be offered by a doctor. A psychologist's report will not satisfy the prerequisite. 'Mental condition' is not defined but is not restricted to the four forms of mental disorder within the ambit of MHA 1983 (mental illness, psychopathic disorder, mental impairment or severe mental impairment). This thus gives this treatment measure much greater flexibility than a measure under the 1983 Act but a psychiatric probation order will not be appropriate if the offender does meet the criteria for compulsory detention in hospital for treatment under MHA 1983 s37.

Kind of Treatment 'The treatment required by any such order shall be such one of the following kinds of treatment as may be specified in the order':

(a)   treatment as a resident patient in a mental hospital;

(b)   treatment as a non-resident at such institution or place as may be specified in the order; and

(c)   treatment by or under the direction of such duly registered medical practitioner or chartered psychologist (or both) as may be so specified;

'but the nature of the treatment shall not be specified in the order except as mentioned in para (a), (b) or (c) above': para 5(3).

The court must thus phrase the requirement carefully from within the range of options offered by para 5(3). It is thus not lawful to include a requirement of treatment 'as may be directed by the supervising probation officer'.

Other Prerequisite: Arrangements for Treatment 'A court shall not ... include a requirement ... unless it is satisfied that arrangements have been or can be made for the treatment intended to be specified in the order (including arrangements for the reception of the offender where he is required to submit to treatment as a resident patient)': para 5(4)(a).

Procedural Requirement: Consent The offender must 'express his willingness to comply with such a requirement': para 5(4)(b).

Use In 1999, of 813 psychiatric orders made, 506 specified non-residential treatment, 257 specified treatment 'under direction' and only 50 required in-patient treatment.

6. Treatment for Drug or Alcohol Dependency

Schedule 2 para 6(2) empowers the court to include a requirement that the offender:

'shall submit, during the whole of the community rehabilitation period or during such part of that period as may be specified in the order, to treatment by or under the direction of a person having the necessary qualifications or experience with a view to the reduction of the offender's dependency on drugs or alcohol.'

Much of the market share of this kind of additional requirement, as regards drug dependency, is being absorbed by the drug treatment and testing order (DTTO), introduced by CDA 1998. If the court has been notified by the Home Secretary that arrangements are available for DTTOs in the area to be specified in the proposed order, then para 6 shall apply as if it does not apply to drug dependency. In other words, if DTTOs are available then para 6 shall have application only in respect of alcohol dependency.

Criterion The court must be satisfied of the following (para 6(1)):

(a)   the offender is dependant on drugs or alcohol;

(b)   that dependency caused or contributed to the offence for which the order is proposed: and

(c)   that dependency is 'such as requires and may be susceptible to treatment'.

Para 6 does not specify on what basis or evidence the court must be satisfied of these matters. There is no requirement that there should be evidence from either a medical practitioner or a person qualified or experienced in substance dependency. 'Dependency' is defined as including 'having a propensity towards the misuse of drugs or alcohol': para 6(9). Note in respect of (b) above that the offence for which such an order is proposed need not have been directly drug or alcohol related, nor need the offence have been committed under the influence of drugs or alcohol.

Kinds of Treatment Para 6 is clearly based on the provisions in para 5 for treatment for mental condition and echoes that paragraph by specifying that the treatment for dependency shall be—

'such one of the following kinds of treatment as may be specified in the order' (para 6(3)):

(a)   treatment as a resident in such institution or place as may be specified in the order;

(b)   treatment as a non-resident in or at such institution or place as may be so specified; and

(c)   treatment by or under the direction of such person having the necessary qualifications or experience as may be so specified;

but the nature of the treatment shall not be specified in the order except as mentioned in (a), (b) or (c) above.'

No definition is provided of what shall count as the necessary qualifications or experience, which is hardly surprising, given the comparative newness, flexibility and lack of regulation in this field. The question may be posed whether it would be lawful to phrase the requirement thus: 'to submit to treatment as directed by the supervising probation officer'. (The Probation Inspectorate (1997) noted the questionable use of imprecise orders purportedly made under para 6, such as: 'attend treatment as required'; 'receive treatment for drug problem if the probation officer decides'.) It seems clear that a probation officer may be a person with the necessary qualifications and experience, but not simply by being a probation officer. It is submitted that the court would need to be satisfied of the officer's special suitability for work of this nature. Further, the purpose behind the phrasing of such a proposed requirement is usually not with a view to the supervising officer themselves undertaking or overseeing the treatment but gaining the discretion and flexibility to arrange some form of treatment for the offender. It is clear in the context of para 5 that the medical practitioner or psychologist will be directly providing or supervising the treatment offered and, by analogy, the same expectation arises in the context of para 6 requirements. In other words, the scope of para 6(3)(c) extends only to situations where the 'person' takes direct responsibility for the treatment. The provision is not fulfilled if the person (in this instance, the probation officer) refers the probationer to a third person who then exercises their own discretion as to the nature and kind of treatment to be pursued. It is thus submitted that the wording above is not a lawful variation. If the wording is unsoundly cast, enforcement may well be a practical impossibility. Further support for this interpretation comes from the following prerequisite of which the court must be satisfied.

Prerequisite: Treatment Arrangements Para 6(4)(a) specifies that the court shall not impose a treatment requirement of this nature 'unless it is satisfied that arrangements have been or can be made for the treatment intended to be specified in the order (including arrangements for the reception of the offender where he is required to submit to treatment as a resident)'. Though the 1998 Act extended the flexibility of this prerequisite by including the words 'or can be' above, it is submitted that if the nature and location of the proposed treatment is yet to be determined and remains simply a notional possibility (as in the case of an requirement worded so as to give the supervising officer flexibility to direct the offender to receive some form of treatment at some stage), this could not satisfy the court that the necessary arrangements have been or can be made. It is also important that the proposed treatment is sufficiently meaningful and clear to the offender so that their informed consent (see below) may be given.

Procedural Requirement: Consent The offender must express their 'willingness to comply with such a requirement': para 6(4)(b).

Use In 1999, of 2,982 orders imposed containing drug/alcohol dependency requirements, 1,582 were for non-residential treatment, 1,124 were 'as directed' and 276 specified residential treatment. A recent thematic inspection report on probation work with drug users (HM Inspectorate of Probation, 1997) noted how few probation areas were making any significant use of para 6 requirements, though sentencers indicated that they would welcome more proposals for such orders.

7. Curfew Requirement

Schedule 2 para 7, inserted by CJCSA 2000 s47, empowers a court to 'include a requirement that the offender remain, for periods specified in the requirement, at a place so specified'. This provision enables a court to make what is in effect a curfew order in tandem with a probation order, albeit within a single order, and the paragraph is modelled on the statutory provisions for curfew orders, now contained in PCC(S)A 2000 s37. A curfew requirement may not be included 'if the community sentence includes a curfew order': para 7(6).

Duration As with a curfew order, a requirement may specify different places or different periods but shall not specify periods which fall outside the period of six months from the date of the order, or periods which amount to less than two hours or more than 12 hours in any one day. Requirements shall, as far as practicable, be such as to avoid conflict with the offender's religious beliefs, working hours or educational attendance, and with the requirements of any other community order to which he is subject.

Prerequisite As with a curfew order, before including a requirement the court 'shall obtain and consider information about the place proposed to be specified ... (including information as to the attitude of persons likely to be affected by the enforced presence of the offender)': para. 7(7).

Monitoring The order 'shall include provision for making a person responsible for monitoring the offender's whereabouts during the curfew periods specified in the requirement'. Further, the court making the order has power under s36B to include a requirement of electronic monitoring of the offender's compliance (see page 136). This will invariably be added when making a curfew requirement and hence monitoring will be undertaken by an approved electronic monitoring contractor.

8. Exclusion Requirement

Schedule 2 para 8, inserted by CJCSA 2000 s48, empowers a court to include a requirement 'prohibiting the offender from entering a place specified in the requirement for a period so specified of not more than a year'. There is no specified minimum period.

'Place' includes an area: para 8(10). A requirement of this nature is closely based on the exclusion order made under PCC(S)A 2000 s40A, a new form of community order in its own right, also introduced by CJCSA 2000 s39. The requirement can be continuous throughout the order, subject to the overall limit of a year, or can be for specified periods or days. Different places may be specified for different periods or days. The provisions in para 8, such as in respect of monitoring arrangements and avoidance of conflict with other commitments, are essentially identical to those in s40A and so need not be repeated here, albeit that exclusion may be more likely to be ordered as a feature of a probation order rather than as a stand-alone sentence. Allied to this provision, the court is likely to use its powers under s36B to make electronic monitoring requirements (see page 136) to allow the offender's compliance to be checked. Section 36B(4) specifies that where the court proposes to include an electronic monitoring requirement and there is a person other than the offender without whose co-operation it will not be practicable to secure such monitoring, the requirement shall not be included without that person's consent.

Drug Abstinence Requirement

Separate from powers to impose additional requirements under Sch 2, CJCSA 2000 s49 amends PCC(S)A 2000 s42(2) by inserting a provision either requiring or enabling a court to include a new form of requirement, designed to address the problems posed by drug misusing offenders by compulsory abstinence and testing. This measure is allied to the new power to impose a drug abstinence order (see page 169). A community rehabilitation order shall not include such a requirement if the order includes a requirement in respect of drugs under Sch 2 para 6 or if the community sentence imposed on the offender includes a DTTO or a drug abstinence order (s42(2D)).

Nature of the Requirement The requirement is twofold (s42(2A)):

(a)   to abstain from misusing specified Class A drugs;

(b)   to provide, when instructed to do so by the responsible officer, any sample mentioned in the instruction for the purpose of ascertaining whether he has any specified Class A drug in his body.

Mandatory Requirement A court must include a requirement if the following set of conditions is satisfied:

PCC(S)A 2000 s42(2B)

(a)   that the offender was aged 18 or over on the date of his conviction for the offence;

(b)   that, in the opinion of the court, the offender is dependent on or has a propensity to misuse specified Class A drugs; and

(c)   that the offence is a trigger offence.

'Trigger offences' are listed in CJCSA 2000 Sch 6:

Theft Act 1968 Offences: theft, robbery, burglary, aggravated burglary, TWOC, aggravated vehicle-taking, deception, going equipped.

Offences under Misuse of Drugs Act 1971: production/supply (s4), possession with intent to supply (s5(3) and possession (s5(2)) of a controlled drug if Class A.

Discretionary Requirement A court may include a requirement if conditions (a) and (b) in s42(2B) above are satisfied and, in addition, the court is of the opinion that 'the misuse by the offender of any specified Class A drug caused or contributed to the offence', (albeit that it is not a 'trigger offence'): s42(2C).

Instructions Giving instructions as to the provision of samples shall be in accordance with guidance given by the Home Secretary.

COMMUNITY (SERVICE) PUNISHMENT ORDERS

First introduced by CJA 1972, now regulated by PCC(S)A 2000 ss46–50 (formerly PCCA 1973 ss14–15), the community service order has long had wide appeal as a community-based punishment that is demanding yet also reparative, with some prospect also of providing rehabilitative gains for the offender. The order, formally defined by PCC(S)A 2000 s163, requires the offender to 'perform unpaid work' in accordance with the provisions of s47. The order has been renamed as the community punishment order by CJCSA 2000 s41.

In addition to being a community order or sentence, a community punishment order in a modified form can be imposed: (i) as a penalty for breach of a community order (Sch 3), (ii) as an option in the face of fine default (C(S)A 1997 s35) and (iii) as a punishment instead of a fine for 'petty persistent offenders' (see page 193).

Power to Impose a Community Punishment Order: PCC(S)A 2000 s46

Courts to which Available Crown Court, magistrates' courts, youth courts.

Minimum Age 16.

Nature of Offence Any offence punishable by imprisonment (s46(1)).

Agency Responsible for Supervision See 'Procedural Prerequisites and Requirements' (iv) below.

Pre-Sentence Report? Mandatory (but see page 133).

Procedural Prerequisites and Requirements

(i) A court shall not make an order 'unless, after hearing (if the court thinks it necessary) an appropriate officer, the court is satisfied that the offender is a suitable person to perform work under such an order': s46(4). 'Appropriate officer' is defined in respect of an offender aged 18 or older as a probation officer or local authority social worker; where the offender is aged under 18, a YOT member may also act in this capacity.

(ii) 'A court shall not make an order unless it is satisfied that provision for the offender to perform work under such an order can be made under the arrangements for persons to perform work under such orders which exist in the petty sessions area in which he resides or will reside': s46(6).

(iii)   Before making an order, the court shall explain to the offender in ordinary language the purpose and effect of the order (and in particular the requirements of the order under s47), the consequences of failure to comply with the order and the court's power to review the order on the application of either the offender or the responsible officer: s46(10).

(iv)   The order shall specify the petty sessions area in which the offender resides or will reside, and where the offender is aged under 18 and supervision is to be undertaken by a YOT, shall also specify the local authority within whose area the offender resides or will reside: s46(9).

Responsible Officer The functions of 'responsible officer' are discharged, in the case of an offender aged 18 or older, by an officer of a local probation board appointed for or assigned to the PSA specified in the order. If the offender is aged under 18, a member of the YOT for the local authority specified in the order may also act.

Length The number of hours that the offender may be required to work under a community punishment order shall be specified in the order and 'shall be in the aggregate (a) not less than 40; and (b) not more than 240': s46(3).

Duration Subject to exercise of power to amend the order by extending the period of performance, the work shall be performed 'during the period of 12 months beginning with the date of the order but, unless revoked, the order shall remain in force until the offender has worked under it for the number of hours specified in it': s47(3). Under s46(11), the court which makes the order is required to give copies of the order to a probation officer assigned to that court (or to a YOT member if the offender is aged under 18) who shall give a copy to the offender and the 'responsible officer' (see above). Supply of a copy of the order to the offender is 'not a prerequisite to the coming into force of the order; the order comes into force as soon as the court has pronounced the sentence' and is enforceable accordingly: *Walsh v Barlow* [1985] 1 WLR 90.

Aggregate Hours in Different Orders Section 46(8) specifies in respect of two or more orders imposed on the same sentencing occasion:

Where a court makes CSOs in respect of two or more offences of which the offender has been convicted by or before the court, the court may direct that the hours of work specified in any of those orders shall be concurrent with or additional to those specified in any other of those orders, but so that the total number of hours which are not concurrent shall not exceed the maximum specified in s46(3)(b) (i.e. 240 hours).

The court should make clear whether it is imposing orders that are intended to run concurrently or consecutively and if it fails to do so, it will avoid subsequent confusion if the probation officer in court seeks clarification of the court's intention. The position is less clear cut where the offender is dealt with on separate sentencing occasions. The leading authority is *R v Siha* (1992) 13 Cr App R(S) 588. The offender was initially sentenced to 180 hours. Six months later, he was sentenced to a further order for 90 hours. The Court of Appeal stated that though PCCA 1973 s14(3) (the predecessor of s46(8)) did not prevent the imposition of consecutive orders on different occasions which together total more than 240 hours, 'it is highly desirable that there should not be in existence at the same time orders which cast upon the offender a liability to perform more than 240 hours consecutively'. Because information was not available to the Court of Appeal about the number of hours worked or outstanding under the initial order of 180 hours, the Court reduced the second order from 90 hours to 60 hours to ensure that the consecutive total still to be worked did not exceed 240 hours.

In the light of *Siha,* the following propositions appear valid, drawing analogy with concurrent and consecutive custodial sentences:

(i) If a court sentencing an offender to two or more CS/CPOs in respect of offences dealt with on the same sentencing occasion does not specify that the hours shall be worked consecutively, it shall be presumed that the orders are concurrent.

(ii) If a court imposing a further CS/CPO upon an offender already subject to an existing order fails to specify that the fresh order is consecutive to the existing order, it shall be presumed that the fresh order is concurrent and overlaps with the existing order. It is likely that the second court will intend its further order to be consecutive, if clarification is sought, unless there are concerns about the aggregate liability to which the offender will be subject, as outlined next.

(iii) If a court imposing a further CS/CPO upon an offender already subject to an existing order intends the fresh order to be consecutive to the existing order, it shall limit the number of additional hours so that the aggregate of the fresh order together with the number of hours remaining to be worked under the existing order does not exceed 240. Some courts in such circumstances may choose to respect the ceiling of 240 hours intended by Parliament as the maximum commitment that an offender should be subject at any one time to the extent of declining to impose a fresh consecutive order that has the effect of bringing into effect orders that together total in excess of 240 hours, irrespective of how many hours the offender has actually worked under the existing order. If that 'pure' interpretation is adopted, this could markedly restrict the second court's powers of sentence, e.g. if the offender is already subject to an order of 240 hours, no further consecutive hours could be imposed, even though the offender has already worked 200 hours under that existing order. Such a stance would appear to allow only a further concurrent order of 40 hours. This seems an unjustified restriction and in such circumstances it would appear preferable that the second court could impose a consecutive order of up to 200 hours, thus still respecting the 240 hour ceiling for the number of hours in total to which the offender should be subject at any one time.

Tandem Measures

Section 35(2) specifies that 'a community sentence shall not consist of or include both a probation order and a CS/CPO'. This clearly prevents a court from imposing probation and CS orders as a sentence for a single offence but it had been assumed that there is no objection to imposing probation for one offence and CS for a separate offence, as had been held to be lawful prior to the 1991 Act (*R v Harkess* (1990) 12 Cr App R(S) 366).

However, in *Gilding v Director of Public Prosecutions* (1998) *The Times* 20 May, the Divisional Court ruled that there is no power to impose the two sentences in tandem (in this case a 12 month probation order and 180 hours CS). Schiemann LJ stated that 'the rationale appears to be that the length of time which could be imposed under a community service order which was significantly more than under a combination order would be so demanding on the offender that he would not be able to pay proper attention to the probation requirements imposed at the same time'.

PCC(S)A 2000 s69(5) prevents the making of an action plan order where the court proposes to pass a community punishment order. The Act does not regulate the mix of a CPO and a supervision order for the same (or different) offence(s) but, by analogy, this combination would appear inappropriate. There appears nothing in law or principle to prevent the making of a CPO and a curfew order for either a single offence or different offences. A CPO should not be imposed on the same occasion as an immediate sentence of custody, whether for a single or different offences: *R v Starie* (1979) 69 Cr App R 239.

Requirements of a Community Punishment Order

Section 47(1) specifies that an offender in respect of whom a CPO is in force shall:

(a) keep in touch with the responsible officer in accordance with such instructions as he may from time to time be given by that officer and notify him of any change of address; and

(b) perform for the number of hours specified in the order such work at such times as he may be instructed by the responsible officer.

Such instructions 'shall, so far as practicable, be such as to avoid (a) any conflict with the offender's religious beliefs or with the requirements of any other community order to which he may be subject; and any interference with the times, if any, at which he normally works or attends a school or other educational establishment': s47(2). The Act remains supplemented by CSCOR 1992 (SI 1992/2076), a statutory instrument with full legal status which, in particular, requires the offender to comply with reasonable directions by the supervisor as to the manner in which work is to be performed and with rules imposed by the supervisor as regards the workplace (r4(1) – see Stone, 1999). For scope for a court to include an electronic monitoring requirement, see page 136.

Drug Abstinence Requirement

CJCSA 2000 s49(2) amends s47 to insert a new sub-section empowering a court when making a community punishment order to include a drug abstinence requirement, if one or other of two sets of specified conditions is satisfied. This provision is in identical terms to that pertaining to inclusion of a drug abstinence requirement, as defined by s42(2A), in a community rehabilitation order (see page 155). If the set of conditions contained in s42(2B) is satisfied, such a requirement is obligatory; if the set of conditions in s42(2C) is satisfied, a requirement is discretionary. However, this power may not be exercised if the community sentence incorporating the community punishment order includes either a DTTO or a drug abstinence order: s47(B). The provisions of s42(2E) and (2F) (as regards giving instructions under this kind of requirement) apply also in this context: s47(3C).

Sentencing Practice

Though a number of Court of Appeal decisions prior to implementation of CJA 1991 indicated that longer periods of community service could validly be regarded as an 'alternative to custody', akin to shorter terms of imprisonment, such a notion is at odds with the framework of sentencing introduced by that Act. Since implementation, there have been very few appeal cases interpreting the appropriate use of community service orders and cases predating the Act have to be viewed guardedly in determining their continuing applicability and relevance. However, this measure has been considered of particular merit in the context of criminal damage: e.g. *R v Ferreira* [1988] 10 Cr App R(S) 343 (spraying graffiti on London Underground carriages – 'They have done this wanton damage and it behoves them to do some service to the public to put it right'). Ashworth (1995:279) characterised CS as a measure 'reserved for those who commit moderately serious offences, much too serious to warrant a mere fine but insufficiently serious for custody'. The Court of Appeal in *R v T* [1999] 2 Cr App R(S) 304 identified the demands of CS as more punitive in nature than a probation order and thus able to match more serious offences within the community sentence band (see page 131).

Use

In 1997, CSOs were imposed upon 8% of offenders sentenced for indictable offences in magistrates' courts and upon 12% of such offenders in the Crown Court.

Management and Enforcement

For details of the administration of CSOs and provisions governing the amendment, breach and revocation of orders, see Stone (1999). In 1999, 29% of offenders subject to CSOs were the subject of breach proceedings, with 2.7% being sentenced to immediate custody as a consequence (*Criminal Statistics* Table 7.24).

COMMUNITY PUNISHMENT AND REHABILITATION ORDERS

Introduced by CJA 1991 s6(4)(c) and s11 and now regulated by PCC(S)A 2000 s51, the combination order (as it was previously titled) blends familiar elements of probation supervision and unpaid community service work within a single community order. When first proposed, much hope was expressed that the combination order would be viewed as a 'high tariff', 'top of the range' community order, appropriately imposed only where a particularly demanding or high level of restriction is considered necessary in respect of offences that approach or even cross the 'so serious' threshold. It was sometimes suggested that it would be deployed primarily by the Crown Court. Hopes for such a special niche in the community sentencing framework have not been realised (see below) and, in practice, it appears that this innovatory order has been absorbed without acquiring any clearly defined tariff status. As Ashworth (1995) suggests, one possible explanation is that where magistrates have received a PSR that proposes probation but also indicates that community service is also a possibility (or vice versa), they may have opted to impose a combination order rather than choosing one or other of the singleton alternatives. The order was given the new if unwieldy name of 'community punishment and rehabilitation order' (CPRO) by CJCSA 2000 s42.

The statute makes little detailed provision for the CPRO order in its own right, thus requiring reference to the relevant provisions pertaining to probation orders and CSOs. Section 51(4) specifies that ss41–42 and ss46–47 shall apply in relation to combination orders:

(a)   in respect of the community rehabilitation element, as if it were a community rehabilitation order; and

(b)   in respect of the community punishment element, as if it were a community punishment order.

This is usually a logical process, as the following outline seeks to demonstrate.

Power to Impose a CPRO

Courts Crown Court, magistrates' courts, youth courts.

Nature of Offence As in the case of a community punishment order, any offence punishable with imprisonment other than murder. CDA 1998 inserts a new s11(1A) which states that the reference in s11(1) to an offence punishable with imprisonment 'shall be construed without regard to any prohibition or restriction imposed by or under any enactment on the imprisonment of young offenders'.

Minimum Age 16.

Supervising Agency Though previously supervised exclusively by the Probation Service, this monopoly was ended by CDA 1998 which provided that in the case of an offender aged under 18, supervision may be exercised by a member of a youth offending team established by the local authority within whose area it appears to the court that the offender resides or will reside. This is now regulated by PCC(S)A 2000 s41(5)(b) and s46(5)(b).

Length and Duration (i) Community rehabilitation element: 'not less than 12 months nor more than three years' (s51(1)(a)). This longer minimum term than would otherwise apply to a community rehabilitation order is clearly designed to reflect the period within which community punishment should be completed (see page 157).

(ii) Community punishment element: 'in the aggregate not less than 40 hours nor more than 100 hours' (s51(1)(b)). Note the shorter maximum number of hours, intended to avoid overloading the demands of a CPRO.

Criteria As in the case of a community rehabilitation order, the court should be of the opinion that 'the making of the order is desirable in the interests of:

(a)   securing the rehabilitation of the offender; or

(b)   protecting the public from harm from him or preventing the commission by him of further offences' (s11(3)).

Pre-Sentence Report? Mandatory (but see page133).

Other Procedural Prerequisites The court must comply with the prerequisites that pertain to community rehabilitation and community punishment orders, as detailed on pages 138 and 156, i.e. being satisfied that the defendant is a suitable person to perform community punishment; explaining the purpose and effect of the order in ordinary language etc. Note that the offender's consent is no longer required: C(S)A 1997 s38(2).

Additional Requirements Additional requirements may be included in a CPRO as adjuncts to the community rehabilitation element in exactly the same manner as in a community rehabilitation order. The court will need to relate the overall restriction of liberty to the seriousness of the offence and also have regard to the question of compatibility between the various competing demands of the proposed order. Priority would appear to lie with the demands of the community punishment element as this is an essential feature of a CPRO. If the sentencer wishes to ensure that additional requirements are included that do not fit readily with the demands of community punishment, then the preferable course would appear to be a community rehabilitation order.

Aggregate Community Punishment Hours The same principles and approach applies to CPROs as to community punishment orders (see page 157), except that the lower aggregate ceiling of 100 hours applies instead of 240 hours.

Tandem Measures

PCC(S)A 2000 s35(2) specifies that 'a community sentence shall not consist of or include both a community rehabilitation order and a community punishment order', except as elements within a CPRO. By implication, a CPRO cannot lawfully be combined with either a community rehabilitation order or a community punishment order for the same offence. In the light of *Gilding v DPP* (see pages 141 and 159) this mix appears unlawful also in sentencing for separate offences. In any event, if the second order that the court proposes is a community punishment order, the sentencer will need to have regard to the maximum permissible aggregate of 100 hours, the ceiling set by Parliament as the maximum considered compatible with community rehabilitation commitments. It would seem wrong in principle to seek to combine a CPRO with a supervision order as this would juxtapose two distinct statutory regimes for supervision purposes. It appears technically proper for a CPRO to be combined with a curfew order for a single offence, though this may create difficulty in the event that one order is later revoked with a view to re-sentence while the other order remains in force. The new scope to make curfew an additional requirement in a community rehabilitation order under Sch 2 para 7 will avoid such problems.

The court is not permitted to make either an action plan order or a reparation order where it proposes to make a CPRO: s69(5)(b) and s73(4)(b). A CPRO cannot be imposed simultaneously with an immediate term of custody (see discussion at page 139) or a suspended term of imprisonment (see page 140).

DRUG TREATMENT AND TESTING ORDERS

Introduced by CDA 1998 ss61–64 as an additional community order, the drug treatment and testing order (DTTO) is now governed by PCC(S)A 2000 ss52–58. The order seeks to offer sentencers a more purposeful approach to drug misusing offenders, requiring courts to take an active role in their progress during sentence by conducting periodic reviews. This measure is intended to replace power to impose a probation order with an additional requirement of treatment for drug dependency under PCC(S)A 2000 Sch

2 para 6. To be eligible, an offender need not be 'dependent on drugs'; having 'a propensity to misuse drugs' will suffice. DTTOs were piloted in three areas (Gloucestershire, Liverpool and Croydon) for 18 months from 30 September 1998 and were implemented nationally from 2000, in the light of an evaluation study (Turnbull *et al*, 2000).

Power to Impose a DTTO: PCC(S)A 2000 s52

Courts to which Available Crown Court, magistrates' courts, youth courts.

Minimum Age 16.

Nature of Offence Any offence, imprisonable or otherwise, other than murder or one that attracts an automatic life or minimum custodial sentence under C(S)A 1997 ss2(2), 3(2) or 4(2), committed on or after 30 September 1998.

Duration The 'treatment and testing period', to be specified in the order, is of the same permissible length as a probation/community rehabilitation order, i.e. a minimum of six months and a maximum of three years. The Home Secretary retains the power to amend the minimum and maximum terms.

Criterion The court must be satisfied (s52(3)):

(a)   that the offender 'is dependent on or has a propensity to misuse drugs; and

(b)   that his dependency or propensity is such as requires and may be susceptible to treatment.'

This criterion is rather like the criterion to be satisfied before a requirement of treatment for drug dependency can be included in a community rehabilitation order (Sch 2 para 6) but is buttressed by a provision allowing sampling, subject to the offender's consent (s52(4)). However, this provision has since been largely superseded by the separate provisions of PCC(S)A 2000 s36A introduced by CJCSA 2000, authorising a court to order pre-sentence drug testing (see page 136) in respect of offenders aged 18 or older, without requiring consent. In consequence s52(4) has been amended to read:

For the purpose of ascertaining for the purposes of s52(3) whether the offender has any drug in his body (in a case where, at the time of his conviction, he was aged under 18), the court may by order require him to provide samples of such description as it may specify; but the court shall not make such an order unless the offender expresses his willingness to comply with its requirements.

For the consequences under PCC(S)A 2000 s79(3) where a juvenile defendant declines to express their willingness, see page 135.

Pre-Sentence Report? Mandatory (but see page 133).

Procedural Prerequisites

(i)   This measure is not available to the court unless it has been notified by the Home Secretary that 'arrangements for implementing such orders are available in the area proposed to be specified in the order and the notice has not been withdrawn': s52(5). Once notification has been given, the power to make a Sch 2 para 6 requirement in a probation order ceases: Sch 2 para 6(2).

(ii)   Additionally, the court shall not make a DTTO 'unless it is satisfied that arrangements have been or can be made for the treatment intended to be specified in the order (including arrangements for the reception of the offender where he is required to submit to treatment as a resident)': s53(3). The nature of the treatment under a DTTO is outlined below.

Explanation and Consent Before making a DTTO, the court 'shall explain to the offender in ordinary language': (a) the effect of the order and its requirements; (b) the consequences that may follow in the event of failure to comply; (c) the power of the court to review the order on the application of either the offender or the responsible officer; (d) that the order will be periodically reviewed under the provisions of s54 (s52(6)). 'The court shall not make the order unless the offender expresses his willingness to comply with its requirements': s52(7). For the consequences under PCC(S)A 2000 s79(3) where the defendant declines to express their willingness, see page 135.

Specified PSA A DTTO shall specify the PSA in which it appears to the court making the order that the offender resides or will reside: s54(1). The consequence is that a probation officer assigned to the specified PSA has responsibility for supervision of the offender and enforcement of the order.

Court Responsible for the Order The court which is 'responsible' for a DTTO (for the purposes of Review Hearings etc.) is ordinarily the court which makes the order (s54(7)(b)) but where the order is made by a magistrates' court where the PSA specified in the order (see above) is not the area for which the court acts, the court has discretion ('if it thinks fit') to include in the order that the court responsible for the order shall be a magistrates' court acting for that specified area: s54(9).

Provision of Copies of Order The court 'shall forthwith give copies of the order to a probation officer assigned to the court' who shall give a copy to the offender, to the 'treatment provider' (see below) and to the responsible officer: s57(1) and (4).

Fulfilling Procedural Requirements: the Tower Bridge Judgement

R (on the application of Inner London Probation Service) v Tower Bridge Magistrates' Court (2001) *The Times*, 21 May illustrates the care which courts must exercise in satisfying statutory prerequisites. A pre-sentence report prepared for a magistrates' court identified that a defendant convicted of shoplifting was a persistent offender with a history of drug dependency who was at high risk of further offending. Two probation orders imposed in the past two years had failed because of his chaotic mode of life associated with drug misuse. The reporter suggested that he might benefit from a drug treatment and testing order. However, after adjournment for a specialist assessment, the DTTO team advised the court that, because the offender wished to give priority to his employment and was thus unwilling to attend daily, he was not suitable for a DTTO. The offender requested either a suspended sentence or deferment of sentence but the district judge indicated that the only options were a DTTO or immediate imprisonment. Faced with this choice, the offender (who was representing himself) agreed to 'submit' to a DTTO. A probation officer on duty at court requested the opportunity to consult the senior officer of the DTTO team, reporting back that the defendant was definitely not suitable for such an order. The district judge nevertheless made a DTTO for 12 months. The Probation Service sought judicial review, challenging the court's decision on the basis that the court did not explain to the offender the effect of the order and obtain his consent, as statutorily required by PCC(S)A 2000 s52(6) and (7) before such an order can be made.

Upholding the challenge, the Divisional Court stated that 'unless the requirements of the DTTO have been clearly explained to the offender in court, it will generally be difficult for the court to be satisfied that his expressed willingness (if any) to comply with the requirements is genuine and meaningful'. Unless the court can be so satisfied, 'it may be difficult for the court to be satisfied that his dependency or propensity to misuse drugs may be susceptible to treatment' (s52(3)(b)). Further, the sentencer must be satisfied that arrangements have or can be made for the treatment to be specified in the order (s53(3)). This aspect had not been addressed in the specialist assessment, doubtless because the offender was found to be unsuitable for a DTTO. 'Although the court is entitled to assume that the Probation Service will loyally seek to give effect to the court's orders in so far as it is able to do so', there was no basis before the court on which the court could be so satisfied. That in itself was fatal to the sentence imposed.

Though the sentencer knew that the offender had read information about DTTOs, the court was still required to explain the proposed order in ordinary language and there was insufficient basis for believing this had happened. Additionally, the defendant's 'willingness' had been expressed in less-than-positive terms, 'submitting to the order and giving it a go, no doubt in the realisation that if he did not, he would go to prison'. The court was also faced with conflicting information about the offender's susceptibility to treatment. 'His reluctance to grasp the opportunity when it was first offered was discouraging, or should have been.'

Quashing the DTTO, supported in its decision by the news that the offender had failed to attend appointments made under the order, the Divisional Court indicated that:

> 'because of the strict and arduous requirements of a DTTO, any court should be slow to act against the conclusions of a reasoned probation service assessment unless it has cogent reasons for doing so. If it thinks that there are cogent reasons for disagreeing ... the court would be well advised to ask the person who made the unfavourable assessment, or some representative of the unit, to attend court so that the court can discuss matters as they then present themselves to the court.'

Where a court disagrees with a DTTO assessment and proceeds to make an order, it should express the reasons for its conclusions so that those responsible for the order can understand the factors which the court had in mind.

Requirements of a DTTO

The obligations of the order are fourfold:

(i) *'The Treatment Requirement':* 'a requirement that the offender shall submit, during the whole of the treatment and testing period to treatment by or under the direction of a specified person having the necessary qualifications or experience ("the treatment provider") with a view to the reduction or elimination of the offender's dependency on or propensity to misuse drugs': s53(1). As applies in regard to a requirement of treatment within a probation order, the treatment to be specified must be one of a number of precise options, in this case the two provided by s53(2):

The required treatment for any period shall be—

    (a)   treatment as a resident in such institution or place as may be specified in the order; or

    (b)   treatment as a non-resident in or at such institution or place, and at such intervals, as may be so specified;

but the nature of the treatment shall not be specified in the order except as mentioned in (a) or (b) above.

The statutory provisions do not identify the nature of the 'necessary' qualifications or experience to be offered by the treatment provider. The absence of an additional treatment option, available under a Sch 2 para 6 requirement ('treatment by or under the direction of such person ... as may be specified') should avoid the risk of the kind of loose, ambiguous and unlawful requirements that have been purported to be made under para 6 (see page 153). Regulation by the Home Office should ensure that this treatment provision is pursued in a more rigorous way.

(ii) *The Testing Requirement:* 'a requirement that, for the purpose of ascertaining whether he has any drug in his body during the treatment and testing period, the offender shall provide during that period, at such times or in such circumstances as may (subject to the provisions of the order) be determined by the treatment provider, samples of such description as may be so determined': s53(4). This provision gives considerable discretion to the treatment provider, the court's (mandatory) power being to 'specify for each month the minimum number of occasions on which samples are to be provided': s53(5). Test results must be communicated to the supervising probation officer (see below). Note that the requirement is simply to provide samples, not to produce samples that indicate the absence of controlled drugs.

(iii) *The Supervision Requirement:* A DTTO shall (s54(2) and (4)):

    (a)   provide that, for the treatment and testing period, the offender shall be under the supervision of a responsible officer, i.e. a probation officer appointed for or assigned to the PSA specified in the order;

    (b)   require the offender to keep in touch with the responsible officer in accordance with such instructions as he may from time to time be given by that officer, and to notify him of any change of address; and

    (c)   provide that the results of the tests carried out under the testing requirement shall be communicated to the responsible officer.

Supervision is, however, a limited exercise, and s54(5) specifies that it

shall be carried out only to the extent as may be necessary for the purpose of enabling him—

(a)   to report on the offender's progress to the court responsible for the order;

(b)   to report to that court any failure by the offender to comply with the requirements of the order; and

(c)   to determine whether the circumstances are such that he should apply to that court for the revocation or amendment of the order.

(iv) *Periodic Review Requirement:* A DTTO shall require the offender to attend review hearings by the court responsible for the order (s54(6)), as outlined below.

Periodic Review Hearings

An integral feature of a DTTO is the provision for the order 'to be reviewed periodically at intervals of not less than one month', 'at a hearing held for the purpose by the court responsible for the order': s54(6)(a) and (b). Before each hearing, the responsible officer shall report 'in writing on the offender's progress under the order': s54(6)(d). Each report shall include (i) the test results communicated to the officer and (ii) the views of the treatment provider as to the treatment and testing of the offender: s54(6)(e).

Amendment of Order At a review hearing, the court, after considering the responsible officer's report, 'may amend any requirement or provision of the order': s55(1). Power of amendment is restricted by s55(2)(b) in that the court cannot either reduce the treatment and testing period below the minimum of six months or increase the period above the maximum of three years. Further, the order may only amend the treatment or testing requirements if the offender expresses willingness to comply with the requirement as amended: s55(2)(a). Additionally, the court shall not amend the order while an appeal against the order is pending, except with the offender's consent: s55(2)(c).

Unwillingness to Comply with Proposed Amendment If the offender fails to express willingness to comply with the proposed amendment, the court may: (a) revoke the order; and (b) deal with him, for the offence in respect of which the order was made, in any manner in which it could deal with him if he had just been convicted by the court of the offence: s55(3). In dealing with the offender under s55(3)(b), a court shall take into account the extent to which the offender has complied with the requirements of the order, and may impose a custodial sentence notwithstanding anything in PCC(S)A 2000 s79(2) (i.e. the normal threshold criteria for a custodial sentence): s55(4).

Where the DTTO was imposed by a youth court in respect of an offender aged under 18 in respect of an indictable only offence, the court dealing with the offender under s55(3)(b) shall have power to impose a Level 5 fine and/or to deal with the offender as if s/he had just been convicted of an offence punishable with imprisonment not exceeding 6 months: s55(5).

Review Without a Hearing If the court at a review hearing is of the opinion that the offender's progress is satisfactory, the court may amend the order to provide for each subsequent review to be made by the court without a hearing, i.e. without the offender's attendance: s55(6). For the purposes of a review without a hearing, the 'court' means, in the case of the Crown Court, a judge of the court, and in the case of a magistrates' court, a single justice: s55(9). If at a subsequent review without a hearing the court is of the opinion that the offender's progress is no longer satisfactory, the court may require the offender to attend a hearing at a specified time and place: s55(7) and (8).

Enforcement of DTTOs

Apart from the special enforcement provisions pertaining to DTTOs through periodic review proceedings, enforcement powers are exercised through PCC(S)A 2000 Sch 3 which is applicable to DTTOs, in a modified form where necessary to reflect the special nature of this order The most significant difference is that jurisdiction in DTTO enforcement proceedings lies with the court that made the order, Crown Court or magistrates' court, not with a court acting for the PSA specified in the order.

DTTOs in Practice

Evaluation by Turnbull *et al* (2000) of the use of this order in the three trial areas can be summarised thus:

Selection: Before a DTTO can be made, offenders have to pass through a variety of selection processes: referral to the specialist team for assessment; consent; recommendation as suitable; agreement of sentencing court. Nearly three-quarters of those proposed to courts as suitable were given a DTTO. In Croydon, of 125 referrals 41% were considered unsuitable. Six offenders declined consent and the courts rejected 15 of the 57 orders proposed. In Liverpool, of 146 referrals, 112 were proposed as suitable (eight declined consent) and the court rejected 44, imprisoning 36. In Gloucestershire, of 257 referrals, under a half (119) were proposed as suitable of which 100 were given a DTTO.

Testing: Though the evaluation report does not make clear what courts ordered as the minimum number of tests per month, the frequency of tests varied, from three times a week throughout the order in Croydon to three or four tests in the first month and two/three a month thereafter in Liverpool. The majority view was that twice weekly testing in the first month was appropriate, more frequent testing being expensive and largely redundant.

Expectations of Offenders: The pilot sites had widely differing expectations of offenders' progress. The Gloucester project expected rapid progress to drug-free status whereas the other two programmes took what may be regarded as a more realistic view and expected a gradual progress towards abstinence. To expect offenders to be completely drug-free in a matter of weeks was regarded as 'pushing them too far'.

Court Reviews: The data for scrutiny was not complete but in Croydon and Liverpool reviews were held monthly while in Gloucestershire the initial review was held after a month with subsequent reviews as recommended by the DTTO team, ranging between one month and three months. Those attending residential rehabilitation programmes were expected to attend less frequently in all three areas. Almost all reviews were attended by the offender, with hearing length ranging from one to 70 minutes (average nine minutes). Though sentencers expressed a strong belief that there should be continuity so that offenders appeared for review before the sentencers who imposed the order, this happened routinely only in Liverpool. The outcome of reviews was 'no change' in 80% of hearings.

Enforcement: The scope for non-compliance is higher than in respect of a probation/CR order and lapses occurred, breach prosecutions occurring in 28 of 42 orders made in Croydon; in 29 of 68 cases made in Liverpool and in 63 of 100 cases made in Gloucestershire. The ensuing revocation rate as a percentage of orders made was 28% in Liverpool, 40% in Croydon and 60% in Gloucestershire.

DRUG ABSTINENCE ORDERS

Introduced by CJCSA 2000 s44, amending PCC(S)A 2000 by inserting ss58A-58B, the drug abstinence order is a new form of community order that seeks to combat drug-related crime by requiring the offender (s58A(1)):

(a)   to abstain from misusing specified Class A drugs; and

(b)   to provide, when instructed to do so by the responsible officer, any sample mentioned in the instruction for the purpose of ascertaining whether he has any specified Class A drug in his body.

Power to Make a Drug Abstinence Order: PCC(S)A 2000 s58A

Courts having Power Crown Court, magistrates' courts.

Offence Any offence, imprisonable or not.

Age of Offender Aged 18 at time of conviction.

Criteria A court shall not make an order unless (s58A(1)):

(a)   in the opinion of the court, the offender is dependent on, or has a propensity to misuse, specified Class A drugs; and

(b)   the offence in question is a trigger offence or, in the opinion of the court, the misuse by the offender of any specified Class A drug contributed to the offence in question.

A 'trigger offence' is one listed in CJCSA 2000 Sch 6 (see pages 155-156). The criteria is not unlike the criteria to be satisfied before a DTTO may be imposed but is more precise in regard to the type of offence which can attract a drug abstinence order and the narrowness of the type of drug misuse, being restricted to Class A substances. Courts will be able to reach the opinions specified in s58A(3) by means of the new power provided by s36A to order pre-sentence drug testing, as outlined at page 136.

Length As with a community rehabilitation order, the period specified shall be not less than six months and not more than three years.

Explanation Before making the order, the court shall explain to the offender the effect of the order, the consequences of breach and the scope for the order to be reviewed under Parts III and IV of PCC(S)A Sch 3.

Specified PSA Under s54(1), applied to drug abstinence orders by s58B(2), the order shall specify the PSA in which it appears to the court that the offender resides or will reside.

Responsible Officer/Supervisor See below.

Copies of Orders Section 54B(2) specifies that s57 (which regulates the supply of copies of a DTTO: see page 164) shall apply to drug abstinence orders, with the exception of: s57(2) (dealing with copies of any amendment of the order at a periodic review); s57(3A) (detailing arrangements for supplying copies of an order following amendment where a different court is now specified as responsible for the order); s57(4)(b) (which relates to 'treatment providers' and therefore not relevant in this context).

Requirements of the Order

In addition to requirements to (a) abstain from misusing one or more Class A drugs as specified, and (b) to submit samples for testing to monitor compliance with (a), in accordance with rules that the Home Secretary may make under s58A(8), the offender shall (c) be under the supervision of a person, being a person of a description determined by the Home Secretary: s58A(4). The person responsible for this supervision is the 'responsible officer' for enforcement purposes: s58A(5).

These provisions are augmented by s58B(2) which specifies that s54 (which governs the supervision of DTTOs: see page 166) shall apply to drug abstinence orders as if reference in s54 to DTTOs were to this kind of order. The aspects of s54 which are specifically excluded from cross-application are: s54(2) and (3) (which relate to supervision by a probation officer and the designation of 'responsible officer'); s54(6) (which provides for periodic reviews of a DTTO by the court – there is thus no equivalent scope for drug abstinence orders). Accordingly, an offender subject to a drug abstinence order is required to keep in touch with the responsible officer as instructed and to notify that officer of any change of address: s54(4)(a). The results of tests on samples provided by the offender under the order shall be communicated to the supervising officer: s54(4)(b). Supervision by the responsible officer is confined to the three responsibilities set by s54(5)(a)–(c) (see page 167).

CURFEW ORDERS

A sentencing innovation introduced by CJA 1991 and now regulated by PCC(S)A 2000 ss37–40, the curfew order has obvious parallels with the little-used power to impose a 'night restriction' requirement in a supervision order (see page 181) but is a free-standing, all age group, community order that requires the offender 'to remain, for periods specified in the order, at a place so specified': s37(1). This sentencing power was subjected to pilot trials from 1995, initially in three areas, before being rolled out nationally in 2000, following the implementation of Home Detention Curfews as an innovative feature of Early Release under CDA 1998. The curfew order is often referred to colloquially as 'tagging' because of the requirement of electronic monitoring that may be (and in practice invariably is) included in the order.

C(S)A 1997 s43 extended use of the curfew order to allow it to be imposed as a community order for young offenders aged under 16, again on a trial basis in the first instance, and as a penalty for fine default and, instead of a fine, upon 'petty persistent offenders' (see page 189).

Power to Impose a Curfew Order: PCC(S)A 2000 s37

Courts to which Available Crown Court, magistrates' courts, youth courts.

Minimum Age Originally 16, the minimum age is now 10, albeit that offenders aged under 16 are subject to a lower maximum duration (see below) and sentencers must follow an additional procedural requirement (see below).

Nature of Offence Any offence. Though often viewed as semi-custodial or as a community order that is particularly restrictive of liberty, s37 does not confine this penalty to imprisonable offences.

Length, Duration and Location The periods specified in the order must not 'fall outside the period of six months beginning with the day on which it is made': s37(3)(a). (Note that the maximum length of a curfew order made for fine default is 180 days.) Where the offender is aged under 16, the maximum duration is three months: s37(4)). The hours for which the offender may be curfewed are expressed as a negative: the order 'shall not specify periods which amount to less than two hours or more than 12 hours in any one day' (s37(3)(b)). The periods of curfew do not have to run in continuous daily blocks of time but can be specified on an entirely flexible basis as the court sees fit, in the light of the offender's commitments and any purpose that the court may be seeking to achieve (see 'absence of rationale', below). The absolute minimum order, in theory at least, is for two hours on one day only. The maximum is for 12 hours per day, daily for six months (i.e. 2,184 hours, or half that number in the case of a juvenile). There is thus considerable range of sentencing discretion. The periods can combine part of the morning , afternoon and evening, provided that these add up to at least two hours in any day. The periods can be daily but could be only for certain days of the week, such as at weekends. The sentencer can provide a gap in the timetable if this is thought fit, e.g. to allow the offender to go on holiday (though the forgoing of holiday might be regarded as a valid or inescapable part of the punishment). Different periods and different places may be specified for different days (s37(3)) and there is nothing in s37 that restricts the place(s) so specified to the offender's home, though in most instances that will be the specified place. This certainly makes the process of electronic monitoring more straightforward.

Aggregate and Overlapping Orders Unlike PCC(S)A 2000 s46(8) in respect of community service orders, s37 does not make reference to the maximum aggregate commitment to which an offender shall be liable or to the issue of concurrent or additional liability for two or more offences. This may prompt uncertainty in the event that the offender is dealt with for more than one offence on the same sentencing occasion or stands to be further sentenced while still subject to a curfew order imposed on an earlier occasion. It appears clear that Parliament sought to set a maximum for the potential restriction of a defendant's liberty of 12 hours per day at any one time and that it thus be unlawful to impose two or more sets of curfew hours for different offences that in aggregate total in excess of that maximum. Thus if X has committed three offences of theft from vehicles at night, it would not be open to the court to impose three separate nightly curfews of 4pm to 10pm, 10 pm to 4 am and 4 am to 10 am, as this would total 18 hours. Similarly, if X is made subject to a nightly 10 hour curfew, 8pm to 6am, for four months for an offence of night-time burglary and then two months later stands to be sentenced for day-time shoplifting, it is submitted that it would not be open to the court to impose a further curfew order with immediate effect of daytime curfew 9am to 6pm, as this would amount to an aggregate curfew of 19 hours. It would, however, be open to the court to specify that the second period of curfew should take effect in two months time after the earlier order is completed. Though the period specified must not fall outside a period of six months from the date of the order, the court is not obliged to require the order to take immediate effect. There is thus scope for what amounts to a consecutive curfew order and for the offender to be subject to curfew for an aggregate period exceeding six months. Similarly, if X is subject to curfew for six hours daily for offence A and during the life of that order stands to be sentenced for offence B, the court could impose a further curfew for six further hours with immediate effect as this would be within the permissible maximum.

Avoiding Legitimate Commitments The periods set for curfew 'shall, so far as practicable, be such as to avoid any conflict with the offender's religious beliefs or with the requirements of any other community order to which s/he may be subject, and any interference with the times, if any, at which s/he normally works or attends school or other educational establishment': s37(5). The demands of other commitments do not present an absolute veto to proposed curfew requirements, only in so far as is 'practicable'.

Absence of Rationale Unlike the provisions for making a community rehabilitation order, s37 does not require the sentencer to consider that the making of a curfew order is likely to achieve any purpose such as the protection of the public or the reduction of offending by the defendant. In other words, though this may be an informal hope of the sentencer, there is nothing in the formal powers of the court that prevents the imposition of a curfew order as a simple restriction of liberty, regardless of whether there is any pattern to the timing of the defendant's crimes or any periods of time that present a greater risk of re-offending.

Procedural Prerequisites Before making a curfew order, 'the court shall obtain and consider information about the place proposed to be specified in the order (including information as to the attitude of persons likely to be affected by the enforced presence there of the offender)': s37(8). The section does not specify how the court should secure this information though this is most conveniently and reliably obtained through a PSR. Note that the provision does not formally require the consent of any person whose co-operation is essential for the curfew order to be viable (particularly when the demands of electronic monitoring are also considered), though this seems a clear aspect of 'attitude' that should be assessed. In the case of an offender aged under 16, the court must additionally 'obtain and consider information about his family circumstances and the likely effect of such an order on those circumstances': s37(9). *National Standards* (2000, para B9) specify that where a PSR proposes a curfew order, it must include 'details of the suitability of the proposed curfew address and its likely effects on others living at the address'.

Explanation Before making the order, the court 'shall explain in ordinary language' (a) the effects of the order (including any electronic monitoring requirements), (b) the consequences of failure to comply, (c) the court's power to review the order on the application of either the offender or responsible officer: s37(10). The original requirement that the offender should express willingness to comply was abolished by C(S)A 1997 s38(2)(c).

Supervision The order 'shall include provision for making a person responsible for monitoring the offender's whereabouts' during curfew periods, as notified to the court by the Home Secretary. In practice, oversight is linked inextricably to the electronic monitoring arrangements and the designated person is a representative of one of the companies contracted to undertake this task.

Enforcement Jurisdiction The order is not required to specify a PSA but jurisdiction in enforcement proceedings lies with a court acting for the PSA in which the 'place' specified in the order is situated: PCC(S)A 2000 Sch 3 para 1(2)(a).

Electronic Monitoring

A curfew order may include requirements for securing the electronic monitoring of the offender's whereabouts during the curfew periods. This provision, formerly contained in s38, is now available within the generic power of s36B (see page 136). In reality, this option is standard for curfew orders so that oversight is primarily achieved by electronic surveillance, the offender wearing a PID (personal identification device) that transmits a signal to a HMU (home monitoring unit) installed in the offender's home, linked by telephone to the contractor's monitoring centre. If the offender is absent from home during a curfew period, so that the signal is transmitted to the HMU, this is automatically relayed to the monitoring centre for appropriate action.

Tandem Measures

A curfew order is not compatible with a sentence of immediate custody or a suspended sentence of imprisonment, even for a separate offence (s118(6)). It is unlawful to seek to combine a curfew order with a discharge for the same offence. As regards the imposition of a curfew order together with another community order for the same offence there is some basis for doubting the merits of this course in that if one order is revoked or discharged with a view to re-sentencing, it is difficult for the re-sentencing court to approach its task if the other order remains in force. There is additional doubt about combining a curfew order with a supervision order for a single or separate offences, given that the court has power to include a night restriction requirement (see page 181) in the latter which could be seen as a more compatible way of blending such measures. The likelihood of questionable combinations is much reduced as a consequence of the new power to include a curfew requirement in a community rehabilitation order (Sch 2 para 7) and to order the electronic monitoring of community orders generally under s36B.

Use

The experience of curfew orders during the first two years of the trial period in the three areas where electronic monitoring has been piloted, reported by Mair and Mortimer (1996) and Mortimer and May (1997), indicated that the average length of orders has been around 3.3 months. The shortest order made in the first year was for eight hours on each Saturday for 10 weeks. A clear relationship emerged between the length of order/number of hours subject to curfew and the likelihood of revocation following non-compliance. During the second year, 82% of orders were successfully completed. The offences most commonly resulting in curfew orders were: theft/handling (28%); burglary (19%); driving whilst disqualified (13%).

EXCLUSION ORDERS

Introduced by CJCSA 2000 s43 as an amendment to PCC(S)A 2000, inserting ss40A–40C, the exclusion order is a new form of community order designed to extend statutory control over an offender's whereabouts, not by curfew confinement to a specified place but by prohibiting him from entering a place specified in the order. 'Place' is explicitly stated to include 'an area': s40A(12).

Power to Impose an Exclusion Order: PCC(S)A 2000 s40A

Courts to which Available Crown Court, magistrates' courts, youth courts.

Minimum Age The minimum age is 10, albeit that offenders aged under 16 are subject to a lower maximum duration and to a special procedural requirement (see below).

Nature of Offence Any offence, imprisonable or not.

Length, Duration and Location The prohibition may extend for 'not more than one year': s40A(1). In relation to an offender aged under 16 at time of conviction, a lower maximum of three months applies: s40A(4). There is no specified minimum duration. Though the order may require the offender not to enter one specified place throughout the extent of the order, such as where the order is intended to offer protection in their home or workplace to a person at risk from the offender, the order (a) 'may provide for the prohibition to operate only during the periods specified in the order' and (b) 'may specify different places for different periods or days': s40A(3). Thus if the person at risk is considered to require protection both at work and at home, the order could specify each location but at different times, to fit with their anticipated movements. It does not appear possible within s40A(3) for more than one place to be the subject of prohibition at the same time. If this interpretation is correct, it would seem open to the court to impose more than one exclusion order, each specifying a different place, in respect of the same offence.

Procedural Requirement: Juvenile's Family Circumstances Before making an order in respect of an offender aged 16 at conviction, the court shall obtain and consider information about his family circumstances and the likely effect of such an order on those circumstances.

Avoidance of Interference with Legitimate Commitments So far as practicable, the requirements shall avoid conflict with the offender's religious beliefs or interference with his normal work hours or times of attendance for education, or with the requirements of any other community order to which he may be subject: s40A(5).

Explanation Before making the order, the court shall explain to the offender the effect of the order, the consequences of failure to comply and the power of the court to review the order under Sch 3.

Enforcement Jurisdiction The order shall specify the PSA in which the offender resides and jurisdiction lies with a court acting for that PSA.

Monitoring Arrangements Before a court may make an order, it has to be notified by the Home Secretary that arrangements for monitoring the offender's whereabouts are available in the area in which the specified place is situated. Under the generic powers of s36B, empowering the electronic monitoring of requirements in community orders, the court may, and invariably will, include such a requirement in an exclusion order, and monitoring will thus be undertaken by a company contracted to take responsibility for electronic monitoring in that area. Where an electronic monitoring requirement is proposed to be included in an exclusion order and this would not be practicable without the co-operation of a person other than the offender, the requirement shall not be included 'without that person's consent': s36B(3).

'Affected Person' Where the consent of a person is required in pursuance of s36B(3) (above) or a prohibition in the order is included for the purpose (or partly for the purpose) of protecting a person from being approached by the offender, the person has the status of 'affected person' and, in consequence, has the right to apply for the order to be reviewed under Parts III and IV of PCC(S)A 2000 Sch 3 and shall be given 'any information relating to the order which the court considers appropriate for him to have': s40A(11)(b).

ATTENDANCE CENTRE ORDERS

Designated a community order within the scope of CJA 1991, the attendance centre order (ACO) is now regulated by PCC(S)A 2000 ss60–62 (formerly CJA 1982 s17).It may also feature as a requirement of an action plan order (s70(1)(c)). This measure may be regarded as a somewhat tangential non-custodial measure as it has attracted little controversy, has a limited age range and is managed separately from more 'mainstream' orders of the court. It remains to be seen whether it maintains a significant market share as a stand alone order in youth justice sentencing.

In essence an ACO requires the offender to attend at a specified centre for such number of hours as may be specified: s60(1). The measure has had appeal to sentencers as (a) a means of imposing loss of liberty during prime weekend leisure time as a tangible penalty upon a young person not felt to require more sustained supervision; (b) a measure that the offender has to comply with personally, that may encourage the development of constructive leisure pursuits in a disciplined environment; (c) a means of bringing the young offender into positive contact with police officers (who normally staff centres). In a climate where we may be developing greater crime-reductive expectations of sentence-based intervention in the lives of young people, it may be that the ACO has less appeal than before.

In addition to its status as a community order, the ACO is available as a measure for eligible fine defaulters and for breach of supervision orders, action plan and reparation orders and also of orders regulated by PCC(S)A 2000 Sch 3 (where the offender is of an eligible age – under 21). The outline that follows addresses only its availability as a community order.

Power to Impose an ACO: PCC(S)A 2000 s60

Courts to which Available Crown Court, magistrates' courts, youth courts.

Nature of Offence Any imprisonable offence: s60(1)(a).

Eligible Age Though not a statutory differentiation, in practice the order is available to: males 10 to under 21 (depending on availability of centre); females: 10 to under 18.

Length The minimum and maximum number of hours in aggregate for which attendance may be ordered is expressed somewhat complexly by s60(3), varying primarily according to the offender's age but with a secondary degree of discretion according to what the court considers appropriate:

(i)   The aggregate number of hours shall not be less than 12, except where the offender is under 14 and, in the opinion of the court, 12 hours would be excessive, having regard to the offender's age or other circumstances: s60(3).

(ii)   The aggregate number of hours shall not exceed 12 except where the court is of the opinion, having regard to all the circumstances, that 12 hours would be inadequate: s60(4).

(iii) Where the court is of the opinion that 12 hours would be inadequate, the aggregate number of hours shall not exceed 24 hours where the offender is under 16, or 36 hours where the offender is not less than 16: s60(4).

This can be distilled as follows:

Age	Minimum Hours	Maximum Hours
10–11	12 (unless excessive)	24 (if 12 inadequate)
12–15	12	24 (if 12 inadequate)
16–20	12	36 (if 12 inadequate)

An offender shall not be required to attend at a centre on more than one occasion on any day, or for more than three hours on any occasion: s60(10).

Aggregate of Sentences on Different Sentencing Occasions 'A court may make an ACO in respect of an offender before a previous ACO made in respect of him has ceased to have effect, and may determine the number of hours to be specified in the order without regard:

(a)   to the number specified in the previous order; or

(b)   to the fact that that order is still in effect': (s60(5)).

In other words, the court can impose such hours as it sees fit on separate sentencing occasions, without having to have formal regard to the accumulating aggregate, though the court will doubtless wish to consider the overall impact of the total demand upon the young offender.

Procedural Prerequisite The court may impose an ACO only if:

(i)   it has been notified by the Home Secretary that a centre 'is available for the reception of persons of the offender's description': s60(1);

(ii)   it is 'satisfied that the centre ... is reasonably accessible to the offender, having regard to his age, the means of access available to him and any other circumstances': s60(7).

Centres are categorised as 'junior' or 'senior'. 'Junior' centres are designated for under 18s, though 16 and 17 year old boys may be allocated to a 'senior' centre, i.e. one taking young men up to age 20. Some but not all junior centres receive girls aged under 18. There are no senior centres for young women and thus this sentence is not available for female young adults. As regards accessibility, the *National Standard for Attendance Centres* (1995) specifies that offenders should not be expected to travel more than one hour or 10 miles (one way), whichever is the more, though 'courts may consider that less demanding travelling requirements are appropriate to younger attenders'. Travelling time does not count towards completion of the order.

Pre-Sentence Report? Not mandatory.

Distribution of Order The clerk of the court imposing an ACO shall deliver or send a copy of the order to the officer in charge of the specified centre and to the offender at the offender's usual or last place of abode: s60(11).

Agency Responsible for Supervision Responsibility rests with 'the officer in charge' of the specified centre. No agency has exclusive responsibility for centre provision and separate arrangements apply to each centre. Responsibility has commonly been exercised by an officer (or retired officer) of the local police force.

Tandem Measures

It appears wrong in principle to seek to combine an ACO with custodial sentence. It is also illogical and unlawful to combine an ACO with a discharge for a single offence. Where a court proposes to make an attendance centre order as a community sentence, it shall not make an action plan order: s69(5)(b). Otherwise, it appears possible to combine an ACO with another non-custodial sentence even for the same offence, though it appears undesirable to pair two community orders for the same offence as this will create difficulties in the event of revocation/discharge and re-sentence in respect of one order while the other remains in force.

SUPERVISION ORDERS

Introduced by CYPA 1969 as a distinctive and very flexible form of statutory supervision for juveniles, the supervision order was designated a community order by CJA 1991 and is now governed by PCC(S)A 2000 ss63–67. The order lost its exclusivity when the 1991 Act empowered courts to impose probation orders on offenders aged 16, thus overlapping the two forms of statutory community supervision as regards defendants aged 16–17. The future market share of the supervision order, in competition with the action plan order, remains to be seen but the supervision order would appear more appropriate where (a) the factors associated with offending are complex and need longer assessment; (b) there are several welfare issues at stake requiring significant input over time, in collaboration with other agencies; (c) lasting change is thus unlikely to be achieved within three months intervention.

Power to Impose a Supervision Order: PCC(S)A 2000 s63

Courts to which Available Crown Court, youth courts.

Eligible Age 10 to under 18.

Nature of Offence Any offence, imprisonable or otherwise.

Length The order runs for three years from the date on which it is made, or for such shorter period as may be specified: s63(7). There is thus no specified minimum length.

Supervising Agency The court has power to specify that supervision shall be exercised by (a) a local authority, (b) a probation officer, or a member of a youth offending team: s63(1). A local authority should not be designated 'unless the authority agree or it appears to the court that the supervised person resides or will reside in the area of the authority': s64(1). Where a probation officer is designated, the supervisor shall be a probation officer assigned to the PSA specified in the order: s64(2). If a YOT member is designated, the supervisor shall be a member of the team established by the local authority within whose area it appears to the court that the supervised person resides or will reside: s64(3).

Pre-Sentence Report? Mandatory if the proposed order will include any additional requirements authorised by PCC(S)A 2000 Sch 6 (but see page 133).

Consent The consent of the offender is not required before a supervision order can be imposed, except in the very limited instance of an additional requirement of treatment for mental condition under Sch 6 para 6, as detailed below.

Core Requirements

The essential consequence of an order is to place the offender under the supervision of the designated supervisor (s63(1)) who is then under a duty 'to advise, assist and befriend the supervised person': s64(4). Section 63(6) specifies that an order 'may contain such prescribed provisions as the court making the order considers appropriate for facilitating the performance by the supervisor of his functions under s64(4), including any prescribed provisions for requiring visits to be made by the offender to the supervisor'. In furtherance of this scope, as prescribed in Rules made under MCA 1980 s144, MC(C&YP)R 1992 r29(3) empowers the following requirements to be included in the standard order:

(a) That he shall inform the supervisor at once of any change of his residence or employment;

(b) That he shall keep in touch with the supervisor in accordance with such instructions as may from time to time be given by the supervisor and, in particular, that he shall, if the supervisor so requires, receive visits from the supervisor at his home.

Tandem Measures

If the court proposes to make a supervision order, it is not able to make either a reparation order (s73(4)(b)) or an action plan order (s69(5)(b)), on the same sentencing occasion. It appears either unlawful or improper in principle to combine a supervision order with:

a community rehabilitation order; a CPRO; or custody, either for the same offence or separate offences. To blend a supervision order with a community punishment order for a single offence for a 16 or 17 year old is not explicitly prohibited but this appears contrary to the spirit and intention of the current legislative framework. That combination for different offences was possible for 16 year olds before CJA 1991 and has not been subject to any Court of Appeal comment. To combine a supervision order with a curfew order for the same offence is questionable, given that there is scope for a supervision order to include an additional night restriction requirement. Under PCC(S)A 2000 s36B, introduced by CJCSA 2000 s52, a court may include electronic monitoring of requirements in supervision orders and can thus strengthen the enforceability of a night restriction requirement.

Additional Requirements

1. *General Power* Section 63(6) gives a general power to the court to include requirements but this should not be used to side-step the provisions of the Act to impose a range of specifically identified requirements. In practice, little use is made of this general power and by far the most important and utilised provisions are those now contained within PCC(S)A 2000 Sch 6. The court is generally able to combine Sch 6 requirements as it sees fit (Sch 6 para 8), subject to certain limitations as outlined below.

2. *To Comply with Supervisor's Directions* Under Sch 6 para 2(1) (formerly CYPA 1969 s12(2) and often referred to under the old law as 'Discretionary Intermediate Treatment'), the court may require the supervised person 'to comply with any directions given from time to time by the supervisor, requiring him to do all or any of the following things:

(a) to live at a place or places specified in the directions for a period or periods so specified;

(b) to present himself to a person or persons specified in the directions at a place or places and on a day or days so specified;

(c) to participate in activities specified in the directions on a day or days so specified'.

A requirement of this nature shall not be included unless the court is satisfied that a scheme is in force under s66 (regulating local authority facilities of this nature) for the area where the offender resides: para 2(2). The requirement shall be subject to any requirement under para 6 to receive treatment for mental condition.

Under this paragraph it is for the supervisor to decide whether and to what extent he exercises any power to give directions conferred on him and to decide the form of the directions: para 2(4). The discretion of the supervisor is limited as follows:

(a) para 2(2) specifies that no directions may involve the use of facilities which are not within a scheme in force under s66;

(b) para 2(7) specifies that directions shall, so far as practicable, avoid conflict/ interference with work, education, religious beliefs and the requirements of any other community order;

(c)   para 2(5) specifies that the total number of days for which the supervised person may be required to comply with directions shall not exceed 90, or such lesser number as the order may specify. In totting up the number of days, the supervisor is permitted to disregard any day for which directions were given but the supervised person failed to comply: para 2(6).

This provision embraces the original concept of IT introduced by the 1969 Act and has the scope to give the supervisor very wide and interventive discretion, the court having little sense of or say in how this will be exercised. In practice, s12 is used to require the offender to engage in activities rather than, for example, to reside away from home, and this 'version' of the supervision order is often perceived as of lesser tariff weight than a requirement imposed under para 3 (see below).

3. *Specified Activities Requirements* Under para 3(2) (formerly CYPA 1969 s12A(3)(a) and often referred to as stipulated Intermediate Treatment), the court can require the supervised person to undertake all or any of the requirements which can s/he can be directed to do under para 2(1)(a)–(c) (see above), shall not exceed 90 days, including any days when the offender is subject to a reparation requirement under para 3(2)(d) or to a night restriction requirement under para 3(2)(e) (para 3(3)) or such lesser number of days as may be specified in the order. Such a requirement may not be included in a supervision order that imposes an additional requirement under para 2: para 3(1). As a further restriction on the court's power, para 3(5)(c) and (d) specify that a requirement under para 3(2) shall not require the supervised person to reside with a specified individual (a requirement that *can* be imposed under para 2(1)), nor include a requirement for mental treatment (for which separate provision is made by para 6).

Procedural Prerequisites (i) The court may not include requirements under para 3(2) unless (para 3(4)):

(a)   it has first consulted the supervisor as to—

(i)   the offender's circumstances; and

(ii)   the feasibility of securing compliance with the requirements,

and is satisfied, having regard to the supervisor's report, that it is feasible to secure compliance with them;

(b)   having regard to the circumstances of the case, it considers the requirements necessary for securing the good conduct of the supervised person or for preventing a repetition by him of the same offence or the commission of other offences; and

(c)   if the supervised person is under 16, it has obtained and considered information about his family circumstances and the likely effect of the requirements on those circumstances.

(ii) The court shall not include any requirement that would involve the co-operation of a person other than the supervisor and the supervised person unless that other person consents to its inclusion: para 3 (5)(a).

180

Repeal of CYPA 1969 s12D Provisions The old provisions of s12D which empowered the court in certain instances to impose a s12A(3)(a) requirement instead of a custodial sentence were repealed by CDA 1998, as a consequence of the changes the 1998 Act introduced to CYPA 1969 strengthening the court's general powers to deal with breach of a supervision order by allowing re-sentence for the original offence.

4. *Night Restriction* Under para 3(2)(e), the court can require the supervised person to remain for specified periods between 6pm and 6am either at a place specified in the order or at one of several places so specified. The place (or one of the specified places) shall be where the supervised person lives: para 4(1). The supervised person may leave the place of restriction if accompanied by their parent or guardian, or their supervisor or some other specified person: para 4(6). Only nine orders made under Probation Service supervision in the five years 1994–98 included such a requirement.

Length and Duration The requirement shall not restrict the person for longer than 10 hours on any one night (para 4(2)) and the restriction shall not be imposed for more than 30 days (para 4(3)) and the total days for which the offender shall be subject to para 3(2) requirements (excluding any 'refraining' requirement) shall not exceed 90 days: para 3(3). The days so restricted must not fall outside the first three months of the order: para 4(4).

Procedural Prerequisites The same as apply under para 3(4) and (5) in respect of a specified activities requirement (see above).

5. *Refraining from Activities* Under para 3(2)(f), the court can require the supervised person to refrain from participating in activities specified in the order, on a specified day or days occurring within the period of the order, or during the whole or any specified portion of the order. The usual aggregate maximum length under para 3(2) does not apply: para 3(3). Only four orders made under Probation Service supervision in the five years 1994–98 included such a requirement.

Procedural Prerequisites The same as apply under para 3(4) and (5) in respect of a specified activities requirement (see above).

6. *Reparation Requirement* Under para 3(2)(d), the court can require the supervised person 'to make reparation specified in the order to a person or persons so specified or to the community at large', otherwise than by payment of compensation: para 3(2). The total number of days to which the offender shall be subject to para 3(2) requirements (excluding 'refraining' requirements') is 90 days: para 3(3).

Procedural Prerequisites The same as apply under para 3(4) and (5) in respect of a specified activities requirement (see above). In addition, para 3(5)(b) specifies that no requirement to make reparation to any person shall be included in an order 'unless that person (i) is identified by the court as a victim of the offence or a person otherwise affected by it; and (ii) consents to the inclusion of the requirement.'

7. *'Named Person' Residence Requirement* Under para 1 the court may require the supervised person 'to reside with an individual named in the order who agrees to the requirement' being made. Such a requirement 'shall be subject to any such requirement authorised under paras 2, 3, 6 or 7'.

8. *Residence Requirement: Local Authority Accommodation* Under para 5 the court may require the supervised person to live for a specified period not exceeding six months in local authority accommodation, provided that certain conditions specified by para 5(2) are satisfied:

(a) a supervision order has previously been imposed on the defendant;

(b) that supervision order imposed (i) a requirement under paras 1, 2, 3 or 7; or (ii) a local authority residence requirement;

(c) he 'fails to comply with that requirement, or is found guilty of an offence committed while that order was in force'; and

(d) the court is satisfied (i) that the failure to comply with the requirement, or the behaviour which constituted the offence, was due to a significant extent to the circumstances in which the supervised person was living (this prerequisite does not apply if the previous supervision order included a local authority residence requirement); and (ii) the imposition of a local authority residence requirement will assist in his rehabilitation.

The requirement shall designate the local authority that will receive the offender and this shall be the authority in whose area the offender resides: para 5(3). The court may include in the requirement a stipulation that the supervised person shall not live with a named person (para 5(5)), thus restricting the local authority's discretion, e.g. to place the young person with a member of their family. Where a para 5 requirement is imposed the court may also include any of the requirements contained in paras 2, 3, 6 and 7: para 5(9).

Procedural Prerequisites The court must first consult designated local authority: para 5(4). Additionally, a requirement may not be imposed on a defendant who is not legally represented unless he was granted a right to representation under the Criminal Defence Service or that right was withdrawn because of his conduct or he has refused or failed to seek such representation: para 5(7).

9. *Mental Treatment Requirement* Under para 6 (formerly CYPA 1969 s12B), the court can require the supervised person to receive treatment for his mental condition, on the evidence of a registered medical practitioner approved under MHA 1983 s12 and where satisfied that arrangements have been or can be made for the treatment in question. The provisions of para 6 are almost identical to those which pertain to a requirement of treatment for mental condition in a community rehabilitation order under PCC(S)A 2000 Sch 2 para 5 (see page 151). Where the defendant has attained the age of 14, this kind of requirement may not be imposed unless he consents to its inclusion: para 6(3)(b). Such a requirement shall not continue in force after the supervised person attains the age of 18: para 6(3).

10. *Educational Requirement* Under para 7 (formerly CYPA 1969 s12C(1)), the court may require a supervised person of compulsory school age to comply with such arrangements for his education as may from time to time be made by their parent (being arrangements approved by the local educational authority). This requirement may not be included in an order including a para 2(1) requirement.

Procedural Prerequisite (i) The authority must be consulted in advance about the proposed requirement (para 7(3)(a)); (ii) the court must be satisfied that, in the view of that authority, 'arrangements exist for the supervised person to receive efficient full-time education suitable to his age, ability and aptitude and any special educational needs he may have' (para 7(3)(b)); (iii) the supervisor must first be consulted about the defendant's circumstances; (iv) the court must be satisfied that the proposed requirement is 'necessary for securing the good conduct of the supervised person or for preventing a repetition of the same offence or the commission of other offences': para 7(5).

Intensive Supervision and Surveillance Programmes

Commencing in 2001, the Youth Justice Board is funding programmes targeting persistent young offenders, defined as those who have been charged or warned for an imprisonable offence on four or more separate occasions within the 12 months preceding their current court appearance and who have previously received at least one community or custodial penalty. YOTs have been invited to bid for grants to provide this resource. ISSPs are not exclusive to community sentences and may be pursued during the community supervision element of a detention and training order or as part of a bail supervision package. However, this form of intervention is probably most likely to be encountered as part of a community sentence. As ISSPs are intended to last at least six months, only supervision and community rehabilitation orders will stand to benefit. The aim is to provide a structured supervision programme during the first three months of at least five hours a day (weekdays) plus access to support during evenings and weekends. After three months face-to-face contact must be maintained for at least an hour each weekday. Additionally, the whereabouts of subjects must be checked at least twice daily. The package is intended to combine education, reparation, offending behaviour coursework and family support. The publicity offered by the Board clearly anticipates that requirements will be included in the two kinds of eligible community order to facilitate ISSPs but does not detail the precise legal provisions regarded as suitable for this purpose. The ambitious schedule of contact and demands appears to exceed the scope of additional requirements under either Sch 3 (allowing an aggregate of specified activities of 60 days in community rehabilitation orders) or Sch 6 (an aggregate of 90 days in supervision orders).

ACTION PLAN ORDERS

This new community order, introduced by CDA 1998 ss69–70 and now regulated by PCC(S)A 2000 ss69–72, requires a child or young person to comply with an 'action plan', defined as 'a series of requirements with respect to his actions and whereabouts': s69(1)(a). The nature and extent of those requirements and directions are detailed below but it will be seen that the APO can incorporate elements already familiar in supervision orders (specified activities, education arrangements) and ACOs, together with new ingredients of reparation and avoiding specified places, in a versatile regulatory cocktail. This sentence is the subject of detailed Home Office guidance (*Guidance Document: Action Plan Order*, 2000) as well as the rubrics set for youth justice workers by the *National Standards for Youth Justice* (Youth Justice Board, 2000).

Power to Impose an APO: PCC(S)A 2000 s69

Courts to which Available Crown Court, youth courts.

Nature of Offence Any offence, imprisonable or otherwise, other than one for which the sentence is fixed by law.

Eligible Age 10 to under 18.

Ineligible Defendants and Incompatible Measures An APO cannot be imposed (s69(5)) if either:

(a) the offender is already the subject of such an order (though he remains eligible if he has previously received an APO that has been completed); or

(b) the court proposes to pass on him one of the following—

    (i) a custodial sentence;

    (ii) a community rehabilitation order;

    (iii) a community punishment order;

    (iv) a community rehabilitation and punishment order;

    (v) a supervision order;

    (vi) an attendance order.

(Eligibility is unaffected if the defendant is already subject to an order listed.)

Criterion to be Satisfied The court must be of the opinion that making an order is 'desirable ... in the interests of securing the offender's rehabilitation or of preventing the commission by him of further offences': s69(3).

Length Compliance with the action plan is 'for a period of three months beginning with the date of the order': s69(1)(a). This suggests that the order remains in force until the expiry of that period though it is possible that the offender will have fulfilled the requirements of his plan before the expiry date. In that case, what residual obligations remain? The generic supervision demands of the *National Standards for Youth Justice* specify that 'minimum contact arranged with the offender must be twice-weekly' during the 'first 12 weeks of the order' (thus covering virtually the entirety of the action plan order) but can an offender who has completed his plan be subject of enforcement proceedings if he does not keep appointments fixed in accordance with the *Standards* rubric? This is further addressed below under 'Requirements'.

Pre-Sentence Report? Not mandatory but s69(6)(a) specifies that the court 'shall obtain and consider a written report by a probation officer, a social worker of a local authority social services department or a YOT member, indicating:

(i) the requirements proposed by the reporter to be included in the APO;

(ii) the benefits to the offender that the proposed requirements are designed to achieve; and

(iii) the attitude of a parent or guardian of the offender to the proposed requirements'.

In addition, s69(6)(b) specifies that where the offender is under 16, the court shall obtain and consider 'information about the offender's family circumstances and the likely effect of the order on those circumstances'. The *Guidance Document* (Home Office, 2000: para 3.7) adds that the report should also indicate: (i) the hours likely to be involved in completing the requirements and how these will fit in with school and work commitments and any religious observance (see s70(5)); (ii) that the consent of the victim has been obtained, where direct reparation is proposed; (iii) the officer who will be responsible for supervising the plan.

Other Procedural Prerequisite The court must have been notified by the Home Secretary that arrangements for implementing APOs are available in the area to be named in the order (and that the notice has not been withdrawn): s69(7).

Explanation Before making an APO, the court 'shall explain in ordinary language (a) the effect of the order and the proposed requirements; (b) the possible consequences of non-compliance; (c) the court's power to review the order on the application of the offender or the responsible officer: s69(11).

Specified PSA The order shall name the PSA in which it appears that the offender resides or will reside: s69(8). This is necessary in order to identify the court having jurisdiction for the purposes of enforcement proceedings (see below).

Responsible Officer The order shall specify which of the following shall act as the responsible officer: a probation officer; a local authority social worker; a YOT member (s69(4)).

Permitted Requirements and Directions

Under s70(1), the offender may be required 'to do all or any of the following things:

(a) to participate in activities specified in the requirements or directions at a time or times so specified;

(b) to present himself to a person or persons specified in the requirements or directions at a place or places and at a time or times so specified;

(c) to attend at an attendance centre specified in the requirements or directions for a number of hours so specified (not applicable unless the offence is imprisonable in the case of a person aged 21 or over: s70(2));

(d) to stay away from a place or places specified in the requirements or directions;

(e) to comply with any arrangements for his education specified in the requirements or directions;

(f) to make reparation specified in the requirements or directions to any person or persons so specified or to the community at large;

(g) to attend any hearing fixed by the court under s71'.

Additionally, s69(1)(b) 'places the offender ... under the supervision of the responsible officer' for the period of the order and s69(1)(c) requires him 'to comply with any directions given by the responsible officer with a view to implementation of that plan'. This gives the supervisor greater explicit authority to manage the order than applies under a reparation order (see page 201) but does not place the offender under an intrinsic obligation to notify the responsible officer of any change of address, though it would appear to follow that the officer could give an early direction that the offender should do so as this can be argued to be 'with a view to implementation of the plan'. But in the light of *National Standards* expectations of minimum twice-weekly contact (see above), will the supervisor be able to give enforceable directions that the offender continues to keep appointments once the plan is complete since such directions will no longer be related to the plan's implementation? If not, then the supervisor can only fall back on the general scope under s69(1)(b) to 'supervise' the offender and this does not appear to place the supervisor in a sound position in enforcement proceedings.

Such requirements and directions lawfully given under ss69 and 70 'shall, so far as practicable, be such as to avoid (a) any conflict with the offender's religious beliefs or with the requirements of any other community order to which he may be subject; and (b) any interference with the times, if any, at which he normally works or attends school or any other educational establishment': s70(5).

The Home Office *Guidance Document* (2000: para 4.2) illustrates the kind of activities that may be specified, involving intervention relevant to the defendant's offending and related lifestyle. A requirement of type (d) may aim to keep the offender away from places where he 'may have been accustomed to meet people who adversely influenced his behaviour' or from the victim's property' but careful thought should be given to the enforceability of such a requirement. The Document places emphasis on the care to be used in making arrangements for direct reparation to avoid exploiting or pressuring individual victims (see page 202 where these safeguards are noted in the context of reparation orders).

Optional Review Hearing within 21 Days

Immediately after making an APO, the court *may* (a) fix a further hearing, for a date not more than 21 days after the making of the order; and (b) direct the responsible officer (RO) to make, at that hearing, a report (not specified to be in writing) 'as to the effectiveness of the order and the extent to which it has been implemented': s71(1).

At a review hearing the court shall consider the RO's report and may, on the application of the RO or the offender, vary the order. The order may be varied either by (i) cancelling any provision included in it; or (ii) inserting in it (either in addition to or in substitution for any of its provisions) any provision that the court could originally have included in it: s71(2).

It remains to be seen whether courts will opt to order a review hearing as a routine way of maintaining oversight of APOs. It appears that there is power to fix only a single hearing, at time of sentence, to occur within the first three weeks of the three month period, and that the court cannot order any further review at any later stage in the order. Failure to attend for the hearing will constitute a failure to comply with the order.

Enforcement

Though an APO is a community order as defined by PCC(S)A 2000 s33(1), enforcement is regulated not by PCC(S)A 2000 Sch 3 but by a separate code, shared with reparation orders, contained in Sch 8.

6
OTHER DISPOSALS AND ANCILLARY
SENTENCING POWERS

This chapter corrals together a raft of measures that may be used either (i) where the court is able to exercise powers that fall short of a community sentence because the offence does not meet the 'serious enough' threshold test or because mitigation allows the offence to be dealt with in a milder way, or (ii) in addition to a custodial/community disposal as an ancillary sentencing power. The distinction between community sentences and other non-custodial sentences encompassed in the original CJA 1991 framework has been blurred by the subsequent introduction of non-community disposals for juveniles of an actively demanding, interventive nature and by power to impose community service/punishment and curfew orders as an alternative to a fine.

DISCHARGES
Absolute Discharge

Power to make an absolute discharge is now governed by PCC(S)A 2000 s12(1)(a).

Availability In any criminal court dealing with an offender of any age for any offence (except murder or where sentence falls to be imposed as a minimum custodial sentence or an automatic life sentence under PCC(S)A 2000 ss109–111).

Criterion As for a conditional discharge (see below).

Tandem Measures As for a conditional discharge (see below).

Principle As this measure causes the conviction to stand alone without any obligation or specific consequence beyond the finding of guilt, it is most likely to be imposed in the following circumstances (see Wasik, 1985):

- the offence is of a very minor or technical nature;

- the offender had very low culpability or pro-social motivation but in circumstances that do not provide a defence in law;

- the offender has suffered indirect punishment or collateral losses as a result of their crime of such a nature that direct punishment is not appropriate;

- the offender is being dealt with for a number of offences and an absolute discharge serves as a convenient disposal for a less serious matter, avoiding any clash with the effect of any substantial penalty imposed (the equivalent of imposing 'no separate penalty').

Use Absolute discharges were imposed for indictable (excluding motoring) offences upon 0.8% of offenders sentenced in magistrates' courts and only 0.1% of offenders in the Crown Court in 1998.

Conditional Discharge

Power to make a conditional discharge is now governed by PCC(S)A 2000 s12(1)(b). The limited legal consequences of a conviction followed by discharge are specified by s14, as explored fully in Wasik (1997).

Availability In any criminal court dealing with an offender of any age for any offence (except murder or where sentence falls to be imposed as a minimum custodial sentence or an automatic life sentence under PCC(S)A 2000 ss109–111), with the following exceptions.

Ineligibility CDA 1998 introduces three important limits to this wide discretion:

(a) Any child or young person who has been given a formal warning under CDA 1998 s53 and is convicted of an offence within two years of the warning shall not be eligible to receive a conditional discharge unless the court 'is of the opinion that there are exceptional circumstances relating to the offence or the offender which justify' such a disposal: CDA 1998 s54(4).

(b) Where a person contravenes the terms of an anti-social behaviour order, 'it shall not be open to the court by or before which he is convicted to make a (conditional discharge) in respect of the offence: CDA 1998 s2(11).

(c) The same restriction as in (b) will apply in respect of contravention of a sex offender order: CDA 1998 s3(9).

Criterion The court 'is of the opinion, having regard to the circumstances including the nature of the offence and the character of the offender, that it is inexpedient to inflict punishment': s12(1).

Condition That the offender commits no offence (imprisonable or not) during such period, not exceeding three years from the date of the order, as may be specified: s12(1)(b). Note that there is no minimum period in law, though any period is unlikely to be less than six months.

Procedure The court must explain to the offender 'in ordinary language' that if s/he commits another offence during the discharge period s/he shall be liable to be sentenced for the original offence: s12(4).

Tandem Measures Costs; Compensation Order; Forfeiture Order; Endorsement or Disqualification from Driving; Recommendation for Deportation.

Principle The conditional discharge has been characterised as a 'threat' (Ashworth, 1995) or 'a mild penalty in the form of a warning' (Blackstone's). In *R v Watts* (1984) 6 Cr App R(S) 61 – where a conditional discharge was imposed in place of a suspended sentence upon an appellant who had permitted cannabis smoking in her home but who otherwise had led an 'honest and perfectly respectable life' for 15 years – the Court of Appeal said that the offence required 'some sanction to prevent her from permitting a repetition'. A conditional discharge may be the appropriate disposal where the offence is insufficiently serious to justify a fine (though most fined offenders are unlikely to seek to appeal against their sentence). Thus in *R v Jamieson* (1975) 60 Cr App R 318, a fine of £300 imposed for theft of a half-bottle of whisky on a man of previous good character and with substantial personal mitigation was varied to a conditional discharge. It is less clear whether this measure is flexible enough to be used at any level of seriousness in place of punishment, perhaps where the court wishes to avoid a specific penalty or where the offence crosses either the 'so serious' or the 'serious enough' threshold but there are reasons why a custodial or community sentence should be avoided, given the particular circumstances of the offender. The measure has the advantage of keeping the court's sentencing powers intact for a later date, and thus may be preferred to a fine if the offender is not 'suitable' at this stage for a community sentence.

Use Conditional discharges were imposed for indictable (excluding motoring) offences upon 20% of offenders sentenced in magistrates' courts and 3% of offenders in the Crown Court in 1998.

Breach See page 229.

FINANCIAL ORDERS AND MEASURES FOR PETTY PERSISTENT OFFENDERS

Fines

By far the most common penalty imposed in criminal proceedings, the fine is simply an order that the offender shall pay a sum of money to the State. A fine should represent a 'hardship', one of the objectives being to 'remind the offender that what he has done is wrong': *R v Olliver* (1989) 11 Cr App R(S) 10.

Power to Fine

Magistrates' Courts On convicting of an either way offence, the court may fine the offender a sum not exceeding the 'prescribed sum', which at present is £5,000 (MCA 1980 s32(9)), unless the statute creating the offence specifies a different maximum. The maximum fine for a summary offence varies according to the level on the 'standard scale' specified by CJA 1982 s37(2), a device that allows the actual maxima to be varied in line with inflation by order of the Home Secretary. The current maxima, fixed in 1991, are as follows:

Level on Scale	Amount
1	£200
2	£500
3	£1,000
4	£2,500
5	£5,000

For defendants aged under 18, the maximum sum that may be imposed by a magistrates' court is subject to a special ceiling (PCC(S)A 2000 s135). In instances where an adult could be fined a sum exceeding £1,000, the amount for a youth shall not exceed £1,000. Where the defendant is aged under 14, and the court could otherwise have imposed a sum exceeding £250, the fine shall not exceed that sum.

Crown Court The Crown Court has general discretion under PCC(S)A 2000 s127 upon conviction on indictment to 'impose a fine instead of or in addition to dealing with (the offender) in any other way in which the court has power to deal with him, subject however to any enactment requiring the offender to be dealt with in a particular way'. This discretion applies also where the offender has been committed for sentence under MCA 1980 s38. There is no statutory maximum to the amount of fine that may be imposed either upon an adult or a youth. However, where the Crown Court is dealing with an appeal from a magistrates' court or is sentencing upon breach of a conditional discharge imposed by the lower court, the maximum amount available to the justices applies.

Determining the Amount of a Fine

Seriousness of Offence The amount of any fine 'shall be such as, in the opinion of the court, reflects the seriousness of the offence': s128(2). The court should thus have regard to aggravating and mitigating factors in the normal way. A defendant pleading guilty and thus having the benefit of s152 (see page 16) is therefore not likely to receive the maximum fine. Some cases would seem to be insufficiently serious to attract a fine at all – see *R v Jamieson* (1975) detailed on page 188. *R v Cleminson* (1985) 7 Cr App R(S) 128 illustrates an instance where a fine (of £1,000 imposed for handling stolen goods) was reduced (to £150) on the basis that the original sum was excessive, judged by the gravity of the crime.

Financial Circumstances of the Offender Before fixing the amount of any fine, 'a court shall inquire into (the offender's) financial circumstances' (s128(1)) and, in fixing the amount, 'a court shall take into account the circumstances of the case including, among other things, the financial circumstances of the offender so far as they are known, or appear, to the court': s128(3). This requirement to take account of financial circumstances can have 'the effect of increasing or reducing the amount of the fine': s128(4). However, while a court is able to increase the amount of a fine to take account of an offender's advantageous financial circumstances, it must retain a sense of proportionality in regard to the seriousness of the offence. Thus in *R v Jerome* [2001] 1 Cr App R(S) 316 where an offender convicted of handling stolen computer equipment value £2,739 ran a successful business, fine of £10,000 was reduced to £6,000 to reflect more appropriately the scale of the offence.

The amount of a fine should not be fixed on the assumption that another person – even the offender's spouse – will help to pay it (*R v Charambous* (1984) 6 Cr App R(S) 389). The fine should reflect the offender's own means, not their family's. Note that if the offender is liable to fine in respect of a number of offences, the aggregate amount should be reviewed by the sentencer to ensure that the overall sentence remains proportionate to the totality of their offending: CJA 1991 s28(2)(b).

If an offender is affluent and thus able to meet a fine without any inconvenience, even where the amount reflects their ability to pay, it would be wrong in principle to impose a custodial or community penalty in its place if the court considers that a fine is the proper sentence to reflect the seriousness of the offence. Equally, an offender convicted of an offence of sufficient seriousness to attract a custodial or community penalty should not be dealt with by a fine simply by reason of their capacity to meet a substantial sum. In other words, a rich defendant should not be able to 'buy their way out of prison' (*R v*

Markwick (1953) 37 Cr App R 125). However, note the case of *R v Olliver and Olliver* (1989) 11 Cr App R(S) 10 where two brothers convicted of wounding and ABH against a police officer, matters that often attract custodial sentences, were fined and ordered to pay compensation. The Court of Appeal supported this disposal, noting that they ran a carpentry business on which the jobs of 23 employees depended and to imprison them would jeopardise the livelihoods of their workers.

Financial Circumstances Order

To assist the court in making such inquiry PCC(S)A 2000 s126(1) empowers a court to make a 'financial circumstances order' (FCO) following conviction. This requires the defendant to give 'such a statement of his financial circumstances as the court may require', within such period as may be specified: s126(3). Where a magistrates' court has been notified (under MCA 1980 s12(4) that a defendant intends to plead guilty without personal appearance, the court may nevertheless make an FCO: s126(2). Failure to comply with an FCO without reasonable excuse is punishable by a fine not exceeding Level Three. Knowingly or recklessly making a false statement or knowingly failing to disclose any material fact in an FCO is punishable with three months imprisonment or a fine not exceeding Level Four: s126(4) and (5). Where an offender has failed to comply with a s126(1) order or has otherwise failed to co-operate with the court in its inquiry into his or her financial circumstances, and the court considers that it has insufficient information to make a proper determination of their financial circumstances, 'it may make such determination as it thinks fit': s128(5).

Fine and Compensation

Where a court considers it appropriate to impose a fine and also to make a compensation order but the offender has insufficient means to pay both, the court 'shall give preference to compensation (though it may impose a fine as well)': PCC(S)A 2000 s130(12). Thus the amount of fine may be mitigated by the need to give priority to compensation.

Period of Payment

The Lord Chancellor's Department practice guidelines (1996) indicate that payment should be expected immediately if the court is sure that the offender has sufficient means to pay forthwith. If this is not possible, the court can either allow time for payment or agree to payment though a series of regular instalments. Scope for the Crown Court to allow time for payment and payment by instalments is provided by PCC(S)A 2000 s139(1)(a) and (b). Fines should be capable of being paid off within a reasonable time. A number of Court of Appeal decisions in the 1980s suggested that the sum should be payable within 12 months (and thus that the total amount should be set so that it could be realised in full via a feasible instalment rate). However, in *R v Olliver and Olliver* (1989) (detailed above), Lord Lane CJ stated that this was not a rigid rule and that sums that may take a longer period can be justified:

> 'There is nothing wrong in principle in the period of payment being longer, indeed much longer than one year, providing it is not an undue burden and so too severe a punishment having regard to the nature of the offence and the offender. Certainly ... a two year period will seldom be too long and in an appropriate case three years will be unassailable ...'.

Tandem Measures

A fine can in law be imposed compatibly with most other measures for a single offence, the principal exception being where the defendant is given a discharge, absolute or conditional. The old prohibition against combining a fine with a probation order for a single offence no longer applies now that probation is a sentence. Courts are generally reluctant to combine a fine with an immediate custodial sentence, for the same or different offences, though may do so if this is considered a means of removing the offender's profit from their offending, if no other means (such as a confiscation order) is appropriate. In 'exceptional circumstances' justifying a suspended term of imprisonment, a court is encouraged by PCC(S)A 2000 s118(5) to consider adding a fine.

Enforcement at Point of Sentence

For post-sentence enforcement powers in respect of fines, see Stone (1999). However, detailed here are measures that that may be exercised at point of sentence.

Crown Court In every instance where the Crown Court imposes a fine, the court is required to fix a term of imprisonment to be served in default: s139(2). The default period is determined according to a table of *maximum* periods applicable to the amount of the fine, specified by s139(4):

Not exceeding £200	7 days
£200+ to £500	14 days
£500+ to £1,000	28 days
£1,000+ to £2,500	45 days
£2,500+ to £5,000	3 months
£5,000+ to £10,000	6 months

Longer terms up to a maximum of 10 years apply for sums exceeding £10,000. Where more than one fine is imposed, consecutive terms may be fixed. No defendant upon whom a fine is imposed may be committed to imprisonment or detention forthwith unless in the case of an imprisonable offence s/he appears to have the means to pay the sum forthwith, or it appears that s/he is unlikely to remain long enough at a place of abode in the UK to enable payment to be enforced by other methods, or on that sentencing occasion the defendant is sentenced to immediate imprisonment or other custodial sentence, or is already serving a custodial sentence: PCCA 1973 s139(3).

Magistrates' Courts A magistrates' court may:

- order the defendant to be searched and any money found taken towards payment, though not if the court is satisfied that the money does not belong to the defendant or that the loss would be injurious to the defendant's family;

- where time to pay is allowed, set a review date at which the rate of payment can be scrutinised and any change of circumstances be assessed;

- where (a) the offence is imprisonable and the defendant appears to have sufficient means to pay forthwith, or (b) the defendant appears unlikely to remain long enough at a place of abode in the UK to enable enforcement by other methods, or (c) the defendant is sentenced to immediate imprisonment or detention for that or another offence or is already a serving prisoner, either—

(i)   issue a warrant of commitment for default in making payment forthwith, or

(ii) set a term of imprisonment or detention to be served in the event of default (MCA 1980 s82);

- make a money payment supervision order (MCA 1980 s88);

- on the defendant's application, make an attachment of earnings order (AEA 1971 s1(3));

- where default is made in paying forthwith, issue a warrant of distress or direct the issue of such a warrant but postpone its effect on conditions;

- where default is made in paying forthwith, order the defendant's detention under MCA 1980 s135 (see page 226).

Power to Order Parent to Pay

Where a person aged under 18 is convicted of any offence and the court is of the opinion that the case would best be met by the imposition of a fine or costs, or compensation order, the court has power under s137 to order that the sum shall be paid by the offender's parent/guardian. If the juvenile is aged under 16 then the order must be made unless the court is satisfied that the parent/guardian cannot be found or that 'it would be unreasonable to make an order for payment, having regard to the circumstances of the case'. No order should be made without first giving the parent an opportunity to be heard: s137(4). Before exercising this power, the court may make a financial circumstances order (see page 191) with respect to the parent: s136.

Use

Fines were imposed in 1999 on 34% of offenders sentenced for indictable offences in magistrates' courts and upon 3% of such offenders in the Crown Court.

Alternatives to Fine for Petty Persistent Offenders

In circumstances where either the Crown Court or a magistrates' court is minded to impose a fine, PCC(S)A 2000 s59 (formerly C(S)A 1997 s37) empowers the court to make either a community punishment order (from 40 hours to 240 hours) or a curfew order with electronic monitoring upon a defendant aged 16 or older, even though the offence does not cross the 'serious enough' threshold, as normally required by PCC(S)A 2000 s35(1) before a community sentence can be imposed (s59(4) states that either order may be imposed 'not withstanding anything in s35(1) or (3)(b)'). It is not open to a court to impose both measures as a double-headed alternative to a fine.

Non-Imprisonable Offence Section 59(1) states that it applies where 'a person is convicted of an offence ...', not 'an offence punishable by imprisonment' as specified in PCC(S)A 2000 s46(1) (see page 156). It appears clear from the provisions of s59(6) (which adapts the wording of s46(1) for this purpose) that s59 is intended to offer a new sentencing option in respect of all offences.

Applicable Criteria Each of the following conditions specified in s59(2) must be satisfied, qualifying the defendant as a 'persistent petty offender':

(a)   that one or more fines imposed on the offender in respect of one or more previous offences have not been paid;

(b)   if a fine were imposed in an amount which was commensurate with the seriousness of the offence, the offender would not have sufficient means to pay it.

By 'previous offences', s59(2)(a) appears to mean offences previously dealt with prior to the current sentencing exercise, not necessarily offences committed prior to the offence(s) being dealt with on the present occasion. 'Sufficient means to pay it' in s59(2)(b) appears to mean 'sufficient means to pay it out of disposable income within an appropriate reasonable period', not 'sufficient means to pay it at once'.

Community Punishment Order Before imposing a CS/CPO in these circumstances, the court must be satisfied, after hearing (if the court thinks necessary) an appropriate officer, that the offender is a suitable person to perform work under such an order: s46(4)). The sentencing court may face some difficulty in determining how many hours to impose of a measure that is normally intended to impose a restriction of liberty for an offence of intermediate level of seriousness. Some guidance may be drawn from the parallel provisions of C(S)A 1997 s35 which sets a top ceiling of 100 hours for non-payment of a fine exceeding £500, with a lower ceiling of 60 hours for a fine exceeding £200 and 40 hours for a fine not exceeding £200.

Curfew Order Before making such an order, the court 'shall obtain and consider information about the place proposed to be specified in the order (including information as to the attitude of persons likely to be affected by the enforced presence there of the offender)': s37(8). As in respect of CSOs in this context, the court has to determine the appropriate number of days to restrict the offender's liberty for an offence of lesser seriousness. Regard to C(S)A 1997 s35 (curfew orders for non-payment of fines) may indicate that the scale supplied there could set a ceiling as follows: intended fine not exceeding £200 – 20 days; £200+ <£500 – 30 days; £500+ <£1,000 – 60 days.

If Community Punishment and Curfew not Appropriate If the court concludes that neither order is appropriate for the offender, despite their inability to pay the fine deemed appropriate for the offence(s), the court has little option but to impose a reduced (and thus more realistic) fine or a conditional discharge (or perhaps disqualification from driving under PCC(S)A 2000 s146 – see page 222).

This measure was subject to pilot trials in two areas (Greater Manchester and Norfolk) from 1 January 1998, as reported by Elliott & Airs (2000).

Compensation Orders

A compensation order in criminal proceedings is intended as a convenient and speedy means of providing recompense to victims in straightforward cases without the need for resort to civil remedies.

PCC(S)A 2000 s130(1) empowers a court to make an order requiring the offender 'to pay compensation for any personal injury, loss or damage resulting from' the offence of which he is convicted or any other offence which is TIC. Additionally, the order may require the offender to make payments for funeral expenses or bereavement in respect of a death resulting from an offence, other than a death arising from a RTA. In respect of a Theft Act offence where property is recovered, any damage occurring while the property was out of the owner's possession shall be treated as having resulted from the offence, 'however and by whomsoever the damage was caused': s130(5). Section 130(3) makes clear that a compensation order is a clear expectation as 'a court shall give reasons, on passing sentence, if it does not make such an order' in a case where it is empowered to do so.

Amount of Compensation Compensation shall be of 'such amount as the court considers appropriate', having regard to the evidence and representations made by the prosecution and defence: s130(4). Section 131(1) limits the amount that may be ordered by a magistrates' court to £5,000 for each offence. If compensation is ordered in respect of any TIC offences, the magistrates must not exceed in aggregate the statutory maximum for the conviction offence(s): s131(2). Thus if an offender is convicted of an offence for which compensation of £1,000 is ordered, the maximum in respect of any TICs will be £4,000. The court must have regard to the means of the offender 'so far as they appear or are known to the court': s130(11). If the defence mitigates on the basis that the offender is able to pay a substantial sum in compensation, the advocate is obliged to check that the necessary means exist to fulfil this offer. Co-defendants can properly be required to pay different sums in compensation, despite equal responsibility for the loss or damage, if their capacity to pay is different. Where an offender has obtained substantial financial advantage from his offending, a court is entitled to assume that the money is still available to the offender unless he can produce convincing evidence to the contrary. The court may order a financial circumstances order (see page 191) to require the offender to give information to assist the court. If the prosecution can show that the offender had substantial assets in the recent past, the court will be able to assume that those assets remain available to be used to meet a compensation order unless the offender can show why those assets are no longer available to him: *R v Houghton and Maisey* [2001] 1 Cr App R(S) 337.

Compensation Order as Sentence or Ancillary Measure Because an order may be made 'instead of or in addition to' another sentence or order of the court, it is clear that it may be a free-standing disposal in its own right, though it is more usually imposed ancillary to another measure.

Compensation as Priority over Fine Where a court considers it appropriate to impose both a fine and make a compensation order, preference shall be given to compensation (s130(12)), though the court may impose a fine as well. A fine should thus be reduced or even disposed with to enable compensation to be paid where the offender's means prevent the imposition of the full amount of both financial demands.

Sentencing Principles The following general points can be drawn from case authority:

- Compensation orders are appropriate only where the issue of loss is straightforward and the amount can be readily ascertained.

- If the prosecution and defence are unable to agree the amount of the victim's loss, the court should not make an order unless it has received evidence. Merely hearing representations is not enough. However, complex inquiries into the scale of loss are not appropriate in this arena. Though the standard of proof that should apply in such determinations is not explicit, it appears that the court should be satisfied as to the extent of loss at least on a balance of probabilities.

- Assessment of personal injury is particularly complex and sentencers proposing to make such orders should satisfy themselves as to the proper evidential basis on which they are proceeding. In *R v Smith* [1998] 2 Cr App R(S) 400, a case of domestic violence ABH inflicting an eye injury, the Crown Court had ordered £4,000 compensation on the basis that permanent scarring had been caused. There was no up-to-date medical evidence from the victim as to her current condition and a complete absence of any prognosis regarding her facial injuries. In the light of the Judicial Studies Board guidelines on the assessment of personal injuries, the Appeal Court reduced the amount to £1,000.

- Personal injury or damage includes terror or distress directly occasioned by the offence.

- Compensation is not precluded by the fact that the offender has not profited or gained from the offence.

- The order should be precise, making clear which sums relate to which offence. A 'global' sum should not be ordered unless the offences were committed against the same victim. If there are co-defendants, separate orders should be made in respect of each of them.

- An order should be realistic in the sense that there is a realistic possibility of the order being complied with, and should not be oppressive in effect.

- An order should not involve payment by instalment over an unreasonable length of time. As Lord Widgery CJ stated in *R v Bradburn* (1973) 57 Cr App R 948, the order 'should be sharp in effect rather than protracted'. But in *R v Olliver* (1989) 11 Cr App R(S) 10, the Court of Appeal indicated that an order could properly be payable over a period of up to three years – 'a two year period will seldom be too long'.

- While an order may properly be combined with an immediate custodial term where the offender has the means to pay or has clear prospects of meeting payment on release, this will often be an inappropriate proposition and it may be wrong in principle for an order to be hanging over the offender's head on release if this would inhibit their resettlement and possibly increase the risk of re-offending.

Use

In 1999 compensation orders were made in respect of 16% of offenders sentenced for indictable offences by magistrates' courts (average order £207) and 7% of such offenders sentenced at the Crown Court (average order £1,411).

Recovery of Defence Costs Order

Under the *Criminal Defence Service (Recovery of Defence Costs Orders) Regulations 2001* (SI 2001/856), at the conclusion of proceedings against a defendant whose representation has been funded by the Legal Services Commission 'the judge shall consider whether it is reasonable to make a RDCO in all the circumstances of the case, including any other financial order or penalty' (r.11). Making such an order depends on the defendant's resources and is means tested (if income does not exceed £24,000 per year, income is not taken into account nor is the first £3,000 of capital). An RDCO may not be made against a funded defendant who has appeared in the magistrates' court only, or is committed for sentence, or is appealing against sentence to the Crown Court, or (other than in exceptional circumstances) has been acquitted: r.4. Where the judge considers an order is or may be reasonable but considers that further information is required, the matter may be adjourned to enable further information to be obtained.

REFERRAL AND REPARATION ORDERS

This section combines the two forms of interventive sentence available for juvenile offenders that fall outside the category of community sentence despite restricting the offender's liberty, and reflect the wish to engage actively with this age group about the consequences of their offending, without being tied by conventional considerations of offence seriousness.

Referral Orders

This new sentence, introduced by YJCEA 1999 ss1–15, and now governed by PCC(S)A 2000 ss16–27, is intended to be the standard form of sentencing response for young offenders on first conviction, based on principles of 'restorative justice': making good the harm caused, taking responsibility for the offence, gaining re-integration into the community. The emphasis is on challenging the offender about their behaviour at an early point in his offending career when he may be considered receptive to such restorative initiatives. The sentence aims to increase the prospective impact on the offender by referring him to a youth offender panel, established by the YOT, which seeks to 'reach agreement with the offender on a programme of behaviour the aim (or principal aim) of which is the prevention of re-offending by the offender': s23(1). (The agreement is known as a 'youth offender contract': s23(6).) This is hoped to have more impact on a young offender than a conventional sentencing exercise in court. This is thus a complex exercise involving procedures and meetings outside the court arena. The account that follows deals primarily with the powers and sentence of the court making the order. For more detail of the panel process, see Ball *et al* (2001). The measure is being piloted in a number of trial areas from 1 June 2000 to 31 December 2001.

Power to Make a Referral Order

Courts to which Available youth courts; other magistrates' courts. The Crown Court can make this order only when exercising its appellate jurisdiction but can remit the offender to a youth court if it considers a referral order to be appropriate.

Offence Eligibility Any offence, imprisonable or otherwise, other than one for which the sentence is fixed by law, where the court is not proposing to impose a custodial sentence or a hospital order or an absolute discharge: s16(1).

Age Eligibility 10 to under 18 (at the time when the court is *dealing with* the person).

Compulsory Referral Conditions If the following conditions specified by s17(1) are satisfied, the court is required by s16(2) to make a referral order:

(a)   the offender pleaded guilty to the offence and to any connected offence;

(b)   he has never been convicted by or before a court in the United Kingdom of any offence other than the offence and any connected offence; and

(c)   he has never been bound over in criminal proceedings in England and Wales or Northern Ireland to keep the peace or to be of good behaviour.

An offence is 'connected' with another if the offender falls to be dealt with for it at the same time as he is dealt with for the other offence (whether or not he is convicted of the offences at the same time or by or before the same court): s16(4). If the offender has been conditionally discharged on the occasion of a previous court appearance, this counts as a conviction despite the limiting provisions of s14(1): s17(5)(a).

Discretionary Referral Conditions If the following conditions specified by s17(2) are satisfied, the court has the discretion under s16(3) to make a referral order:

(a)   the offender is being dealt with by the court for the offence and one or more connected offences;

(b)   although he pleaded guilty to at least one of the offences mentioned in paragraph (a) above, he also pleaded not guilty to at least one of them;

(c)   he has never been convicted by or before a court in the United Kingdom of any offence other than the offences mentioned in paragraph (a) above; and

(d)   he has never been bound over in criminal proceedings in England and Wales or Northern Ireland to keep the peace or to be of good behaviour.

For the definition of 'connected' offences, see above. These two sets of criteria are intended to insure that the referral order is not deployed where the offender has denied either his single offence or all offences, as the order is intended to achieve progress with those who acknowledge their offending, to some extent at least.

Length and Duration The court does not specify the length of the order as such. Rather, s18(1)(c) states that the order 'shall specify the period for which any youth offender contract taking effect between the offender and the panel ... is to have effect (which must be not less than three months nor more than twelve months)'.

Relationship of Order to Offence Seriousness There is no statutory provision for the court to have regard to the seriousness of the offence, the aim being to deal appropriately with the risk of re-offending (s23(1)). However, the court has scope to reflect the seriousness of the offence in the length of period specified (see above) even if this does not relate necessarily to the extent of demands during the period set.

Two or More Offences If the court is dealing with the offender for two or more connected offences and makes a referral order in respect of each, the orders have the effect of referring the offender to a single panel but the periods specified under s18(1)(c) may be different: s18(5). The court may direct the period specified in one order to run 'concurrently with or be additional to that specified in any other order' but the total period for which a contract shall have effect must not exceed 12 months: s18(6). Each order shall be treated as 'associated with' any other.

Prior Prerequisite: Notice of Availability A court may not make a referral order unless notified by the Home Secretary that arrangements for implementing such orders are available in the area in which it appears to the court that the offender resides or will reside: s16(5).

Requirement The sole requirement under the order itself is that the offender shall 'attend each of the meetings of the panel'. The requirements of the contract will then be negotiated at the first panel meeting. The order does not place the offender under the supervision of any specified person or agency.

Specified Youth Offending Team The order shall specify the YOT responsible for implementing the order (s18(1)(a), being the team having such responsibility in the area in which it appears to the court that the offender resides or will reside (s18(2). The consequence is that jurisdiction in enforcement proceedings lies with a youth court acting for the named PSA.

Explanation On making a referral order the court shall explain to the offender in ordinary language (a) the effect of the order and (b) the consequences that may follow if no youth offender contract takes effect between the offender and the panel or if the offender breaches any of the terms of any such contract.

Effect of Order on Other Sentencing Powers If the court makes a referral order it may not deal with the offender for the offence or any 'connected offence' in any of the following 'prohibited ways' specified by s19(4):

(a) any community sentence;

(b) fine;

(c) reparation order;

(d) conditional discharge.

Further, the court may not make any of the following orders in connection with the offence or offences: binding over of the offender or of the parent/guardian (s150); parenting order (CDA 1998 s8). The intention is to delegate fully to the panel, giving it maximum discretion in determining the appropriate response to the offender's offending and circumstances. For good measure, s73(4) and s69(5) specify that a court shall not make either a reparation order or an action plan order if it proposes to make a referral order. However, the court retains discretion to make any other ancillary order for which the offender is eligible, including: costs, compensation order, forfeiture order, exclusion order, disqualification from driving. Where a court is required under s16(2) to make a referral order, the court may not exercise power under s1 to defer sentence (see page 58): s19(7). However, s16(2) and s16(3)(a) do not affect a court's power or duty to act as follows: remit to another court under s8; adjourn for inquiries under MCA 1980 s10(3); remand under MHA 1983 ss35, 38, 43 or 44 for reports, make an interim hospital order or commit to Crown Court with a view to a restriction order to be attached to a hospital order (s19(7)).

Parental Attendance at Panel Meetings As a secondary power when making a referral order, a court may make an order requiring 'the appropriate person(s)' to attend meetings of the youth offender panel: s20(1). The court is required to make such an order in respect of 'at least one appropriate person' where the offender is aged under 16 when the referral order is made (s20(2)); in the case of older offenders the court has discretion. However, such an order shall not be made if the court is satisfied that 'it would be unreasonable' to require such attendance: s 20(3)(a). Additionally, the court should not make such an order 'to an extent which the court is satisfied would be unreasonable': s20(3)(b). Each person who is a parent or guardian of the offender is an appropriate person (s20(4)) but in the case of an offender who is 'a child looked after by a local authority' (under the Children Act 1989), 'appropriate person' means a representative of the local authority concerned and each parent/guardian with whom the offender is allowed to live: s20(5).

Panel Proceedings

The meetings and proceedings of the youth offender panel are regulated by ss23–27 but are not detailed here, save that s23(2) specifies that the terms of the programme agreed with the offender 'may, in particular, include provision for any of the following:

(a)   the offender to make financial or other reparation to any person who appears to the panel to be a victim of, or otherwise affected by, the offence, or any of the offences, for which the offender was referred to the panel;

(b)   the offender to attend mediation sessions with any such victim or other person;

(c)   the offender to carry out unpaid work or service in or for the community;

(d)   the offender to be at home at times specified in or determined under the programme;

(e)   attendance by the offender at a school or other educational establishment or at a place of work;

(f)   the offender to participate in specified activities (such as those designed to address offending behaviour, those offering education or training or those assisting with the rehabilitation of persons dependent on, or having a propensity to misuse, alcohol or drugs);

(g)   the offender to present himself to specified persons at times and places specified in or determined under the programme;

(h)   the offender to stay away from specified places or persons (or both);

(i)   enabling the offender's compliance with the programme to be supervised and recorded.'

However, 'the programme may not provide for (a) the electronic monitoring of the offender's whereabouts; or (b) for the offender to have imposed on him any physical restriction on his movements': s23(3).

Enforcement

Enforcement of referral orders is governed by the dedicated provisions of PCC(S)A 2000 Sch 1 (formerly YJCEA 1999 Sch 1), detailed in respect of non-compliance in Stone (1999). The separate provisions governing re-offending during the period of referral are detailed below.

Further Convictions During Referral

Part Two of PCC(S)A 2000, Sch 1 deals with instances where an offender aged under 18 who is subject to a referral order appears before a youth court or other magistrates' court to be dealt with for an offence, provided: (i) that the offender's compliance period is less than 12 months and (ii) the occasion when the referral order was made was the only other occasion in which the offender has been dealt with for an offence by a court in the United Kingdom. These provisions can be summarised as follows.

(a)   If the further offence (and any associated offence) was committed *before* the referral order, the court *may* sentence the offender by making an order extending the compliance period: para 11.

(b)   If the offence was committed *after* the referral order, an order extending the compliance period may be made under para 12, but only if the court is satisfied on the basis of a report (by the panel or, if no contract has yet taken effect, the relevant youth offending team) that that there are exceptional circumstances which indicate that despite re-offending since referral to the panel, extension of the compliance period is likely to prevent further re-offending. Home Office Guidance (para 4.12) suggests that extension is 'most likely to be a satisfactory outcome where the re-offending occurs close to the outset of the referral period, or where the re-offending is in respect of a very minor offence'. If of that opinion, the court must state its reasons in open court: para 12(2)(b). An order extending the offender's compliance period must not cause it to exceed 12 months in aggregate: para 13(1). Revocation of a referral order under Sch 1 para 5(2) on referral back by the panel has the effect of revoking any related order made under paras 11 or 12: para 5(3).

Irrespective of whether the further offence was committed before or after the referral order was imposed, or whether the offender has attained the age of 18, where a court decides to deal with the further offence other than by making (i) an extension order under paras 11 or 12 (if the offender is of an eligible age), or (ii) an absolute discharge, that order of the court shall have the effect of revoking the referral order: Sch 1 para 14(2). The court may then deal with the offender for the offence for which the referral order was imposed, in any manner in which s/he could have been dealt with for that offence by the court which made the order, provided it appears in the interests of justice to do so: para 14(3). In dealing afresh with the original offence, account shall be taken of the extent of the offender's compliance with the terms of their contract: para 14(4).

Reparation Orders

A new sentence for young offenders, introduced by CDA 1998 ss67–68 and now regulated by PCC(S)A 2000 ss73–75, the reparation order embodies the belief expressed in the consultation paper *No More Excuses* (Home Office, 1997, para 4.13) that reparation can be:

'a catalyst for reform and rehabilitation and can also benefit victims – who may receive compensation, an apology or the chance to ask offenders why they committed the offence and to say how it made them feel.'

The sanction thus seeks to place victim-offender mediation on a statutory footing, to make young offenders face the consequences of their misbehaviour in a more direct and instructive way, and to allow them to 'make good' in kind rather than by financial recompense. The statute clearly expects this sentence to be imposed if available for an eligible young offender, as s73(8) specifies that 'the court shall give reasons if it does not make a reparation order in a case where it has power to do so.'

Status of the Reparation Order The reparation order is not included in the list of community orders at PCC(S)A 2000 s33(1) that can constitute or form part of a community sentence, and it is thus anomalous as a sentence that restricts the offender's liberty but is not subject to the test of the 'serious enough' threshold or the other provisions of ss35–36 regulating community sentences. Given also that the statute specifies that reparation can be a requirement of either a supervision order or an action plan order, it appears that the reparation order is intended for 'comparatively minor offences committed by relatively inexperienced young offenders' (*Justice of the Peace*, 28 February 1998).

Nature of Reparation

Though the spirit of reparation has the individual victim in mind, reparative initiatives of that nature may not be appropriate, either if there is no direct or personal victim or if that person is unwilling to receive reparation. The statute thus empowers the court to order the offender 'to make reparation specified in the order (a) to a person or persons so specified; or (b) to the community at large': s73(1) (to be known in future as 'community payback'). 'Any person so specified must be a person identified by the court as a victim of the offence or a person otherwise affected by it.'

The scope for reparation is explored in a Home Office *Guidance Document* (2000) which suggests that tasks might involve:

'a letter of apology, a meeting or restorative conference at which the nature and consequences of the offence are discussed and the offender apologises directly to the victim, or several hours per week of practical activity which benefits the victim or the community at large. Wherever possible, the nature of the reparation should be linked to the offence or type of offence for which the reparation is to be made.'

It is emphasised that a victim must give willing and informed consent to any form of direct reparation and that reparation should not be considered where there is any possibility that the victim might be put at risk by further contact with the offender. Detailed guidance is given as regards liaison with victims, pre-sentence and thereafter, and this is amplified by the relevant provisions of *National Standards for Youth Justice* (Youth Justice Board, 2000). In translating such safeguards into reality, practitioners may encounter problems in fulfilling such authoritative expectations within the limited timescale of court listings and sentencer expectations. In consequence, indirect reparation schemes or reparation through work of wider community benefit may be more readily offered, and the reparation order could be viewed as a junior form of the community service/punishment order. For fuller detail, see Ball *et al* (2001). As regards the statutory provision requiring victim/affected person consent, see below.

Power to Make a Reparation Order

Courts to which Available Crown Court, youth courts.

Offence Eligibility Any offence, imprisonable or otherwise, other than one for which the sentence is fixed by law.

Age Eligibility 10 to 18.

Length and Duration The 'work' ordered by the court shall not require 'more than 24 hours in aggregate' (s74(1)(a)) and the required reparation 'shall be made within a period of three months from the date of the making of the order': s74(8)(b). Requirements shall, so far as practicable, avoid (a) conflict with the offender's religious beliefs or with the requirements of any community order to which s/he may be subject, and (b) interference with their normal work hours or attendance at school or another educational establishment: s74(3). The statute leaves in some doubt what is the fate of the order when hours remain outstanding when the period of three months has elapsed. Parallels with the community service/punishment order come to mind but there is no equivalent provision to s47(3) to the effect that 'the order shall remain in force until the offender has worked under it the number of hours specified in it'. If the analogy nevertheless holds good, it can be argued that the offender's obligations continue beyond the three month timespan if hours remain to be completed.

Relationship of Requirements to Offence Seriousness Requirements specified in the order 'shall be such as in the opinion of the court are commensurate with seriousness of offence, or the combination of the offence and one or more offences associated with it': s74(2).

Supervision Reparation 'shall be made under the supervision of the responsible officer', as specified in the order (s74(8)(a)), i.e. a probation officer, a LASSD social worker or a YOT member: s74(5). In practice, responsibility will invariably be exercised by a YOT member. Note that reparation requirements are set by the court, not determined by the supervisor, though the court will be guided by the proposals in the report before it (see below). Note too that the statute does not make any provision for the conduct of supervision; for example, it does not require the offender to 'keep in touch' with their supervisor as instructed or notify change of address. This presumably reflects the intention that the order should entail a brief reparatory experience rather than a sustained process but appears to place the supervisor in a rather restricted position in the event of non-compliance. In this respect, too, the legislation relating to CS/CPOs is rather more helpful to those exercising supervision.

Prior Prerequisite: Notice of Availability A court may not make a reparation order unless notified by the Home Secretary that arrangements for implementing such orders are available in the PSA proposed to be named in the order: s73(6).

Procedural Prerequisite: Report and Victim Attitude Though a PSR is not a statutory requirement before making a reparation order, s73(5) specifies that before making an order 'a court shall obtain and consider a written report by a probation officer, a LASSD social worker or a YOT member, indicating:

(a)   the type of work that is suitable for the offender; and

(b)   the attitude of the victim or victims to the requirements proposed to be included in the order'.

The attitude of the proposed beneficiary mentioned in (b) above is clearly crucial, to ensure both sensitivity to the victim perspective and the viability of the proposed requirements. This is reflected in s74(1)(b) which specifies that a reparation order shall not require the offender 'to make reparation to any person without the consent of that person.'

Explanation In common with other community-based sentencing provisions, s73(7) requires the court before it makes a reparation order to explain to the offender in ordinary language (a) the effect of the order and its proposed requirements, (b) the consequences that may follow failure to comply, and (c) the power of the court to review the order on the application of either the offender or the responsible officer.

Petty Sessions Area The order shall name the PSA in which it appears that the offender resides or will reside: s74(4). The consequence is that jurisdiction in enforcement proceedings lies with a youth court acting for the named PSA.

Tandem Measures

PCC(S)A 2000 s73(4) specifies that a court shall not make a reparation order if it proposes:

(a)   to pass a custodial sentence on the offender; or

(b)   to make the offender subject to any of the following—

    (i)   a CSO;

    (ii)   a combination order;

    (iii)   a supervision order including ss12–12C requirements;

    (iv)   an action plan order.

The prohibition under (b) appears clearly to prevent such combinations either for a single offence or for more than one offence dealt with on the same sentencing occasion. This provision appears to allow the option of a probation or curfew order, or a supervision order without additional requirements, or a fine, alongside a reparation order for a single offence or more than one offence.

Enforcement

Enforcement of reparation orders is governed by the dedicated provisions of PCC(S)A 2000 Sch 8, which applies also to action plan orders. Sch 8 empowers 'the appropriate court' (i.e. a youth court acting for the named PSA) to discharge or vary the order, and to penalise the offender for failure to comply, including power to discharge the order and re-sentence for the original offence (or to return the offender to the Crown Court if the order was made by that court). Enforcement provisions are detailed in Stone (1999).

RESTITUTION, FORFEITURE AND CONFISCATION

Restitution Orders

Power to order restitution, formerly governed by TA 1968 s28, is now regulated by PCC(S)A 2000 ss148–149 and applies 'where goods have been stolen'.

Purpose To restore goods stolen or unlawfully removed to the person entitled to them or, if the goods are not recovered, to restore to that person the cash or goods equivalent.

Courts Crown Court, magistrates' courts, youth courts.

Offences A 'stealing' offence includes not just theft and related offences where theft is a constituent element (such as burglary and robbery) but also deception, handling and blackmail. The provision applies equally to TIC offences.

Powers Under s148(2) the court may:

(a) Whether upon application or at the court's own initiative, order anyone having possession or control of the goods to restore them to any person entitled to recover them from him. That person need not be the convicted offender and could be a purchaser in good faith.

(b) On the application of a person entitled to recover from the convicted person any other goods directly or indirectly representing the original stolen goods, as the proceeds of any disposal or realisation, order those other goods to be delivered or transferred to the applicant. Such an order should not cause the entitled person to recover more than the value of the original goods.

(c) Whether upon application or at the court's own initiative, order that a sum not exceeding the value of the original goods shall be paid to the entitled person out of any money in the possession of the convicted offender and taken from him on his apprehension. It is not necessary to establish that the money is the proceeds of the offence, simply that it belongs to the offender. Similarly, the fact that the offender gained a smaller sum than the value of the goods does not prevent an order for a greater sum out of any money taken from the offender.

A restitution order may be made even where the passing of sentence is in other respects deferred.

Principles An order should not be made unless the basis for making it is clear and has been established before sentencing. A criminal court is not a suitable forum in which to deal with complex issues of title and so an order will only be appropriate where title to goods is straightforward. However, 'in appropriate cases, where the evidence is clear, it is important that the court should make proper use of the powers ... since this can frequently avoid unnecessary expense and delay in the victim receiving the return of their property': *R v Calcutt* (1985) 7 Cr App R(S) 385.

Forfeiture and Deprivation

Courts have a general power under PCC(S)A 2000 s143 to order the forfeiture of property connected with the commission of an offence, together with other statutory powers specific to certain offences.

General Power

This power is of particular applicability if the offence consists of the unlawful possession of property but is also available if the property was used in committing or facilitating the offence or was intended to be used for that purpose. The property must have been lawfully seized from the offender, or was in his possession or under his control, at time of apprehension or summons.

PCC(S)A 2000 s143

(1) Where a person is convicted of an offence and the court by or before which he is convicted is satisfied that any property which has been lawfully seized from him, or which was in his possession or under his control at the time when he was apprehended for the offence or when a summons in respect of it was issued—

  (a) has been used for the purpose of committing, or facilitating the commission of, any offence, or

  (b) was intended by him to be used for that purpose,

  the court may (subject to subsection (5) below) make an order under this section in respect of that property.

(2) Where a person is convicted of an offence and the offence, or an offence which the court has taken into consideration in determining his sentence, consists of unlawful possession of property which—

  (a) has been lawfully seized from him, or

  (b) was in his possession or under his control at the time when he was apprehended for the offence of which he has been convicted or when a summons in respect of that offence was issued,

  the court may (subject to subsection (5) below) make an order under this section in respect of that property.

In considering whether to make an order, the court shall have regard to the value of the property and to the likely financial and other effects on the offender of the making of the order (taken together with any other order that the court contemplates making): s143(5).

Principles Case law indicates the following considerations:

* Forfeiture should be ordered only where the facts are straightforward and would thus not be appropriate where the property is in joint ownership.

* The power should not be used to forfeit property used in the commission of

an offence by some other person and s43(1)(a)(i) should be read as ' ... any offence by him'.

- Though forfeiture may be regarded primarily as a preventive measure, it may well have a punitive impact and the court should have regard to the totality of sentence (see page 27). If forfeiture would 'overdo the punishment' (*R v Buddo* (1982) 4 Cr App R(S) 268) or would have a disproportionately severe impact on the offender, an order would be inappropriate. Alternatively, the primary sentence may need to be scaled down, as *R v Priestley* [1996] Crim LR 356 illustrates. The deprivation order in that case was in respect of property and money worth in excess of £35,000. The Court of Appeal held that the totality principle required the term of imprisonment to be reduced or discounted from four to three years.

Forfeiture can be used routinely in respect of, say, tools used to break into property, duplicate car keys or radio equipment used to monitor police communications, but may become more problematic if, for example, a vehicle is used in the course of crime.

Effect of Forfeiture Forfeiture deprives the offender of any property rights but does not affect the rights of any other person. The order causes the property to pass into the possession of the police, subject to the provisions of the Police Property Act 1897. A claimant seeking to recover the property may apply to the court and must satisfy the court that s/he did not know and had no reason to suspect that the property was likely to be used for a criminal purpose. If no claim is made within six months, the property can be disposed of by sale. Where the offence in question caused loss or injury that would have justified a compensation order but for the offender's lack of means, the proceeds of sale can be used as compensation.

Other Statutory Powers

Prevention of Crime Act 1953 Permits the forfeiture and disposal of any weapon concerned in the offence of possessing an offensive weapon in any public place without lawful authority or excuse.

Firearms Act 1968 Section 52 empowers a court to order forfeiture of any firearm or ammunition when sentencing the offender to imprisonment or YOI, or to a probation order including an additional requirement that the offender does not possess, use or carry a firearm. This power applies even if the offence in question did not involve a firearm.

Obscene Publications Act 1964 Permits forfeiture of articles intended for publication for gain.

Misuse of Drugs Act 1971 Following conviction of any offence under this Act or a drug trafficking offence under DTOA 1986, the court may order 'anything shown to the satisfaction of the court to relate to the offence to be forfeited and either destroyed or dealt with' as the court may order: s27(1). Such property may include money, though this power should be distinguished from the Crown Court's power under DTA 1994 (see page 208).

Use

In 1999, forfeiture orders were made in respect of 10% of offenders sentenced for indictable offences by magistrates' courts and 14% of such offenders at the Crown Court.

Confiscation Orders

In cases where the offender has obtained property as a result of or in connection with the commission of an offence (other than drug trafficking offences, for which confiscation is regulated separately: see below), CJA 1988 s71 empowers the Crown Court (or a magistrates' court in very limited circumstances – see below), in addition to dealing with an offender in any other way, to make an order requiring the defendant to pay such sum as the court thinks fit. In assessing the amount of an offender's realisable property, the court has to determine the amount that might be realised, even though the market value of property in which the offender has an interest may not be certain and the court may not be aware of the exact extent of any encumbrances upon the property in favour of third persons. The court is not in a position to determine the extent of such interests and its decision is not binding upon any third parties but is simply resolving matters between the defendant and the Crown: *R v Harvey* (1998) *The Times* 14 October, in which the Appeal Court held that in making an order for £492,947 the judge was entitled to ignore the question whether there was a legal charge on the defendant's house of £350,000.

Crown Court Available where the sum involved is at least £10,000 on conviction of any indictable offence, where the court is satisfied that the offender has benefited to that extent from that offence or from that offence taken together with some other offence of which s/he is convicted in the same proceedings, or which is TIC. Now that many more offenders may be subject to committal for sentence under PCC(S)A 2000 s3 (under 'plea before venue' provisions – see page 64), CDA 1998 s83 clarifies that following such committal the Crown Court shall have powers under s71 as if the defendant was convicted on indictment. Schedule 9 of the 1998 Act specifies that s83 does not apply where the offence was committed before the commencement of that section (30 September 1998).

Magistrates' Courts In the same circumstances as apply in the Crown Court and also in respect of the following summary offences: relating to sex establishments; relating to video recordings of unclassified works; use of unlicensed premises as a cinema; relating to use of premises for entertainment, etc.

The prosecution must give written notice to the court that an order of at least £10,000 could be made against the offender. The making of an order is left out of account in determining the appropriate sentence or other manner of dealing with the offender, i.e. the totality principle does not apply.

Confiscation Orders under Drug Trafficking Act

Now consolidated under the provisions of DTA 1994, power to make a confiscation order in drugs trafficking cases is intended to ensure that the convicted drug trafficker is deprived of the benefit of any proceeds from their criminal activities and has been described as 'intentionally draconian' to remove ill-gotten gains: *R v Dickens* [1990] 2 QB 102.

Process Available only to the Crown Court, the power may be exercised either on the request of the prosecution or upon the Court's own initiative. Though the provisions of the Act will normally be complied with prior to sentence, the Court may postpone determination until after sentencing if it requires further information before proceeding: DTA 1994 s3.

Statutory Assumptions A person is deemed to have benefited from drug trafficking 'if he has at any time received any payment or other reward in connection with drug trafficking carried on by him or another person': s2(3). In determining first whether the defendant has so benefited, the Court 'shall make the required assumptions' (s4(2)) specified in s4(3), namely:

(a) that any property appearing to the Court—

    (i) to have been held by the defendant at any time since his conviction, or

    (ii) to have been transferred to him at any time since the beginning of the period of six years ending when the proceedings were instituted against him,

    was received by him, at the earliest time at which he appears to the Court to have held it, as a payment or reward in connection with drug trafficking carried on by him;

(b) that any expenditure of his since the beginning of the period was met out of payments received by him in connection with drug trafficking carried on by him; and

(c) that, for the purpose of valuing any property received or assumed to have been received by him at any time as such a reward, he received the property free of any other interests in it.

Once the prosecution has established a prima facie case to support the facts on the basis of which the assumptions are made, the defence may seek to rebut any of the assumptions by showing, on a balance of probabilities, that the assumption is not justified in respect of a particular item.

Though the Court is entitled to have regard to the general extent of the offender's assets for the purposes of making a confiscation order, the primary sentence imposed on the offender should be based on the offences of which s/he is convicted and it is wrong in principle for a heavier sentence to be imposed on the basis of what is established in the course of a DTA inquiry. Thus in *R v Callan* (1994) 15 Cr App R(S) 574 the Appeal Court held that it was wrong to deny an offender with no previous convictions credit for previous good character despite a finding under statutory assumptions that he had been involved in drug dealing prior to his conviction offences. If as in *R v McNulty* (1994) 15 Cr App R(S) 606 a defendant has pleaded guilty to supplying drugs on the basis of supplying only to friends and DTA inquiries indicate commercial dealing activities, a *Newton* hearing should be conducted to establish the basis for sentencing on the footing of 'beyond a reasonable doubt'. Where an offender was found in possession of controlled drugs and gives no credible explanation of how they came into his possession, a court may infer that the drugs were purchased for cash and that this expenditure was made from the proceeds of drug trafficking: *R v Dellaway* [2001] 1 Cr App R(S) 265.

Amount to be Recovered by Confiscation Order The amount of the order 'shall be the amount the Court assesses to be the value of the defendant's proceeds of drug trafficking' (s5(1)). But if the Court is satisfied that 'the amount that might be realised' is less than that value, the sum specified shall be either (a) the amount appearing to the Court to be the amount that might be realised, or (b) a nominal amount, where it appears that the amount that might be realised is nil: s5(3). The burden rests on the defendant to show, on a balance of probabilities, that the realisable amount is less than the value of their proceeds. The 'amount that might be realised' is defined as 'the total of the values at the time of all the realisable property held by the defendant', less the satisfaction of any 'obligations' (e.g. mortgage repayments) payable in respect of the property: s6(1).

Term in Default It is mandatory for the Court to fix a term of imprisonment or detention in default of payment, the maximum terms being the same periods as apply in respect of non-payment of fines (see page 192). Serving the specified term does not remove liability under the confiscation order: s9(5). If any sum under an order is not paid by the date specified, the defendant is liable in addition to pay interest for the period for which it remains unpaid.

Use

In 1999 of 6,577 offenders sentenced under the Drug Trafficking Acts confiscation orders were made in 1,009 cases (15%), in 682 instances for sums under £1,000, the average amount ordered being £15,964.

EXCLUSION AND DISQUALIFICATION ORDERS

Exclusion from Licensed Premises Orders

Under LP(ECP)A 1980 s1, a court may make an 'exclusion order' for a specified period, in addition to any sentence imposed for the offence or, where the offence was committed in England and Wales, in addition to an absolute or conditional discharge.

Qualifying Offence An offence committed on licensed premises (on-licence) where the court is satisfied that in committing that offence, the offender 'resorted to violence or offered or threatened to resort to violence'. The statutory provision does not specify that an order may be made only upon application by the prosecution (or the victim). It is thus open to the court to make an order on its own initiative. In *R v Penn* [1996] Crim LR 360 (see below) the Court of Appeal disapproved of the making of an order on the application of the local Licensed Victuallers Association, stating that it is undesirable for application to be made by someone who is not a party to the proceedings or a victim. An interested third party should make representations to the prosecution. It is nevertheless open to the writer of a PSR to address the possibility unprompted in their report, though it may be sensible first to approach the prosecution to see what view, if any, is taken of the suitability of this measure.

Effect of Order The offender is prohibited from entering those premises or any other specified premises, 'without the express consent of the licensee of the premises or his servant or agent'. A copy of the order shall be sent by the court to the licensee(s) of the premises concerned. In *R v Grady* (1990) 12 Cr App R(S) 152 the court's order specified any licensed premises 'within the county of Norfolk'. The order was quashed on appeal not because of its wide purported ambit but on the basis that such orders are intended for those who make a nuisance of themselves in public houses to the annoyance of other customers and possible danger to the licensee (here the offender was deemed not such a person being a woman of mature years of previous good character). It is nevertheless open to doubt whether a such a blanket order, unrelated to specific premises, is lawful (though the author has known a magistrates' court to make an order purporting to apply to all public houses in a small market town). The better view is that the order should specify the premises affected. In *R v Penn* (see above) an order (for 18 months covering 20 premises) was considered manifestly excessive for a man of 37 with no previous convictions for drink and violence convicted of unlawful wounding (a pub fight in which the landlord was apparently cut with a knife), especially given that he had been on bail for 18 months with a condition not to enter pubs in the area.

Length of Order Minimum of three months; maximum of two years.

Breach Entering premises in breach of the order is a summary offence, punishable by a fine not exceeding £200 and/or one month imprisonment. On conviction, the court shall consider whether the order should continue, be varied (by removing the name of any premises) or terminated, as it thinks fit. There is no power to extend the order.

Football Banning Orders

Under FSA 1989 s14A (as amended by F(D)A 2000) (replacing the provisions of POA 1986 s30) a court may impose a football banning order in addition to any sentence or conditional discharge for a 'football-related offence' where satisfied that the conviction is in connection with a 'regulated football match'. The court is under a duty to make a banning order where it is satisfied that there are reasonable grounds to believe that the issue of an order would help prevent violence or disorder at or in connection with regulated football matches. Where it has power to make an order but does not do so, it must state in open court why it is not satisfied that such reasonable grounds exist. (For more details of this complex legislation, see *HOC 34/2000: Home Office Guidance on Football-Related Legislation*. See also page 149 where a probation/community rehabilitation order is made for a football-related offence.

Qualifying Offences

Football-related offences are listed in FSA 1989 Sch 1, including any offence involving the use or threat of violence to another person or property or of threatening behaviour (POA 1986 s5), or the use, carrying or possession of an offensive weapon or firearm, or any offence under the Football Offences Act 1991 (which includes indecent or racialist chanting, throwing objects at or towards the pitch). The offence must have been committed in the period of 24 hours before the start of and after the end of a regulated match. For offences committed away from the ground itself, the court must issue a 'declaration of relevance' that the offence related to football matches. The court must normally be satisfied that the prosecution gave notice to the defence at least five days before trial that it is proposed to show that the offence was football-related, unless the defendant waives the giving of such notice or the court is satisfied that, notwithstanding lack of full notice, the interests of justice do not require more notice to be given.

Regulated Matches

This refers to any match regulated under the FSA 1989 and the F(D)A 2000. In respect of matches played in England and Wales, this means any association football match in which one or both teams represents a club which is a member of the Football League, the Football Association Premier League, or the Football Conference.

Effect of Order

The offender is forbidden from entering any premises for the purpose of attending any regulated football match. Additionally, save in exceptional circumstances which make such a requirement inappropriate, the offender is obliged, on the occasion of regulated football matches which are played outside England and Wales to report to a named police station and, unless confirmed to the contrary, submit their passport in advance of reporting requirements. (The requirement to surrender their passport comes into effect when the enforcing authority – The Football Banning Orders Authority – issues the banned person with a notice relating to a match outside the UK.) The offender is also required to report initially to a designated police station within the period of five days from the date of order (in the case of those receiving a custodial sentence, within five days of release from prison), so that the police may agree the location of the station for subsequent reporting/surrender of passport. The court may also order that a photograph of the defendant may be taken for enforcement purposes and the offender may be required to attend a specified police station within seven days for this purpose. A banning order may, if the court making the order thinks fit, impose additional requirements on the person in relation to any regulated football matches. A banning order preventing a UK national from leaving the country to attend a regulated match abroad is not contrary to the individual's freedom of movement under European Community law, nor a disproportionate response because the state is entitled to conclude that very firm measures are justified to confront 'the various sickening ills of football violence': *Gough v Chief Constable of Derbyshire* (2001) *The Times*, 19 July.

Duration

(a)   Where an immediate custodial sentence is imposed, a minimum of six years and a maximum of ten years.

(b)   In all other cases, a minimum of three years and a maximum of five years.

Enforcement

Breach Breach of an order is a summary offence punishable by a Level Five fine and/or six months' imprisonment.

Variation of Requirements On the application of the offender or prosecutor, the court has power to vary the order so as to impose, replace or omit any requirement.

Application to Terminate The offender may apply to a court acting for the PSA in which the order was made for the order to be terminated, after a minimum of at least two-thirds of the specified banning period has elapsed. On hearing such an application, the court must have regard to the applicant's character, his conduct since the order was made and the nature of the offence which led to the order. If the application is refused a further application may not be made for a further six months.

Travel Restriction Orders

The Criminal Justice and Police Act 2001 introduces a power for the Crown Court to impose travel restrictions on drug trafficking offenders. Under s33, the power is available where the offender receives a custodial sentence of four years or longer on conviction of a drug trafficking offence committed after commencement of the Act. In those circumstances the court has a duty to consider whether it would be appropriate to make such an order and, if it determines that an order is not appropriate, to state its reasons. An order prohibits the offender from leaving the United Kingdom during the period specified. The order may contain a direction that the offender surrenders any UK passport held by him to the court.

Qualifying Offences A drug trafficking offence for this purpose is defined by s34(1) to mean either (i) an offence under MDA 1971 s4(2) or (3) (production and supply of controlled drugs) or s20, or (ii) an offence under CEMA 1979 s50(2) or (3) (improper importation), s68(2) (exportation), or s170 (fraudulent evasion).

Length of Order For a minimum of two years (no specified maximum) from the date of the offender's release from custody (not including any temporary release).

Revocation and Suspension Section 35 provides that the offender may apply to the court either for the revocation of the order or for its temporary suspension. A revocation application cannot be made until after a 'minimum period' has elapsed since the period of prohibition began. The length of that period varies according to the length of the order: (a) four years or less requires a minimum of two years; (b) over four years but under ten years requires a minimum of four years; (c) ten years or longer requires a minimum of five years. The court shall not revoke the prohibition unless it considers this appropriate, having regard to the offender's character, his conduct since the order and the nature of the offences which prompted the order.

The offender may apply for suspension of the prohibition at any time after the making of the order and the length of suspension shall be for such period as the court may determine. This provision specifies no statutory criterion (such as 'exceptional compassionate grounds' as applies in respect of an early release licence condition not to leave the UK) for the exercise of this power.

Disqualification of Company Director

Under CDDA 1986 ss1 and 2 a court has power to make a disqualification order on a defendant convicted of an indictable offence, whether on indictment or summarily, committed in connection with the promotion, formation, management or liquidation of a company, or in connection with the receivership or management of a company's property. In some instances the court is required to impose such an order; in other instances the power is discretionary. The consequence is that the offender must not be a director, administrator or liquidator of a company, a receiver or manager of a company's property, or in any way, directly or indirectly, be concerned or take part in the promotion, formation or management of a company for the period specified. The maximum period of disqualification is five years (magistrates' court) or 15 years (Crown Court).

Contravention of a disqualification order is an offence punishable on indictment by a maximum of two years imprisonment.

Disqualification Regarding Animals

Dangerous Dogs: Destruction and Disqualification

Upon conviction of an offence under DDA 1991 s1 (control and possession of a dog bred for fighting) or s3(1) or (3) (failing to keep a dog under proper control) or of an offence under an order made under s2, a court may order the destruction of any dog concerned in the offence (a destruction order is mandatory in respect of an offence under s1 or an 'aggravated offence' – i.e. where the dog injures any person – under s3): s4(1)(a). The court may also order the offender to be disqualified from having custody of a dog, for such period as the court thinks fit: s4(1)(b). Contravention of a disqualification order is a summary offence punishable by a Level Five fine.

Disqualification from Working with Children

CJCSA 2000 ss28–29 introduce a mandatory power to disqualify an offender from working with children, s28 dealing with those aged 18 or over when the relevant offence was committed and s29 with those aged under 18 on commission of that offence. In each instance the measure applies where:

(a) the offender is convicted of 'an offence against a child', as listed in Sch 4 of the Act, (or receives a hospital/guardianship order without conviction) and

(b) a 'qualifying sentence' (i.e. a custodial sentence, including a detention and training order, of 12 months or longer) is imposed for that offence by a 'senior court' (i.e. the Crown Court, Court of Appeal or a court-martial).

In respect of s28, the court must order the offender to be disqualified from working with children unless the court is satisfied, having regard to all the circumstances, 'that it is unlikely that the individual will commit any further offence against a child' (s28(5)). If the court does not make an order, it must state its reasons for not doing so (s28(6)). In respect of s29, the court must order the offender to be disqualified from working with children if it is satisfied, having regard to all the circumstances, 'that it is likely that the individual will commit any further offence against a child' (s29(4)). If the court makes an order, it must state its reasons for doing so (s29(5)).

Disqualification from Driving

Disqualification from driving primarily arises under RTOA 1988 as an incapacitative measure where the offender's standard of driving or road use has raised cause for concern. The measure also has obvious deterrent potential as the capacity to drive is a valued asset. Disqualification under this legislation may be either a discretionary or obligatory penalty, depending on the offence for which the defendant now stands convicted and/or their driving record. Disqualification cannot be imposed in the defendant's absence. Disqualification cannot be imposed either on the same or subsequent sentencing occasion to run consecutively to another period of ban. Disqualification commences from the point at which the order is imposed.

Disqualification may also be imposed by the Crown Court PCC(S)A 2000 s146 for car-related crime and, under more controversial powers introduced by C(S)A 1997 s39 and now translated to the 2000 Act, by any court as an optional penalty irrespective of the nature of the offence. These measures are discussed at page 222 after the main RTOA provisions have been outlined.

Obligatory Disqualification: Nature of Offence

Disqualification is obligatory upon conviction of the following, as listed in RTOA 1988 Sch 2:

- causing death by dangerous driving;
- causing death by careless driving when under the influence of drink/drugs;
- dangerous driving;
- driving/attempting to drive/in charge of vehicle with excess alcohol;
- driving/attempting to drive/in charge of vehicle when unfit to drive through drink/drugs;
- failing to provide specimen for analysis required to ascertain ability to drive or proportion of alcohol in driver's body;
- manslaughter by driving;
- aggravated vehicle taking (even if not driving the vehicle).

Length of Disqualification Where disqualification is mandatory, the basic *minimum* period of ban is *12 months*: RTOA 1988 s34(1). However, in certain instances the minimum period is specified as longer:

- offence of manslaughter, death by dangerous driving, or death by careless driving when under the influence of drink/drugs: *two years* minimum.
- defendant has had more than one previous ban for 56 days or longer imposed within three years immediately preceding the date of their current offence: *two years* minimum.
- defendant convicted of—

    (a) death by careless driving when under the influence of drink/drugs, or

    (b) driving/attempting to drive whilst unfit, or

    (c) driving/attempting to drive with excess alcohol, or

    (d) failing to provide a specimen (as above),

    and has within the 10 years immediately preceding the date of their current offence been convicted of any such offence: *three years* minimum.

Note that there is no specified maximum period of ban, even by a magistrates' court, and the court is empowered to set such period as it 'thinks fit' (see below).

'Special Reasons' Though disqualification is obligatory, s34(1) specifies that the court may opt not to impose a ban at all or to impose a shorter period of disqualification less than the minimum that would otherwise apply if the court 'thinks fit' 'for special reasons'. As in respect of a court's discretion not to endorse a defendant's licence, 'special reasons' must relate to the facts of the offence, not to mitigating factors associated with the offender's circumstances. The Divisional Court has characterised a 'special reason' as 'a mitigating or extenuating circumstance not amounting in law to a defence to the charge, yet directly connected with the commission of the offence': *Whittal v Kirby* [1947] KB 194. Thus the offender's long record of clean driving, their reasons for needing to drive because of their occupation or their family circumstances, or their physical disability, will not count. Instances that may amount to a special reason include: drinks laced without the defendant's knowledge, driving with excess alcohol in an emergency where there was no practicable alternative, or where the vehicle has been driven a very short distance to move it to safety or to avoid obstruction, particularly in circumstances where the driver was unlikely to encounter other road users. The onus lies upon the defendant to establish the circumstances on a balance of probabilities. The court is not obliged to reduce or avoid the period of disqualification even if the reasons are established.

Obligatory Disqualification for Repeated Offences: 'Totting Up'
Under the penalty points system applicable to road traffic offences, a driver (often described as a 'totter') who shows repeated disregard for the law by committing offences of themselves not sufficiently serious to warrant disqualification is penalised by obligatory disqualification on accumulating 12 or more points within a three year period. Points imposed for the current offence(s) are added to any other points imposed in respect of offences committed within three years of the current offence (unless those previous points have been dealt with or 'wiped' by reason of an earlier 'totting up' ban). If the accumulated total amounts to 12 or more, the court is obliged to disqualify: RTOA s35.

Length of Disqualification The standard *minimum* period of disqualification is for 6 months. However, in the following instances the applicable minimum is longer under s35(2)(b):

- One previous ban of 56 days or longer imposed within three years of the commission of the current offence, whether imposed for an offence carrying obligatory disqualification, under 'totting up' provisions or as a discretionary measure: minimum of 12 months.

- Two or more periods of disqualification imposed within three years of the commission of the current offence: minimum of two years.

Note, however, that a previous disqualification does not count if it was imposed for an offence of:

- theft of a motor vehicle;

- taking without owner's consent or allowing self to be carried in a vehicle so taken;

- going equipped for theft involving a motor vehicle;

- attempting to commit any of the above offences,

or if that disqualification was imposed under *PCCA 1973 s44* (see below) or RTOA 1988 s26 (interim disqualification: see below): s35(5).

Mitigating Circumstances If the court considers that 'there are grounds for mitigating the normal consequences of conviction', it may order disqualification for a shorter period or no disqualification at all: s35(1). However, s35(4) specifies that no account may be taken of:

- 'any circumstances that are alleged to make the offence(s) not a serious one'; or

- 'hardship, other than exceptional hardship'; or

- any circumstances that were taken into account by a court (as recorded on the court register) within the three year preceding period in ordering the offender to be disqualified for a shorter period or not ordering them to be disqualified.

Unlike the 'special reasons' provisions considered above, mitigating circumstances may (and usually will) relate to the circumstances of the offender and are likely to concern 'exceptional hardship', commonly arising from the offender's employment and potential loss of livelihood if unable to drive. Clearly the hardship must go beyond the hardship that befalls anyone who is deprived of the convenience of driving, and courts are likely to take particular note of hardship that will impact upon persons other than the driver.

Discretionary Disqualification

Power to disqualify at the court's discretion arises on conviction for any road traffic offence that carries power of endorsement of licence where liability to 'totting up' disqualification does not arise. There is no statutory minimum or maximum term of discretionary ban. The Appeal Court has indicated that discretionary disqualification should 'generally be restricted to cases involving bad driving, persistent motoring offences or the use of vehicles for the purposes of crime': *R v Callister* [1993] RTR 70. Speeding offences may attract discretionary disqualification. Speeding carries 3–6 penalty points. The Magistrates' Association Guidelines (2000) suggests that disqualification should be considered (for a period up to 56 days) if the offender's excess speed was in the following range according to the applicable speed limit that was exceeded:

Speed Limit	Excess Speed
20–30 mph	21–30 mph
40–50 mph	26–35 mph
60–70 mph	31–40 mph

Discretionary disqualification may also be imposed for the following offences under TA

1968 even though they are not endorsable offences: stealing or attempting to steal a motor vehicle; TWOC or attempted TWOC or, knowing it to have been taken, driving the vehicle or allowing oneself to be carried in it; going equipped for theft or taking of motor vehicles.

Length of Disqualification

Apart from the statutory minima applicable to obligatory disqualification, a court has wide discretion in determining the period of ban, The Magistrates' Association Guidelines (2000) offer guidance in respect of speeding (see above), excess alcohol (see Stone, 2000: 62), dangerous driving ('at least 12 months') and refusing an evidential specimen (suggesting a minimum of 18 months). (Disqualification is also mentioned as a consideration without advice regarding length in respect of careless driving, driving whilst disqualified by court order and failing to stop/report.) Walker and Padfield (1996) suggest that the Court of Appeal is unlikely to uphold a determinate period exceeding 10 years and *Blackstone's Criminal Practice* indicates that the Court generally considers that 'lengthy disqualifications tend to be counter-productive and often hamper the offender in the job market, sometimes leading to further crime and, in particular, driving whilst disqualified'. Decisions of the Appeal Court have suggested a particular concern that long bans can be counter-productive if imposed on younger drivers 'seemingly incapable of leaving vehicles alone' who cannot reasonably be expected to adhere to such restraint (e.g. *R v Thomas* [1983] 1 WLR 1490). The Court has also been concerned about the imposition of lengthy disqualification at the same time as a custodial sentence as this may have an adverse effect on 'the defendant's prospects of effective rehabilitation upon his release from custody': *R v Russell* [1993] RTR 249. However, the Court has also acknowledged the sentencer's duty to protect the public which may indicate the need to seek to keep the offender from driving until they have acquired greater discretion and consideration.

Disqualification for Life Such indeterminate ban has been held to be inappropriate and wrong in principle in the absence of psychiatric evidence or evidence of many previous convictions indicating that the offender will be a danger to the public indefinitely if allowed to drive: *R v King* (1992) 13 Cr App R(S) 668. *R v Buckley* (1994) 15 Cr App R(S) 695 illustrates an uncommon instance where the second arm of the *King* guidance was found to be satisfied. The offender had an appalling driving record, including six convictions for reckless driving, and demonstrated an 'astonishing readiness to imperil the public'.

Reduced Disqualification on Completion of Approved Course

Under RTOA 1988 s34A (introduced by RTA 1991) where a defendant aged 17 or older is convicted of a drink-drive offence and obligatorily disqualified under s34 (see above) for a period of *not less than 12 months*, the court may make an order that the period of disqualification shall be reduced if, by the date specified in the order, the offender satisfactorily completes an approved re-training course.

Eligible Offences Death by careless driving under the influence of drink or drugs; driving/ in charge under influence of drink/drugs; excess alcohol; failing to provide a specimen (i.e. offence under RTOA 1988 ss3A (though see below under 'experimental period'), 4, 5 or 7).

Course One approved by the Home Office for the purposes and specified in the order. The court must be satisfied that a place is available. Each course has a 'manager' nominated by the Secretary of State. In turn, the manager nominates a 'course organiser'. The provisions of ss34A–34C are supplemented by the Road Traffic (Courses for Drink-Drive Offenders) Regulations 1992.

Explanation and Consent The effect of the order must be explained to the defendant in ordinary language, including the obligation to meet the fees of the course prior to its commencement, and the defendant must agree to the order.

'Reduced Period' The reduction shall be 'a period specified in the order of not less than three months and not more than one-quarter of the unreduced period': s34A(3). Thus if the ban is for 12 months, the reduced period shall be for three months. If the ban is for 18 months, the reduced period must be for a period of between three months and four-and-a-half months, as determined by the court.

Specified Date The date specified in the order as the latest date for completion of a course 'must be at least two months before the last day of the period of disqualification as reduced by the order': s34A(5). Thus if the ban period is for 12 months with a reduction period necessarily of three months, the course must be completed within seven months and the specified date will thus be the date that marks a period of seven months from the date of disqualification. If the ban period is for two years, thus affording a reduction period of between three and six months, the specified date will be the conclusion of 16–19 months, depending on the period set.

Supervising Court The order shall name the PSA (or, if the order was made by a district judge, the Commission Area) in which the offender resides or will reside: s34A(6). The 'supervising court' is a court acting for that PSA (or Commission Area).

Effect The order reducing the ban period comes into effect when a certificate of completion is received by the clerk of the supervising court: s34B(1). If the certificate is received within the period of reduction, the ban ends on the date that the certificate is received.

Enforcement Though the organiser of the course has no power to require or instruct the offender to participate, the organiser does have the power to refuse to give a certificate if the offender's participation is deemed not to be satisfactory: s34B(4) and (5):

  (4) A course organiser shall give the certificate mentioned in s34B(1) to the offender not later than 14 days after the date specified in the order as the latest date for completion of the course, unless the offender fails to make the due payment of the fees for the course, fails to attend the course in accordance with the organiser's reasonable instructions or fails to comply with any other reasonable requirements of the organiser.

  (5) Where a course organiser decides not to give the certificate ... he shall give written notice of his decision to the offender as soon as possible and in any event on later than 14 days after the date specified in the order as the latest date for completion of the course.

A notice issued under s34B(5) shall be treated as given if it was sent by registered post or recorded delivery addressed to the offender at their last known address, notwithstanding that it was returned as undelivered or was for any other reason nor received by them: TR(CDDO)R 1992 para 5.

Application by Offender for Declaration If the offender wishes to challenge the organiser's decision not to give a certificate, they may apply to the supervising court 'for a declaration that the course organiser's decision not to give a certificate was contrary to s34B(4)' and, if successful, the granted application has the same legal effect as the receipt of a certificate by the relevant clerk: s34B(6). Such an application must be made within 28 days of receipt of notice under s34(5). Under RTOA 1988 s41A, a court has power to suspend a disqualification pending the hearing of such an application. If the course organiser neither gives a certificate nor issues notice of decision not to issue a certificate, the offender may, within 28 days, apply to the supervising court 'for a declaration that the course organiser is in default; and if the court grants the application s34A shall have effect as if the certificate had been duly received': s34B(7).

Experimental Period RTA 1991 s31 provides that ss34A–34C shall operate for an experimental period during which no order under s34A shall be made in respect of a conviction under RTA 1988 s3A (causing death by careless driving under influence of drink/drugs) nor except by a *magistrates' court* in a designated area. The experimental period was extended to the end of 1999. At the present time 26 PSAs have been designated for this purpose.

Disqualification Pending Passing of Driving Test

RTOA 1988 s36 empowers the sentencer to order not only a period of disqualification but also to order that the offender remains disqualified until they have passed 'the appropriate driving test', irrespective of whether they have previously passed the driving test. In some instances exercise of this power is mandatory rather than merely discretionary. On completion of the specified ban period, the offender may drive as a provisional licence holder subject to the normal restrictions and requirements of the 'Learner' driver, e.g. with 'L' plates and under supervision. If the offender drives without such adherence, they can be charged with driving whilst disqualified.

Mandatory Order On conviction and disqualification for: manslaughter by driver of motor vehicle; death by dangerous driving; dangerous driving (s36(1) and (2)). In such instances, the 'appropriate' test is 'an extended driving test' which is longer (minimum of 60 minutes) and more rigorous than the standard test (regulated by Motor Vehicles (Driving Licences) Regulations 1987 (SI 1987/1378) as amended by SI 1992/1318). If an offender is subject to such an order, a further order of this nature shall not be made while they remain subject to the initial order: s36(7)(b). In *R v Lauder* (1998) *The Times* 5 November, the Court of Appeal reminded sentencers that an order under s36, though 'little known and often overlooked', must be made. In the case in question the offender had been convicted of dangerous driving. Though dismissing his appeal against sentence, the Court noted the omission of a s36 order but was unable to make such an order at the appeal stage as this would be contrary to the rule that the Appeal Court could not pass a more severe sentence than the Crown Court (see page 240).

Discretionary Order Available to a court under s36(4) on conviction and disqualification for any road traffic offence carrying obligatory or discretionary disqualification. In this instance, the 'appropriate' test is the standard driving test. In exercising this discretionary power, s36(6) specifies that a court 'shall have regard to the safety of other road users'. The Court of Appeal has indicated that an order of this nature should be imposed only upon evidence that the defendant's ability to drive is in question and should not be used simply as an additional punishment – only where the court considers that through age or infirmity or in the circumstances of the offence, the defendant may not be a competent driver: *R v Buckley* (1988) 10 Cr App R(S) 477. In *R v Bannister* [1991] RTR 1, the Appeal Court indicated that competence to drive includes having proper regard for other road users in addition to control of a vehicle. Thus in *R v Miller* (1994) 15 Cr App R(S) 505 use of the power was upheld in respect of a 'grossly incompetent' driver convicted of careless driving who had never passed a driving test and had numerous convictions for road traffic offences, including 10 for driving whilst disqualified.

Expiry Disqualification under s36 'shall be deemed to have expired on production to the Secretary of State of evidence ... that the person disqualified has passed the test in question since the order was made': s36(8).

Interim Disqualification

In circumstances where a court has power to impose a period of disqualification after conviction, it may exercise power under RTOA 1988 s26 to impose an interim disqualification ('the first order'), i.e. where the court:

- commits the defendant to Crown Court for sentence;

- remits the matter to another magistrates' court for sentence;

- defers sentence;

- adjourns the case, e.g. for preparation of a PSR.

An interim ban continues until the case is concluded (but ceases to have effect at the end of six months if it has not ceased to have effect meantime: s26(4)). Any period of interim disqualification counts towards the completion of any disqualification imposed as part of the ultimate sentence. Only one such order may be imposed in the course of proceedings.

Appeal Against Disqualification

RTOA 1988 s38 specifies that a person disqualified by order of a magistrates' court under ss34–35 may appeal against the order in the same manner as against a conviction. Any court that imposes disqualification may, if it thinks fit, suspend the disqualification pending an appeal against the order.

Disqualification under PCC(S)A 2000 s147

Power of disqualification is available to the Crown Court, whether on conviction or on committal for sentence, in respect of an offence punishable on indictment by two years or longer, where a motor vehicle was used for the purpose of committing or facilitating the commission of an offence. The offender does not need to have been the driver of the vehicle and the vehicle need not have been directly involved in the crime provided that its use in some way facilitated the offending. 'Facilitating' an offence includes the 'taking of any steps after it has been committed for the purpose of disposing of any property to which it relates or of avoiding apprehension or detection': s147(6). This power also applies in respect of an offence of common assault or any other offence involving an assault, 'committed by driving a motor vehicle', for example by using the vehicle as a weapon to run down the victim, and includes an offence of aiding, abetting, counselling or procuring, or inciting the commission of, an assault. The period of disqualification is 'for such period as the court thinks fit'. When imposing disqualification under s147, a court should take account of the effect of the disqualification on the offender's employment prospects on his release from any custodial sentence also imposed: *R v Wright* (1979) 1 Cr App R(S) 82, reiterated in *R v Liddey* [1999] Crim LR 340, where a ban for five years imposed following conviction for evading excise duty was considered manifestly excessive; 12 months' disqualification was substituted.

Disqualification under PCC(S)A 2000 s146

Under s146(1) 'the court by or before which a person is convicted of an offence committed after 31 December 1997 may, in addition to or instead of dealing with him in any other way, order him to be disqualified, for such period as it thinks fit'. This discretion is available irrespective of the nature of the offence and disqualification can be an ancillary measure or a sentence in its own right. The power is available as an ancillary disposal even in cases that attract an automatic life sentence or a custodial sentence of a minimum length under PCC(S)A 2000 ss109, 110 or 111: s146(2). A court making a s146 order shall require the offender to produce any licence held by them: s146(4). The power is not open to a court unless it has been notified by the Secretary of State accordingly: s146(3).

The measure was piloted in selected areas from 1 January 1998, after its initial enactment by C(S)A 1997 s39. When the measure was proposed in Parliament, the Magistrates' Association and Justices' Clerks Society expressed concern that disqualification in non-driving cases could be imposed too readily as punishment disproportionate to the seriousness of the offence. The Magistrates suggested that such a ban should be imposed only for offences serious enough to merit a community sentence. The Government emphasised the value of enhancing the flexibility of courts' powers without such specific restriction but acknowledged (House of Commons, 10 December 1996) that:

'It is important that the courts regard disqualification ... as a heavy penalty, especially if someone is employed. There will be occasions when they will not apply this penalty if it may result in a person losing their job, because that may seem disproportionate.'

Removal of Disqualification

A driving disqualification may be lifted on the application of the individual subject to ban, under the provisions of the Road Traffic Offenders Act 1988 s42. Application cannot be made where the disqualification was ordered to run until the offender passes 'the appropriate driving test' under RTOA 1988 s36(1) (s42(6)).

Court with Jurisdiction Application is made to the court which imposed the disqualification (s42(1)). This may thus be the Crown Court, to which application should be made direct, not via a magistrates' court. There is no provision to allow application to the applicant's local court if that is not the court which imposed the ban. Application is probably most appropriately made in writing in the first instance to the Clerk to the Justices or the Chief Clerk of the relevant Crown Court centre.

Period to Elapse Prior to Application No application can be made before the expiry of the relevant period from the date of disqualification, determined as follows (s42(3)):

(a)   two years, if the disqualification is for less than four years;

(b)   one half of the period of disqualification where that period is for four years or longer but less than ten years;

(c)   five years, if the disqualification is for ten years or longer.

It is thus not possible to seek the early removal of disqualification imposed for a term of two years or less. The hearing may be fixed prior to the expiry of the minimum period provided that the application is not heard until after that period has elapsed.

Criteria to be Considered The court should have regard to (s42(2)):

(a)   the character of the person disqualified and their conduct subsequent to the order; and

(b)   the nature of the offence attracting the disqualification; and

(c)   any other circumstances of the case.

Decision The court has discretion either to remove the disqualification 'as from such date as may be specified in the order', which could thus be at some future date rather than the date of the application, or to refuse the application. Whether the application is successful or refused, the applicant may be ordered to pay the whole or any part of the cost of the application, in any case where the disqualification was imposed in respect of an offence involving mandatory endorsements. Where the application is refused, a further application may not be made within three months of the date of refusal (s42(4)).

Procedure No specific procedure is specified by s42 but it is usual for the police to be notified of the application and given the chance to respond to it. A commonly adopted form of procedure is for the police (or CPS) to outline the facts of the offence leading to disqualification and give details of the applicant's driving record. The applicant is then able to give evidence in support of their application, and may be cross-examined with the leave of the court. Thereafter, the applicant or their legal representative may address the court.

Revocation of Newly Qualified Driver's Licence

Though not a sentencing measure, it is convenient to outline here the provisions of RT(ND)A 1995, implemented in 1997. This measure introduced a probationary period of two years from date of passing the driving test. Where the new driver accumulates six or more penalty points for offence(s) committed during the probationary period (even if conviction arises outside of that period), licence is revoked, not by the court but by the DVLA authority, acting on receipt of details from the court (including the offender's licence), which then sends notice of revocation to the offender which takes effect from five days of the date of issue. The offender is then entitled to drive as a provisional licence holder until they pass a re-test. The critical date for revocation purposes is the date of the offence(s) that attracts the required number of points, not the date of conviction. Conviction may arise after the expiry of the probationary period but if the offence was committed in the probationary period, liability will still accrue.

Any penalty points imposed which lead to revocation remain effective for the usual three year period and are not 'wiped' as a consequence of revocation. On re-gaining their full licence, the offender is not subject to a further probationary period (otherwise some drivers could be endlessly subject to the revocation rules). If the driver appeals against their conviction or penalty points, and the Secretary of State is notified thus, licence is temporarily restored pending outcome. If appeal is successful, a new licence is issued, and the probationary period continues to run unless it has meantime expired.

OTHER MEASURES

Recommendation for Deportation

On sentencing an offender aged 17 or over, who is not a British citizen (or a Commonwealth citizen having right of abode in the United Kingdom), for an offence punishable by imprisonment, a court may make a recommendation that the offender be deported: IA 1971 s6(3). An exception arises in respect of a Commonwealth citizen or a citizen of the Irish Republic who was resident in the UK when the 1971 Act came into effect (1 January 1973) and who has been ordinarily resident within the UK for at least the five years immediately prior to date of conviction. Having refugee status does not provide grounds in itself for avoiding an order.

Procedure A defendant should be given a minimum of seven days notice in writing that the court is considering such a recommendation and the defence should be given the opportunity to make representations. A court should not make a recommendation without a full inquiry into the circumstances and should give reasons for deciding to make such a recommendation. In *R v Rodney* [1996] 2 Cr App R(S) 230 where the Crown Court had recommended deportation in respect of an offender convicted of supplying crack cocaine to undercover police officers, the Court of Appeal set aside the recommendation because the judge, despite making proper inquiry, had failed to give any reasons for it. The Court indicated that it is 'of crucial importance for sentencers to give their reasons in a little detail'. However, in *R v Bozat* [1997] 1 Cr App R(S) 270 the Appeal Court indicated that though failure to give reasons renders a recommendation liable to be quashed, and that reasons are important in fairness to defendants and to assist the Secretary of State, *Rodney* should not be interpreted to mean that such failure will always lead to quashing on appeal. It is still open to the appeal court to supply its own reasons if it thinks a recommendation is appropriate (see below).

Criterion The relevant consideration is usually posed as whether the offender's continued presence in the UK would be detrimental to the community. As expressed by the Court of Appeal in *R v Nazari* [1980] 1 WLR 1366, 'the more serious the crime and the longer the record, the more obvious it is that there should be an order'. The Court illustrated the proper approach by suggesting that an offence of shoplifting would not normally justify a recommendation but if the offender had been involved in a series of such offences or was part of an organised gang of thieves, a recommendation could be appropriate. A clear consideration is whether the offender poses a continuing risk of further serious offending. The fact that an offender is living on social security has been held not to be relevant to the question of detriment to the community: *R v Serry* (1980) 2 Cr App R(S) 336. The Court in *Nazari* indicated that a court should not seek to take account of the alleged or assumed harshness of the political regime to which a deported person might return and the defendant's fear of that regime (see *R v Chen* (2001) *The Times* 17 April) as this is not an issue that the courts can have adequate knowledge and that should be a matter for the Home Secretary.

However, courts have considered evidence of the special hardship that deportation is likely to cause the individual in the light of their personal circumstances, for example a young person facing return to a country of which he knows little and where family ties have ceased. Thus in *R v Dudeye* [1998] 2 Cr App R(S) 430 the Appeal Court set aside a deportation order imposed on a young Somali man, aged 18 at the time of his offence, a s18 wounding by stabbing a woman aged 50 in attempting to steal her handbag. He had left Somalia at age 9 because of the civil war in that country, being granted refugee status in the UK, and there was no evidence that he retained any connection with the country. Neither parent lived there and he had no realistic prospect of establishing himself there successfully, even leaving aside the continuing problems of civil disorder. Deportation was thus inappropriate, despite the serious nature of his offence. Courts have also been prepared to take into account the likely harmful impact of deportation upon third parties, in particular the offender's spouse or dependants.

Among decisions where the community detriment test has been found not to be satisfied:

R v David (1980) 2 Cr App R(S) 362: theft of passport by man with previous convictions but all arising outside the UK and none in last eight years.

R v Ariquat (1981) 3 Cr App R(S) 83: indecent assault by 19 year old offender who had sexual intercourse with a girl aged 15, believing she was over 16.

R v Tshuma (1981): arson causing damage value £3,000 but committed under emotional stress, with an assessment that he was very unlikely to re-offend.

R v Bozat (see above): Though the Appeal Court considered that two of the three men, members of the Kurdish Workers Party, convicted of conspiracy to set fire to various Turkish establishments by petrol bombing, satisfied the criterion, it quashed the recommendation respecting the youngest of the three, aged 18, noting that he had lived in this country since he was 13, his parents were permanently resident here and his offending had been under the influence of older men. The Court observed that recommendations should not be made as a matter of course but only after careful consideration of the criteria.

R v Tangestani-Nejad (1998, unreported): ABH committed by a landlord against one of his tenants by striking him with a hammer on the ear. In recommending deportation, the judge had referred critically to his criminal record (an ABH nine years earlier, some handling and deception some years previously, and failing to disclose property as a bankrupt) and to his unscrupulous practice as a landlord. The Court of Appeal did not consider his record worrying enough to warrant deportation and said that his ethics as a landlord were not material to the case and should not have been taken into account in deciding whether he met the criterion.

Relationship to Sentence A recommendation is ancillary to sentence which should be determined first on its own merits. A recommendation can be lawfully combined with any other disposal though is unlikely to follow a community sentence, given the criterion justifying such a recommendation.

Consequence The decision whether to deport is a matter for the Home Secretary, taking into account the full range of considerations, including the political regime of the person's home country and any further representations made on the person's behalf.

European Community and Human Rights Deportation of an EC national interferes with the fundamental right of free movement of workers (Article 39 – previously 48 – of the Treaty of Rome) and of the right to respect for private life (ECHR Article 8). Thus deportation should be considered more circumspectly in such instances and should be justified only on the basis of a genuine and sufficiently serious threat affecting one of the fundamental interests of society. Additionally, deportation must be proportionate in the sense of being appropriate and necessary for the attainment of the public policy objective sought and also must not impose an excessive burden on the individual concerned. These principles were expounded by the Court of Appeal in *B v Secretary of State for the Home Department* [2000] 2 CMLR 1086 (not a case where deportation was recommended but treated as such) where an Italian national had been convicted of prolonged sexual assault of his daughter, attracting five years' imprisonment, having an earlier conviction for non-sexual assault of his son. In conducting the balancing exercise, the court had no difficulty concluding that he had clearly acted in a manner contrary to public policy but determined that deportation was not proportionate. He had grown up and lived all his adult life in the UK where his parents lived and his ties were still substantial, despite the severance of his links with his children in the light of his offending. His links with Italy were much more tenuous in comparison.

Detention at Court or Police Station

Though a magistrates' court may normally impose imprisonment for a minimum of five days, MCA 1980 s135 confers a special power to order the detention of an offender aged 21 or more within the precincts of the courthouse or a police station for a period during the day of sentence. This form of detention must not extend beyond 8pm and must not be exercised so as to deprive the offender of a 'reasonable opportunity of returning to his abode' that night. Typically, the court may order detention until the court concludes its sitting that day. Note that this does not count as a custodial sentence for the purposes of Part One of PCC(S)A 2000 s79–83 and so the normal criteria, restrictions or requirements do not apply.

Binding Over

Under JPA 1968 s1(7) any 'court of record having a criminal jurisdiction' (thus including both magistrates' courts and the Crown Court) has:

> as ancillary to that jurisdiction, the power to bind over to be of good behaviour, a person who or whose case is before the court, by requiring him to enter into his own

recognisances or to find sureties or both, and committing him to prison if he does not comply.

This ancient and flexible measure with origins in common law and JPA 1361 is primarily used as a preventive measure without requiring a conviction (or following acquittal) in respect of any person before the court whether as accused, witness or complainant. It may also be employed as a sentencing measure following conviction and is outlined here in that context alone. A survey of court practice conducted for the Law Commission found that only 25% of bind-overs were imposed as a sentence. As a sentence, a bind-over can be characterised as a suspended fine (Ashworth, 1995: 256). The wording of s1(7) appears to indicate that a bind-over should be imposed as an ancillary measure rather than as the court's primary disposal but *Blackstone's Criminal Practice* (E11.2) reports that some courts feel at liberty to impose bind-overs without any additional penalty or order. There is no power to impose specific conditions beyond 'being of good behaviour and keeping the peace'.

Period of Recognisance Though the period for which the order should run is not subject to statutory limit, this should be determined by the court at its discretion. A period of 12 months is often specified.

Amount of Recognisance Again, no maximum is specified in statute and the sum payable in default could thus exceed the maximum fine for the offence.

If the sum is other than a trivial amount, the court should inquire into the defendant's means and allow relevant representations by the defence: *R v Central Criminal Court, ex parte Boulding* [1984] QB 813.

Refusal to Enter into Recognisance As s1(7) indicates, the sanction is committal to prison, subject, in respect of a magistrates' court, to its maximum powers of imprisonment. Imprisonment ceases if the person subsequently agrees to be bound over.

Default If the offender is subsequently adjudged to have failed to comply with the order, the court which made the bind-over may require the sum specified to be forfeited, in whole or in part. There is no power to impose a term of imprisonment instead (unless imposed for any fresh offence committed, though forfeiture may be ordered without such conviction upon complaint in civil proceedings and upon proof on a balance of probabilities) but in making a forfeiture order the court must fix a term of imprisonment or detention to be served in default of payment.

Binding Over to Come Up for Judgement

Separate from the power outlined above, the Crown Court has a common law power to bind a convicted defendant to come up for judgement. The power is exercised in lieu of sentence, not in addition to sentence. The defendant is required to enter recognisances for a specified period, as above, but the court has the power to impose specific conditions. The ambit of such conditions are not restricted and seem very much at the court's discretion. In *R v Williams* (1982) 4 Cr App R(S) 239 a condition that an 18 year old British-born offender of UK nationality but of Jamaican parents, convicted of theft, should accompany his mother to Jamaica and not return to the UK for five years – in effect, a temporary exile or deportation of a UK citizen – was upheld as lawful in principle, albeit disapproved of by the Court of Appeal on its particular facts. Lord Lane CJ stated that such a condition should be imposed 'very sparingly' and only to ensure that an offender goes to a country of which he is a citizen and where he is habitually resident.

Consent The defendant's consent is required before this measure can be adopted.

If required to return to court for breach of a condition the bound over defendant may be sentenced for the original offence even though not convicted of a further offence. The measure has obvious parallels with deferment of sentence and a conditional discharge.

The Law Commission (1994) recommended the abolition of binding over as anomalous, unduly wide in extent and no longer serving any justifiable purpose. The measure nevertheless retains support among the magistracy and some members of the judiciary because of its flexibility.

Sex Offender Orders

Requirements of notification to the police following conviction of a sexual offence (or on being found either not guilty by reason of insanity or unfit to plead) are detailed in Stone (1999). Though the obligation arises without need for this to be ordered by the sentencing court, SOA 1997 s5(2) specifies that where the court by which the offender is convicted (or so found) states in open court that on that date he has been so convicted etc. and that the offence is a sexual offence for the purposes of the Act, and certifies those facts, the certificate shall be evidence of those facts. The usual practice in the Crown Court is for the court to announce the consequences of the conviction and in many instances to require the offender immediately to sign a notice of their ensuing obligations.

No Separate Penalty

Where an offender has been convicted of more than one offence, the sentencer has the option to dispose of one or some of those offences by specifying that 'no separate penalty' (NSP) is being imposed for that matter. This has advantages in instances where the court is dealing with several offences and it is not considered necessary or appropriate to sentence for one or more (usually the more minor) offences in the light of the powers exercised in respect of the other offences. A common instance arises where a magistrates' court is dealing with a substantial number of road traffic offences and it appears unnecessary to penalise every violation instance. Thus if the defendant has been stopped for driving while disqualified, with no insurance and a fraudulent vehicle excise licence, it may be considered appropriate to 'NSP' associated offences of no MOT certificate or a defective tyre. It is possible for the court in such instance to order endorsement of licence, which may be an obligatory measure but otherwise to specify NSP.

Another instance in which NSP can be a convenient course arises where the main penalty ordered by the court is not available for one or more of the other offences, e.g. in the Crown Court when detention under CYPA 1933 s53(3) is ordered for the main offence but is not a legal option for other matters to be dealt with. The 'NSP' device may also be adopted where a custodial sentence is imposed for further offences and an existing community order is revoked though, strictly speaking, simple revocation without re-sentence is an option in such circumstances under CJA 1991 Sch 2 paras 7 and 8.

7
BREACH OF EARLIER MEASURES

This chapter combines issues that may be faced and powers that may be exercised at point of sentence where the defendant is being dealt with for offences commmitted during the operational period of an earlier disposal and thus stands to be dealt with for the offence attracting that earlier disposal. The two kinds of earlier disposal relevant in this context are conditional discharge and suspended sentence of imprisonment. For enforcement in response to failure to comply with other disposals or re-offending prior to the expiry of earlier immediate custodial sentences, see Stone (1999).

Breach of Conditional Discharge

A conditional discharge is breached in only one way: by the conviction of the discharged person of a further offence by a court in Great Britain during the operational period of their discharge, and their being 'dealt with' for that further offence (PCC(S)A 2000 s13(1)). 'Breach' is not a term used in the relevant legislation but is simply a convenient shorthand term for commission of a further offence triggering consideration of the conditional discharge. The pertinent date is that of the further offence, not of the ensuing conviction or the point at which the breach is dealt with. Breach can be dealt with at either of two points of consideration:

(i)   upon conviction in England and Wales of a further offence;

(ii)   after conviction in Great Britain of a further offence has been notified to the court which imposed the discharge and that court requires the offender to appear to be dealt with.

Note that a court with jurisdiction to deal with breach is not obliged to deal afresh with the original offence. If it chooses not to do so, the conditional discharge continues in existence as before and can thus be breached by a further offence.

Upon Conviction of a Further Offence

Jurisdiction and power to deal with the breach, i.e. sentence afresh for the original offence, depends on whether the conditional discharge was imposed by a magistrates' court or the Crown Court. In essence, only the Crown Court can deal with a discharge made by that Court but the Crown Court can deal with a magistrates' court discharge.

Crown Court Conditional Discharge If the offender is convicted before the Crown Court of a further offence, the Crown Court has obvious jurisdiction to address the breach and 'may deal with him, for the offence for which the order was made, in any way in which it could deal with him if he had just been convicted by or before that court of that offence' (s13(6)). If the offender is convicted of a further offence before a magistrates' court, that court 'may commit him to custody or release him on bail until he can be brought or appear before the Crown Court' (s13(5)(a)).

When committing an offender under this provision, a magistrates' court may also commit the defendant to the Crown Court under s6 (see page 65) to be dealt with for any other offence of which he is convicted that the magistrates' court has jurisdiction to deal with. Thus the offender may be dealt with at Crown Court not only in respect of the offence subject to conditional discharge but the further offence which has breached that discharge, even though that is a matter which, if standing alone, would have been dealt with summarily. If the offence for which the conditional discharge was imposed by the Crown Court is a summary offence, the magistrates' court's powers under s6 are limited to committing any other offence only if it is imprisonable or punishable by the committing court with disqualification from driving.

Magistrates' Court Conditional Discharge If a magistrates' court convicts the offender of a further offence and the discharge was imposed by that court, the court has clear jurisdiction to address the breach and 'may deal with him, for the offence for which the order was made, in any way in which it could deal with him if he had just been convicted by or before that court of that offence' (s13(6)). If the offender is convicted of a further offence before a different magistrates' court from that which imposed the conditional discharge, the new court does not have automatic jurisdiction to deal with the original offence but may do so 'with the consent of the court which made the order' (s13(8)). Permission can be obtained by telephone if necessary to expedite proceedings and, if secured, allows the new court to deal with the offender 'for the offence for which the order was made, in any manner in which the court could deal with him if it had just convicted him of that offence' (s13(8)).

If an offender subject to a magistrates' court conditional discharge is convicted before the Crown Court of a further offence (or is dealt with by the Crown Court for a further offence upon committal for sentence – see page 62), the Crown Court's powers to deal with the offender for the offence for which the order was made are restricted to 'any way in which the magistrates' court could deal with him if it had just convicted him of that offence' (s13(7)).

Young Offender If an offender is conditionally discharged by a magistrates' court (including a youth court) for an offence triable only on indictment at Crown Court in the case of an adult but dealt with by a lower court because the offender was aged under 18, any court which subsequently deals with the breach after s/he has attained the age of 18 has the power to (a) impose a fine not exceeding £5,000 and/or (b) 'deal with the offender for the offence in any way in which a magistrates' court could deal with him if it had just convicted him of an offence punishable with imprisonment for a term not exceeding six months': s13(9). So, for example, if an offender aged 17 is given a conditional discharge for robbery by a youth court and subsequently appears before the Crown Court aged 18 for sentence for a further offence committed during the period of discharge, the Crown Court's powers in respect of the robbery are limited to a maximum of six months YOI detention. This is thus a specified exception to the usual discretion to deal with the offender as if s/he had just been convicted of the pertinent offence.

Upon Notification

If an offender has been convicted of a further offence by a court in any part of Great Britain and the new court either lacks jurisdiction to address the breach (e.g. a Scottish court or a fresh magistrates' court which did not secure consent to deal with the breach from the original magistrates' court) or opts not to exercise jurisdiction, the court which imposed the conditional discharge should be notified. The Crown Court (in respect of a discharge made by that Court) or a justice acting for the relevant sessions area (in respect of a discharge made by a magistrates' court acting for that PSA) may either issue a summons requiring the offender to appear before the court or a warrant for the offender's arrest. The relevant procedure is specified as follows:

PCC(S)A 2000 s13

(3)   A justice of the peace shall not issue a warrant under this section except on information and shall not issue a warrant under this section except on information in writing and on oath.

(4)   A summons or warrant issued under this section shall direct the person to whom it relates to appear or to be brought before the court by which the order for conditional discharge was made.

On the offender's appearance before the relevant court, the court's powers are as outlined in the preceding section dealing with powers upon conviction, i.e. to deal with the person for the offence for which the order was made, 'in any manner in which the court could deal with him if it had just convicted him of that offence' (s13(8)), subject to the special provision relating to young offenders, as detailed above.

Putting the Breach to the Offender

If a court considers that an offender's further conviction constitutes a breach of a conditional discharge, it is necessary for the breach to be put to the defendant for their acceptance or denial of that breach. If the breach is denied, e.g. the defendant does not accept that they are subject to conditional discharge or claims that the breach has already been dealt with, the breach must be proved according to the normal rules of evidence. The offender's claim will thus be checked and, given the scope for error or omissions in criminal record-keeping, may well be vindicated. If the breach is admitted or proved, the prosecution will be expected to provide the court with details of the original offence.

Role of the PSR Writer

If a PSR is requested in respect of the further offence, the issue of whether this conviction constitutes a breach of conditional discharge will normally be established prior to the request. If so established, the PSR writer will be expected to address the earlier offence as part of the report's ambit. The front sheet of the report should identify the original offence which now stands to be sentenced rather than referring merely to 'breach of conditional discharge', for the court has no powers to deal with 'breach' other than by dealing afresh with the original offence, or by taking no action and leaving the conditional discharge undisturbed.

Given the gaps which can occur in a defendant's criminal record, which may not be fully up to date, the PSR writer may become aware of an outstanding and now breached conditional discharge, unbeknown to the court, perhaps being alerted to this issue by the defendant. The PSR writer should then draw this to the court's attention within the report and preferably by a separate advance note to the court, particularly in cases where permission to deal with the breach is required. The PSR writer may not have details of the original offence to which to refer but sometimes may have these on file. If so, the relevant documents should be made available with the report to the court duty officer in case these need to be loaned to the prosecution which may not have this information. Without this information it may be necessary to adjourn the case to allow details to be obtained.

Dealing with the Original Offence

If a court deals with the original offence by passing sentence for it, the conditional discharge terminates, though any ancillary order accompanying the discharge, e.g. for compensation or costs, forfeiture, disqualification from driving or licence endorsement, remains valid. It is clearly possible for the court to impose a further conditional discharge which then runs from the date of the fresh order. The *Criminal Statistics for England and Wales* (1999, Table 7.24) indicate that around 12% of those conditionally discharged were dealt with for breach of their order, of whom 15% received a sentence of immediate custody for the original offence.

Activation of Suspended Sentence

A suspended term of imprisonment may be activated, varied or at least addressed where the offender is convicted of an offence punishable with imprisonment, committed during the operational period of suspension (PCC(S)A 2000 s119(1)), hereinafter referred to as a 'further offence'. This is sometimes loosely referred to as a 'breach of suspended sentence' but this is not a statutory term. If the offender is convicted by a magistrates' court of an offence punishable with imprisonment only on indictment, this does not count as a further offence for activation purposes. A TIC offence does not count, either, as it is not a 'conviction'.

Conviction for a further offence will count if it occurs in any court in Great Britain (England, Wales or Scotland). A Scottish court has no jurisdiction to deal with a suspended sentence in England and Wales but is required to give written notice of the conviction to the court which imposed the suspended term (s121(3)).

Jurisdiction to Deal With Suspended Sentence

Jurisdiction, as specified by s120, is summarised in the following table. Note that a magistrates' court has no power to deal with a suspended sentence imposed by the Crown Court but 'may, if it thinks fit, commit (the offender) in custody or on bail to the Crown Court' (s120(2)(a)). A magistrates' court is thus not obliged to commit the offender but, if it does not, it 'shall give written notice of the conviction to the appropriate officer of the Crown Court' (s120(2)(b)). The Crown Court may then issue either a summons requiring the offender to appear before it or a warrant for the offender's arrest (s121(1)).

Court convicting of further offence	*Court passing suspended sentence*	*Jurisdiction*
Crown Court	Crown Court	Yes
Crown Court	Magistrates' Court	Yes
Magistrates' Court	Magistrates' Court	Yes
Magistrates' Court	Crown Court	No, but may commit to or shall give notice to the Crown Court

Note also that a magistrates' court has power to deal with a suspended sentence imposed by another magistrates' court and, unlike the provisions relating to conditional discharge (see page 230), is not required first to seek the consent of the other court.

When committing an offender under s120(2)(a), a magistrates' court may also commit the defendant to the Crown Court under s6 to be dealt with for any other offence of which s/he is convicted that the magistrates' court has jurisdiction to deal with. This includes the further offence which has breached the suspended sentence, even though that is a matter which, if standing alone, would have been dealt with summarily. If, unusually, the offence for which suspended sentence was imposed by the Crown Court is a summary offence, the magistrates' court's powers are limited by s6(3) to committing any other offence only if it is imprisonable or punishable by the committing court with disqualification from driving. Note that if the magistrates' court deals with the further offence by absolute or conditional discharge, this will prevent the Crown Court from activating the suspended sentence because this will not count as a 'conviction' for activation purposes (*R v Moore* [1995] 2 WLR 728). *Stone's Justices Manual* (2001 para. 3-776) advises magistrates' courts to refrain from making this kind of order (or deferment of sentence) and instead to commit the defendant to the Crown Court in all matters so that the case can be dealt with as a whole. It would also seem inadvisable for the magistrates' court to suspend sentence for the further offence.

Options in 'Dealing With' the Offender

A court with jurisdiction to deal with an offender in respect of a suspended sentence '*shall* consider his case and deal with him by one of the following methods' (italics added): s119(1):

(a) the court may order that the suspended sentence shall *take effect* with the original term *unaltered*;

(b) it may order that the sentence shall take effect with the *substitution of a lesser term* for the original term;

(c) it may by order *vary the original order* under s118(1) by substituting for the period specified therein a period ending not later than two years from the date of the variation; or

(d) it may make *no order* with respect to the suspended sentence.

The court cannot deviate from these options. It should not, for example, purport to impose a community rehabilitation order for the original offence.

Dealing First with Further Offence The court should first sentence the offender for the fresh offence, determining the appropriate disposal before addressing the question of the suspended sentence (*R v Ithell* [1969] 1 WLR 272). The further offence and the offence which attracted the suspended sentence are not 'associated offences' within the definition of PCC(S)A 2000 s161(1) for the purposes of weighing the seriousness of the further offence. The decision at this stage may determine the subsequent question of whether to activate the suspended term.

- Where the court imposes an absolute or conditional discharge for the further offence, though this will count as a conviction for activation purposes because the discharge is made in the same proceedings (PCC(S)A 2000 s14(1)), it would nevertheless seem contradictory to impose a discharge (i.e. where 'it is inexpedient to inflict punishment') and at the same time to activate a custodial sentence (*per* Sedley J in *R v Moore* [1995] 1 WLR 728).

- Where the further offence is dealt with by a non-custodial sentence, the authority of *R v McElhorne* (1983) 5 Cr App R(S) 53 supports the view that it is normally inappropriate to activate the suspended sentence. Quashing the activation of a suspended term of two months imposed for possession of heroin, decided at the same time as making a community service order for possession of cannabis, Skinner J in the Court of Appeal observed:

  'although it is wrong to say that the court can never bring a suspended sentence into operation when it passes a non-custodial sentence for the substantive offence, it is correct to say that in this particular instance it was wrong to do so.'

- If the court defers sentence in respect of the further offence, it would be contradictory to the spirit of deferment simultaneously to activate the suspended term.

Activation as Normal Consequence Where the court imposes imprisonment for the further offence, the Court of Appeal has made clear that activation of the suspended term is the normal consequence, in the absence of exceptional circumstances. Further, the suspended term should normally be ordered to run consecutively to the prison sentence for the further offence, subject to the totality principle (see page 27).

The court may be prepared to deviate from the usual presumption of activation in either of the following circumstances:

- *Nature of Further Offence* Though the Court of Appeal has often observed that the fact that the further offence is dissimilar to the original offence or is of an entirely different character does not justify a departure from the normal consequences of activation, this may carry weight with the court, particularly where the later offence is 'comparatively trivial'. If the new offence is of relatively limited seriousness, it may well be that it will attract a non-custodial sentence and thus activation may be avoided on that basis, as outlined above.

Alternatively, the relative triviality of the new offence may justify activation for a lesser term (option (b) above).

- *Timing of Further Offence* If the new offence was committed late in the operational period of suspension, the court may be willing to avoid activation, either in full or at all, or may consider that the suspended term can run concurrently rather than consecutively with the new sentence.

Making No Order If the court opts to make 'no order' under option (d) above, it has nevertheless 'dealt with' the offender. It would thus not be possible for the magistrates' court which imposed a suspended sentence to issue a summons or warrant under s121(1) to bring the offender before it if it is notified that another magistrates' court has convicted that offender of a further offence where that court exercised option (d). If, however, the other court did not 'deal with' the breach of suspended sentence, e.g. because it was unaware that the offender was subject to suspended sentence, it would then be open for the original court to exercise its powers under s121(1).

If the court dealing with the suspended sentence exercises either option (c) or (d), the suspended sentence continues in existence either as varied (under option (c)) or in its original form (under option (d)).

Recent Consequences of Breach The *Criminal Statistics for England and Wales* (1999, Table 7.24) indicate that in that year 14% (down from 22% in 1995) of those subject to suspended sentence were dealt with for breach, of whom 79% received immediate imprisonment for the original offence.

8
POST-SENTENCE: VARIATION, APPEAL AND REVIEW OF LENIENCY

This chapter seeks to summarise the scope for a sentence to be reconsidered, either by the sentencing court because of second thoughts or by a higher court on appeal. Though there is no general provision in this jurisdiction for the prosecution to appeal against sentence, the narrower ambit for the Attorney-General to refer a sentence to the Court of Appeal on grounds of undue leniency is also summarised.

Varying or Rescinding Sentence

Both the Crown Court and a magistrates' court have power to vary or rescind its decision as to sentence or other order, under PCC(S)A 2000 s155 (Crown Court only) and MCA 1980 s142(1) (as amended by CAA 1995 s26) (magistrates' courts). The previous limitation upon this power under MCA 1980 that it had to be exercised within 28 days has ceased to apply under the variations introduced in the 1995 Act (s26(7)).

Extent of the Power

PCC(S)A 2000 s155

(1)   Subject to the following provisions of this section, a sentence imposed, or other order made, by the Crown Court when dealing with an offender may be varied or rescinded by the Crown Court within the period of 28 days beginning with the day on which the sentence or other order was imposed or made or, where subsection (2) below applies, within the time allowed by that subsection.

(2)   Where two or more persons are jointly tried on an indictment, then, subject to the following provisions of this section, a sentence imposed, or other order made, by the Crown Court on conviction of any of those persons on the indictment may be varied or rescinded by the Crown Court not later than the expiry of whichever is the shorter of the following periods, that is—

   (a)   the period of 28 days beginning with the date of conclusion of the joint trial;

   (b)   the period of 56 days beginning with the day on which the sentence or other order was imposed or made.

MCA 1980 s142(1)

A magistrates' court may vary or rescind a sentence or other order imposed or made by it when dealing with an offender if it appears to the court to be in the interests of justice to do so; and it is hereby declared that this power extends to replacing a sentence or order which for any reason appears to be invalid by another which the court has power to impose or make.

The scope of this power is wide and may be used in the following instances, by no means confined to correcting minor errors in sentencing:

- To replace an invalid sentence or one which the court had no power to pass with a lawful sentence, e.g. where a young person aged 15 at the time of conviction is mistakenly sentenced to a community punishment or community rehabilitation order, as may happen if sentence is passed after their 16th birthday.

- To replace a sentence which the court had power to pass but which was crucially flawed in some procedural way. For example, a court may seek to impose a community rehabilitation order that includes a requirement with which the defendant must express his willingness to comply (e.g. to receive treatment for mental condition) and it may become apparent subsequently that obtaining consent was overlooked.

- To increase sentence where the court feels that the original sentence was imposed on a factually incorrect basis. The reported cases illustrating this possibility concern instances where the offender had made claims in mitigation which caused the court to take a lenient view but which rapidly proved to be ill-founded. Thus in *R v Hart* (1983) 5 Cr App R(S) 25 a suspended prison sentence imposed on the strength of the offender's claim that he was going abroad with his girlfriend to start afresh was replaced with an immediate term when it came to light that this was untrue and had been invented simply to sway the court. Likewise, in *R v McLean* (1988) 10 Cr App R(S) 18, sentence of immediate custody was increased when the offender who had promised the judge that he was remorseful and intent on changing his ways promptly escaped from custody through an inadvertently open door. (The situation posed in *McLean* should be distinguished from instances where the offender misbehaves in court immediately after sentence, for example by abusive language towards the sentencer, which is not a valid ground for variation: *R v Powell* (1985) 7 Cr App R(S) 247.) It is not difficult to think of instances where community sentences are imposed on the strength of good intention or mitigation which soon evaporates or proves to be groundless. However, unlike the position with custodial sentences, the court retains some oversight of the order and the opportunity to re-sentence in any subsequent breach or revocation proceedings (which are likely to follow in some instances of bogus assurances) and it would usually seem preferable for the court to exercise control by those means. Although the court certainly has the discretion to increase sentence when exercising variation powers, the Court of Appeal has indicated that this should be done only in exceptional circumstances which undermine the whole basis of the original sentence (per Woolf LJ in *McLean*).

- To impose a different form of sentence in the light of new information that becomes available to the court. Thus in *R v Sodhi* (1978) 66 Cr App R 260 a prison term was replaced by a hospital order in the light of psychiatric opinion that the offender was suffering from paranoid psychosis. Though it would seem unfortunate for a court to go ahead with sentencing when information of this important nature is pending, there may be rare instances where new information transforms the basis of judging the offender's suitability for a particular community sentence. This situation may, however, be dealt with more appropriately and flexibly, without worry of time limit, by revocation proceedings. The offender's misconduct in the dock after sentence has been passed does not provide basis for increasing sentence as the court should deal with any contempt separately: *R v Powell* (1985) 7 Cr App R(S) 247. Variation includes the scope to add a further order to the sentence already passed: *R v Reilly* [1982] QB 1208 where a criminal bankruptcy order was imposed on top of a term of imprisonment.

Procedure for Variation

There is no precisely defined procedure for bringing such exceptional instances to the court's attention. *Stone's Justices Manual* (2001, 1-2235) suggests that in a magistrates' court an application may be made by the offender or the prosecution or the court may, of its own motion, reconsider a sentence. If the matter is raised other than by the offender, s/he should be given notice of when the court proposes to consider reviewing sentence. Variation should take place in open court and the defendant or his legal representative should have an opportunity to address the court. Variation should normally be in the presence of the defendant (unless the circumstances imply waiver of that right, for example, he has absconded) but variation in his absence will not be ruled unfair or unlawful if the defendant's advocate is present (*R v Shacklady* (1987) 9 Cr App R(S) 258). The previous rule in magistrates' courts that the varying court should consist of the same magistrates who dealt with the case originally or at least the majority of that Bench has been repealed. Variation or rescission under s155 must be by the court as constituted when the sentence or order was imposed or made, save that where the court included one or more magistrates, power may be exercised in the absence of one or more of those justices: s155(4).

Outside the 28 day Period

Unlike a magistrates' court disposal, a Crown Court sentence may not be varied after the expiry of the 28 day limit. The matter will then have to be taken on appeal by the usual route to the Court of Appeal. Where the Court rescinds its order within the time limit but delays making a further order, for example to allow further inquiry, the new order must be imposed within the same time limit: *R v Dunham* [1996] 1 Cr App R(S) 438. However, the Crown Court has an inherent jurisdiction, separate from its power under s155, to remedy formal mistakes in its record and so corrections of a very minor, technical nature, not altering the substance of the sentence or order or changing the length or requirement of an order, can be dealt with by exercise of that inherent jurisdiction.

Effect of New Sentence

PCC(S)A 2000 s155(5) and MCA 1980 s142(5) specify that the sentence or other order as varied shall take effect from the beginning of the day on which it was originally imposed or made, unless the court otherwise directs.

Appeal against Sentence

Appeals against conviction are outside the scope of this book but the following provides a brief outline of the process of appeal against sentence (though appeal can, of course be against both).

Appeal from the Crown Court

CAA 1968 s9 provides for appeal against any sentence or order (other than one fixed by law) following conviction on indictment, including against sentence for any additional summary offence committed to the Crown Court under CJA 1988 s41. CAA 1968 s10 makes parallel provision for appeal against sentence where the offender has been dealt with for a matter of which s/he was summarily convicted, most prominently following committal for sentence. Appeal under s10 is available only if:

(a)   the offender has been sentenced to custody for six months or longer; or

(b)   the sentence is one which the magistrates' court had no power to impose; or

(c)   the court has recommended deportation, or disqualification from driving, or has activated a suspended sentence, or ordered to be returned to custody under PCC(S)A 2000 s116 (see page 89).

The restriction in (a) above (s10(3)) means that an offender committed to Crown Court for sentence who receives a penalty less than six months but within the power of the magistrates' court is left without scope to appeal (see *R v Gatehouse* [2001] Crim LR 416).

Notice of Appeal Notice of application for leave to appeal must be given within 28 days from date of sentence using the appropriate form and accompanied by the grounds of appeal. The time for giving notice may be extended by the Court of Appeal either before or after the 28 days have elapsed but the Court has indicated that extension will require very good reasons.

Leave to Appeal CAA 1968 s11 provides that appeal can only proceed if (i) the appellant is granted leave to appeal by the Court of Appeal or (ii) if the sentencing judge has granted a certificate that the case is fit for appeal against sentence. The Court of Appeal has indicated that such certification should only be granted if there is a 'particular and cogent' ground of appeal and, in practice, this arises very rarely. Leave to appeal may be granted by a single judge and this is the normal 'clearing house' for appeals against sentence, being a private consideration of the papers without attendance of advocates or the appellant. If leave is refused, the appellant has the right to have their application determined by the court but notice of renewed application must be served within 14 days of receipt of notification of refusal.

Powers of Court of Appeal

If the Court of Appeal considers that the appellant 'should be sentenced differently for an offence for which s/he was dealt with by the court below', the court may (CAA 1968 s11(3)):

(a)   quash any sentence or order which is the subject of the appeal; and

(b)   in place of it pass such sentence or make such order as they think appropriate for the case and as the court below had power to pass or make when dealing with him for the offence;

but the court shall so exercise their powers ... that, taking the case as a whole, the appellant is not more severely dealt with on appeal than he was dealt with by the court below.

This sub-section thus answers the obvious question in many would-be appellant's minds: 'will I end up worse off?' The test is whether the substitute sentence constitutes an increase when weighed 'as a whole'. This means that if the offender was sentenced for two or more matters, it is possible that the Appeal Court could increase the penalty in respect of one of those offences provided that the total impact is less or the same as that imposed by the Crown Court. Among decisions on the 'as a whole' principle:

- A suspended term of imprisonment cannot be replaced by an immediate term of shorter duration, even if time spent on custodial remand would allow the appellant's immediate release.

- A hospital order with an added indeterminate restriction order under MHA 1983 s41 is not more severe than a sentence of three years imprisonment, because a hospital order is not punitive but therapeutic in intention (this decision may be re-considered as it appears unduly swayed by the rationale rather than the impact of such a measure).

- If a term of imprisonment is reduced, it is legitimate for the Court to add a fine or to impose or increase a period of disqualification.

There is, nevertheless, one factor which acts as a deterrent to prospective appellants. The Appeal Court can direct that an appellant who has been in custody will not be able to count their custodial time between trial and hearing of appeal towards the calculation of their time served. Such a direction will normally be made by the single judge in refusing leave to appeal. In a *Practice Note* in February 1980 (1980) 70 Cr App R 180 the Lord Chief Justice stated:

'In order to accelerate the hearing of appeals in which there is some merit, single judges will ... give special consideration to the giving of a direction for loss of time whenever an application for leave to appeal is refused ... such a direction will normally be made unless the grounds are not only settled and signed by counsel, but also supported by the written opinion of counsel.'

This potential sanction is clearly aimed at disgruntled offenders embarking on DIY appeals without the backing of their legal representatives.

Legitimate Grounds for Appeal As summarised by the Court of Appeal in *R v Johnson* (1994) 15 Cr App R(S) 827, appeal against sentence will normally only succeed in one of three instances:

(i)   Where the sentence is unlawful, e.g. where the sentencer purported to impose a term of YOI on an offender aged under 18 in excess of the maximum period of 24 months.

(ii)   Where the sentence is wrong in principle.

(iii)   Where the sentence was excessive.

Usually (ii) and (iii) are approached together, using the time-honoured double criterion of whether the sentence is 'wrong in principle or manifestly excessive'. Wrongness in principle relates to instances where the sentencer adopted the wrong form of sentence, e.g. where the appellant argues that their offence did not qualify for a custodial sentence by the 'so serious' criterion or that they should not have received a longer-than-commensurate term because there was no proper basis to regard them as presenting a serious risk to the public. As regards excessiveness, the Appeal Court has repeatedly indicated that it will not interfere simply because the sentence is at the heavy end of the range of legitimate discretion, being somewhat more severe than the court would personally have felt justified. The appellant will normally only succeed if their sentence was outside the broad range of penalty appropriate for the crime.

The court in *Johnson* indicated a further basis for a valid appeal: 'exceptional cases where an incident in the course of proceedings gives rise to the appearance of injustice or creates a justified sense of injustice on the party of the offender'. Such instances include cases where the offender's hopes of a non-custodial sentence were legitimately raised – so-called *Gillam* cases (see page 52). A further instance of 'injustice' may arise from the judge's sentencing remarks, as in *Johnson* itself. This was a case of street robberies of post office workers and the sentencer had indicated that he was aware of Court of Appeal practice in such instances but did not agree with this trend and did not propose to follow such guidance. Though the sentence actually imposed, though stiff, was at the upper end of the accepted bracket and would not normally be interfered with, in this instance the sentencer had given the impression that he was applying some personal tariff of his own. In the light of these 'unfortunate' sentencing remarks, some reduction of sentence was necessary. Additionally, the sentencer's failure to order a *Newton* hearing to resolve uncertainties of fact may provide valid grounds for appeal as illustrated by *R v Oakley* (outlined at page 48). Another basis for a sense of injustice may lie in a marked disparity of sentence between two or more co-defendants without apparent justification or a failure to differentiate between co-offenders whose culpability is distinguishable(see page 36). Note that a failure to follow technical procedure, such as a failure to obtain a pre-sentence report or to indicate that a PSR is not considered necessary (see page 77), will not be readily regarded as a sound basis for appeal. The important consideration will be whether there are valid grounds for imposing the sentence in question, not penalising the sentencer for their errors or oversights.

Bail Pending Appeal Court of Appeal has power to grant bail pending appeal (CAA 1968 s19(1)(a)) and applications are normally considered by the single judge when considering whether to grant leave to appeal. If application is refused, application may be renewed, in the same way as in seeking leave to appeal, to the Court by giving notice within 14 days. The Court has adopted a cautious approach, the general stance being to ask: 'Are there exceptional circumstances driving the court to the conclusion that 'justice can only be done by the granting of bail?' The Crown Court may grant bail under SCA 1981 s81 in any instance where it has granted a certificate that a case is fit for appeal.

Appeal to the Crown Court
An appeal against a magistrates' court sentence may be made to the Crown Court under MCA 1980 s108(1), 'sentence' being defined to include 'any order made on conviction' other than an order to pay costs or an order under PAA 1911 s2 for the destruction of an animal (s108(3)). Leave to appeal is not required. Appeal is commenced by lodging a notice of appeal in writing with the justices' clerk and the prosecutor within 21 days of sentence. The Crown Court has discretion to extend the 21 day limit and to give leave to appeal out of time on receipt of an application in writing specifying the grounds for the application: CCR 1982 r7(5) and (6).

Bail Pending Appeal If the intending appellant is appealing against an immediate custodial sentence, the justices have discretion to grant bail to appear at the Crown Court: MCA 1980 s113(1). There is no presumption of bail under the Bail Act 1976 s4. If the magistrates refuse bail, application may be made to the Crown Court under SCA 1981 s81(1)(b), or to a High Court judge in chambers. Because any custodial sentence imposed summarily is necessarily short, bail is an important consideration as the appellant may well have served all or a large proportion of their sentence pending their appeal hearing. On the other hand, if bail is granted and the appeal is unsuccessful, the appellant will have to face custody knowing that had they not sought bail they might well have completed their term in the interim. Courts may well feel that the better course is to refuse bail but seek to expedite the appeal to resolve matters as quickly as possible (see *Practice Direction (Crown Court: Bail Pending Appeal)*[1983] 1 WLR 1292 which states that the risk of delay cannot alone be a ground for the grant of bail if the chance of a successful appeal is not substantial). For an argument that a sentencing bench is not an appropriate or fair tribunal to judge a bail application pending appeal, see Herling and Dear (2000).

Abandonment of Appeal Abandonment of appeal may be effected by giving written notice to the clerk to the justices, the appropriate officer of the Crown Court and the prosecutor, at least three days before the appeal hearing.

Appeal Process An appeal is heard by a judge who normally sits with two lay magistrates who were not involved in the original decision. The prosecution outlines the facts and presents antecedent evidence; any reports on the appellant prepared for the original sentencing occasion or for the appeal are read; the defence mitigates. If the sentence that the Crown Court considers to be the appropriate sentence differs significantly from the sentence imposed by the lower court, the appeal should be allowed and the sentence of the Crown Court substituted for that imposed by the magistrates. The court should give reasons for its decision.

Powers of the Crown Court Under SCA 1981 s48, the Crown Court has extensive powers to confirm, reverse or vary any part of the decision appealed against, even a part that the appellant has not opted to appeal against. Thus, to answer the obvious concerns of the would-be appellant, the Crown Court may increase sentence and thus has a freer hand than the Court of Appeal (see above). This discretion is subject to the important limitation that the new sentence must not exceed the powers of the magistrates (s48(4)). As a further deterrent against unmeritorious appeals, where an appeal fails the appellant may be ordered to pay the prosecution costs. The Crown Court may also remit the matter back to the magistrates with its opinion, e.g. where it considers that the appellant's plea was equivocal (see page 39).

Case Illustration

Sentence is not often increased on appeal but the following example illustrates circumstances where this can occur. Alan Partridge, aged 30, appealed to the Crown Court against both conviction and sentence for indecent exposure and indecent assault, arising from an incident when he was a hotel guest and admittedly propositioned a 16 year old chambermaid who was servicing his room. She had alleged that he had forcibly kissed her, placed his hand up her skirt and pushed her on to the bed and, as she was leaving the room, had drawn her attention to his exposed penis. He had been sentenced to four months imprisonment for the assault with one month concurrent for the exposure.

Upholding both convictions, the Crown Court indicated that this was a serious assault involving a youthful victim who, in the course of her work requiring her to enter guests' rooms, was obliged to rely on their good behaviour. Mr Partridge had sought to take advantage of that occupational vulnerability and her trust and had now obliged her to undergo the ordeal of giving evidence for a second time. Sentence for the assault was increased to six months.

Appeal to the Divisional Court by 'Case Stated'

An appeal challenging sentence can proceed by the 'case stated' route to the High Court (a Divisional Court of the Queen's Bench Division) seeking an authoritative opinion on a point of law, either from a magistrates' court decision or from a decision of the Crown Court acting in its appellate capacity. The Divisional Court may reverse, affirm or amend the lower court's decision or may remit the case back to the lower court with its opinion, or make any other order it thinks fit. It may thus pass the sentence it considers right, if the test outlined below is satisfied. This procedure is akin to the process of challenge by application for judicial review, as permitted in respect of a Crown Court decision, including sentence, by SCA 1981 s29(3).

From a Magistrates' Court Appeal lies direct from a magistrates' court under MCA 1980 s111(1), either on the initiative of the defence or the prosecution, on the ground either that the sentence imposed was 'wrong in law' or was 'in excess of jurisdiction'. Grounds of this nature are likely to be uncommon in respect of sentencing at summary level. Application in writing must be made within 21 days of sentence, indicating the question of law or jurisdiction on which the High Court's opinion is sought. When the court has drafted its statement of case in response, the prosecution and defence have an opportunity to make representations, within 21 days. The final statement is then sent to the appellant who must lodge it in the Crown Office at the Royal Courts of Justice within 10 days (RSC Order 56, rule 6), also serving a copy and of the notice of entry of the appeal on the respondent. Where the magistrates' court passes an immediate custodial sentence, the appellant may be granted bail pending the appeal hearing under MCA 1980 s113, on terms that unless the appeal succeeds he must appear back at the magistrates' court within 10 days of the Divisional Court's judgement, a specific date to be set by the court after the appeal hearing. If an appellant applies for a case to be stated under s111, he loses any right he otherwise had to appeal to the Crown Court: s111(4).

From the Crown Court A similar process to that described above applies where the Crown Court has dealt with a case on appeal from a magistrates' court and it is claimed that the Court's decision was wrong in law or in excess of jurisdiction, under SCA 1981 s28. In this instance, the task of drafting the statement of case falls to the appellant and is then submitted to the judge who presided when the disputed decision was made. The appeal should be lodged with the High Court within six months of the Crown Court's decision. Pending the hearing, bail may be granted by the Crown Court or a High Court judge (SCA 1981 s81(1)(d)). Where the Crown Court purports to make an order but lacks jurisdiction or power to do so, that decision can be challenged by judicial review despite arising in relation to trial on indictment: *R v Crown Court at Croydon, ex p. London Borough of Harrow* [2000] 1 Cr App R 117 (see Stone, forthcoming).

Grounds of Appeal

In respect of challenges to sentence, the ground can be that although the sentence was within the court's powers of penalty, it was so significantly beyond the normal bounds of discretion as to be 'harsh and oppressive'. The Divisional Court may then feel able to conclude that the court below must have made some error in law, otherwise it would not have reached a decision so grossly out of step with good sentencing practice. The test suggested by *R v Croydon Crown Court, ex parte Miller* (1986) 85 Cr App R 152 was that the sentence imposed can be regarded as 'truly astonishing'. Subsequently, in *R v Truro Crown Court, ex p. Adair* (1997) COD 296, Lord Bingham CJ questioned whether this was an ideal test 'since some people are more readily astonished than others and it would appear a somewhat subjective approach'. Later, in *R v DPP, ex parte McGeary* [1999] 2 Cr App R(S) 263, he stated that 'the departure of the sentencing court from normal standards or levels of practice in sentencing must be so great as to constitute an excess of jurisdiction or an error of law'. It is not enough that the judges in the Divisional Court would have imposed a different sentence, had they been dealing with sentence, either initially or in the Court of Appeal, Criminal Division; the test in this context is rather more stringent for the Court to feel justified in interfering. In *R (on the application of Smith) v Southwark Crown Court* [2001] 2 Cr App R(S) 163, the Divisional Court spoke of intervening where a sentence 'falls outside the broad area of the lower court's discretion'.

The High Court has sought to discourage inappropriate resort to this means of challenging sentence, as in the recent instance of *Allen v West Yorkshire Probation Service Community Service Organisation* (2001) *The Times* 20 February. The appellant had failed to comply with a community service order imposed for common assault and on revocation of the order had been sentenced by the magistrates to three months imprisonment. His appeal to the Divisional Court was based on his claim that he had been wrongly re-sentenced on the basis of his breach rather than the seriousness of the original offence and also that his solicitor should have been granted the adjournment he had requested before the court proceeded to re-sentence so that fuller information could be obtained about the assault, particularly the victim's witness statement. Neither argument was upheld by the Court which went on to state that these were matters that could have been better pursued on appeal to the Crown Court, thus avoiding delay. In this instance the appellant had to face going back to prison, having been freed on bail since March 1999.

Review of Lenient Sentences

Usually, the prosecution has no right to challenge or appeal against a sentence which is considered to be too lenient. However, a limited exception was introduced by CJA 1988 ss35 and 36 which gives the Attorney-General power to refer to the Court of Appeal cases in which it appears that the sentencing by the Crown Court has been 'unduly lenient': s36(1)(a). Section 36(2) goes on to state that 'without prejudice to the generality of s36(1), the condition specified in s36(1)(a) may be satisfied if it appears to the Attorney-General that the judge erred as to his powers of sentencing'. In practice, power of reference is exercised primarily where the judge has passed a legally correct sentence but the Attorney-General considers that judicial discretion has been exercised inappropriately. C(S)A 1997 Sch 4 para 13 amended s36(2) to add that the specified condition may be satisfied also if the court failed to impose a minimum term of custody for a drug trafficking or domestic burglary offence, or a mandatory life sentence under what is now PCC(S)A 2000 ss109-111 (pages 100 and 106). Note that a reference may follow any order made by the Crown Court, other than an interim hospital order (specifically exempted by s35(6)), including a decision to defer sentence (*Attorney-General's Reference No 22 of 1992* (1993) 97 Cr App R 275). Reference may be made even in instances where the sentencer gave an indication prior to conviction that a non-custodial sentence would be imposed, provided that the defendant did not act on that legitimate expectation to his detriment: *Attorney-General's Reference Nos 86 and 87 of 1999* [2001] 1 Cr App R(S) 505 where the judge had told counsel that a custodial sentence would not be imposed, irrespective of whether the accused contested the case or pleaded guilty. They had maintained their not guilty plea. The Court of Appeal added that if prosecuting counsel considers that the level of sentence thus indicated is 'inappropriate', he or she should register dissent and draw the sentencer's attention to any relevant authorities.

Reference can only be made if:

(i)   the offence for which sentence was passed is triable only on indictment, or is an 'either way' offence which the Home Secretary has specifically made subject to this procedure, and

(ii)   the Court of Appeal gives leave.

So far, the power of reference has been extended to only three 'either way' offences, sentenced on or after 1 March 1994 (CJA 1988 (Review of Sentencing) Order 1994):

• indecent assault on a male or female;

• cruelty to or neglect of children (CYPA 1933 s1);

• making threats to kill.

The power does not apply where these offences are sentenced by a magistrates' court but does apply where the offender has been committed to the Crown Court for sentence.

Notice of application for leave to refer a case must be given within 28 days from date of sentence.

When reviewing sentence upon the Attorney-General's reference, the Court of Appeal may quash the Crown Court's sentence and substitute any other sentence that the Crown Court has power to impose. The Court of Appeal has indicated that it will not intervene unless it is of the view that there was some error in principle in the judge's sentence, so that public confidence would be damaged if the sentence were not altered (*Attorney-General's Reference No 5 of 1989* (1990) 90 Cr App R 358). Even where it considers that the sentence was unduly lenient, the Appeal Court has a discretion as to whether to exercise its powers: *Attorney-General's Reference No 4 of 1989* [1990] 1 WLR 41 where the Court was reluctant to attempt a full definition of the circumstances where such discretion might be appropriate but mentioned as 'one obvious instance: where in the light of events since the trial it appears either that the sentence can be justified or that it would be unfair to the offender or detrimental to others for whose well-being the court ought to be concerned'.

In reviewing sentence, the Court of Appeal should thus take account of the position as it now stands, including any indication of the offender's efforts since the original sentence was passed. Thus if a community sentence was imposed, the Court will be able to consider a report from the Probation Service about the offender's response to date. In *Attorney-General's Reference No 4 of 1989*, the court quashed a suspended sentence imposed for incest and replaced it with a three year probation order at a probation officer's suggestion, acknowledging that a custodial sentence would hamper the intensive therapeutic work being undertaken with the family by the Social Services Department. This case illustrates that in exceptional circumstances the Appeal Court may even substitute a lesser sentence. In the youth justice sphere, in *Attorney-General's References Nos 41 and 42 of 2001* (2001, unreported), the Appeal Court declined to increase sentence imposed on two youths for robbery, despite undue lenience, because of the long interlude of some 15 months between arrest and sentence, during which they kept out of further trouble. They had been released after serving their original sentences, obtaining employment, and the girlfriend of one had just given birth.

Where sentence is increased, the Appeal Court normally takes into account in mitigation the fact that the offender has had the anxiety and suspense of awaiting review and the prospect of being sentenced twice over.

Reviewing Community Sentences

Though the Court of Appeal is by no means confined in its discretion to increasing the Crown Court's sentence, this is a very likely outcome. Thus a community sentence imposed for a serious offence may well be challenged and overturned. *Attorney-General's Reference No 27 of 1993* [1994] Crim LR 465 provides an illustration. On pleading guilty to causing grievous bodily harm with intent, for attacking an opposing player during an association football match, the offender had been sentenced to a probation order with a requirement of attending a 'violent offenders' programme'. The Court of Appeal understood 'that it might be in the best interests of the offender that he should be rehabilitated' but 'the idea that conduct involving an intention to do really serious bodily harm is to be dealt with by putting a person on probation should not be allowed to become current'. A period of imprisonment was substituted.

Among more recent examples, in *Attorney-General's Reference No 18 of 1997* [1998] 1 Cr App R(S) 151 the Appeal Court reviewed a combination order including a requirement of an anger management programme imposed on a 26 year old offender of previous good character pleading guilty to an incident of robbery of a video rental shop in the course of which the youthful assistant suffered a minor assault when his assailant banged his head against a shelf. There was no financial motive. A PSR had identified the offender's heightened emotions and great anger at the time of the offence, uninhibited by alcohol. The Appeal Court now had the benefit of a progress report indicating satisfactory completion of the violent offenders' programme and full compliance with the order overall. Though accepting that the offence was at the lower end of the scale, the Court reiterated the serious public dimension to offences of this kind and the need to protect vulnerable staff in retail outlets, to deter and to make plain that offences of this nature call for serious punishment, 'whatever the personal mitigation'. Noting that the minimum sentence ordinarily was one of two years imprisonment, the Court imposed 12 months in recognition of developments since the original sentence and the double jeopardy experienced by an offender facing his first custodial sentence. In *Attorney-General's Reference No 23 of 2000* [2001] 1 Cr App R(S) 155, the Appeal Court set aside a probation order with additional requirements of residence and sex offender groupwork imposed for rape, stating that a non-custodial sentence for this crime cannot be justified except in 'wholly exceptional circumstances'. See also *Attorney-General's Reference No 31 of 2000* [2001] 1 Cr App R(S) 386 and *Attorney-General's Reference No 56 of 2000* [2001] 1 Cr App R(S) 439.

However, in exceptional circumstances, even where the Court of Appeal considers that the sentence was unduly lenient, discretion may be exercised to allow that sentence to stand. Thus in *Attorney-General's Reference No 18 of 1993* [1994] Crim LR 467, a probation order with a requirement that the offender should receive treatment for alcohol dependency, imposed for GBH with intent (aiming a blow with an iron bar at a pregnant woman, instead hitting a small child on her knee), was allowed to continue. The Court took account of a letter from the child's mother asking that no further sentence be imposed and a report from the Probation Service that the offender had responded extremely well to the requirements of the order. In *Attorney-General's Reference No 28 of 2000* [2001] 1 Cr App R(S) 307 the Appeal Court agreed that a probation order for three years with an additional requirement of participation in a sex offender programme imposed for persistent indecent assault of the offender's daughter was unduly lenient but decided not to vary sentence in the light of his efforts since the order was made. Permitting a probation order (including a sex offender programme) imposed for indecent assault to remain in place, the Appeal Court in *Attorney-General's Reference No 46 of 2000* [2001] 1 Cr App R(S) 407 stated that, if the exceptional course taken by the judge were to succeed, that would be of greater benefit to the public than the substitute term it would otherwise impose.

Where sentence is increased, the court almost invariably takes into account in mitigation the fact that the offender has had the anxiety and suspense of waiting for the review and the prospect of being sentenced twice over.

Recent Use of Referral and Outcome

In a House of Commons written answer of 8 December 1999, the Solicitor-General stated that, in 1998, 95 sentences were referred, sentence being increased in 68 (72%) cases, with referral being withdrawn in 10 cases (three cases remaining to be heard). A further answer of 8 January 2001 stated that, in 2000, 85 sentences had been referred and, of 48 heard to date, 43 were held to be unduly lenient, sentence being increased in 36 cases. For a review of referrals since the inception of this power, the implications for sentencing policy and an argument in favour of a general right of appeal by the prosecution, see Henham (1994).

Appendix 1

SPENT CONVICTIONS

The rehabilitation periods for particular sentences specified by the Rehabilitation of Offenders Act 1974 (as amended) are as follows, running from date of conviction:

(a) Sentence of imprisonment (or YOI/Youth Custody, or s53/s91 detention for grave crimes)–

    (i) exceeding 30 months: cannot be spent,

    (ii) exceeding six months but no more than 30 months: 10 years*,

    (iii) for six months or less: 7 years*;

(b) detention and training order on offender aged 15 or over at conviction–

    (i) term more than six months: 5 years,

    (ii) term of six months or less: 3+ years;

(c) detention and training order on offender aged under 15 at conviction/secure training order: 1 year after order ceases;

(d) Borstal (obsolete): 7 years;

(e) Detention Centre (obsolete): 3 years;

(f) combination/community punishment and rehabilitation order: 5 years*;

(g) community service/punishment order: 5 years*;

(h) drug abstinence/ treatment and testing order: 5 years*;

(i) curfew/exclusion order: 5 years*;

(j) probation/community rehabilitation order–

    (i) conviction before 3/2/95: 1 year or until order ceases, whichever is the longer,

    (ii) conviction on or after 3/2/95: 5 years*;

(k) supervision order: 1 year or until order ceases, whichever is the longer;

(l) attendance centre order: 1 year after order ceases;

(m) action plan/reparation order: 2+ years;

(n) referral order–

    (i) if young offender contract takes effect: date when contract ceases to have effect,

(ii)   if young offender contract does not take effect: date when such a contract would have ceased to have effect if it had taken effect;

(o)   fine/compensation order: 5 years*;

(p)   conditional discharge: 1 year or until order expires, whichever is the longer;

(q)   absolute discharge: 6 months;

(r)   bind over: 1 year or until order expires, whichever is the longer;

(s)   hospital order: 5 years or 2 years after order expires, whichever is the longer;

(t)   order imposing disqualification, disability, prohibition or other penalty: date order ceases to have effect.

[Periods marked * are halved if the offender was aged under 18 at date of conviction.]

Custodial sentences of indeterminate length or for terms exceeding 30 months cannot become 'spent'. The length of rehabilitation periods is currently subject to government review.

Appendix 2
SENTENCING FRAMEWORK REVIEW

In July 2001 the Home Office published *Making Punishments Work*, the Report of a Review of the Sentencing Framework for England & Wales directed by John Halliday, commonly known as The Halliday Review. This fundamental rethink of the principles that underpin and inform sentencing and the actualisation of those principles through coherent, transparent disposals is likely to lead to fresh legislation replacing the Criminal Justice Act 1991 and subsequent allied statutes, principally the Powers of Criminal Courts (Sentencing) Act 2000. The aim here is to summarise the main features of *Halliday* in anticipation of such reform. Though the Review concentrates on powers available for sentencing those aged 18 or older, its proposals for general principles are considered relevant for the sentencing of all offenders. The full report can be accessed at: www.homeoffice.gov.uk/cpg/halliday.htm Following publication of the report, the Home Secretary has announced that he intends to put the purpose of sentencing on a statutory footing, introducing three Ps and three Rs: prevention, protection, punishment, reparation, reduction of crime and rehabilitation.

Principles of Sentencing

Critique of 1991 and all that

The principle that severity of sentencing should be proportionate to the seriousness of the criminal conduct in question should be retained. However, 'just deserts' provides a less than adequate guide to 'the selection of the most suitable sentence in an individual case'. The 1991 Act framework, as amended, is insufficiently clear what heed should be paid to criminal record, with consequent inconsistency. Exercise of current discretion to 'take account' of previous convictions is too imprecise and unpredictable. The Act has also been interpreted by sentencers to include deterrence as an aim in sentencing and to cite local prevalence as a justification for more severe penalties, albeit without clear evidence or justification. While any framework must have a clearly expressed threshold governing the use of custody, the value of a lower threshold dividing financial and non-financial community penalties is less clear and may have unintentionally created an impression that fines should be reserved for the least serious offences. Additionally, sentencers are not encouraged to consider issues relating to crime reduction or reparation. Accordingly, the present approach is narrow, muddled, rigid, opaque, over-complex and inconsistent. Outcomes are likely to be improved by targeting resources on offenders most likely to re-offend and commit crimes serious enough to cause concern to local communities. The sentencing framework should promote effective work with offenders, supporting 'What Works' developments and paying greater attention to reparation.

Severity of Sentence

The existing just deserts philosophy or proportionality principle should be modified to take clearer and more predictable account of previous convictions by incorporating a new presumption that severity of sentence should increase when an offender has sufficiently recent and relevant convictions. The justification for this is three-fold (para. 2.7):

- A continuing course of criminal conduct in the face of repeated attempts by the State to try to correct it, calls for increasing denunciation and retribution, notwithstanding that earlier crimes have already been punished.

- Persistent criminality justifies the more intensive efforts to reform and rehabilitate which become possible within a more intrusive and punitive sentence.

- Because previous convictions are a strong indicator of risks of re-offending, this presumption takes such risks into account.

The new presumption would serve to target resources on the offenders who commit a disproportionate amount of crime and are most likely to re-offend. The new presumption must be governed by the proportionality principle, to avoid excessively severe, and therefore unjust, punishments. To do this, clear guidelines demonstrating the 'gearing' between offence seriousness, seriousness of record and bands of acceptable sentences will be needed, building on the guidelines already established or under development.

The principles governing severity of sentence should be as follows (para. 2.8):

- The severity of the punishment should reflect the seriousness of the offence and the offender's criminal history.

- The seriousness of the offence should reflect its degree of harmfulness or risked harmfulness, and the offender's culpability in committing the offence.

- In considering the offender's criminal history, the severity of the sentence should increase to reflect previous convictions, taking account of how recent and relevant they were. The most relevant will be those showing a continuing course of criminal conduct, even when the types of offence committed have been various, as they commonly are.

Completely disparate and remote previous convictions should be given less weight. Present information systems are unlikely to tell a court much about the seriousness of previous convictions so in future a short record of sentence passed and the reasons for it should be kept and become part of an offender's 'dossier', available at any ensuing court appearance.

Guidelines and Entry Points In explaining its preferred approach, the Report states:

'The amount and rate at which a criminal record should (presumptively) increase sentence severity, and subject to what limits, will need to be spelt out in guidelines. Those guidelines should set out presumptive "entry points" for sentences, in relation to offences graded according to described levels of seriousness. Seriousness levels would be defined within, as well as between, categories of offence (so as to distinguish, for example, between defined seriousness levels of different offences of burglary or robbery, and show where they overlapped). The "entry points" would be artificial, in that they would assume, as a basis for structured decision making, no prior adjustment for aggravating or mitigating factors. They would make no allowance, for example, for a guilty plea, which would be dealt with separately in the guidelines, along with other aggravating and mitigating factors not covered in definitions of seriousness.' (para. 2.18)

'The guidelines would then specify the way in which previous convictions should impact on the "entry point". Absence of previous convictions (or a small number that were old or irrelevant) would reduce severity of sentence below the "entry point". Relatively few previous convictions, showing a sufficiently recent disposition to criminality of about the same level of seriousness as the current offence, would justify adopting the "entry point". Larger numbers of previous convictions, of the same or greater apparent seriousness as the current offence, would increase severity of sentence progressively, within a range to be specified.' (para. 2.19)

'To avoid disproportionate outcomes, either too lenient or too severe, the guidelines would indicate the permissible range for a given level of seriousness. The following examples are illustrative only. Where the "entry point", for example, was a prison sentence of 18 months, a first offender might receive a non-custodial sentence, but for an offender sentenced on a large number of sufficiently recent occasions for offences of about the same level of seriousness, the sentence might be three years.' (para. 2.20)

Principled Decision-Taking In applying themselves to the guidelines, sentencers would ask themselves (para. 2.30):

- What is the acceptable range of sentence severity for this case, bearing in mind the seriousness of the current offence or offences, and any increase or reduction to be made on account of presence or absence of previous convictions?

- Within that range, taking account of any other relevant factors that could justify increasing or reducing severity, what sentence would most closely serve the purposes of crime reduction and reparation in this case?

They would consider evidence before them bearing on (para. 2.31):

- The seriousness of the current offence or offences (this should embrace the acts committed, the harm caused or risked, and the culpability of the offender in relation to those).

- The relevance of previous convictions (this would embrace their number, how recent and frequent they were, and the extent to which they demonstrated a continuing course of criminal conduct on the one hand, or serious attempts to 'get out of crime' on the other).

- The assessed likelihood of re-offending and measures most likely to reduce that risk.

Guidelines would help sentencers to establish the relationship between offence seriousness, previous convictions and severity of sentence, and to take account of any other aggravating and mitigating circumstances. These guidelines would look for consistency of approach rather than uniform outcomes, and there would be scope to recognise justifiable disparity, e.g. in cases where the offender has young dependent children. Claims of mitigation by an offender would be subject to challenge by the prosecution and courts would have the discretion not to accept the same claims indefinitely, regardless of persistent offending.

Pre-Sentence Reports PSRs would contain assessments of risk of re-offending, likely levels of resulting harm, and the measures most likely to reduce them (para. 2.32).

Totality Principle The principle allowing several current offences to be treated as a whole for sentencing purposes would be preserved and set out in guidelines. This should mean that, when several offences are sentenced together, the combined effect should be more severe than would have been justified by the most serious offence, but not so severe as to be outside the range for that offence, after taking account of any added severity for previous convictions. Although some have seen this as a 'discount for bulk offending', a cumulative approach would be impractical (para. 2.9).

Imprisonment

Imprisonment should be reserved for cases in which no other sentence would be severe enough. However, the court should also decide whether a prison sentence of 12 months or longer is needed. If a term of that length is not judged necessary, the court would then consider whether a community sentence would meet the needs of punishment, having regard to the needs for crime reduction and reparation and the assessed risks of re-offending. In 'low risk' cases, if a combination of restrictions on liberty (curfew and tagging; compulsory work) and financial penalties would suffice, that would be ordered. But if the maximum loss of liberty and property would fall short of the minimum punishment required, a short prison sentence would be passed.

Imprisonment of Less than 12 Months

All short term prison sentences would mean what they said in terms of time served.

Custody Plus Shorter prison terms need to be substantially reformed to make them more effective in reducing crime and protecting the public. This should be achieved by requiring those who serve short prison sentences to undertake programmes under supervision after release, under conditions which – if breached – could result in swift return to custody. Under such a sentence, the initial period in custody could be any period between two weeks and three months, and the period of supervision could be any period between (a minimum) of six months and whatever would take the sentence as a whole to less than 12 months. Such a sentence would be potentially more punitive in its effect on offenders who breached their conditions than any existing prison sentence of under 12 months.

Plain Custody In the minority of cases where the court identifies no need for a supervisory period, it should be able to order a period of custody without the 'plus', dispensing with post-release supervision. Such terms would be for up to three months (the issue of consecutive terms is left open). This would be appropriate in instances where a first-time offender has a stable secure background and being caught and punished is enough in itself to enable them to learn a lesson from their experience. This form of sentence could also be appropriate for foreign nationals who will return to their home country on release. (Halliday also considers that it may also be appropriate where the offender is so 'recalcitrant and unresponsive that there is simply no point in trying to work with them in the community' but, recognising that this is 'a policy of despair', concludes that courts should not be able to dispense with the 'plus' element on grounds of forecast non-compliance.)

Imprisonment of 12 Months or Longer

- Prison sentences of 12 months or more should continue to be served partly in prison and partly in the community, but conditions of release, and supervision, should continue to the end of the sentence, with liability to recall to prison if conditions are breached. For most offenders release would be at the half-way point of the sentence.

- Before the release of a prisoner, the content of the second half of the sentence should be subject to court review, on the basis of proposals prepared jointly by the prison and probation service, in consultation with other statutory, independent and voluntary sectors.

- Discretionary release should be reserved for violent and sexual offenders who may need to be detained for longer to avoid risks of serious harm to the public.

- Violent or sexual offenders who present a risk of serious harm to the public should be eligible for a new sentence, the effect of which would be to make their release during the second half of the sentence dependent on a decision by the Parole Board. Courts would have power to extend the supervisory part of the sentence.

Intermediate Sanctions

The Review considered the scope for new forms of sentence that would allow an offender to spend part of a custodial sentence out of prison, but considered that this kind of sentence could not be accommodated within existing prison establishments. It proposes further consideration of the range of accommodation, current and potential, that could serve to strengthen 'containment in the community', for example probation hostels. In addition, it recommends that suspended prison sentences should continue to be available only in exceptional circumstances. It also considered that, for imprisonable offences, wider recognition that non-custodial sentences are, in effect, 'conditional' prison sentences would enhance their credibility and effectiveness. Courts should thus have power, when passing a community sentence for an imprisonable offence, to indicate the length of a prison sentence that would be an appropriate starting point for re-sentencing, should breach of the community sentence make that unavoidable.

Non-Custodial Powers

The Review concludes that the proliferation of community orders, each with their own detailed provisions and with a lack of clarity about their individual purpose, has caused such sentencing to become over-complicated and inconsistent. Existing sentences should be replaced by a new generic community punishment order, whose punitive weight would be proportionate to the current offence and any additional severity for previous convictions. The sentence would consist of ingredients best suited to meeting the needs of crime reduction, and exploiting opportunities for reparation, within an appropriately punitive 'envelope'.

A CPO would be made up of elements drawn from (para. 6.6):

- compulsory programmes, aimed at changing offending behaviour, including treatment for substance abuse, and improving skills;

- compulsory work;

- restriction and requirements, including curfew, exclusion, electronic monitoring;

- reparation;

- supervision – to manage and enforce the sentence and support resettlement.

An outline tariff for the ingredients making up the new order is suggested, consisting of three tiers, rising in restrictive severity. At top tier level, it is suggested that enforced work could be for longer than the current maximum of 240 hours.

Financial Penalties

Substantial fines in quite serious cases might be enough to meet the needs of punishment, but history of failure to pay fines would justify using non-financial penalties of appropriate severity. It would not be possible to impose a non-custodial penalty in cases of fine default or in those cases where a fine would simply add to the burden of debt to little effect. An offender who received a non-custodial penalty instead of a fine would be liable to imprisonment for breach. It will be important, therefore, to use this power in a way which does not expose 'poorer' offenders to a greater risk of imprisonment. It should be possible to create degrees of 'punitive' equivalence between the loss of liberty involved in a community penalty and the deprivation of resource involved in a fine. The proposed sentencing guidelines could include illustrations of 'equivalence' between financial and non-financial penalties (para. 6.16).

Discharges

Absolute and conditional discharges would continue as now.

Interim Review Order

To strengthen the current power to defer sentence, a new interim review order could be made for a maximum of six months, subject to undertakings from the offender to meet specified voluntary commitments, such as: reparation, participation in restorative justice schemes, substance misuse programme attendance, residence at a nominated address. On the basis of a report from the probation service at the end of the period, a final sentence would be passed. The activities carried out and the progress shown would act as mitigating factors in any subsequent sentence passed. These changes would clarify, and strengthen, the existing powers to defer sentence, and should increase consistency in the use of these powers.

Penal Code

For a new framework, an Act of Parliament should set out the general principles, specify the newly designed sentences, provide for review hearings, prescribe enforcement procedures and require guidelines to be drawn up. The Act should take the form of a Penal Code, which would be kept continuously available in up-to-date form. New guidelines for the use of judicial discretion will be an essential part of the new framework, in order to avoid unpredictable consequences, for example in the sentencing of persistent offenders. Such guidelines would be set out in a separate, published Code that would apply to all criminal courts.

INDEX